Development of Posture and Gait Across the Life Span

Growth, Motor Development, and Physical Activity Across the Life Span

Harriet G. Williams, Series Editor

Development of Posture and Gait Across the Life Span
Edited by Marjorie H. Woollacott
and Anne Shumway-Cook

Problems in Movement Skill Development
by David A. Sugden and Jack F. Keogh

Development of Eye-Hand Coordination Across the Life Span
Edited by Chantal Bard, Michelle Fleury,
and Laurette Hay

Development of Posture and Gait Across the Life Span

Edited by
Marjorie H. Woollacott
Anne Shumway-Cook

**Growth, Motor Development,
and Physical Activity Across the Life Span
Harriet G. Williams,**
Series Editor

UNIVERSITY OF SOUTH CAROLINA PRESS

Published in Columbia, South Carolina, by the
University of South Carolina Press

Manufactured in the United States of America

First Edition

Second Printing, 1990

Development of posture and gait across the life span / edited by Marjorie H.
    Woollacott, Anne Shumway-Cook. — 1st ed.
        p.   cm. — (Growth, motor development, and physical activity
    across the life span)
    Bibliography: p.
    ISBN 0-87249-629-5
    1. Posture.   2. Gait.   3. Posture disorders—Age factors.   4. Gait
disorders—Age factors.   5. Aging.   I. Woollacott, Marjorie H.,
1946–   . II. Shumway-Cook, Anne, 1947–   .   III. Series.
QP310.3.P.67   1989
612.7'6—dc20   89-9183
                                                                           CIP

Contents

PART III.
Posture and Gait Changes in the Aging Adult

PART IV.
Abnormal Postural Control and the Effects of Training

Contributors

Ann M. Baylor, Ph.D.
Department of Kinesiology and Health Education, University of Texas at Austin, Austin, Texas 78712

Anne Bekoff, Ph.D.
Department of Environmental, Population and Organismic Biology, University of Colorado, Boulder, Colorado 80309

Nina S. Bradley, Ph.D.
Department of Environmental, Population and Organismic Biology, University of Colorado, Boulder, Colorado 80309

Thomas Brandt, M.D.
Neurological Clinic, University of Munich, Klinium Grobhadern, Marchioninistr. 15, 8000 Munich, FRG

Jane Clark, Ph.D.
Department of Physical Education, University of Maryland College Park, Maryland 20742

Rebecca Craik, Ph.D.
Department of Physical Therapy, Beaver College, Glenside, Pennsylvania 19038

Bettina Debu, Ph.D.
Department of Physical Education and Human Movement Studies and Institute of Neurosciences, University of Oregon, Eugene, Oregon 97403

Keith C. Hayes, Ph.D.
Department of Physical Medicine and Rehabilitation, University of Western Ontario, London, Ontario, Canada

Fay Bahling Horak, Ph.D., RPT
Division of Neurootology, Good Samaritan Hospital and Medical Center, Portland, Oregon 97210

Jody L. Jensen Ph.D.
Department of Psychology, Indiana University, Bloomington, Indiana 47405

Contributors

Alar Mirka, M.D.
Division of Neurootology, Good Samaritan Hospital and Medical Center, Portland, Oregon 97210

Walter Paulus, M.D.
Neurological Clinic, University of Munich, Klinikum Grobhadern, Marchioninistr. 15, 8000 Munich, FRG

Edward S. Reed, Ph.D.
College of Humanities, Drexel University, Philadelphia, Pennsylvania 19104

Cindy L. Riach, Ph.D.
Department of Physical Medicine and Rehabilitation, University of Western Ontario, London, Ontario, Canada

Charlotte C. Shupert, Ph.D.
Division of Neurootology, Good Samaritan Hospital and Medical Center, Portland, Oregon 97210

Anne Shumway-Cook, Ph.D., PT
Emanuel Rehabilitation Center, Portland, Oregon 97227

Esther Thelen, Ph.D.
Department of Psychology, Indiana University, Bloomington, Indiana 47405

Beverly D. Ulrich, Ph.D.
Department of Psychology, Indiana University, Bloomington, Indiana 47405

Lynda Werner, Ph.D.
Department of Dance, University of Oregon, Eugene, Oregon 97403

Jill Whitall, Ph.D.
Department of Physical Education, University of Wisconsin, Madison, Wisconsin

Harriet Williams, Ph.D.
College of Health, Motor Control Laboratory, University of South Carolina, Columbia, South Carolina 29208

Marjorie Hines Woollacott, Ph.D.
Department of P.E. and Human Movement Studies and Institute of Neuroscience, University of Oregon, Eugene, Oregon 97403

Preface

Age-related changes in posture and gait have been the focus of a considerable amount of research in the 1980s. Much insight has been gained into the neurophysiological basis for normal postural control in young adults, as well as postural control changes contributing to the development of stability in children. As the percentage of elderly in our population has grown, there has been increasing research on the neural correlates of aging. This research is particularly critical in the area of postural control underlying balance and gait, since the incidence of falls resulting in serious injury increases significantly with age. Research examining postural control in exceptional populations—skilled athletes and the disabled—has also contributed to our increased understanding of the limits of postural ability. Studies examining the effect of peripheral and central nervous-system pathology on postural control benefit both the scientist interested in basic physiological questions and the health-care clinician committed to improving approaches for assessing and treating patients with balance and gait disorders.

A review of the literature reveals a divergence of experimental approaches used in studying questions related to posture and gait. We believe this divergence reflects, in part, the use of fundamentally different models of neural control of posture and movement. A model or theoretical framework of neural control has a pervasive impact on one's scientific approach, and influences both the hypotheses to be tested and the subsequent interpretation of results. This is true for the scientist asking questions about the neural basis for postural control, as well as the clinician designing treatment strategies for the patient with balance disorders.

This volume endeavors to present current research on changes in posture and gait across the line span. The contributing authors have been asked to consider the influence of current models of neural control when presenting research findings in their respective fields. It is our hope that this will stimulate our readers to examine critically their own underlying assumptions regarding developmental changes in posture and gait from infancy to old age. More importantly, we hope this will encourage new approaches to research in the area as well as formulation of new intervention strategies designed to improve posture and gait control.

The book is divided into four parts that progress from theoretical issues through basic research to practical applications of research findings. Chapters in Part I discuss important issues affecting the study of the origins of postural control and gait. The chapter on animal models was included to give a better understanding of the neural circuitry underlying the development of locomotion. In addition, animal research findings can address critical issues in the development of locomotion, for example, whether ontogeny recapitulates phylogeny.

Part II presents basic research on the development of balance and locomotion in children. Changes in postural control underlying the development of stability are discussed, as are age-related changes leading to the development of mature gait. In addition, the postural foundations for voluntary movement in children are examined.

Posture and gait in the aged are the focus of Part III. Research findings on age-related changes in posture control and gait are examined relative to two hypotheses: (1) that aging represents an inevitable linear decline in neural function versus (2) that aging nervous-system function remains optimal unless specific pathology occurs. Issues concerning plasticity in the mature nervous system are also discussed, specifically the effects of exercise on improving function in the elderly.

Finally, Part IV presents information on abnormal postural control and the effects of training on improving equilibrium function. Pathophysiology within the postural control system underlying dysequilibrium in both children and the elderly is discussed. We believe insight into the efficacy of various approaches to improving equilibrium function may be gained from studies on training effects in patient populations as well as skilled athletes.

What is the significance of combining pediatric and geriatric postural control research in one volume? It is known that children and older adults often demonstrate similar postural and locomotor patterns. The underlying cause for similarities in these patterns is unclear. One hypothesis suggests that with aging there is a degradation of higher nervous-system control resulting in a reemergence of developmentally immature patterns of behavior. Alternatively, one can ask, do children and older adults show comparable patterns of behavior because similar constraints engender similar strategies for interacting with the environment? These constraints need not be limited to the nervous system but may reflect limitations within the entire neuromusculoskeletal system.

Results from studies in these two populations suggest a possible commonality of control issues. Thus researchers studying development may choose not to define the limits of their research based on an arbitrary age of their subjects, but rather to examine the individuals' capacity for optimally interacting with the environment, taking into consideration the effects of age-dependent constraints. Clinicians working with both children and the aged can use this information to develop therapeutic strategies independent of age limitation.

Marjorie Woollacott and Anne Shumway-Cook

Development of Posture and Gait Across the Life Span

Part I

Developmental Theories and Their Relationship to the Study of Posture and Gait

1

Changing Theories of Postural Development

Edward S. Reed

What is postural development the development of? Traditionally, it has been limited to the study of the development of input/output neural mechanisms underlying both bodily support and response to perturbation. More recently, postural development has come to be seen as the development of a key functional component of all action systems: that group of diverse processes—perceptual as well as motor—which serves to maintain bodily orientation to the environment and its features. Reflex hierarchy or traditional theories I define as the first sort of approach, whereas those of the second type would be called "action systems" approaches (Reed, 1982).

My own view is that traditional theories are based upon assumptions that are no longer tenable and that the predictions by these theories have been falsified by our recent accumulation of knowledge about posture. This is a controversial claim and therefore deserves close scrutiny. What is not controversial is that views of posture and movement are undergoing considerable change and that some new understanding will emerge to replace a number of traditional views. The particular group of assumptions of the traditional approach that appears most in need of revision concerns the ideas that the central nervous system (CNS) is an input-output mechanism. Throughout the history of neurophysiology there has been a temptation to believe that the environment affects animals by means of physical stimuli that are channeled into specific spinal and cerebral locations, then processed by means of various internal CNS connections, and subsequently channeled back out. Posture has been treated as one of these unitary sensorimotor mechanisms, with local stimuli from muscles, joints, and the inner ear being integrated in the cerebellum and perhaps elsewhere and then channeled out in the form of signals modifying both phasic and tonic reflexes.

Many scientists now believe that this sort of model of neural functioning is oversimplified (Edelman, 1987; Reed, 1989). Neural connections—whether between center and periphery or within the center—are not like electrical wiring diagrams (Easter et al., 1985). Each peripheral region is multiply represented in the center (in both the spine and brain). These representations are not mappings of the body or of the external environment, but complexes where various influences meet and achieve a dynamic equilibrium under the combined constraint of neural architecture and the effects of experience. Sensory signals are not channeled into singular sensory mapping regions but are themselves the results of active exploratory processes involving complex and distributed control of the movements of the head and the hands, and these movements in turn produce specific spatio-temporal patternings of input neural activities throughout the CNS.

In other words, "vicarious function" (Gibson, 1966: Introduction) is the rule. "Variant groups of cells . . . carry out the same functions more or less well" (Edelman, 1987; p. 107), and particular CNS regions are typically implicated in diverse behavioral functions. Traditional motor control theories have assumed that behaviors are built up out of mechanistic units that are expressed in relatively unchanging form in different actions, units such as reflexes and central pattern generators (see Gallistel, 1980, for a summary). To paraphrase Edelman (1987: p. 225), it is not that such units do not exist, but that they do not account for the variability and adaptibility inherent in action from the outset, and which increases with development. When action is treated as the response of a body to a stimulus, and especially when experimental subjects are not required to accomplish their own postural support, then reflexes and other mechanistic units emerge in our laboratories. However, when action is studied naturalistically, as an achievement of an autonomous biological system, and especially when agents are required to accomplish their own postural support, these units disappear (Reed, 1982; Pearson, 1985). This is not to say that action (or the CNS) is indefinitely variable; quite the opposite is the case. The variability in action is, under normal circumstances, tightly constrained. But the specific patterning of actions is *functional* and *ecological,* not mechanistic. Any particular action skill, such as reaching or standing, is subserved by a diversity of mechanisms distributed throughout the nervous system. This great precision and *functional specificity* is achieved through competition and cooperation among the diverse processes.

Although the mechanisms underlying specific anatomical boundaries among variant groups have begun to be understood (Edelman, 1987; Kaas, 1987), we do not as yet have a good idea of the developmental and experiential mechanisms underlying the differentiation of functional specificity among action systems. For this reason the present chapter is focused at a descriptive and not an etiological level. The goal is to contrast the novel description of postural development in terms of functional specificity with the traditional account of posture as based on mechanically specific units. The chapter begins with an outline of the traditional motor approach to posture and continues with a brief description of some milestones in the recent study of posture. Several questions concerning stance are then discussed, followed by a functional analysis of the role of posture in activities of daily life (ADL) in general. Stress is laid on the adaptive and flexible integration of posture and movement.

POSTURAL DEVELOPMENT:
History and Theory

Despite their importance, the phenomena of posture have not fit in well with most accounts of movement. Consequently, we know very little about posture, and much of what is known is obscured by confusion or controversy. The reasons that posture has not been well integrated into studies of motor behavior are largely conceptual. Yet the actual processes hindering our understanding of posture have been primarily experimental. Human movement science, like most branches of psychology and neurophysiology, has inherited a dualistic legacy from Descartes (Reed, 1982b; Greene, 1985). In his *Passions of the Soul* (1649/1986) Descartes went to great lengths to demonstrate that human actions were either mechanical responses to stimuli or voluntary movements of the body to commands issued from the mind or brain. As postures are only rarely isolatable responses (they are most often anticipatory, ongoing, and follow-through in nature) and rarely the result of mental deliberation, they were in effect granted no place to live in the Cartesian universe.

It was not merely the dualistic theory of Descartes that hindered research on posture. The experimental procedures that emerged from Cartesian psychology—what Danziger (1983) calls the paradigm of stimulated motion—ensured that postures would find no place in the laboratories of our science. Reflex responses were studied in pithed or decapitated animals, a procedure pioneered in the eighteenth century (Whytt, 1751) and a staple of modern neuroscience by the present century (Sherrington, 1906). As decorticated animals do not engage in spontaneous behavior, they make an excellent model for studying movements as responses to stimuli but are at best deceptive for the study of posture. Often these decorticated preparations must be supported or placed in special positions (e.g., so that the limb under study is hanging with gravity). The reaction-time methods that emerged when psychologists and brain scientists wanted to study "voluntary" action as opposed to these involuntary responses also offered little potential for understanding posture. According to the Cartesian dogma, voluntary action is opposed to involuntary in that it is stimulated not by external factors, but by the mind—and because the mind has been supposed to be in the brain, the relative timing of different actions supposedly reveals how much "higher" processing is involved. Yet, again, the behaviors that have been studied in this way have been relatively isolated movements of limbs in situations in which the experimental subject has not had to provide his or her own support. As we shall see, a primary function of posture is the integration of movements into coordinated action sequences. Such phenomena simply do not emerge in experimental paradigms devoted to isolated movements under constrained conditions.

The absence of a viable account of posture has meant that motor development has been looked upon primarily as *movement* development. Posture has had a less significant role in both theory and experimental practice, although it has always played a significant role in clinical procedures. It is very misleading to study action development entirely in terms of movement development, because the role played by posture in the development of adaptability in action is central. In this respect, clinical insight has been in the vanguard of our understanding of posture, and research and theory are only beginning to catch up.

If, as has traditionally been done, one assumes that movement is what develops, a number of further questions naturally arise: what are the processes of movement control, and how do these change with maturation and experience? Do we see changes from reflexive to voluntary (programmed) and from voluntary to automatic (habitual, preprogrammed) in the control of movement? If there is a trend away from stimulus-bound, reflexive movement toward more programmed, voluntary movement, is there also a trend toward integrating various sensory systems into motor performance? All these questions were asked in an empirical manner as early as David Hartley's *Observations on Man* (1749) and were central to Alexander Bain's influential theories of the last century.

Despite its longevity, the traditional approach to motor development flies in the face of at least two important classes of fact. First, given anatomical structures often accomplish diverse actions. Even a neonate can and does use her mouth for exploring as well as for nursing (Rochat, 1987). This means that functional differentiation and integration is important from the outset in action development. Studies or theories that focus on mouth movements alone, ignoring what it is the infant is doing with her mouth, will therefore miss important phenomena. The second class of recalcitrant facts that undermines traditional motor approaches is that practice and repetition of behavior leads not to stereotypy of movement, but to *movement variability along with functional invariance*. Both these important classes of phenomena will be addressed below.

TWENTIETH-CENTURY DEVELOPMENTS IN THE STUDY OF POSTURE

Much of the work on posture in the present century can fairly be characterized as an elaboration of Sherrington's (1906) important theory of the neural control of behavior. His was a classic Cartesian theory, treating reflex behavior as a purely mechanical response to stimuli, and voluntary behavior as the activity of unanalyzed higher centers superimposed on the bodily mechanism. Above all, it was Magnus (1924) who applied Sherrington's methods and concepts to the study of posture.

According to Magnus (1924, 1925), the orientation of the head on the trunk is fundamental in vertebrate behavior, because this orientation affects the inner ear and the neck muscles, thus producing stimuli that modulate all the antigravity responses of the trunk and limbs. Head position may also be adjusted so as to improve the biomechanical efficiency of a sitting, locomoting, or standing human being, and at the same time it may facilitate the strength of movements through the intermediation of the tonic neck reflexes.

Using rabbits and other animals, Magnus showed that what he called the "tonic neck reflexes" exert an influence on the entire bodily configuration. By this he meant that static positions of the head in space (i.e., with respect to the force of gravity) facilitated muscle extension and flexion in different parts of the body. In animals, when the head is bent backward, there is an increase of activity in extensors in the forelimbs. Studies with human infants and brain-damaged patients soon showed that, in general, this bending back of the head in humans caused an increase in flexor activity.

The most important work applying and modifying Magnus's work was done in the two decades following the publication of his book. The following is a very brief summary of a number of investigations (Schaltenbrand, 1928; Simons, 1953; Weisz, 1938):

> (1) The head maintains a range of mobility around an equilibrium position, based on the perceived vertical (itself a combination of visual and vestibular information). In traditional thinking this is attributed to a hypothetical unitary mechanism, the "labyrinthine righting reflex."

(2) The body maintains a range of mobility around an equilibrium by which it maintains support of the head. This probably involves kinesthetic as well as vestibular and visual information. In traditional thinking this is attributed to a hypothetical unitary mechanism, the "neck righting reflex."

(3) In standing up and locomoting, the head leads the way: in younger children the head is turned and the arms swing with it to help push off from sitting. The head is then pushed up higher to enable the trunk to become vertical below it. In older children and adults the head is brought forward and up when sitting is achieved from supine position. A continuation of these movements is used in standing.

(4) If the support surface is unsteady or not level (which is to say not orthogonal to the line of gravity), the position of the head is treated as the equilibrium point and the legs, arms, and trunk shift under it.

Despite the usefulness of these studies and their important role in informing clinical practices, they have very real limitations. Chief among them is that they follow Sherrington in treating posture as a static state. For Sherrington, Magnus, and others in their tradition, posture is literally a summation of all the antigravity stretch reflexes in the body. As research has accumulated concerning the relations between posture and movement it has become clear that movement and posture are not separately controlled but tightly integrated. It is almost certain that these dynamically stable states of our bodies exist not because of unitary underlying mechanisms, but rather because they reflect an equilibrium among a complex set of mechanisms.

Perhaps the earliest evidence for the conception of posture as an integral component of voluntary action, and not as a response to stimuli, came from the work of F. M. Alexander (1974), who invented the so-called "Alexander technique" early in the present century. This therapy involves manipulating the body's *posture*—especially the head and neck—so as to result in smoother *movements*. According to Jones's (1965) empirical studies of this technique, Alexander therapists alter the habitual balance of the head so that it is held slightly higher, and its center (the Frankfurt axis) is moved slightly forward, so that the eyes face downward from the horizontal. This is an alteration not in static but in dynamic posture; that is, patients are trained to adopt this posture under a range of conditions (i.e., to develop new coordinations that enable them to keep the head in this pose while sitting, standing, or locomoting). The adjustment of the head in this way apparently has a marked effect on the amount of force required to change postures, making it easier, for example, to rise from a seated posture. It also makes standing up more rapid, direct, and smooth, at least according to the reports of some subjects. Apparently, there is also a change in tonus that is systemic, as well as a change in particular movement characteristics. All these changes in posture are effected by verbal and nonverbal instructions that have the effect of altering habitual dynamic patterns of action that are voluntary, but relatively automatic.

In the past two decades posture has begun to regain its rightful place as a fundamental component of human activity and has therefore been seen as worthy of careful scientific analysis. Yet even with this renewed interest, the negative effects of our Cartesian heritage are still being felt. For instance, the well-known British neurologist Purdon Martin (1977) has emphasized correctly that posture has a separate function from movement and that postures ought not to be conceptualized as a series of movement responses. This sounds like the beginnings of what I here call an *action systems approach*. Yet when it comes to defining the function of posture, Martin offers a definition that is nearly as static and mechanistic as traditional ideas. He treats posture as a "state of the body" comprised of two things; relationships among body parts and "of the body to the ground," specifically "supporting activity against gravity" (1977: 25). Posture should not be seen as a response to or against gravity. Dynamic posture is the result of the functioning of perceptuomotor systems that work *with* gravity to achieve functional action (Bernstein, 1967 cited in Whiting, 1984). Moreover, gravity is by no means the only force relevant to motor control. As Stoffregen & Riccio (1988) show, there are a number of self-generated reactive forces, especially those of the body against local surfaces (stairs, walls, chairs, and other furniture as well as floors!) which must be incorporated into efficacious action. The passenger in a car or subway who maintains an erect posture of his or her head is adapting to these reactive forces, which are due to an accelerating local framework as well as gravity. The result of this integrated neural functioning is not a *state*, but an *act* combining numerous diverse processes. This is demonstrated by the fact that, when an agent's local force framework is suddenly altered, there is at least a brief period of time in which the now-no-longer-adaptive postural activities are maintained despite such potentially dangerous results as whiplash.

Martin (1977), like many other recent writers, also defines postures as reflex or automatic, even though he recognizes that they usually involve "muscular activity in almost the whole body" (and, hence, throughout the CNS). When a term such as "reflex," whose precise meaning is that of a localized peripheral-central arc, is used to refer to systemic neural activity, one can be sure that a deep conceptual confusion exists. This confusion pervades the literature on posture, and in this regard it is interesting to note the lack of agreement in recent years concerning how to label postural phenomena. Consider the following cases. It has been shown that the muscular synergies involved in maintaining an upright posture in response to perturbation are quite similar to those synergies involved in "anticipating" the destabilizing results of voluntary movement of the arms (Nashner & McCollum, 1985). If this is one and the same postural synergy, should it be called a reflex response or a voluntary behavior? Current theorists usually hedge and call it either an adaptable response or a preprogrammed component of voluntary behavior. To make matters more complicated, this same synergy undergoes developmental changes of functional significance (Shumway-Cook & Woollacott, 1985), but these changes may be as much due to perceptual development as to changes in motor-control mechanisms. Is this synergy reflexive or voluntary, is it perceptual or motor, is it automatic or learned? The answer to all these questions seems to be both yes and no when it comes to this and other postural phenomena. Such a confusing circumstance suggests the need for a new set of concepts to enable us to describe posture more adequately. Perhaps the action systems approach offered here will begin to clarify some of these confusions.

The discussion below takes an action systems approach, first with regard to the nature of stance and then with respect to the various ways in which postures form functional units in ADLs. Throughout, the emphasis is on new lines of thinking and research that need to be explored if an adequate theory of postural functioning is to emerge.

STANCE

Gurfinkel (1973) summed up the traditional view of stance control very succinctly: "the stretch reflex occupies the key position in all the conventional schemes of pose regulation, whereas the important role of other sources of afferentation is limited to the formation of descending influences that change the reflex loop gain of the stretch reflexes." Although Gurfinkel's group has demonstrated that the sensitivity of the stretch reflex of triceps surae increases significantly when there is a possibility of falling (Elner et al., 1972), they have also shown that, under normal conditions of quiet stance, no stretch reflex is elicitable in either soleus or gastrocnemius. These latter muscles may have sufficient passive resistance to aid stabilization. Because the parameters of passive muscle stretch are modulated by descending signals, Gurfinkel concludes that stance is regulated by a "preparatory set" of the postural muscles around the ankles and by stretch reflexes whose thresholds and gains are both modifiable by this preparatory process (Gurfinkel, 1973; Bonnet et al., 1976).

In fact, careful observations of the whole body during standing raise questions about whether stance is indeed built up out of a summation of antigravity stretch reflexes. If stance were so constructed, one would expect that patterns of sway would reveal control of the movements of single joints, across which the available stretch reflexes act. For example, one would expect to see that the stretch reflexes around the ankles enabled them to maintain a relatively consistent posture, and similarly with other important joints, such as the knees and hips. Yet "the standing body does not sway about the ankles as a rigid rod, but as a 'reed in the breeze' " (Thomas & Whitney, 1959: 534). Furthermore, the available evidence suggests that only the *ratios* of sway across two or more joints are controlled, not sway at a single joint (Ibid., Table 3). Finally, when there is a functional task beyond that of quiet stance, the postural patterns undergo task-specific reorganizations of an intricate sort. Thus, Arutunyan and his colleagues (1967) found that marksmen did not control any individual joints but nevertheless succeeded in maintaining a remarkably stable position of the tool in their hands. Further studies of the maintenance of postures in the service of the use of hand tools (eating utensils, hammers, and other appliances) would be of both theoretical and practical value.

The most remarkable thing about the task specificity of voluntary action is that it is accomplished through a considerable variety of subsidiary movements, and yet we are rarely conscious of these subsidiary units. Try the following experiment: get a package of ice cream and a spoon, and scoop out a few spoonsful of the ice cream into a bowl. Now, without using either the spoon or the ice cream, replicate the movements made by your shoulder and elbow in scooping. This task is virtually impossible, even for trained occupational and physical therapists. Movement educators and therapists know that it is exceedingly difficult to attend to the subsidiary movements and postures of functional actions. Thus, they make every effort to rehabilitate function using components of normal situations. Yet the traditional theory of motor development holds that when a child learns, for example, to use a spoon, she is learning to construct a series of movements that will enable her to spoon up food. According to the approach advocated here, this is backward: children learn how to act and *then* they learn how to move. The spooning comes first, often clumsily and without good movement control; with functionally rewarding practice the movements of the tool use finally emerge and are selected as comprising the skill, out of the initially large and variable range of possibilities. The present hypothesis is that the development of action is what leads to the ability to coordinate groups of movements within various contexts. Central to this development is the integration of adaptable postures with movements, as is well illustrated even in the task of standing.

Standing is accomplished in a variety of contexts, with various ground surfaces and objects to be held on to or looked at. Standing is also learned in a variety of behavioral contexts: while reaching for objects at varying heights or objects on other surfaces, while attempting to step or being assisted in stepping, or while getting erect from seated or reclining positions, and so on. The locomotor movements found in adults can be found in neonates and other young infants who are well supported (Thelen et al., Chap. 2 of this volume). However, stance and locomotion require not only movements, but functional action. This means movements and postures that are specifically adapted to the local contingencies of gravity, reactive forces, and surfaces of support. "Proper" leg and trunk movements will be of no avail to a 1-year-old human who cannot find the proper posture and support for his (relatively heavy) head. The task of normal stance requires relatively frequent adjustments of weight bearing (Smith, 1954; cited in Rozendal, 1986), and these adjustments must be properly graded and tuned so as to not cause a stumble or fall. Unfortunately, almost all studies of stance have focused on symmetrical static cases, in which there is no real task. Such studies assume that the human upright posture is nothing more than a static head-above-the-neck-above-the-trunk, etc., pose. Yet what the 1-year-old learns is a dynamic skill, one that enables him or her to keep the head and body upright and focused on the stream of action. This is why falling is actually an important part of learning to stand, because through falling one discovers the limits of one's equilibrium.

We are very much in need of studies on dynamic standing at all ages. It is well known that walking undergoes significant changes from birth through adolescence (Bernstein, 1967 as cited in Whiting, 1984), as the stepping movements and overall bodily posture are functionally correlated with the changes in body size and proportions. It is likely that these sorts of changes continue in older adulthood, and it is also likely that significant alterations in stance go along with these developments. Dynamic stance is best conceived of as a perceptuomotor skill in which the CNS is able to detect the limits of reversible action, so that movements and postures that would tend to bring the entire body into an unstable position, or move a portion of the body with sufficient force to establish a disbalancing counterforce, are automatically eliminated. If this is the case, the CNS must continually adapt to bodily changes across the life span and recalibrate its ability to maintain equilibrated stance. How is such recalibration achieved, and does it ever break down? Are sudden changes in bodily configuration (e.g., amputation or serious weakening) too rapid to be adapted to?

THE ROLE OF POSTURE IN
MOTOR FUNCTION

The phenomenon that least well accords with traditional motor theories but that is central to the action systems approach is the *increasing flexibility* of behavior with practice and repetition. Repeated activity produces not "stamped in" responses and stereotypies, but *adaptable skills.* One's ability to accomplish a task is refined and made precise through repetition, but not because repetition develops and locks in a unitary motor mechanism. On the contrary, practice seems inevitably to produce a vicariously ie, (the same unit participates in different types of skills) functioning system, for which a given goal can be reached by diverse means.

According to traditional views, the course of postural development should be one in which primitive self-support mechanisms are made increasingly efficient through a combination of maturation and experience, yielding automatic postural programs of considerable precision. In the cases for which data are available, almost the exact opposite seems to be the case, as the following examples illustrate.

In the case of stepping (Forssberg, 1985; Thelen et al., this volume, Chap. 2), prewalking infants produce stepping movements when they are adequately supported (the so-called "stepping response"). The rhythmic production of this stepping is quite precise (although its temporal structure is not as precise as that of functional mature walking, at least when the latter is performed on a treadmill in a laboratory). The kinematic details of this stepping pattern in prewalking infants are also rather stereotyped: there is no heel strike in front of the body, the hips and knee joints are flexed synchronously in swing phase and hyper-flexed throughout the cycle, and interestingly, extensor muscles seem to be coactivated, so that the ankle is extended prior to contact. Such a pattern is obviously not functional for the generation of propulsive force, but it is precise and stereotyped. Nevertheless, these and other patterns of early stepping break down and are reorganized over the first few years of life, as Bernstein showed in the 1930s (Bernstein, 1967, cited in Whiting, 1984). Mature gait is characterized by considerably increased variability and flexibility among the movements of component joints, but with a corresponding increase in temporal precision of the key phases of the step cycle, such as heel strike and the exertion of propulsive force.

Winter (1985: p. 252) has pointed out that the variability inherent in gait is of considerable value. In normal gait a great variety of forces "can result in the same joint angle history; and, in turn, many combinations of agonist and antagonist muscle forces will result in the same [overall] moment of force." He adds that "this variability is often a synergistic flexibility" enabling adaptive performance, even in the face of pathology. What is learned in learning how to walk is precisely that many different muscle combinations can yield the same functional outcome and that a variety of sources of reactive forces can therefore be put to use in the coordination of efficient gait. What is *not* learned in walking are the movements involved in stepping, muscle activities, or joint rotations. The locomotor action system learns to achieve the goals of locomotion through coordinating a large and diverse set of mechanisms involved in stepping and erect posture. This functional ability can and does get more efficient with practice and development, but not by achieving stereotypy of movement patterns or motor mechanisms. The greater adaptability and efficiency results from practice, creating a CNS in which a very diverse range of perceptuomotor ensembles can be mutually coordinated for a specific functional end.

This same developmental pattern of increasing functional specificity with decreasing stereotypy of pattern has been found in the study of the development of reaching. For example, von Hofsten (1979; von Hofsten & Lindhagen, 1979; von Hofsten, 1986) has studied the changing patterns of reaches for moving objects in 3- to 6-month-old infants. He defined a trajectory component as a unit of the reach in which acceleration is followed by deceleration. Even the youngest infants showed a noticeable tendency to adapt their reaches to the velocity and distance of the object. The reaches performed by these younger infants were the most stereotyped, tending to be constructed out of four or more approximately equal trajectory units. By the time these infants were 6 months old their reaches were much closer to the adult pattern. Overall variability increased, as control over reaching to precise positions and at precise speeds improved. Further, the reaches were comprised of two units, the initial component accounting for about 90% of the desired trajectory and the second being a smaller, "corrective" component. What was learned was how to reach to objects in different places and with different motions, not particular patterns of reaching movements.

Even when reaching is only an incidental part of a different manual skill, development does not appear to be based on the "stamping in" of movement patterns. When Richardson (1932, 1934) studied the task of pulling a string in order to move a lever and thereby obtain a toy in 10-month-olds, she found little evidence that repetition of movements was important in the acquisition of the skill. What appeared to be most important was that the child learn to perceive the results of his or her activity, despite the variability of both circumstances and movements. An important part of this developmental process, I believe, is the child's growing ability to control posture in dynamic ways so as to be able to achieve functional results in a variety of settings despite limited movement control.

The importance of practice and repetition is not so much to stamp in patterns of movement, but rather to encourage the functional organization of action systems. This principle is constant throughout life: the achievement of an action is not the agent's coming to possess an immutable motor program, but rather the development of a skill. This means the ability to use perceptual information so as to coordinate movements and postures in a flexible manner that serves to accomplish the desired task. For example, although many people in their sixties and seventies are less stable when their posture is perturbed than those in their twenties and thirties, many older adults nevertheless learn to adapt to such perturbations as well as do the younger ones (Woollacott, 1986).

The traditional view of posture as the ability of the CNS to "respond" to gravity should give way to a more functional approach, emphasizing not stability but *resilience*: the controlled and flexible use of all the forces acting on our bodies. The emphasis should be not on the achieving of a stable state, but on a dynamic process of continuously symmetricalizing the forces acting on the body so as to control the resultant forces in ways compatible with the task at hand. In the traditional view the sensory systems directly influential on posture are the proprioceptive systems of the musculature and skeleton and the vestibular system; in the present view *all* the perceptual systems can contribute information relevant to the control of posture (Gibson, 1966; Reed, 1982). Recent research has shown that multimodal perceptual functioning is well established in the first half year of life (Gibson, 1987), and this apparently lays a solid foundation for the leading role of perceptual guidance in the development of action. The ability of the developing child to control and maintain postures during the course of activity thus counts as an important index of action development.

RELATION OF POSTURES TO MOVEMENTS

Many of the actions of infants that are studied experimentally are not, strictly speaking, autonomously generated. Without considerable and precise postural support, infants under 6 months of age do not, for example, reach very accurately or rotate their heads to track moving objects with real precision. However, if such infants are in a properly positioned infant chair or held supportively on a caretaker's lap, they can and do produce these behaviors in very wellformed ways. More than anything, such phenomena reflect the necessity of postural control for the facilitation of many movements. Thus posture plays a very important role in the development of truly autonomous action. The infant who requires external support before she can act effectively cannot really be said to act in a functional and adaptive way.

Some clinicians have noted the extraordinary effects of providing postural support on movement patterns in infancy. Amiel-Tisson & Grenier (1980), in particular, claim that even 1- or 2-month-old babies can be made to produce quite mature reaching patterns if their heads are properly supported and positioned. These authors also comment on the improved smoothness of the infant's movements and muscle tone when their heads are thus positioned (all of which is reminiscent of the Alexander technique). Without quantitative measurement, these claims are difficult to evaluate. Nevertheless, several experiments on human and animal infants have produced similar findings. Thelen and Fisher (1982) have shown that when 1-month-old and slightly older infants are submerged up to their chests in warm water, stepping patterns are seen, which would not normally be seen due to the weight of the limb. Fentress (1981) reports that when 2-week-old mice are provided with postural support they produce forelimb movements that appear to be components of adult grooming activities. The baby mice do not, however, make reliable contact with their faces, so the movements are nonfunctional. By way of contrast, Gustafson (1984) showed that postural support can allow the emergence of functional higher level cognitive activity. She took prelocomoting infants and placed them in "baby walker" devices. These children spontaneously reorganized their perceptual scanning of the environment to take in information about objects across the room. Previously out of reach, these toys were now accessible, and the infants—without benefit of prior self-locomotion experience—were able to organize more mature patterns of explorations in accord with their new postural and locomotion abilities.

If postural support can yield such dramatic changes in behavior, it would seem unreasonable to limit our concept of the effects of posture to that of simply a stabilizing mechanism. For example, posture can help to organize behaviors beyond those directly related to the function of stability (i.e., supporting an infant's body can change its visual scanning patterns). We do not know with certainty all the mechanisms underlying postural control, but we can safely say that, whatever mechanisms are involved, they have far reaching consequences on multiple action systems.

Throughout the course of the development of action there appears to be a systematic relation between posture and movement. Postural control of the head-neck-trunk system is a necessary precondition for the development of both smooth visual exploration and functional reaching. Bullinger (1983) has shown that visual tracking of objects in the first month of life is achieved largely through rotation of the trunk and head together. Gradually, this mass-action style coordination is differentiated, and the shoulders, neck, arms, and head can be moved separately, at least to some degree. Finally, at about 4 months, the head and trunk can move independently with some skill when the infant is visually tracking. Owen & Lee (1986: Fig. 3) have shown that eye movements are the *last* component of this coordinated action to develop, after the ability to move the head and trunk independently is intact: at 25 weeks, infants' abilities to track objects with their heads appear to be equal to adults', but their eye movements are less accurate and more irregular. In the case of reaching, similar results have been reported. For example, infants as old as 6 months have been reported to move their hands approximately the same distance when reaching for static targets at different distances—compensating by adjusting their trunks (Harris, 1983: 711). However, by 9 months, reaches are much more mature in form, including anticipatory rotation of the hand to meet static targets in different orientations (Lockman et al., 1984). Thus, some postural ability seems to develop before, or coincident to, the expression of mature movement performance.

Many of the previous studies have examined balance in bilaterally symmetrical tasks. Goldfield (1987) has shown that naturally arising asymmetrical tasks may produce instabilities—which can have the functional outcome of facilitating the development of new action skills. In particular, Goldfield has studied how crawling appears to emerge from instabilities produced by asymmetrical reaching when infants are seated. When a seated baby reaches for an object just barely within reach, or even out of reach, there is a risk that the child will lose balance and fall. Goldfield studied ten infants between 6 and 9 months old for a period of eight to ten weeks. Out of 106 falls from seated position, in 97 of them the infants landed on their *non*dominant hands, suggesting that the infants had been reaching and that the nondominant hand was beginning to play the support role it performs in more mature individuals. In such behavior the integration of posture and movement is complete; the nondominant hand typically playing a postural role as a way of supporting the goals of the reaching movement; and this Goldfield suggests, may initiate the first phase of crawling, with knee and hand support. The learning of an action like crawling is not limited to the acquisition of a movement pattern; instead it is a coordination of a variety of postural and movement subsystems in the service of an environmental goal.

POSTURES AS UNITS OF ACTION

From the functional perspective adopted here, the key to understanding posture control is to determine how posture is related to action. This means treating posture as a component of voluntary acts and analyzing the role posture plays in support of actions. Droulez & Berthoz (1986) provide a nice illustration of how the upright posture is adapted to functional differences derived from the act of holding onto an object while walking. A person holding something that requires careful looking (e.g., a book to be read) will adopt a different relation of the arms to the trunk and head than someone holding an object that requires delicate balance (e.g., a container full of liquid). In the former case, the arms are used to link the object as directly as possible to the head and eyes, whereas in the latter case the arms are freed from the trunk's motion, the elbows being held out and high, so as to maintain a consistent path of the object with respect to gravity and to the inertial forces generated by locomotion. Different postures would presumably be used for other tasks, such as carrying a heavy fragile object or carrying something to be placed in a particular location. There are definite limits to the adaptive flexibility of the postural system, however. Mayer et al (1987) have shown that requiring normal subjects to walk at very slow speeds (>4 sec/step) and with some precision (stepping on target lines) induces "gait deviations" including aberrant stance and head position, tremor, abnormally long single-foot stance, and more. In attempting to support these extreme movement requirements, the postural system reveals some of the limits to its flexibility. Naturalistic analyses of the range of postural support required by different tasks needs to be pursued. We need to know what *range* of postural activities is normal for daily tasks, for only then can experimental "dissection" of posture and movements yield results that will be meaningful to either theorists or clinicians.

The work of Ingvarsson and his colleagues (1986) on pathologies of posture in Parkinsonian patients provides an excellent illustration of this research strategy. They chose an important ADL task in which postural adjustment plays a large role: stooping to pick up a heavy object, then stepping forward to place it on a shelf at about head height. They measured the trajectories of the heel, toe, knee, hip, shoulder, and arm, and used both normals and Parkinson's patients on L-Dopa as controls against which to compare Parkinson's patients off L-Dopa. They established a normal range of posture for this task by documenting that healthy control subjects typically "nest" movements into postures: the act of getting erect preceded the stepping and arm movements by a very short time. The stepping and reaching tended to come together, with the stepping slightly prior to the reaching. Phase portraits of the trajectories revealed that this sequencing was a topologically invariant pattern for this task. Parkinsonian adults off L-Dopa lost the integration of posture and movement, with a very long delay between stepping and reaching, and significant breakdowns of the topological patterning of the movements. Other researchers have documented a loss of functionally specific adaptation of posture to movement in Parkinson's patients (Bazalgette et al., 1986).

It is now well established that when a person is engaged in a goal-directed manual task there is always anticipatory postural activity that functions in a specific way to balance the body for the intended movement and for the direction and intensity of forces it will bring to play upon the body (Belen'kii et al., 1967; Lee, 1980; Cordo & Nashner, 1982; Marsden et al., 1983). In Parkinsonian patients these postural adjustments are rarely anticipatory and often are more in the nature of undifferentiated activity than precisely tuned to the needs of the task.

How have normal adults developed such exquisitely precise action skills whereby an enormous range of postural settings can be deployed to facilitate the function of an action? This should be a key question of future research on postural development. In answering this question we shall have to come to grips with the role of variability in action development. Consider, for example, a toddler who wants to engage in activity at a play table, perhaps manipulating blocks or a puzzle. She brings her tiny chair or stool over to the table, sets it up, and begins to play. But she has not noticed that she has placed the chair a relatively great distance from the table surface. Or perhaps she has noticed this but has not realized its significance. Or perhaps she understands that this situation might create problems, but she is not yet capable of making the appropriate compensatory adjustments. At any rate, she quickly discovers that she "cannot reach" all her toys well enough to play. She gets frustrated and perhaps even complains that she "can't do it." (Or, worse, she acts in a way that she cannot fully control, such as standing on the chair and leaning far over—perhaps causing an accident.)

Indeed, the toddler in this story cannot do it. But what exactly is it that she cannot do? And what is the primary reason for the failure? Casually, we might say that "she cannot reach." Yet reaching is precisely what the child *can* do. What she cannot do is *set up* the situation so that she can use her reaching skills effectively. What the child has not done, may be unable to do, or unable to notice the need to do, is to adjust her "posture" to the task, (that is, her initial spatial orientation) so as to create the conditions that enable smooth, skillful action. Such difficulties in organizing posture-movement appropriate to the task appear to be implicated in a number of kinds of accidents in young children and perhaps even in older adults.

Finally, problems with anticipatory postural adjustments appear to be involved in a variety of so-called "movement disorders," from Parkinsonianism to traumatic brain injury and its sequelae. Unfortunately, there is a paucity of studies examining normal anticipatory postural control in ADLs, so quantitative comparisons of postural deviations—analogous to the important work on gait deviations (Winter, 1985)—cannot yet proceed.

CONCLUSION

We have assumed for too long that motor development is limited to the development of movements and their underlying mechanisms. But movements in isolation from their environmental context are a biological fiction. No functional movement, such as reaching, exists, except as embedded in a complex situation and nested into a given postural setting. Both the environmental context and the postural context affect the nature and success of movements. Moreover, the concept of a single mechanism of movement is also a biological fiction. The neuromuscular components of any task will vary radically when the task is done standing versus seated, for example. From the point of view of the CNS, to learn to act is to organize various ensembles of perceptuomotor components so as to achieve invariant outcomes. The fact that posture and movement are so precisely and functionally integrated provides an insight into how such neural ensembles develop. We should therefore pursue naturalistic analyses of tasks and actions, with special emphasis on the normal range of variability found in postural support for voluntary actions.

What makes our activities functional is their specificity to the ongoing task. This specificity cannot be analyzed if experimentalists insist on using *non*tasks in their studies. In the 1980s there has been a growing awareness of the need to bring functional activity into our laboratories. But the present analysis also underscores the need to study function across a range of natural conditions. A given daily task may be accomplished in a large number of ways; in addition normal adults accomplish ADLs in various ways in different settings. There are, for example, innumerable ways to reach out and fork up a morsel of food. What unites these diverse movements and variable means into a coherent type of action is precisely the task: use a fork to transport food from a table to one's mouth. Someone who was able to accomplish this goal under only very restricted conditions would not be said to know how to use a fork. As has been emphasized throughout this chapter, a key factor in constraining motor variability into functional action is adaptable and flexible nesting of movement and posture. What enables a normal person to be able to use a fork standing, seated, lying down, with different-sized bites, and so on, is the ability to use available perceptual information to adapt both posture and movement allowing use of a fork in any given instance.

Action development consists in large part of the development of this adaptively flexible nesting of movement and posture so as to achieve intended outcomes. (This is what Bernstein meant when he spoke of motor learning as being accomplished by lowering the ban on the number of degrees of freedom deployed in a task.) We should be studying how such flexibility develops in general and, in particular, the role played by postural development across the life span in, first, opening up the possibilities for flexible action and, later, narrowing them down. For both theoretical and practical reasons, then, we need to begin studying postural control in natural contexts. We need to try to learn from the variability inherent in skilled performance as well as from its consistency. And, most especially, we need to discover how the functional attunement of posture to movement variability emerges in the first few years of life and becomes a stable unit of action across the rest of the life span.

REFERENCES

Alexander, F. M. (1974). *The resurrection of the body: The essential writings of F. M. Alexander.* New York: Dell Books.

Amiel-Tisson, C., & Grenier, A. (1980). *Neurological evaluation of the human infant.* New York: Masson.

Arutunyan, G. A.; Gurfinkel, V. S.; & Mirskii, M. L. (1968). Investigation of aiming at a target. *Biophysics, 131*, 642–45.

Bazalgette, D.; Zattara, M.; Bathien, N.; Bouisset, S.; & Rondot, P. (1986). Postural adjustments associated with rapid voluntary arm movements in patients with Parkinson's disease. *Advances in Neurology, 45*, 371–74.

Belenkei, U. Jr.; Gurfinkel, V. S.; & Pal'tsev Jr. (1967). Elements of control of voluntary movement. *Biophysics,* 12: 154–60.

Bernstein, N. (1967). *The coordination and regulation of movements.* London: Pergamon. Reprinted in H. T. A. Whiting (Ed.), *Human motor actions: Bernstein re-assessed.* Amsterdam: North Holland, 1984.

Bonnet, M.; Gurfinkel, V.; Lipchits, M.-J.; & Popov, K.-E. (1976). Central programming of lower limb muscular activity in the standing man. *Aggressologie, 17*, 35–42.

Bullinger, A. (1983). Space, the organism, and objects, their cognitive elaboration in the infant. In A. Hein & M. Jeannerod (Eds.), *Spatially oriented behavior.* New York: Springer-Verlag.

Butterworth, G. (1983). The structure of the mind in human infancy. In L. Lipsitt & C. K. Rovee-Collier (Eds.); *Advances in infancy research* (Vol. 2, pp. 1–30). Norwood, NJ: Ablex.

Cordo, P., & Nahsner, L. (1982). Properties of postural adjustments associated with rapid arm movements. *Journal of Neurophysiology, 47*, 287–302.

Danziger, K. (1983). The origin of the schema of stimulated motion in eighteenth century neuropsychology. *History of Science, 21*, 183–210.

Descartes, R. (1649). *The passions of the soul.* Reprinted in J. Cottingham, R. Stoothoff, & D. Murdoch (Eds.), *Descartes' Philosophical Works.* Cambridge: Cambridge University Press, 1986.

Droulez, J., & Berthoz, A. (1986). Servo-controlled (conservative) versus topological (projective) mode of sensory motor control. In W. Bles & Th. Brandt (Eds.), *Disorders of posture and gait.* Amsterdam: Elsevier.

Easter, S. S.; Purves, D.; Rakic, P.; & Spitzer, N. (1985). The changing view of neural specificity. *Science, 230*, 507–11.

Edelman, G. (1987). *Neural Darwinism.* New York: Basic Books.

Elner, A. M.; Popov, K. E.; & Gurfinkel, V. S. (1972). Changes in stretch reflexes concerned with the control of postural activity of human muscle. *Aggressologie, 13*, 19–23.

Forssberg, H. (1985). Ontogeny of human locomotor control, I. Infant stepping, supported locomotion and transition to independent locomotion. *Experimental Brain Research, 57*, 480–93.

Gallistel, C. R. (1980). *The organization of action.* Hillsdale, NJ: Erlbaum.

Gibson, E. (1987). What does infant perception tell us about theories of perception? *Journal of Experimental Psychology: Human Perception and Performance, 13*, 515–23.

Gibson, J. J. (1966). *The Senses Considered as Perceptual Systems.* Boston: Houghton-Mifflin.

Fentress, J. (1981). Sensorimotor Development. In R. Aslin, J. Alberts & M. Petersen (Eds.), *Development of Perception Vol. 1: Audition, Somatic Perception, and the Chemical Senses.* New York: Academic Press.

Goldfield, E. (1987). Symmetry and asymmetry in the transition from rocking to crawling. Paper presented to the Society for Research in Child Development, April, Baltimore, MD.

Grene, M. (1985). *Descartes*. Minneapolis: University of Minnesota Press.

Gurfinkel, V. S. (1973). Muscle afferentation and postural control in man. *Aggressologie, 14*, 1–8.

Gustafson, G. (1984). Effects of the ability to locomote on infants' social and exploratory behaviors: An experimental study. *Developmental Psychology, 20*, 397–405.

Harris, P. (1983). Infant cognition. In P. Mussen, H. Haith & J. Campos (Eds.), *Handbook of child psychology*, Vol. 2, New York: Wiley.

Hofsten, C. von. (1979). Development of visually guided reaching: The approach phase. *Journal of Human Movement Studies, 5*, 160–78.

Hofsten, C. von. (1986). The emergence of manual skills. In M. Wade & H. T. A. Whiting (Eds.), *Motor development in children: Aspects of coordination and control*. Amsterdam: M. Nijhoff.

Hofsten, C., von, & Lindhagen, K. (1979). Observations on the development of reaching for moving objects. *Journal of Experimental Child Psychology, 28*, 158–73.

Ingvarsson, P.; Johnels, B.; Lund, S.; & Steg, G. (1986). Coordination of manual, postural, and locomotor movements during simple goal-directed motor tasks in Parkinsonian Off and On states. *Advances in Neurology, 45*, 375–82.

Jones, F. P. (1965). Method for changing stereotyped response patterns by the inhibition of postural sets. *Psychological Review, 72*, 411-425.

Kaas, J. (1987). The organization of neocortex in mammals: Implications for theories of brain function. *Annual Review of Psychology, 38*, 129–51.

Lee, W. (1980). Anticipatory control of postural and task muscles during rapid arm flexion. *Journal of Motor Behavior, 12*, 185–96.

Lockman, J. J.; Ashmead, D. H.; & Bushnell, E. W. (1984). The development of anticipatory hand orientation during infancy. *Journal of Experimental Child Psychology, 37*, 176–86.

Magnus, R. (1924). *Körperstellung*. Berlin: Springer.

Magnus, R. (1925). Animal posture (The Croonian Lecture). *Proceedings of the Royal Society of London, 98*, 339–52.

Marsden, C. D.; Merton, P. A; & Morton, H. B. (1983). Rapid postural reactions to mechanical displacement of the hand in man. *Advances in Neurology, 39*, 645–59.

Martin, J. Purdon. (1977). A short essay on posture and movement. *Journal of Neurology, Neurosurgery, and Psychiatry, 40*, 25–29.

Mayer, N.; Ridenour, M.; & Kent, L. (1987). Stride length variability and the average velocity of human gait. Paper presented to the Society for Neuroscience, November, New Orleans, LA.

Nashner, L., & McCollum, G. (1985). The organization of human postural movements: A formal basis and experimental synthesis. *Behavioral and Brain Sciences, 8*, 135–72.

Owen, B. M., & Lee, D. N. (1986). Establishing a frame of reference for action. In M. Wade & H. T. A. Whiting (Eds.), *Motor development in children: Aspects of coordination and control*. Dordrecht: M. Nijhoff.

Pearson, K. G. (1985). Are there central pattern generators for walking and flight in insects? In W. J. Barnes & M. H. Gladden (Eds.), *Feedback and motor control in invertebrates and vertebrates*. London: Croom Helm.

Reed, E. S. (1982a). An outline of a theory of action systems. *Journal of Motor Behavior, 14*, 98–134.

Reed, E. S. (1982b). Descartes' corporeal ideas hypothesis and the origin of scientific psychology. *Review of Metaphysics, 35*, 731–52 (B).

Reed, E. S. (1989). Neural regulation of adaptive behavior. *Ecological Psychology, 1*, 97–118.

Richardson, H. M. (1932). The growth of adaptive behavior in infants: An experimental study of seven age levels. *Genetic Psychology Monographs, 12*, 195–359.

Richardson, H. M. (1934). The adaptive behavior of infants in the utilization of the lever as a tool: A developmental and experimental study. *Journal of Genetic Psychology, 44*, 352–77.

Rochat, P. (1987). Mouthing and grasping in neonates: Evidence for early detection of what hard and soft substances afford for action. *Infant Behavior and Development, 11*, 261–278.

Rozendal, R. H. (1986). Biomechanics of standing and walking. In W. Bles & Th. Brandt (Eds.), *Disorders of posture and gait*. Amsterdam: Elsevier.

Schaltenbrand, G. (1928). The development of human motility and motor disturbances. *Archives of Neurology and Psychiatry, 20*, 720–30.

Sherrington, C. S. (1906). *The integrative action of the nervous system*. New Haven: Yale University Press.

Shumway-Cook, A., & Woollacott, M. (1985). The growth of stability: Postural control from a developmental perspective. *Journal of Motor Behavior, 17(2)*, 131–47.

Simons, A. (1953) Head posture and muscle tone. *Physical Therapy Review, 33*, 409–19.

Stoffregen, T., & Riccio, G. (1988). An ecological theory of orientation and the vestibular system. *Psychological Review*, 95:3–14.

Thelen, E. & Fisher, D. M. (1982). Newborn stepping: An explanation for a disappearing reflex. *Develop Psychology, 18*, 760–75.

Thomas, D. P., & Whitney, R. J. (1959). Postural movements during normal standing in man. *Journal of Anatomy, 93*, 524–39.

Weisz, S. (1938). Studies in equilibrium reaction. *Journal of Nervous and Mental Diseases, 88*, 150–62.

Whytt, R. (1751). *An essay on the vital and other involuntary motions of animals*. Edinburgh: Balfour et al.

Winter, D. (1985). Concerning the scientific basis for the diagnosis of pathological gait and for rehabilitation protocols. *Physiotherapy Canada, 37*, 245–52.

Woollacott, M. (1986). Gait and postural control in the aging adult. In W. Bles & Th. Brandt (Eds.), *Disorders of posture and gait*. Amsterdam: Elsevier.

2

The Developmental Origins of Locomotion

Esther Thelen,
Beverly D. Ulrich,
and Jody L. Jensen

THEORETICAL OVERVIEW:
Dynamical Processes in Movement and Development

Normal human infants walk independently when they are about one year of age. During the preceding year, we can trace their progress toward bipedal locomotion through a series of reasonably well defined "stages," which index increasing levels of skill. Traditionally, psychologists, neurologists, and therapists have interpreted these stages as development from simple reflexes and subcortical motor responses through cortical inhibition of these reflexes to the growing influence of the voluntary or cortical motor control centers.

We present here a different picture of locomotor development. Although there can be no argument that locomotion (and all other skills) reflects maturation of the motor cortex, we believe that much more complex ontogenetic processes also underlie this seemingly linear developmental progression. In this chapter we take the view that upright walking is an *emergent* property of these interacting, complex processes, each of which is necessary, but in itself not sufficient, to determine the skill. Our tasks in such a developmental analysis, then, are to identify the component processes and to suggest how their interaction leads to the observed developmental sequence that culminates in walking.

Our theoretical perspective on the development of locomotion derives from an approach to motor behavior, a dynamical systems view, adapted from the works of Bernstein (1967) and recently given precise elaboration by Kelso, Turvey, Kugler, and their colleagues. These authors, in turn, use concepts from the more general field of synergetics, or nonlinear dynamics (see, for example, Haken, 1983), which deal with cooperative phenomena in a wide variety of physical and biological systems. It is beyond the scope of this chapter to explicate in detail the dynamical principles we use to characterize motor development; readers are referred to the more extended treatments by Kelso & Tuller (1984), Kugler & Turvey (1987), Thelen, Kelso & Fogel (1987), and Thelen (1986b; in press a, b). We present instead a brief synopsis of our assumptions and their implications for studying locomotion in particular.

The fundamental assumption of a dynamical approach is that moving and developing organisms are complex, cooperative systems. Animals that move and develop are composed of many anatomical parts and physiological processes. Every action requires that these component elements act cooperatively. A motor task requires assembling a synergy of muscle groups spanning many body segments and joints; even the most simple finger movement can require adjustments of posture in elements far removed from the moving digit (Marsden, Merton & Morton, 1983). But movement is more than muscles and motoneurons; all the elements of the organism must participate in a cooperative way to ensure a functionally appropriate outcome, including sensory, perceptual, and integrative neural components, vegetative support such as respiration and cardiac function, anatomical elements, and many levels of autonomic processes.

A second fundamental assumption in our approach is that moving and developing systems have certain "self-organizing" properties. By self-organization we mean that these systems can spontaneously form patterns that arise solely from the interaction of the component parts. Thus, when an infant kicks, the trajectory of the movement, which has highly predictable and rhythmical properties, is not coded anywhere in the nervous system. Rather, the trajectory is a function of the assembly of many elements, including the neural substrate, but also the anatomical linkages, the body composition of the infant, his or her generalized activation level, the gravitational conditions, and so on.

Note that this "self-assembly" occurs only within a particular context for the organism. No moving animal exists in a functional or environmental vacuum. All animals live surrounded by fluid or gas and with certain gravitational demands, and with certain functional tasks to accomplish. Thus, it is not enough to ask about the parts and processes of the organism without considering also how those parts and processes are assembled in a context.

The fact that such complex systems "hold together" to form time and space patterns without prior instructions has profound implications for our study of motor development. This means that at any point during development the motor outcome is a product of all the functionally related elements acting cooperatively, rather than of some preexisting code in the nervous system or in some abstract developmental timetable. Given, then, any particular developmental status of the infant or child and a particular context for the assembly of the action, the system can be said to "prefer" a certain range of motor outputs, but these outputs are nowhere prespecified.

When we characterize the motor system as self-organizing, we abandon our notions of motor programs or reflexes as rigidly determined and adopt a view of movement as continua of relative stability and flexibility. The Babinski reflex is perhaps less flexible than an adaptive reach for a toy, but even the reflex is responsive to context. Likewise, single leg supine kicking appears to be a more stable configuration at 2 months, but it is not an obligatory coordination. In our characterization of locomotor development we shall see many examples in which infants prefer certain movement topographies at particular ages and in certain contexts but in which other configurations can also be elicited.

The third important assumption in this approach is that during ontogeny the component structures and processes of a skill develop in an asynchronous and nonlinear manner. That is, some elements show an accelerated developmental course and may be available long in advance of the skill, whereas others mature more slowly. Since all components are necessary for the performance of the skill, earlier components must await the slower, or *rate-limiting*, elements. In Figure 2–1 we depict the developing organism as such a parallel assembly of components, each with a distinct developmental profile. At any point in time the resulting behavior is the cooperative interaction of these elements, specific to and organized by the context (the task and the environment at hand). Thus, for any given task environment and any given developmental status of the components, the organism will prefer a certain behavioral output. Under other conditions, different movement topographies may emerge. Depending on the context, available components may be masked or manifest, since their appearance is a function of the composite assembly.

A fourth important property is characteristic of complex dynamical systems. Shifts from one qualitative behavioral mode to another are often discontinuous. A commonly cited example is quadruped gait (e.g., Kelso, 1982). As a horse, for instance, increases speed in locomotion, it shifts from a walk to a trot to a gallop with no apparent intermediate gait configurations. What is significant is that this shift is accomplished by a continuous scalar of one parameter, the energy delivered to the system. In dynamical terminology, this parameter that can shift qualitative modes is called the *control parameter*. For development this

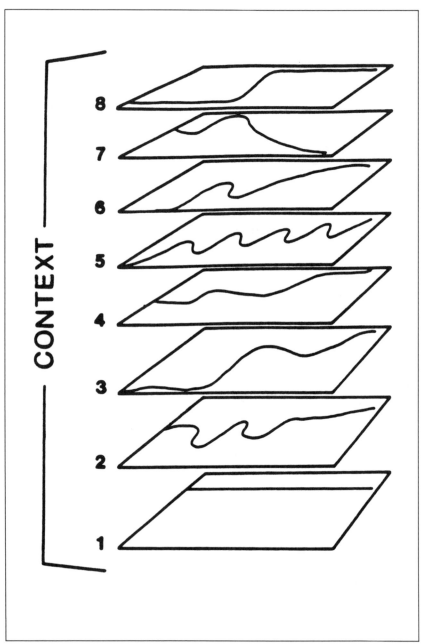

Fig. 2–1. A developing system depicted as a layered system of interacting components, each with its own developmental profile. Outcome at any point in time is context-dependent, indicated by the whole system bracket.

suggests that, although all systems are undergoing change, a small change in only one or a few control parameters can disrupt the entire system sufficiently to have it seek another preferred stable output. At important changes in locomotor development, then, we would expect to identify components that may act as control parameters to engender such shifts. Our model suggests that at different times in ontogeny different subsystems act as control parameters.

Such a dynamical characterization leads to the following analysis of locomotor development. First, we identify likely subsystems or components essential for the assembly of the skill and trace the ontogenetic course of such components. In this way we notice which elements are in place early and which are slower to develop. In particular, we discuss motivation and voluntary control, non-neural components of upright locomotion such as body proportion and composition, pattern generation, and posture and balance. The questions of motivation, voluntary control, and body-build factors have been discussed elsewhere (Thelen, 1984) and we mention them only briefly here. Instead we focus on the components for which there has been significant recent research: developmental origins of pattern generation and posture and balance. We then show how a dynamic systems view can explain locomotion as an emergent, self-organizing process.

COMPONENTS IN A DYNAMICAL VIEW OF LOCOMOTOR DEVELOPMENT

MOTIVATION TO WALK AND VOLUNTARY CONTROL

Independent walking is preeminently a voluntary behavior. This means that the infant must both *want* to travel toward a goal and have the means of translating that desire into directed movements. We could imagine a developmental scenario in which human infants *could* walk independently but did not *want* to. Although there has been little formal study on motivation to locomote, this scenario seems slightly absurd because of our common-sense notion that attention to the goal and the impulse to accomplish it not only come before but drive the appearance of the skill.

Because infants crawl many months before they walk and will locomote in wheeled walkers even before crawling, it seems likely that attention to distant events and the desire to move the body to attain some object or social companion is present long before upright locomotion. Likewise, infants have sufficient voluntary control of the lower limbs to move toward goals at these earlier ages. In crawling, this requires a rather complex interlimb phasing. Thus, neither motivation nor control per se appears to be rate-limiting for locomotion. Nonetheless, we know little about the developmental course of these essential processes.

BODY-BUILD CONTRIBUTIONS TO INDEPENDENT LOCOMOTION

Newborn infants are biomechanically ill-suited for upright locomotion. In addition to their overall motor immaturity, newborns have proportionally large heads and trunks, small weak limbs, and narrow shoulders, all of which are biomechanically disadvantageous and perhaps even prohibitive for upright stance. The first eighteen months are a time of rapid growth, with changes in body proportion and composition that facilitate bipedal walking. The legs become proportionally longer in relation to the trunk, and trunk and limb growth outpaces head growth. Although there is a rapid increase in relative chubbiness in the first few months, there is a marked slimming down by the end of the first year. In addition, changes in the composition of the muscle fibers also promote increased strength (Bayley & Davis, 1935; Eichorn, 1979; Forman, 1966; Shirley, 1931).

In a multicomponent model these anatomical factors are as essential to the final assembly of the behavior as the neurological elements. In the next section we show how simple manipulations of biodynamical parameters such as leg mass can radically alter the movement outcome. There is every reason to believe that the differential growth of the body segments and compositional changes help determine the overall developmental profile of locomotion and may contribute as well to individual variability in attaining this motor milestone.

PRE- AND POSTNATAL PATTERN GENERATION: PRECURSORS TO WALKING

Human locomotion, like legged locomotion in all species, is characterized by precise spatial and temporal patterning of the body segments. This means that the excursions of the joints in one limb are tightly coordinated, as are the cycles of the two limbs. There is an enormous literature describing the kinematic and kinetic parameters of adult locomotion and its presumed neurological basis. We focus here on the developmental precursors to that pattern generation. How do infants assemble their muscles into such functional units?

Newborn infants appear to move in a random and disorganized fashion. However, careful observations have revealed many recognizable and reproducible coordinative patterns even in the newborn period. Some, like rooting, sucking, hand-to-mouth, and grasping, are preferred coordinations elicited by particular stimulus contexts and may serve as early feeding and clinging adaptations. Despite the trend for maturation to proceed in a cephalocaudal direction, highly coordinated movements are also seen in the legs in newborn infants in the form of kicking and stepping. These behaviors are of interest because they appear to be continuous with upright locomotion.

Early coordination in stepping and kicking. When infants are held upright with their trunks tilted slightly forward and their feet resting on a stable surface, they characteristically perform coordinated movements that look similar to mature walking. This so-called newborn "stepping response" has long fascinated pediatricians and neurologists because it seems so paradoxical for a newborn so motorically inept to "walk."

Supine kicking bears a less obvious resemblance to walking. However, the neonate's topographical and temporal patterning of supine kicks is similar to that of newborn stepping and, in several ways, to mature walking. From their kinematic analyses of stepping and kicking in 2-week-old infants, Thelen & Fisher (1982) concluded that these are identical movement patterns differentiated only by the posture in which they are produced. First, both steppng and kicking consisted of four distinct phases with characteristic temporal organization: a flexion phase, a pause between flexion and extension, a steplike forward extension phase, and a between-movement interval. Second, the flexion phase in both actions began with coactive bursts in agonist and antagonist muscles, followed by a passive extension. Third, both action patterns displayed tight temporal and spatial synchrony among hip, knee, and ankle joints; each leg acted as a tightly constrained unit.

In either posture the leg movements of newborn infants "prefer" particular stable modes of organization reflecting the maturational status of the neuromuscular and anatomical components and the motivational state of the infant. Indeed, this stable configuration is likely present even earlier in ontogeny. Heriza (1986) has described coordinated kicking movements in premature infants as early as 28 weeks gestational age identical in topographical organization to the newborn movements. Prechtl (1986) detected alternating flexion and extension movements of the legs during the first half of gestation by ultrasound recordings.

There are a number of striking parallels between these infant action patterns of stepping and kicking and kinematic parameters of mature locomotion. In mature walking a *swing* phase, in which the foot is off the ground and moving forward, alternates with a *stance* phase, in which the foot is in contact with the substrate. Increases in walking speed occur primarily by decreases in the stance phase, while the swing phase remains relatively constant or decreases only slightly (Murray, 1967). In infant kicking and stepping the sum of the flexion phase, pause between flexion and extension, and extension phase is analogous to swing. As with mature walkers, when infants increase kicking or stepping rates, swing phase durations remain almost constant while the between-movement interval, analogous to stance, decreases proportionately (Thelen, Bradshaw & Ward, 1981; Thelen & Fisher, 1982). In addition, most descriptions of infant stepping emphasize the regular, adultlike alternation of the legs (Andre-Thomas & Autgaerden, 1966; Peiper, 1963; Taft & Cohen, 1967). Thelen & Fisher (1982) observed a similar predominance of alternation in both newborn stepping and supine kicking.

There were important differences as well as similarities between these infant action patterns and mature walking. Infant kicking and stepping were more variable in timing than adult patterns. Unlike adults, infants showed a high degree of coactivation of agonist and antagonist muscles during flexion. Infant kicks and steps are characterized by a synchrony among the hip, knee, and ankle joints, whereas in mature walkers these joints enter into the action in a distinct sequence of relative phasing. But most puzzling, infant stepping (although not kicking) disappears by the second month after birth. If these patterns are precursors to upright locomotion, the question becomes, how are they developmentally related?

DEVELOPMENTAL CHANGES IN SPONTANEOUS PATTERN GENERATION

Disappearance of upright stepping. Although step-like leg movements have been reported in fetuses and premature infants, the peak stepping response appears to be at about 1 week of age (Illingsworth, 1972; Touwen, 1976). After the first week of life there is a dramatic decline in the number of steps taken; by 5 or 6 weeks the stepping response is difficult to elicit (Thelen, Fisher & Ridley-Johnson, 1984; Touwen, 1976). Traditionally, this disappearance of stepping has been attributed solely to development of higher cortical centers that inhibit this lower-level—presumably spinal—response. Evidence from several studies suggests a more dynamic explanation.

During the period when stepping naturally disappears, infants are gaining weight rapidly; they are particularly adding adipose tissue in disproportion to muscle. Thelen and colleagues proposed that it is this rapid addition of fat which is responsible for the decrease in stepping: infants' legs become too heavy for their relatively small muscles to lift while upright. This explanation provides an alternative to the well-known results of Zelazo, Zelazo & Kolb (1972), who showed that infants who were encouraged to practice stepping during this period did not lose the ability. Though the experimenters attributed this continuity to instrumental learning, such a systematic exercise program may have increased leg strength and compensated for the rapid fat deposition. Indeed, infants who gained weight most rapidly between the ages of 2 and 6 weeks also took the fewest steps (Thelen et al., 1984). When these researchers submerged 4-week-old infants to chest level in warm water, functionally reducing leg mass, they found that stepping increased dramatically in rate and amplitude. Finally, step rate directly covaries with infant arousal level, a measure of general behavioral activation, suggesting that when more energy is delivered to the muscles, biodynamic limitations can be overcome.

Stepping is clearly a multicausal response in which both neurological and other anatomical elements participate and which self-organizes only within a particular context of posture, fluid medium, and state of activation. In dynamic terminology rapid weight gain acts during normal development as a *control parameter*, shifting the system into a qualitatively new ontogenetic mode—that of no-stepping. However, the no-stepping mode is not predetermined by a code in the central nervous system but emerges from the confluence of organismic conditions and context.

Why, then, does supine kicking persist? Again, the supine posture assembles the system differently, possibly at a biomechanically less-demanding level, so that less force is required to produce the alternating flexion and extension than in the upright posture. That is, the same muscle activation can result in a greater mass moved if working partially with the pull of gravity than entirely against it.

Continuity in leg-pattern generation during the first year. Our claim is that the ability to generate steplike patterns is continuous from the newborn period until independent locomotion, despite the fact that stepping per se disappears. We offer several lines of evidence to support this claim. First, Thelen & Cooke (1987) compared the intralimb coordination patterns and concomitant electromyography (EMG) in stepping at 1 or 2 months of age to that of the same infants 1 and 2 months before independent walking and in the month of the infants' first independent steps. They discovered a *gradual* change in the intralimb patterning. Even by 2 months the tight synchrony of hip, knee, and ankle characteristic of newborn stepping was beginning to dissolve. A more adult-like pattern, in which the knee led the hip in flexion, began to emerge before the onset of walking, but even then some primitive characteristics of newborn stepping remained. Although EMG patterns at walking were more highly differentiated than in the newborn step, much coactivation remained. Even without evidence from the months when normal stepping was suppressed, it looked as if walking coordinative patterns were successively carved out of the more simple newborn patterns. This interpretation contrasts with the discontinuity hypothesis of Forssberg (1985), who suggests that major neurological remodeling soon after the onset of bipedal locomotion is responsible for the emergence of a mature, adult-like gait pattern.

Two additional lines of support for ontogenetic continuity in pattern generation derive from two conditions in which the patterns persist throughout the first year: supine kicking and stepping on a treadmill.

Developmental changes in supine kicking. During the first year the highly synchronous and constrained leg kicks of the newborn become both differentiated into finer actions and integrated with other system components, producing more flexible and adaptive movements. Several trends are evident. First, the intralimb joint correlations, which index the degree of synchrony in movement within the limb, decrease between months 4 and 6 from their initial high level in the newborn, suggesting more individuation. These correlations rise again during the second half of the first year, but by month 10 are again indicating greater individual action. Interlimb organization changes too, from the predominant alternation of the newborn period, to a period of largely unilateral kicks in months 1–4, and back to bilateral coordination, including both alternating and synchronous kicks, by ages 4–6 months. The newborn coactivation of agonist and antagonist muscles seen primarily at the initiation of flexion changes to a biphasic coactivation at both flexion and extension phases, and finally, by 6–9 months into more frequent reciprocal coactivation. As a result, by 7–12 months infants' leg actions show both more individuation in the ability of the joints to work separately and more integration in the ability of the segments to enter into complex phasings needed for crawling and walking (Thelen, 1985; Thelen & Fisher, 1983; Thelen, Ridley-Johnson & Fisher, 1983).

The heterochronous nature of this course of development is striking but not surprising. We can understand this overt behavior only by considering the multiple elements that contribute to it. Kicking does not develop as a unified whole. We see, rather, the systems product of elements each with its own developmental pattern and rate. At different points in time certain elements may mask or facilitate performance in a context, such as the effect of early weight gain. Another important contributor to the uneven course of kicking is the fluctuating dominance of flexor and extensor influences (Thelen, 1985). Gesell (1939) was the first to point out the nonlinear and asynchronous changes in flexor and extensor muscle groups, which lead to a spiral course of development that he called "reciprocal interweaving." Development of voluntary motor centers, control of behavioral arousal, and changes in perception, motivation, and affect may also contribute to the complex picture of kicking.

Stepping on a treadmill. Steplike kicking movements in the supine posture persist throughout the first year and provide a picture of developing coordination in the legs. A second context also allows us to evaluate the mechanisms of pattern generation underlying emergent locomotion. When infants who ordinarily do not step when held upright are supported on a small, motorized treadmill, they will perform well-coordinated, alternating stepping movements (Thelen, 1986a). A recent study in our laboratory showed that this remarkable ability is present very early in life (Thelen, 1988; Thelen & Ulrich, in preparation). We tested nine infants monthly on the treadmill task from ages 1 to 7 months, with some observations continuing until 10 months. When the treadmill was turned on, several infants produced coordinated, alternating steps *at month 1*, or the first time they encountered the treadmill. Although there was considerable variability in the first few months, nearly all the infants were performing treadmill steps well by 4 months of age. Both the number of steps taken and degree of bilateral coordination, as measured by the relative phasing of the two legs (in adults, legs alternate 180 degrees out of phase), improved markedly thereafter. This improvement was dramatic although none of the infants "practiced" on a treadmill and despite the fact that this behavior appeared to be entirely involuntary.

CONTEXT SENSITIVITY

How does the treadmill, a simple mechanical device, elicit stepping in infants normally unable to show such mature-looking coordination? Thelen (1986a) suggested two possibilities: that the mechanical stretch of the leg backward by the moving belt either initiates a reflexive response in the hip or ankle or generates passive viscoelastic forces that, when the leg is released, provide the pendular swing forward.

Although the process by which the treadmill elicits stepping in young infants is unknown, these and other experiments highlight the emergent, context-sensitive nature of leg movements in infants even long before legs are used for voluntary locomotion. On the treadmill, infants at all ages make sensitive adjustments in their step cycle durations to the speed of the treadmill. That is, as the experimenters increased the treadmill speed, infants stepped at a proportionately higher rate, decreasing the duration of their step cycle. This decrease was phase-specific, as it is in other legged animals (Pearson, 1976); the swing phase was affected comparatively little, while the stance phase was inversely proportional to the speed of the treadmill. Such sensitivity was apparent, although not well developed, even in the youngest infants who stepped on the treadmill.

Equally notable is the context-sensitivity of the coordination *between* the legs. In supine kicking, for example, Thelen, Skala & Kelso (1987) found that adding small weights to the legs of 6-week-old infants systematically affected not only the kicks of the weighted leg, but also the frequency and amplitude of the kicks in the unweighted leg. We found a similar bilateral coherence of movement in treadmill stepping. We supported infants on a specially constructed split-belt treadmill, on which one leg could be driven at twice the speed of the other leg. When faced with this discrepant information, infants continued to maintain alternating steps. They did this by decreasing the rate of stepping on the faster belt and increasing it on the slower belt to produce an overall rate that was intermediate between the step rate on either the fast or the slow belt alone (Thelen, Ulrich & Niles, 1987).

In both the kicking and treadmill stepping, infants made involuntary adjustments to perturbations in a two-leg system. In the case of the treadmill, these adjustments were to maintain a near-180-degree alternation, which is essential for upright locomotion. To do this, infants must, at some rather low and nonintentional level, be able to detect information about the dynamic status of one leg and use it to produce a coherent action pattern in both legs. Such self-organization may be a very general characteristic of legged organisms (Kugler & Turvey, 1987).

These findings suggest that the developmental precursors to the coordinative patterns of upright locomotion may not be hard-wired neural networks, but rather "soft-assembled" preferred synergies that coalesce as a function of both task and organism. Changes in these dynamic synergies may occur because the underlying elements change, but the flux is nonlinear.

POSTURE AND LOCOMOTION

Although infants supported on a treadmill can perform complex, coordinated, steplike patterns of movement, they are not walking. They have not combined the pattern generation with the critical ability to independently maintain an upright posture. Throughout the first year, infants must learn to perform adaptive actions within new and increasingly unstable postures. Bipedal locomotion is the most mechanically challenging, as infants are required to provide a stable but shifting base of support while moving forward. This task requires integration of multiple features: coordination of the segments within a dynamic context, muscle strength, and the maturity of postural reflexes and sensory integration.

Postural requirements for bipedal locomotion. Strength and balance are critical features in voluntary motor skills. McGraw (1932) described postural development as acquiring the necessary strength to support an increasing number of body segments against gravity. Strength alone is not enough, however, because instrumental actions require a complementary balance mechanism capable of adapting the posture to contextual demands. As McGraw noted, infants have primitive antigravity abilities at birth, with little or no ability to integrate the actions of the body segments.

Consider even the more simple task of sitting. The trunk, itself composed of thirty-two articulated segments, rests on the pelvic base supported by partially extended legs. The multisegmented arms are connected to the trunk, which is topped by the relatively massive head. The head, trunk, and arms combine to account for 60 to 70% of the total body mass (Schneider, Ulrich, Zernicke & Thelen, in preparation). Initial sitting attempts are characterized by a rounded trunk flexed forward on the thighs, maintained not so much by active muscle strength but by the structure of the articulations, internal volume pressures, and passive muscle stretch. Stable, independent sitting requires sufficient strength to manage a large proportion of the body mass and the equilibratory mechanisms to integrate a large number of segments.

Upright posture is immeasurably more difficult. It is the multiple link structure of thigh, leg, and foot that now supports the trunk. These additions increase the degrees of freedom and provide for flexible postures and movements. However, each joint also is a site of potential structural collapse. Thus, strength is again crucial for sufficient extensor tone to support the total body weight. Integration of control of the segments is even more critical for standing posture because the base of support has diminished and the height of the center of mass increased, factors contributing to reduced stability.

Sitting and standing require only static equilibrium, that is, maintaining the center of mass within the established, stationary base of support. Locomotion, however, requires dynamic equilibrium, or maintaining the erect posture over a constantly changing base of support (Raibert & Sutherland, 1983). Indeed, human bipedal gait is a complex pattern of segmental rotations about all three orthogonal axes of motion (Saunders, Inman & Eberhart, 1985; Sutherland, Olshen, Cooper & Woo, 1980). The system must shift the center of mass from one support to the next, provide for forward propulsion, absorb the landing impact, and control alternate flexor-extensor patterns of multiple segments. Biomechanical complexity notwithstanding, it is not the lack of this pattern-generating capability that constrains the onset of upright independent locomotion. What is required for dynamic stability is the acquisition of strength and the skill of judicious management of self-generated and reactive forces.

Development of postural responses. To successfully move through an environment, an animal must know both about that environment and about its own progress through that environment. Humans obtain such knowledge through their visual, vestibular, and somatosensory systems. Is the onset of independent walking delayed due to immaturity of these sensory functions or inability to process these multiple sensory inputs? Research suggests that appropriate postural responses to information from these sensory modalities is functional, although not fully mature, in advance of walking.

In natural situations people know about moving in the world by integrating information from all three modalities: their eyes, their vestibular apparatus, and by the information conveyed by contact with the support surface. Since these modalities may not develop synchronously, researchers have used ingenious experimental designs to isolate the sensory input to postural responses. Lee & Aronson (1974) created the "moving room" to present subjects with visual information of movement but no corresponding vestibular or somatosensory signals. They did this by moving the walls of the "room" while the subject remained on the detached, stationary floor. When Lee & Aronson tested new walkers, 13–16 months of age, in the moving room, they found that the infants showed directionally appropriate sway patterns, sometimes overcompensating and falling backward, when the walls were moved toward them. Thus, optical flow patterns suggesting forward movement dominated the vestibular and somatosensory inputs suggesting stability.

More recent work has shown that postural corrections in response to visual flow predate the onset of independent walking. Butterworth & Hicks (1977) demonstrated the same sensitivity to visual flow and appropriate postural adjustments in infants who could sit alone but could not stand independently. Other work has confirmed that these postural compensations were a function of the visual flow simulating self-movement rather than just the looming effect of the front wall moving toward the infant. These investigators found correct postural responses in 14- and 18-month-old infants to global flow (the whole room moved) and peripheral flow (only the side walls moved). The infants did not respond to movement of only the front wall, suggesting that they did not perceive central flow as specifying self-movement. In additional experiments these investigators detected appropriate postural movements to global and peripheral retinal flow in infants as young as 7 months. Infants appear to respond to information specifying self-motion long in advance of upright locomotion.

With the moving room, experimenters manipulate the visual flow field. Another instructive paradigm for studying early postural responses has been to perturb the support surface. Subjects stand or sit on a platform that can be moved suddenly forward or backward. Researchers can then monitor subjects' muscle contraction patterns in response to the visual, vestibular, and somatosensory signals of the resulting postural instabilities.

Such experiments have demonstrated that functional, directionally appropriate postural responses to support-surface translations are established by the time infants stand and walk independently. Not surprisingly, the response pattern of the 1-year-old is different from that of an adult. Adults show precisely timed distal-to-proximal synergies (dorsal or ventral, depending on direction of the platform perturbation) and a repertoire of responses of varying complexity (Nashner & McCollum, 1985). Infants, in contrast, depend heavily on more simple monosynaptic reflex responses and coactivation of antagonist muscles, and they generally overcompensate for the perturbation (Berger, Quintern & Deitz, 1985; Haas, Diener, Bacher & Dichgans, 1986; Shumway-Cook & Woollacott, 1985). As would be expected, refinements to the response pattern occur with increasing age and experience. Overcompensations are eliminated and more complex strategies for balance control appear (Haas et al., 1986; Forssberg & Nashner, 1982). Despite the developmental changes in refinement and elaboration yet to come, the new walker has a sufficiently integrated system to compensate for postural perturbations inherent in upright locomotion.

Postural responses, like other skills, are the product of complex, dynamic, and task-dependent developmental processes. When Woollacott (1986) subjected 4-month-old infants seated in an infant seat to a platform translation, their EMG responses in postural muscles were poorly organized. Yet when she removed vision as a source of movement information (infants wore opaque goggles), Woollacott found that the EMG patterns from the postural muscles of the neck and trunk showed appropriate directionally specific patterns. Similarly, although postural responses to platform perturbation in independent sitters were well organized, the same infants looked disorganized when perturbed in a supported stand (Woollacott, 1986). It appears that in both cases the postural system attempted to organize itself *around the task*, which is the maintenance of stability. When deprived of the dominant visual mode, infants were capable of using the available somatosensory and vestibular input. When faced with the more complex task demands of the standing posture, infants could not assemble stable coordinations that were possible in sitting. Tasks called forth preferred responses that depended on the infant's maturational and motivational status in a self-organizing and emergent fashion. We argue in the next section that locomotion itself is such a self-organizing phenomenon whose emergence is paced not by the maturation of a specific bipedal locomotion generator, but by the functional readiness of the rate-limiting parameters such as strength and dynamic balance.

TASK DYNAMICS:
PUTTING IT ALL TOGETHER

Dynamical systems produce behavior as a result of the cooperativity of all the elements. In development some of these elements may be functionally ready before others, but the system must await the slowest component before the target behavior can be exhibited. A small change in this slowest component can act as a control parameter, that is, the impetus driving the system into the new form. We have suggested here that many of the components of locomotor skill are indeed functional in advance of the infant's first steps alone. Steplike within- and between-leg pattern generation, sensitive to dynamic context, may be available from birth and certainly by the second half of the first year when infants are in facilitative contexts. This, in turn, is a product of increasingly independent joint articulations, as infants are released from the tight intralimb synergies of the newborn period and become capable of more complex control. Infants also have sensitivity to optical flow and the ability to make postural compensations in static situations early in the second half of the year. Motivation to move toward a distant object and some level of voluntary control over the legs is by necessity present at the time of creeping and crawling. What are the control parameters, then, that push the infant into independent, upright locomotion? This question requires that we return to the issues of balance and strength.

Consider the infant's first method of independent forward progress: creeping or crawling. In creeping, the trunk is supported on the floor and the infant achieves progression with push/pull actions of the arms and legs. Balance is not a consideration because there is no opportunity for the center of mass to fall outside the base of support. The same may be true for crawling. To crawl, the infant assumes a four-point posture on hands and knees and must lift at least one limb from the support surface to establish a new base of support. With a four-point stance it is possible to move from one static balance position to another by moving only one limb at a time, achieving a tripod stance during each limb swing phase. There are no demands for *dynamic* balance (Raibert & Sutherland, 1983). Indeed, the infant appears to crawl in just such a tripod-based fashion (Inman, Ralston & Todd, 1980). Benson (1985, 1987) has analyzed the hand-knee interaction of the four-point crawling posture. To maximize their stability, infants should minimize the overlap in movement phases of successive limbs (try not to have two limbs in the air simultaneously) and seek a tripod stance between each limb movement. Benson found that once the infant achieved hands-and-knees posture, the limb-alternation pattern tended toward knee 1, hand 1, knee 2, hand 2, where 1 and 2 are the opposite sides of the body. This pattern minimizes the demands of strength and balance better than any pattern requiring simultaneous movement of two limbs or one of hand, hand, knee, knee. Although the latter coordination can provide the stable tripod stance, the infant would have the head and shoulders ahead of both hand supports, which is a muscularly weak position. As the child gains experience in crawling, two support limbs (diagonal or ipsilateral) may be unloaded simultaneously, allowing for greater speed but less stability.

When infants crawl, they use all the elements needed for walking except erect stance and dynamic balance. When the infant becomes biped and attempts to walk, maintaining balance requires the careful management of many forces and torques acting on the system. To maintain the upright posture, the net angular impulse applied to the trunk must be zero, otherwise the trunk segment may be subject to an angular acceleration that thrusts it into disequilibrium (Raibert, 1986). This is no small feat. Walking is often described as a series of intentional falls, separated by brief moments of dynamic equilibrium as the center of mass rotates over the base of support (Alexander, 1984; Mann, Hagy, White & Lidell, 1979). Thus, walking may also be described as a series of force-absorption and propulsion phases—a modulation of oscillating forces.

We make the argument here that it is the *task* of managing these complex propulsive forces—the linear components of forward propulsion, the rotational components of the coordinated moving segments, the inertial properties of a linked system, and the forces necessary to counteract gravity—while maintaining balance and moving forward that organizes the elements into independent locomotion. The infant on the verge of walking alone *can* maintain static balance, she *can* produce exquisitely patterned interlimb and intralimb coordinations when on the treadmill, she recognizes the information in the optic flow field and from her vestibular organs and the soles of her feet, and she wants to cross the room. She will not walk, however, until two component elements become sufficiently developed to shift the system into the new phase. These control parameters are likely extensor muscles strong enough to support the body weight on a single-limb base of support and balance mechanisms able to compensate for the shift of weight from leg to leg. When these abilities reach some just-above-threshold value and the infant can balance momentarily on one leg, the dynamic events of locomotion can self-organize. The trailing leg acquires the necessary viscoelastic stretch for the pendular swing forward and sufficient time to move in front of the center of gravity to establish a new base of support. The swing leg is also strong enough to absorb the force of foot strike and create propulsion for the next step.

The engaging toddle of the new walker has a number of coordinative elements in common with more mature walking, but there are also important differences: more simple joint rotation patterns, without heel strike and knee and hip flexion waves at the initiation of stance (Sutherland et al., 1980), increased variability in the interlimb phasing (Clark, Whitall & Phillips, in press), increased cadence, decreased stride length, hyper-rotation and hyper-flexion in stance (Burnett & Johnson, 1971), lack of upper limb coordination (Sutherland et al., 1980), and excessive stiffness or co-contraction of the muscles (Okamoto & Goto, 1985). All of these can be attributed to the barely adequate strength and dynamic balance elements.

Infants organize locomotion around the task with what they have available. They walk, although it is not efficient or skilled at first. Their abilities to produce highly coordinated patterns are masked by the demands of the newly acquired posture. Remarkably, when these demands are reduced by support or other mechanical means, the underlying coordination is revealed. The treadmill is a prime example. Another striking example of task organization is provided by Clark, Whitall & Phillips (in press), who supported new walkers by holding their hands and saw significant reduction in the variability of interlimb phasing. Even the underlying EMG patterns show more organization when postural stability is provided, changing from a high degree of coactivation in unsupported walkers to a more reciprocal pattern (Kazai, Okamoto & Kumamoto, 1976; Okamoto & Goto, 1985). The ability of experimenters to elicit more mature walking performance by substituting for missing postural and balance elements is good evidence that some combination of strength and dynamic balance is the developmental control parameter for independent walking.

Once walking is in place, gradual improvement in the strength and balance components allows for the underlying coordinative patterns to become fully manifest and for the step cycle to become more adaptable to environmental perturbation. As Bernstein (1967) suggested, this process undoubtedly includes the more effective use of the viscoelastic and inertial properties of the legs, so that unnecessary muscle contractions can be eliminated. Decreased cadence, increased stride length, a smaller base of support, more elaborated joint rotations, and a more dynamically flexible step will "fall out" of this increase in stability. The refinement of the pattern is a result of the cooperative assembly of the system in its dynamical context. What develops is the whole system, not just the central pattern-generating elements.

In summary, we have taken a dynamical systems approach and identified components that appear to contribute to the onset of independent, upright locomotion. As we traced the ontogeny of those components, we have suggested that specific elements act as control parameters for the onset of walking: in particular, the attainment of certain threshold capabilities for strength and balance. There is good evidence that the limb pattern-generating abilities and sensory processing skills necessary for integrating knowledge about the environment with knowledge of self-movement are established in functional, albeit rudimentary form, in advance of walking onset. The task of weight-bearing in the upright posture *and* the management of the segmented body during forward progression add complex demands. We argued that the system waits for the acquisition of sufficient strength to counteract gravity and the integrative capacity for organizing multiple segments in dynamic conditions. With these in place, walking is truly emergent.

ACKNOWLEDGMENTS

Preparation of this chapter and some of the research reported here were supported by National Science Foundation Grant BNS 85-09793, National Institutes of Health Grant RO1 HD 22830, and a Research Career Developmental Award to Esther Thelen.

REFERENCES

Alexander, R. McN. (1984). Walking and running. *American Scientist, 72,* 348–54.

Andre-Thomas, & Autgaerden, S. (1966). *Locomotion from pre- to post-natal life*. London: Spastics Society and William Heinemann.

Bayley, N., & Davis, F. C. (1935). Growth changes in bodily size and proportions in the first three years: A developmental study of sixty-one children by repeated measurements. *Biometrika, 27,* 26–87.

Benson, J. B. (1985). The development of crawling in infancy. Paper presented to the International Society for the Study of Behavioral Development, Tours, France.

Benson, J. B. (1987). New lessons on how infants learn to crawl. Paper presented at the biannual meeting of the Society, or Research in Child Development, April, Baltimore, MD.

Berger, W.; Quintern, J.; & Dietz, V. (1985). Stance and gait perturbations in children: Developmental aspects of compensatory meachanisms. *Electroenphalography and Clinical Neurophysiology, 61,* 385–95.

Bernstein, N. (1967). *Co-ordination and regulation of movements*. New York: Pergamon Press.

Bertenthal, B. I., & Campos, J. J. (In press). A systems approach to the organizing effects of self-produced locomotion during infancy. In C. RoVee-Collier & L. P. Lipsitt (Eds.), *Advance in Infant Research, 6,* Norwood, NJ: Ablex Publishers.

Bertenthal, B. I., & Dai, D. L. (submitted). Visual-vestibular integration in early development.

Burnett, C. N., & Johnson, E. W. (1971). Development of gait in childhood: Part II. *Developmental Medicine and Child Neurology, 13,* 207–15.

Butterworth, G., & Hicks, L. (1977). Visual proprioception and postural stability in infancy. A developmental study. *Perception, 6,* 255–62.

Clark, J. E., & Phillips, S. J. (1987). The step cycle organization of infant walkers. *Journal of Motor Behavior, 19,* 421-33.

Clark, J. E.; Whitall, J.; & Phillips, S. J. (1988). Human interlimb coordination: The first 6 months of independent walking. *Developmental Psychobiology, 21,* 445-56.

Eichorn, D. H. (1979). Physical development: Current foci of research. In J. D. Osofsky (Ed.), *Handbook of infant development*. New York: John Wiley.

Foman, S. J. (1966). Body composition of the infant. In F. Falkner (Ed.), *Human development*. Philadelphia: W. B. Saunders.

Forssberg, H. (1985). Ontogeny of human locomotor control. I. Infant stepping, supported locomotion, and transition to independent locomotion. *Experimental Brain Research, 57,* 480–93.

Forssberg, H., & Nashner, L. M. (1982). Ontogenetic development of postural control in man: Adaptation to altered support and visual conditions during stance. *Journal of Neuroscience, 2,* 545–52.

Gesell, A. (1939). Reciprocal interweaving in neuromotor development. *Journal of Comparative Neurology, 70,* 161–80.

Haas, G.; Diener, H. C.; Bacher, M.; & Dichgans, J. (1986). Development of postural control in children: Short-, medium-, and long-latency EMG responses of leg muscles after perturbation of stance. *Experimental Brain Research, 64,* 127–32.

Haken, H. (1983). *Synergetics: An introduction*. 3rd Ed. Heidelberg: Springer-Verlag.

Heriza, C. (1986). The organization of spontaneous movements in premature infants. Ph.D. dissertation, Southern Illinois University.

Illingsworth, R. S. (1972). *The development of the infant and young child: Normal and abnormal.* 5th ed. London: Livingstone.

Inman, V. T.; Ralston, H. J.; & Todd, F. (1980). *Human walking.* Baltimore, MD: Williams & Wilkins.

Kazai, N.; Okamoto, T.; & Kumamoto, M. (1976). Electromygraphic study of supported waling of infants in the initial period of learning to walk. *Biomechanics, V,* 311–18.

Kelso, J. A. S. (Ed.) (1982). *Human motor behavior: An introduction.* Hillsdale, NJ: Erlbaum.

Kelso, J. A. S., & Tuller, B. (1984). A dynamical basis for action systems. In M. S. Gazzaniga (Ed.), *Handbook of cognitive neuroscience* (pp. 321–56). New York: Plenum Press.

Kugler, P. N., & Turvey, M. T. (1987). *Information, natural law and the self-assembly of rhythmic movement.* Hillsdale, NJ: Erlbaum.

Lee, D. N., & Aronson, E. (1974). Visual proprioceptive control of standing in human infants. *Perception & Psychophysics, 15,* 529–32.

Mann, R. A.; Hagy, J. L.; White, V.; & Lidell, D. (1979). The initiation of gait. *Journal of Bone and Joint Surgery, 61-A,* 232–39.

Marsden, C. D,; Merton, P. A.; & Morton, H. B. (1983). Rapid postural reactions to mechanical displacement of the hand in man. In J. E. Desmedt (Ed.), *Motor control mechanisms in health and disease* (pp. 645–59). New York: Raven Press.

McGraw, M. B. (1932). From reflex to muscular control in the assumption of an erect posture and ambulation in the human infant. *Child Development, 3,* 291–97.

Murray, M. P. (1967). Gait as a total pattern of movement. *American Journal of Physical Medicine, 46,* 290–333.

Nashner, L. M., & McCollum, G. (1985). The organization of human postural movements: A formal basis and experimental synthesis. *Behavioral and Brain Sciences, 8,* 135–72.

Okamoto, T., & Goto, Y. (1985). Human infant pre-independent and independent walking. In S. Kondo (Ed.), *Primate morpho-physiology, locomotor analyses and human bipedalism* (pp. 25–45). Tokyo: University of Tokyo Press.

Okamoto, T., & Kumamoto, M. (1972). Electromyographic study of the learning process of walking in infants. *Electromyography, 12,* 149–58.

Pearson, K. (1976). The control of walking. *Scientific American, 235,* 72–86.

Peiper, A. (1963). *Cerebral function in infancy and childhood.* New York: Consultants Bureau.

Prechtl, H. F. R. (1986). Prenatal motor development. In M. G. Wade & H. T. A. Whiting (Eds.), *Motor development in children: Aspects of coordination and control* pp. 53–64). Dordrecht: Martinus Nighoff.

Raibert, M. H. (1986). Symmetry in running. *Science, 231,* 1292–94.

Raibert, M. H., & Sutherland, I. E. (1983). Machines that walk. *Scientific American, 248,* 44–53.

Saunders, J. B. de C. M.; Inman, V. T.; & Eberhart, H. D. (1953). The major determinants in normal and pathological gait. *Journal of Bone Joint Surgery, 35-A,* 543–558.

Schneider, K.; Ulrich, B. D.; Zernicke, R.; & Thelen, E. (in preparation). Determination of limb kinematics and dynamics in supine infant kicking.

Shirley, M. M. (1931).*The first two years: A study of twenty-five babies. Vol. 1. Postural and locomotor development.* Minneapolis: University of Minnesota Press.

Shumway-Cook, A., & Woollacott, M. H. (1985). The growth of stability: Postural control from a developmental perspective. *Journal of Motor Behavior, 17,* 131–47.

Sutherland, D. H.; Olshen, R.; Cooper, L.; & Woo, S. (1980). The development of mature gait. *Journal of Bone and Joint Surgery, 62-A,* 336–-53.

Taft, L. T., & Cohen, H. J. (1967). Neonatal and infant reflexology. In J. Hellmun (Ed.), *Exceptional infant. Vol. 1. The normal infant.* Seattle: Special Child Publications.

Thelen, E. (1948). Learning to walk: Ecological demands and phylogenetic constraints. In L. P. Lipsitt (Ed.), *Advances in infancy research,* Vol. 3, pp. 213–50. Norwood, NJ: Ablex.

Thelen, E. (1985). Developmental origins of motor coordination: Leg movements in human infants. *Developmental Psychobiology, 18,* 1–22.

Thelen, E. (1986a). Treadmill-elicited stepping in seven-month-old infants. *Child Development, 57,* 1498–506.

Thelen, E. (1986b). Development of coordinated movement: Implications for early human development. In M. G. Wade & H. T. A. Whiting (Eds.), *Motor skills acquisition* (pp. 107–24). Dordrecht: Martinus Nijhoff.

Thelen, E. (1988). Dynamical approaches to the development of behavior. In J. A. S. Kelso, A. J. Mandell & M. R. Shlesinger (Eds.), *Dynamic patterns in complex systems.* Singapore: World Scientific Publishers.

Thelen, E. (in press). Self-organization in developmental processes: Can systems approaches work? In M. Gunnar (Ed.), *Systems in development: The Minnesota Symposium on Child Psychology,* Vol. 22. Hillsdale, NJ: Erlbaum.

Thelen, E.; Bradshaw, G.; & Ward, J. A. (1981). Spontaneous kicking in month-old infants: Manifestations of a human central locomotor program. *Behavioral and Neural Biology, 32,* 45–53.

Thelen, E., & Cooke, D. W. (1987). The relationship between newborn stepping and later locomotion: A new interpretation. *Developmental Medicine and Child Neurology, 29,* 380–93.

Thelen, E., & Fisher, D. M. (1982). Newborn stepping: An explanation for a "disappearing reflex." *Developmental Psychology, 18,* 760–75.

Thelen, E., & Fisher, D. M. (1983). The organization of spontaneous leg movements in newborn infants. *Journal of Motor Behavior, 15,* 353–77.

Thelen, E.; Fisher, D. M.; & Ridley-Johnson, R. (1984). The relationship between physical growth and a newborn reflex. *Infant Behavior and Development, 7,* 479–93.

Thelen, E.; Kelso, J. A. S.; & Fogel, A. (1987). Self-organizing systems and infant motor development. *Developmental Review, 7,*39–65.

Thelen, E.; Ridley-Johnson, R.; & Fisher, D. M. (1983). Shifting patterns of bilateral coordination and lateral dominance in the leg movements of young infants. *Developmental Psychobiology, 16,* 29-46.

Thelen, E.; Skala, K.; Kelso, J. A. S. (1987). The dynamic nature of early coordination: Evidence from bilateral leg movements in young infants. *Developmental Psychology, 23,* 179–86.

Thelen, E., & Ulrich, B. D. (in preparation). Hidden precursors to skill: Treadmill stepping during the first year.

Thelen, E.; Ulrich, B. D.; & Niles, D. (1987). Bilateral coordination in human infants; Stepping on a split-belt treadmill. *Journal of Experimental Psychology: Human Perception and Performance, 13,* 405–10.

Touwen, B. (1976). *Neurological development in infancy.* London: Spastics International and Heinemann.

Woollacott, M. H. (1986). Postural control and development. In H. T. A. Whiting & M. G. Wade (Eds.), *Themes in motor development* (pp. 3–19). Boston: Martinus Nijhoff.

Zelazo, P. R.; Zelazo, N. A.; & Kolb, S. (1972). "Walking" in the newborn. *Science, 177,* 1058–59.

3

Development
of Locomotion:
Animal Models

Nina S. Bradley
and Anne Bekoff

Locomotor behavior is characterized by a number of similarities across species, including humans. This suggests that physiological mechanisms and/or biomechanical factors underlying the control of locomotion may also be similar across species. Though ethical and technical considerations limit our ability to study locomotion in humans, research techniques and conditions can be readily adapted to study locomotion in animals (in this chapter the term *animal* refers to all species excluding man). In some animals it is possible to observe the development of locomotor behavior from the onset of embryonic movements to the establishment of adult motor behaviors. This is a significant advantage, because evidence suggests that the neural circuitry underlying the control of embryonic movements may also serve locomotion. Therefore, by studying embryonic and young animals, we are able to further our understanding of how locomotion is established during development in humans.

The forms of locomotion in vertebrates vary from axial movements, such as swimming in fishes, to multiple limb movements that include swimming, flying, and bipedal or quadrupedal stepping in higher vertebrates. We will, however, limit most of our discussion to bipedal and quadrupedal stepping behaviors, for there are many similarities in these two forms of locomotion across species. For example, the step cycle for a limb during both forms of locomotion is characterized by a stance phase (period of weight support) and a swing phase (period of advancement), and the timing of these phases is coordinated between/among limbs. Also, each phase is characterized by a pattern of activity in muscle synergists and antagonists that is similar for both forms of locomotion.

To consider the use of animal models for study of locomotor development, we will first discuss the advantages that such models afford. Next, embryonic motor development will be explored with respect to changes in neural function and central organization underlying coordinated limb movements. The emergence of locomotion will then be discussed in regard to the continuum of developing motor coordination. Finally, we will consider how a centrally driven pattern generator for coordinated limb movements might be modulated to produce motor behaviors in addition to locomotion.

ADVANTAGES OF ANIMAL MODELS TO THE STUDY OF LOCOMOTOR DEVELOPMENT

There is considerable information on posture and gait in humans, as evidenced by other chapters of this book; however, ethical and technical considerations limit the extent to which the development of coordinated movement can be studied in humans. Although the use of animal models does not eliminate such concerns, experimental procedures can be more readily adapted to address ethical and technical issues.

ETHICAL AND TECHNICAL RESEARCH CONCERNS ADDRESSED IN ANIMAL MODELS

It is essential that research methods do not compromise the physical health of either human or animal subjects. For instance, ethical guidelines do not permit the physical health of human subjects to be risked by the experimental application of invasive or pharmacological procedures. Similarly, the physical health of animals cannot be compromised by research methods that may result in pain and suffering. For this reason, guidelines developed by agencies and institutions that fund or provide research facilities place constraints upon the methodological designs to be used in animal studies. These significant concerns can be readily addressed in animals, however, by providing routine care in a clean, well-maintained environment that is closely supervised by a veterinarian. If experimental procedures are likely to cause animals pain or discomfort, suffering can be avoided by administering an anesthetic or by performing a decerebration to eliminate cerebral function so that afferent input can no longer be experienced. (Decerebration is further discussed below.) It is also important that all experimental animals are healthy, because data obtained from unhealthy animals are likely to differ from data from healthy animals, and such discrepancies can lead the researcher to draw inappropriate conclusions.

It is essential that research methods do not compromise the emotional health of either human or animal subjects. For instance, infants or young children may be easily stressed by the presence of new faces, a new environment, novel testing conditions, or disruptions in the daily routine imposed by a testing schedule. Animals can also become stressed by new persons and procedures or a change in environment and routine. However, when studying animals, the researcher has significantly more control over the subjects' environment so that these stresses can be minimized. For example, animals can be more readily acclimated to change than infants, because changes can be gradually introduced as part of an animal's daily activities prior to their implementation in an experiment. Human subjects could be similarly acclimated to new activities and environments, but researchers rarely have sufficient access to human subjects to make such procedures practical. Finally, it is important that methods in developmental studies do not compromise the emotional health of a subject's family. In human studies, research methods must not compromise parent-infant bonding nor undermine the ability or confidence of parents to care for their child. Similarly, in developmental studies of mammals not yet weaned from their mothers, consideration must be given to the possible impact of procedures upon maternal-young interactions and the mother's ability to care for her young.

There are also a number of practical advantages to the use of animal models for study of locomotor development. Because animals are typically maintained in or near the research facilities, the researcher can directly supervise and control possible factors such as diet and exercise. The proximity of the animals also increases the opportunity to collect data at several stages of development in a single subject, and the more measurements obtained per subject, the smaller the sample size required to detect significant findings. However, if a large population sample is required, some animal species can be more readily obtained than human subjects. Additionally, in comparison to humans, most animals complete the developmental process in a relatively short period of time; thus, data collection can also be completed in a shorter period. Ultimately, the combined impact of these advantages can be a reduction in the financial costs as compared to a similar study conducted with human subjects.

METHODS COMMONLY EMPLOYED TO STUDY LOCOMOTION IN ANIMAL MODELS

The successful outcome of any study is determined in large part by the researcher's ability to control testing conditions. In both infants and young animals, for example, behavioral state (level of arousal) is especially difficult to control. Yet it is an important variable to consider, because it can significantly influence a number of movement parameters in infants (Thelen, Ridley-Johnson & Fisher, 1983). Similarly, in young animals, behavioral state can facilitate or inhibit the expression of motor skills (Bradley & Smith, 1988a). Because the researcher has more ready access to animal subjects, however, a number of technical approaches can be applied to control subject-dependent variables. To control for behavioral state, for example, animals can be selected by their willingness to be handled and by establishing a daily routine of experiment-related activities.

One of the most important advantages of the use of animal models, however, is the ability to use research methods that permit more direct study of behavior and physiological mechanisms. This is exemplified by the use of electromyography (EMG) to record muscle activity. Though EMG is frequently employed to study locomotion in humans, it can be more fully utilized in animal studies to perform detailed analyses of muscle activity under a number of conditions. In humans, EMG recordings are performed using either surface or fine-wire electrodes. The accuracy of EMG records obtained from surface electrodes, however, is limited by such factors as the electrical resistance of skin and subcutaneous tissues and the electrical influence of active muscles adjacent or superficial to the muscle of interest (Loeb & Gans, 1986). Fine-wire electrodes can be directly inserted into a muscle, but placement is difficult to maintain during movement, and even minor displacements of the electrode can produce electrical artifacts.

In newborn or adult animals, in contrast, using sterile procedures and an anesthetic, EMG electrodes can be surgically implanted in superficial or deep muscles of interest and maintained for a period of weeks to months (e.g., Bradley & Smith, 1988a). Surgically implanted, the electrodes can be positioned to lie in parallel with the muscle's fibers to reduce electrode displacement and electrical artifacts during contractions. Additionally, because the electrodes run subcutaneously to a common connecting plug located on a stationary surface, such as the pelvis or head, the animal can comfortably move about the testing area. In chick embryos flexible, suction electrodes can be inserted through an opening in the eggshell and placed on the surface of muscles exposed by dissection to study EMG activity during normal, unrestrained movements at the earliest stages of discernible movement (Fig. 3–1).

A benefit exclusive to animal models is the use of methods that eliminate various sources of input to the nervous system to examine physiological mechanisms and their contributions to the control of locomotion. By surgically removing one or more different inputs to the nervous system, under anesthesia, different experimental (reduced) preparations are created. Reduced preparations commonly used to study the control of locomotion include decerebration, spinal transection, deafferentation, and fictive preparations. Decerebrations eliminate input from the cerebral hemispheres to more caudal neural structures. Spinal transections eliminate input from all neural centers

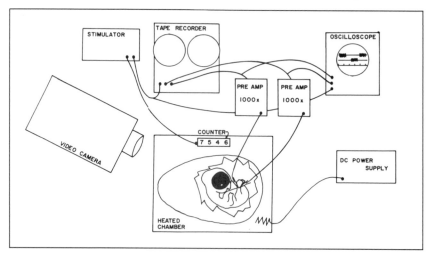

Fig. 3–1. Experimental setup for recording EMG and behavior during motility in chick embryos. Extracellular suction electrodes are inserted through a hole in the eggshell and placed on individual muscles to record EMG activity that is amplified, displayed on an oscilloscope, and stored on magnetic tape. A simultaneous video recording is made through the hole in the shell with a counter in the visual field that also marks time on the magnetic tape to permit synchronization of EMG and video records. (From Bekoff, 1978)

rostral to the transection. Deafferentations eliminate afferent input from peripheral sensory receptors in a particular region such as those in a single hindlimb.

The fictive preparation is also used to reduce the possible sources of input to the nervous system. It usually includes decerebration or spinal transection and pharmacologically induced paralysis (Deliagina, Feldman, Gelfand & Orlovsky, 1975). Paralysis eliminates all movement-generated afferent input to the cord. However, position-dependent and tactile afferent input are retained and can be manipulated under controlled procedures to determine their effects on motor output. A particular advantage to using the fictive preparation is that immobilization permits the recording of activity within individual cells (intracellular recordings). As a result, the fictive preparation has become one of the most common preparations for studying the cellular physiology of neural mechanisms for locomotion.

EMERGENCE OF EMBRYONIC MOTILITY AND
COORDINATED MOTOR PATTERNS

At the onset of embryonic motility, simple axial motions occur in most vertebrates. They are progressively replaced by complex axial motions, and in higher vertebrates, complex limb motions subsequently emerge. Here, we will first present a brief overview of the stages that characterize the development of embryonic motility in birds and mammals. Emphasis will be placed on chick embryos and kitten fetuses, as they are among the most commonly studied animals in the developmental literature. In addition, we will discuss what has been learned from animal models about the neural mechanisms that underlie embryonic motility. For a more comprehensive review, the reader is referred to Bekoff (in press).

STAGES OF EMBRYONIC MOTILITY

In most vertebrates the first movements to occur are simple lateral motions, commonly referred to as *head flexures,* which slowly displace the head to one side of the trunk. Observed soon after the muscles are able to contract, the flexures are initiated by contractions at a few axial segments of the anterior trunk (or neck) region followed by a period of relaxation (Hamburger, 1963; Windle & Griffin, 1931). There is no apparent coordination between the right and left sides during the flexures, and there is no predictable sequential ordering of right and left head flexures. In most vertebrates early head flexures are triggered by neurogenic processes (for review, see Bekoff, 1985). However, they are typically initiated in the absence of apparent external stimuli (Hamburger, 1963), and in many species initial flexures occur in advance of the first sensory-elicited responses (Hooker, 1952).

As the more posterior myotomes develop contractile capability, they are also recruited during contractions of the ipsilateral anterior region. The resulting motion is referred to as a *C-coil.* The C-coils, like head flexures, can occur spontaneously, and contractions to one side occur independently of those to the contralateral side. The C-coils are subsequently replaced by undulatory axial movements referred to as *S-waves* (sometimes called *early swimming* or *alternating flexures*). Emergence of the undulations is probably due to the development of a phase lag (temporal sequencing) in ipsilateral axial contractions. Contractions begin at the neck region, progress caudally, and are coordinated with contralateral axial contractions (Coghill, 1929). Although the S-wave is not a functional locomotor behavior, because the motions do not achieve forward progression, it has been suggested that this movement is a precursor to axial swimming in fishes and amphibians and that it plays an important role in hatching in these lower vertebrates (for review, see Bekoff, in press).

At the S-wave stage, embryonic motor patterns in birds and mammals diverge from those for fishes and amphibians. Instead of developing into swimming, the S-wave motions are replaced by a new kind of motor pattern called *Type I motility* (Hamburger, 1963). Type I motility is characterized by low-amplitude, jerky movements of all body parts with established neuromuscular connections (Hamburger, 1963). Behavioral observations indicate that Type I movements in one body part are not coordinated with those in other body parts. At onset, the frequency of Type I motility is low, but it gradually increases until it occurs almost continuously and then again becomes less frequent as the embryonic period comes to a close (Fig. 3–2). Type I motility appears to occur spontaneously (in the absence of external stimuli) and is generally thought to function to ensure adequate activity important to the development of musculoskeletal tissues and their articulations. This is supported by the observation that, when motility is inhibited in chick embryos by the administration of curare, limb deformities result resembling those of arthrogryposis (Drachman & Coulombre, 1962).

During the final quarter of the embryonic period, birds and mammals begin to develop motility patterns that appear smooth and coordinated. For example, chick embryos display this new pattern, called *Type III motility,* in preparation for, and during, hatching (Hamburger & Oppenheim, 1967). During hatching, the legs synchronously and repeatedly thrust against the inner surface of the egg, as the upper trunk rotates and the head thrusts backward to strike the beak against the shell (Bakhuis, 1974; Hamburger & Oppenheim, 1967). During the last quarter of the fetal period, kittens begin to display synchronous or alternating flexions and extensions of the forelimbs (Windle & Griffin, 1931) and alternating steps in the hindlimbs that resemble walking (Brown, 1915). By the end of the embryonic period, rats also display alternating strokes of the forelimbs or hindlimbs (Bekoff & Lau, 1980) and diagonal coupling of forelimb and hindlimb motions typical of trotting overground (Bekoff & Trainer, 1979).

CENTRAL GENERATION OF EMBRYONIC MOTILITY

It is generally held that initial embryonic motility occurs spontaneously and is generated by central neural circuitry (Hamburger, 1963). That is, independent of sensory information, circuitry within the central nervous system is capable of producing the patterned output that characterizes embryonic motility. The motor patterns are thought to be centrally generated, because behavioral studies indicate that there is no apparent external trigger to initiate motility during its earliest expression (Hamburger, 1963; Windle & Griffin, 1931). Further, in birds there is evidence to suggest that initial motility precedes the completion of peripheral reflex loops (Bekoff, Stein, & Hamburger, 1975; Hamburger & Balaban, 1963; Oppenheim, 1972). These behavioral

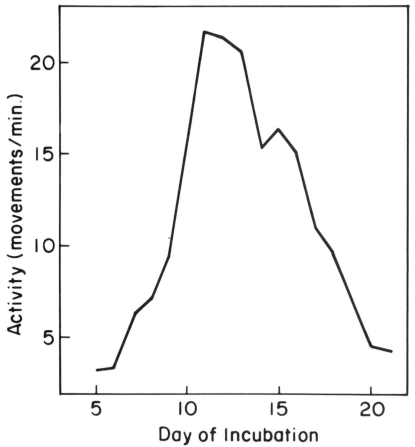

Fig. 3-2. Frequency of body movements in embryonic chicks. The number of body movements per minute increases in frequency, up to a peak at 13 days, then progressively decreases over the remainder of the embryonic period. (From Bekoff, 1981)

observations are substantiated by anatomical studies indicating that the ventral portion of spinal reflex pathways, that is, the connection between motoneuron and muscle, is the first established (Windle & Orr, 1934). Synaptic connections from interneurons to motoneurons are the next to be established, and afferent connections from the dorsal root to the interneurons are the last link of the spinal reflex arc established (Okado, 1981; Saito, 1979; Stelzner, Martin & Scott, 1973).

Even when sensory input is potentially available during early embryonic motility, it does not appear to contribute significantly to the modulation of initial motor output. In chick embryos, behavioral observations indicate that sensory manipulations following completion of the reflex arc (Oppenheim, 1972) and deafferentations of the limbs (Hamburger, Wenger, & Oppenheim, 1966; Narayanan & Malloy, 1974a,b) do not alter Type I motility. Similarly, behavioral observations in fetal kittens indicate that sensory manipulations do not alter initial motility patterns (Windle & Griffin, 1931) despite evidence suggesting that the reflex arc is completed at the onset of motility in fetal mammals (Narayanan, Fox & Hamburger, 1971). Further, evidence in the kitten indicates that the sensory receptors for these pathways have limited ability to encode peripheral information even during initial postnatal development (Ferrington, Hora & Rowe, 1984). Thus, during the embryonic period afferent pathways are probably too immature to modulate motility patterns, but this remains to be tested.

The notion that initial embryonic motility is centrally generated is further supported by evidence indicating that essential neural circuitry for producing the motor patterns is located in the spinal cord and is not dependent upon descending input from the brain. Numerous behavioral studies document the persistence of Type I motility in the limbs of embryonic chicks (Hamburger, Balaban, Oppenheim & Wenger, 1965; Oppenheim & Narayanan, 1968; Oppenheim, 1975), fetal rats (Hooker & Nicholas, 1930), and fetal sheep (Barron, 1941), as well as hindlimb stepping in fetal kittens (Brown, 1915) following spinal transection. The few electrophysiological reports available appear to substantiate these behavioral observations. Stepping-related motoneuron activity is observed in larval frogs after spinal transection (Stehouwer & Farel, 1985), and in chick embryos, EMG patterns characteristic of Type I motility persist after spinal transection (Landmesser & O'Donovan, 1984). The EMG patterns in these embryos continue to persist when the spinal cord is further isolated following deafferentation (Landmesser & O'Donovan, 1984).

The early establishment of spinal circuitry for embryonic motility is also indicated by the apparent regional specificity of output patterns for different levels of the neuraxis (Narayanan & Hamburger, 1971; Straznicky, 1963; Szekely, 1976). If the brachial segments are transplanted to the lumbosacral region in chick embryos, then, after hatching, the legs move synchronously in patterns of abduction and adduction typical of wing flapping (Narayanan & Hamburger, 1971). If lumbosacral segments are transplanted to the brachial region, then, after hatching, motion of each wing appears coordinated with that of the homologous leg; synchronous flapping of the two wings is not preserved (Straznicky, 1963).

EMERGENCE OF LOCOMOTION

Evidence indicates that the basic neural circuits for locomotion are established during the earliest stages of embryonic motility. During the embryonic period these circuits produce coordinated motor output patterns that resemble those characterizing normal locomotion in adult animals. This is despite the fact that at a behavioral level there is little resemblance between embryonic motility and locomotion. Our current understanding of these data leads us to argue that the basic neural network for locomotion is established very early in development, but expression of this circuitry may be contingent upon secondary factors intrinsic and/or extrinsic to the animal.

FROM EMBRYONIC MOTILITY TO LOCOMOTION: BEHAVIORAL ASSESSMENTS

Behavioral observations suggest that there is a sequence to the emergence of locomotion and that much of the sequence can be observed during early stages of embryonic development. As stated earlier, it is thought that the C-coil and S-wave motility patterns develop into swimming in lower vertebrates. In higher vertebrates it appears that locomotor behaviors emerge from embryonic motility patterns as brachial and lumbosacral neural circuits for limb movement are established and become coordinated with each other. There appear to be some variations in the behavioral sequences that describe the establishment of patterned limb movement, but the lack of agreement across behavioral studies may be partly due to differences in experimental methods. In some studies spontaneous motility was observed, whereas in others observations were based on sensory-evoked motility. Here we will review those sequences in the development of limb coordination that appear to be most common in higher vertebrates and that have been observed during spontaneous motility. The conditions under which observations are made are critical to determining the locomotor abilities of developing organisms, and this issue will be discussed later.

Detectable limb movements emerge in a cephalocaudal sequence such that motility is first seen in forelimb pairs and then hindlimb pairs (Narayanan et al., 1971). Initial limb movements appear to occur only in conjunction with trunk movements but soon appear to be initiated independently of trunk movements. Within a limb the first detectable movements occur at the proximal limb joint, and with further development the movements include distal joints. For example, in the frog, the first limb motion to occur is extension at the hip (Stehouwer & Farel,

1985). Knee motions, when they first occur, appear to be independent of motions at the hip. Shortly thereafter, motions at these two joints are initiated synchronously. Motions at the ankle are the last to be established and integrated with proximal limb movements. Although motions of the various segments of the limb now appear coordinated, motions of the limb do not appear to be coordinated with those of other body parts, a finding consistent with observations of Type I motility in the chick.

Generally, interlimb coordination is thought to emerge after the establishment of individual limb movements. However, in some cases, bilaterally coordinated limb movements and individual limb movements appear to be simultaneously established. In frogs, for instance, non-repetitive movements such as isolated hip extension (Stehouwer & Farel, 1985) as well as flexion and extension of the entire limb (Stehouwer & Farel, 1984) emerge simultaneously as unilateral and bilateral movements. Rhythmical flexion and extension movements, however, initially occur in a single hindlimb. Bilateral rhythmical movements subsequently emerge; the hindlimbs are first coordinated in an alternating (stepping) pattern that is eventually replaced by a synchronous (kicking) pattern (Stehouwer & Farel, 1984).

The sequential emergence of alternating and synchronous hindlimb patterns is also observed in other animals. During overground progression in the first two postnatal weeks, rabbits advance the limbs alternately to step, but by the end of the first month they advance the limbs synchronously to hop (Viala, Viala & Fayein, 1986). In kittens, alternating hindlimb movements appear in the final quarter of the fetal period (Brown, 1915) during the same period that independent hindlimb motions are first observed (Windle & Griffin, 1931). Synchronous thrusting of the hindlimbs (in response to tail pinching) is first reported to occur in newborn kittens (Langworthy, 1929). In chicks, both alternating and synchronous hindlimb patterns are present by the middle of the embryonic period (Cooper, 1983; Watson, 1987). Toward the end of the embryonic period, distinct synchronous hindlimb thrusting is used for hatching, and alternating stepping, characteristic of locomotion, is not initiated until hatching has been completed.

These behavioral studies suggest that specific progressions characterize motor development. Further, they imply that the neural circuitries producing these motor patterns are also sequentially assembled within a similar time period. However, a note of caution is warranted when interpreting such findings. We now know that behavioral observations do not necessarily reflect the state of neurological organization. In chick embryos, for instance, motoneurons can be activated to produce the patterned output for locomotion, but the pattern is not readily apparent in the corresponding limb motions (Bekoff, 1976; Watson, 1987). Thus, the motility patterns typically considered to be assembled in developmental sequences need to be reexamined with electrophysiological methods in a number of animals.

LOCOMOTOR CIRCUITRY ESTABLISHED PRIOR TO LOCOMOTOR BEHAVIOR

The presence of motor output patterns resembling those for locomotion in very young embryos suggests that the neural circuitry underlying the control of locomotion is functional at the earliest stages of embryonic motility. Further, circuits established during these early stages have an innervation pattern that is consistent with the adult pattern. For example, at the onset of embryonic limb movements, dorsally located motoneurons selectively activate developing axial muscles, while laterally located motoneurons selectively activate developing limb muscles (Stehouwer & Farel, 1983). Thus, the coordination of limb and trunk movements observed during embryonic motility appears to be the result of a common input to both groups of motoneurons. Neurogram recordings in frog tadpoles indicate that activity of axial and limb motoneurons can even be coordinated before limb structures are established (Stehouwer & Farel, 1985).

Evidence for the early emergence of neural circuitry for locomotion is also seen in the interlimb and intralimb patterns of motoneuron output. In frog tadpoles, recordings from motoneurons innervating left and right hindlimbs indicate that the neural mechanisms for stepping (alternating pattern) are functional early in embryonic development before hindlimb structures differentiate (Stehouwer & Farel, 1985). These same recordings indicate that the mechanisms for kicking (synchronous pattern) are not expressed until late in embryonic development. Similarly, recordings from motoneurons to antagonist hip muscles indicate that the intralimb pattern of alternating activity in antagonist muscles is present at the earliest period in which the peripheral nerves can be successfully dissected. In chicks, EMG recordings indicate that ankle agonist muscles are coactivated and antagonist muscles are reciprocally activated by embryonic day 7 (Bekoff, 1976). By day 9, ankle muscles are coactivated with synergist muscles at the knee (Fig. 3–3) and hip (Bradley & Bekoff, 1987). Further, by day 10, synchronous and alternating patterns of activity are recorded from left and right hip flexor muscles or from ankle extensor muscles (Cooper, 1983). Thus, by the middle of the embryonic period in the chick, the neural circuits determining motoneuronal output are already producing patterned muscle activity within and between limbs even though movements appear uncoordinated (Type I motility). These EMG patterns are also similar to the patterns that will be used for hatching and locomotion at the end of the embryonic period (Bekoff, 1976, 1986).

The most detailed study of early neuromuscular patterns in mammals to date was carried out in newborn kittens (Bradley & Smith, 1988a). Records obtained from EMG electrodes surgically implanted at birth indicate that patterned muscle activity both within a hindlimb and between hindlimbs is present by 3 postnatal days of age when kittens are stepping overground, on a treadmill, and in midair when held with the hindlimbs pendent (airstepping). Specifically, ankle flexor muscles are reciprocally activated with ankle extensors, and ankle extensor muscles are coactivated with knee extensor muscles in patterns that

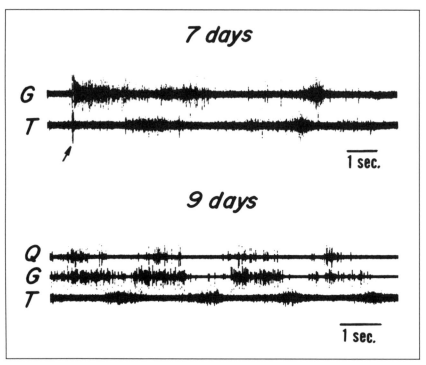

Fig. 3–3. Hindlimb neuromuscular patterns during embryonic motility in chicks. *7 days*: Reciprocal activation between leg antagonist muscles is observed in EMG records of the gastrocnemius lateralis (*G*, ankle extensor) and tibialis anterior (*T*, ankle flexor) following an initial burst of coactivity (*arrow*). *9 days*: Coactivation of synergist muscles of the leg and thigh is observed in EMG records of the quadriceps (*Q*, knee extensor) and gastrocnemius. (Adapted from Bekoff, 1976)

closely resemble those for locomotion in adult cats. Additionally, activity in left and right ankle extensor muscles includes sequences of alternating bursts coincident with bouts of alternating steps. Thus, kittens demonstrate the ability to produce the neuromuscular patterns for stepping at 3 postnatal days, despite the fact that locomotion is awkward and poorly sustained. Behavioral observations suggest that these neuromuscular patterns may be established early in the fetal period and expressed during fetal motility (Brown, 1915; Windle & Griffin, 1931), but this remains to be determined.

DELAYED EXPRESSION OF LOCOMOTOR POTENTIAL IN NORMAL DEVELOPMENT

The failure to observe adult locomotor behavior in embryonic and young animals may be due to the absence of environmental factors that are required to initiate or support the behavior. In other words, the necessary neural circuitry may be assembled and sufficiently competent physiologically to produce locomotion earlier in development than typically acknowledged. However, the behavior may not be expressed until factors external to the animal are present; possible factors include motivational cues or postural support. For example, chicks do not spontaneously initiate coordinated wing flapping until the end of the first postnatal week, but if dropped 2 meters, newly hatched chicks will flap their wings synchronously during the descent (Provine, 1981). Similarly, if a textured mat is placed along the bottom of the aqueous-filled container, frog tadpoles will initiate steps several days earlier than normally observed (Stehouwer & Farel, 1984). Finally, if posturally supported, postnatal rats will initiate grooming with the forelimbs earlier than normal (Fentress, 1981). Thus, in these instances neurological mechanisms were sufficiently established to produce coordinated limb behaviors several days earlier than normally observed if adequate environmental conditions were provided to trigger and/or sustain the behaviors. Conversely, in the absence of these conditions the behaviors were not observed until a more advanced level of development was achieved.

In other instances the expression of locomotor circuitry in young animals may be dependent upon the removal or overcoming of factors that otherwise inhibit expression of the circuitry. Kittens, for example, do not readily initiate weight-supported steps with their hindlimbs until the third postnatal week (Bradley & Smith, 1988a) and do not shake a hindlimb to remove an irritant from the paw (paw-shake response) until the fourth postnatal week (Bradley & Smith, 1985). However, if the spinal cord is transected at the thoracic level at birth, extended bouts of hindlimb stepping (Bradley & Smith, 1988b) and the paw-shake response (Bradley & Smith, 1985) are readily initiated weeks earlier than in normal littermates. These findings suggest that spinal circuits for locomotion and paw shaking are assembled and can produce these behaviors prior to the time they are usually expressed, but that input from rostral neural centers normally inhibits expression of these behaviors during initial postnatal development.

Observations suggest that normal kittens will not initiate some behaviors until postural mechanisms are sufficiently established to accommodate shifts in center of gravity imposed by the movements. For example, during the first two postnatal weeks the normal kitten assumes a wide-based quadrupedal stance characterized by tremor and rocking motions of the entire trunk (Bradley & Smith, 1988a; Villablanca & Olmstead, 1979). To lift and advance one limb, the other three limbs must accommodate a relatively large forward and lateral shift in the center of gravity in addition to the postural displacements resulting from the tremor and rocking motions. Thus, locomotion is not readily observed in newborns because postural control mechanisms are immature. If, however, postural support is provided, newborn kittens will initiate stepping one to two weeks earlier than typically observed (Bradley & Smith, 1988a).

Immaturity of the various limb structures is another factor that may account for the failure to observe locomotion in embryonic and young animals. As discussed above, electrophysiological recordings in the larval frog indicate that hindlimb motoneurons are activated in patterns that will be typical of later coordinated limb movements before hindlimb structures have formed. Obviously, if the limb structures are not yet present, observation alone cannot confirm whether the locomotor circuits are functional. Furthermore, once the limbs develop, a discrepancy is observed between the coordinated motoneuron activity and apparently random limb movements. This discrepancy may also be due to the immaturity of peripheral structures. For example, immature contractile properties in limb muscles and mass parameters of developing limb segments are likely to alter the biomechanical factors that underlie resultant limb motions. It may also be that peripheral sensory receptors and/or afferent fibers may be insufficiently developed to respond to cues that normally initiate some behaviors. The latter two issues will be further considered in the final section of this chapter.

MODULATION OF A BASIC CENTRAL PATTERN GENERATOR

As researchers have begun to examine other rhythmical limb movements in addition to locomotion, questions have arisen as to how the nervous system might organize neural circuits, also referred to as *pattern generators,* to produce multiple rhythmical movements. A few investigators have taken the position that the more economical approach to organizing the nervous system might be to establish a single pattern generator, or a group of unit burst generators representing the various joints of each limb, that could be variably modulated to produce several different rhythmical limb movements (for review, see Grillner, 1981). Berkinblit and colleagues (1978a, b), for example, suggested that a single pattern generator, located in the lumbosacral cord, may control both scratching and locomotor movements in the cat. Further, it has been suggested that this same pattern generator controls paw shaking in cats (Smith et al., 1986). In chicks, it has been suggested that a single pattern generator, or shared elements of that generator, controls the leg movements of embryonic motility, walking, and hatching (Bekoff, 1986; Bekoff, Nusbaum, Sabichi & Clifford, 1987).

To account for the production of multiple rhythmical behaviors by a single pattern generator, Smith and colleagues (1986) proposed that a given set of initial conditions, for example, a triggering stimulus and ensemble of afferent inputs, potentiates specific connections within the pattern generator. By differentially activating subsets of the neural circuitry that comprise the pattern generator, unique sets of output features (e.g., cycle period, burst durations, and onset latencies) can be produced for each of several different behaviors. In this final section we will explore some of the ways a single pattern generator might be modulated to produce different output features for locomotion and other rhythmical limb movements.

DESCENDING NEURAL MODULATION OF PATTERN GENERATOR OUTPUT

Descending neural inputs to the lumbosacral circuits from the brainstem and more rostral portions of the spinal cord can modulate the output of a pattern generator in several different ways. During development, as previously discussed, descending neural inputs may inhibit expression of a behavior that is organized at the spinal level until environmental factors are met that trigger or support expression of the behavior (Bradley & Smith, 1988b, c). The idea that some behaviors may be inhibited by rostral neural centers in the immature animal is a somewhat different view from that traditionally held regarding early motor development. The traditional view is that (primitive) behaviors organized at lower levels of the neuraxis are expressed during initial development and are eventually inhibited as descending neural networks become myelinated (Langworthy, 1933). Consistent with this notion, descending inputs appear to reduce the frequency of bouts of motility as the embryonic period comes to a close in normal chicks (Bekoff, 1981), sheep (Barron, 1941), rats (Narayanan, Fox & Hamburger, 1971), and humans (Prechtl, Fargel, Weinmann & Bakker, 1979). However, as discussed previously, the early expression of prolonged stepping bouts and paw shaking following spinal transection in kittens suggests that descending neural inputs may also function in some instances to inhibit expression of limb movements until the requisite postural mechanisms are established (Bradley & Smith, 1988c).

Thus, although descending inputs may inhibit expression of some rhythmical limb movements, it appears that descending neural inputs may also activate components of the pattern-generating network to initiate locomotor-related behaviors during development. If these inputs are removed by experimental procedures, specific interventions are required to initiate and sustain some rhythmical limb behaviors. For example, following spinal transection at birth, sensory inputs, such as tail pinching and paw contact with the moving belt of a treadmill, are frequently required to initiate and sustain stepping behaviors in kittens (Bradley & Smith, 1988b). Cats that are spinal-transected as adults, in contrast to kittens, do not typically require these sensory inputs to initiate and sustain stepping behaviors (Giuliani & Smith, 1985). Specific interventions are required to initiate rhythmical movements in adult animals, however, if descending inputs are eliminated under acute surgical conditions. Pharmacological agents, such as Nialamide and Dopa, are required to initiate hindlimb stepping in acutely spinal-transected cats (Grillner & Zangger, 1979) and rabbits (Viala & Vidal, 1978). Similarly, in acutely decerebrated preparations, electrical stimulation of the brainstem is required to initiate chewing in guinea pigs (Chandler & Goldberg, 1982), and stimulation of the spinal cord is required to initiate scratching in cats (Deliagina et al., 1975). Thus, in some cases descending inputs appear to be important for initiating and sustaining pattern-generator output in the developing nervous system but not in the mature nervous system except under acute surgical conditions.

The presence of descending neural inputs during the developmental period may also be critical to secure normal function of the pattern generator beyond the developmental period. The chick, for instance, appears to develop normal Type I motility patterns following spinal transection at embryonic day 2 (Oppenheim, 1975). However, convulsivelike behavior develops in these animals after embryonic day 17, suggesting that function of the underlying neural circuitry subsequently deteriorates. EMG recordings from limb muscles in isolated hindlimb-spinal cord preparations suggest that motoneuron output is initially unaffected by transections performed at 8 to 10 embryonic days (Landmesser & O'Donovan, 1984). The EMG patterns in these animals, however, have not been examined at later gestational or posthatching ages. Similarly, in kittens, it appears that descending input to the lumbosacral cord may be important for establishing a stable stepping rhythm both within and between hindlimbs (Bradley & Smith, 1988b).

There is evidence in kittens and adult cats that descending neural inputs modulate pattern-generator output to meet specific behavioral requirements. For example, descending input appears to determine some of the differences observed in the temporal characteristics and EMG patterns for scratching in normal kittens (Bradley & Smith, 1988c) and cats (Abraham and Loeb, 1985) compared to decerebrate cats (Deliagina et al., 1975). It is thought that these differences are due in part to the different scratching strategies employed by normal animals but not available to decerebrate animals (Bradley & Smith, 1988c). Descending neural inputs also appear to modulate motoneuron recruitment patterns. In normal cats, for example, the slow-twitch motor units of the soleus muscle (ankle extensor) are not recruited during the rapid ankle oscillations characteristic of paw shaking (Smith, Betts, Edgerton & Zernicke, 1980). However, these slow-twitch units are recruited during paw shaking in cats following spinal transection, suggesting that descending neural inputs, when intact, selectively control motor-unit recruitment. Whether descending inputs selectively control motor-unit recruitment during the developmental period, when motor-unit properties are being established, is yet to be determined.

SENSORY MODULATION OF PATTERN-GENERATOR OUTPUT

Like descending inputs, sensory inputs also modulate and adapt pattern-generator output to meet specific behavioral requirements. Sensory input appears to be important in initiating motor behavior in the young animal as demonstrated following forelimb deafferented in fetal and neonatal monkeys (Taub, 1976). Following unilateral deafferentations, the monkeys rarely initiated use of the deafferented forelimb under unrestrained conditions. The animals only began to use the deafferented limb if the intact forelimb was restrained, or after the intact limb was also deafferented. These observations suggest that sensory inputs normally function to activate motoneuron output to the forelimb muscles and that, if sensory inputs are removed, forelimb muscles are not activated unless functional demands are sufficiently great.

In some instances sensory inputs appear to either trigger or permit expression of pattern-generator circuitry to produce rhythmical limb movements in young animals earlier in the developmental period than observed under conditions of spontaneous behavior. For example, sensory inputs related to free-falling can initiate wing flapping in newly hatched chicks a week in advance of its normal expression (Provine, 1981). Similarly, sensory inputs related to buoyancy appear to initiate or permit expression of coordinated limb movements for swimming in rat pups approximately one week in advance of the use of coordinated limb movements to locomote overground (Bekoff & Trainer, 1979).

Sensory inputs can also modulate pattern-generator output to meet specific behavioral requirements by altering the phasing of inter-limb neuromuscular patterns. The importance of sensory feedback in modulating pattern-generator output is readily studied in spinal-tran-sected or decerebrated cats. During treadmill locomotion, for instance, interlimb coordination can be varied in spinal-transected cats by chang-ing the belt speed; at slow speeds the hindlimbs step alternately, typical of walking and trotting gait patterns, whereas at faster speeds the hindlimbs step synchronously, typical of galloping (Forssberg, Grillner & Halbertsma, 1980). Modulation of interlimb responses can also be seen in decerebrate cats when a sensory perturbation is applied during treadmill locomotion. Specifically, if a cutaneous stimulus is applied to one hindlimb during swing, the swing phase will be prolonged ip-silaterally and stance phase contralaterally; if the stimulus is applied during stance phase, the stance phase will be prolonged ipsilaterally and swing phase contralaterally (Gauthier & Rossignol, 1981). There is also evidence that sensory inputs, particularly those related to loading and unloading the limbs, modulate interlimb coordination during tread-mill locomotion in the developmental period (Bradley & Smith, 1988b). In this study spinal-transected kittens took synchronous steps when hindlimb weight support was negligible. In contrast, the kittens took alternating steps when weight support was clearly apparent.

Neuromuscular patterns that characterize intralimb coordination can also be modulated by sensory input. The application of an electric current to different loci along the surface of a turtle's carapace (Mortin, Keifer & Stein, 1985) or a frog's back (Berkinblit, Feldman & Fukson, 1986) will initiate different hindlimb neuromuscular patterns for scratching that correspond to the hindlimb strategy required to reach the area stimulated. Sensory input due to motion-dependent feedback can also modify intralimb neuromuscular patterns and is exemplified by the hindlimb paw-shake response in cats (Smith, Hoy, Koshland, Phillips & Zernicke, 1985). In normal cats and in some spinal cats, paw shaking is characterized by a *mixed* muscle synergy (vastus lateralis, a knee exten-sor, is coactivated with tibialis anterior, an ankle flexor). If motion of the hindlimb is perturbed during the response, or if feedback is eliminated by deafferentation, vastus lateralis is no longer distinctly coactive with tibialis anterior. Rather, the vastus lateralis is not activated during the response, is variably activated in poorly defined bursts, or is coactivated with hip and ankle extensor muscles. Motion-dependent feedback may also modulate neuromuscular patterns during the development of rhythmical movements. For example, evidence in kittens suggests, as in adults, that neuromuscular patterns can be modified by sensory inputs due to limb motions during the paw-shake response and that sensory inputs may play a critical role in determining whether motor output is expressed as an immature or mature pattern (Bradley & Smith, 1988c). It remains to be determined whether it is the immaturity of the sensory system and/or the feedback of immature limb motions that perpetuates the expression of immature movement patterns.

BIOMECHANICAL MODULATION OF PATTERN-GENERATOR OUTPUT

As discussed in the previous section, sensory inputs due to motion-dependent feedback can modify the output of spinal networks that produce rhythmical limb movements. The rhythmical limb movements (and resulting motion-dependent feedback) are also the product of biomechanical factors. Biomechanical factors include forces resulting from muscle contractions, gravity, and inertial interactions that arise during movement because each body segment is linked to other body segments. Thus, when the nervous system activates limb muscles to contract and motion is initiated at one or more joints, mechanical interactions arise between adjacent limb segments as well as distant body segments (Hoy, Zernicke & Smith, 1985; Hoy & Zernicke, 1985, 1986). For example, during the swing phase of locomotion in the cat, paw motions contribute to the net forces at both the knee and ankle (Hoy & Zernicke, 1985). For a more comprehensive discussion of basic biomechanics, the reader is referred to Hoy & Zernicke (1985, 1986) and Smith & Zernicke (1987).

It has been suggested that the intersegmental dynamics of morphologically immature limbs may also play a critical role in modulating the output of central pattern generators during development (Bradley & Smith, 1988c). Because biomechanical interactions are determined, in part, by the mass parameters of each body part and these parameters are constantly changing during development, developing animals must contend with constantly changing biomechanical interactions. How young animals contend with these biomechanical interactions during motor development is an area yet to be studied. Further, it is yet to be determined when and how biomechanical interactions first begin to modulate the output of central pattern generators during the developmental period.

SUMMARY AND CONCLUSIONS

Animal models have provided us with a great deal of information about the development of locomotion. We now know that the circuitry underlying locomotion develops very early in ontogeny, typically during the embryonic period. The circuitry underlying embryonic motility and locomotor-related behaviors is located in the spinal cord. Further, regionally specific output patterns develop in the cervical cord for forelimb movements and in the lumbosacral cord for hindlimb movements. Initial output of the spinal pattern-generating circuitry appears to occur spontaneously to ensure normal morphological development, and at this time pattern-generator output is apparently insensitive to sensory input. It also appears that pattern generators can be established in the absence of descending and peripheral neural inputs. In the late embryonic to postembryonic period, pattern generators become mutable to descending and peripheral inputs, and this permits modification of the patterned locomotor output to meet environmental demands.

Parallels in anatomical, physiological, and behavioral development of animals and humans suggest that experimental results in animal studies and the issues they raise are relevant to understanding locomotor development in humans. It is well known that newborn infants display stepping behaviors, and recent advances in ultrasound recording of fetal movements suggest that stepping may be established very early in development (de Vries, Visser & Prechtl, 1982). The early establishment of fetal stepping suggests that there may be findings in the chick embryo that are relevant to the development and control of stepping in humans. Are stepping movements in human fetuses produced by patterned motor output to the legs? Is the motor output to the legs produced by a central pattern generator located in the spinal cord? Are the stepping movements spontaneously generated? Are they altered by descending or sensory input? It has been suggested that advances in the assessment (and understanding) of fetal movements such as stepping may eventually have diagnostic value (de Vries et al., 1982). In sum, animal models have been particularly valuable in providing a stimulus for generating new ideas about motor development and how to study it.

REFERENCES

Abraham, L. D., & Loeb, G. E. (1985). The distal hindlimb musculature of the cat. Patterns of normal use. *Experimental Brain Research, 58,* 580–93.

Bakhuis, W. J. (1974). Observations on hatching movements in the chick (*Gallus domesticus*). *Journal of Comparative and Physiological Psychology, 87*, 997–1003.

Barron, D. H. (1941). The functional development of some mammalian neuromuscular mechanisms. *Biological Reviews, 16*, 1–33.

Bekoff, A. (1976). Ontogeny of leg motor output in the chick embryo: A neural analysis. *Brain Research, 106*, 271–91.

Bekoff, A. (1978): A neuroethological approach to study of the ontogeny of coordinated behavior. In G. Burghardt & M. Bekoff (Eds.), *The development of behavior: Comparative and evolutionary aspects* (pp. 19–41). New York: Garland Press.

Bekoff, A. (1981). Embryonic development of chick motor behavior. *Trends in Neuroscience, 4*, 181–84.

Bekoff, A. (1985). Development of locomotion in vertebrates: A comparative perspective. In E. S. Gollin (Ed.), *Comparative development of adaptive skills: Evolutionary implications* (pp. 57–94). New York: Erlbaum.

Bekoff, A. (1986). Ontogeny of chicken motor behaviors: Evidence for multi-use limb pattern generating circuits. In S. Grillner, P. S. G. Stein, D. G. Stuart, H. Forssberg, R. M. Herman, & P. Wallen (Eds.), *Neurobiology of vertebrate locomotion* (pp. 433–53). Hampshire, England: Macmillan.

Bekoff, A. (in press). Neural basis for the development of motor behavior in vertebrates. In W. M. Cowan (Ed.), *Handbook of physiology, developmental neurobiology*. New York: Oxford University Press.

Bekoff, A., & Lau, B. (1980). Interlimb coordination in 20-day rat fetuses. *Journal of Experimental Zoology, 214*, 173–75.

Bekoff, A.; Nusbaum, M. P.; Sabichi, A. L.; & Clifford, M. (1987). Neural control of limb coordination in the chick. I. Comparison of hatching and walking motor output patterns in normal and deafferented chicks. *Journal of Neuroscience, 7*, 2320–30.

Bekoff, A.; Stein, P. S. G.; & Hamburger, V. (1975). Coordinated motor output in the hindlimb of the 7-day chick embryo. *Proceedings of the National Academy of Science, 72*, 1245–48.

Bekoff, A., & Trainer, W. (1979). The development of interlimb coordination during swimming in postnatal rats. *Journal of Experimental Zoology, 83*, 1–11.

Berkinblit, M. B.,; Deliagina, T. G.; Feldman, A. G.; Gelfand, I. M.; & Orlovsky, G. N. (1978a). Generation of scratching. I. Activity of spinal interneurons during scratching. *Journal of Neurophysiology, 41*, 1040–57.

Berkinblit, M. B.; Deliagina, T. G.; Feldman, A. G.; Gelfand, I. M.; & Orlovsky, G. N. (1978b). Generation of scratching. II. Nonregular regimes of generation. *Journal of Neurophysiology, 41*, 1058–69.

Berkinblit, M. B.; Feldman, A. G.; & Fukson, O. I. (1986). Adaptability of innate motor patterns and motor control mechanisms. *Behavior and Brain Sciences, 9*, 585–638.

Bradley, N. S., & Bekoff, A. (1987). Emergence of flexion and extension muscle synergies in the hindlimb of chick embryos. *Society for Neuroscience Abstracts, 13*, 1504.

Bradley, N. S., & Smith, J. L. (1985). Early onset of hindlimb paw-shake responses in spinal kittens: A new perspective in motor development. *Developmental Brain Research, 17*, 301–3.

Bradley, N. S., & Smith, J. L. (1988a). Neuromuscular patterns of stereotypic hindlimb behaviors in the first two postnatal months. I. Stepping in normal kittens. *Developmental Brain Research, 38,* 37–52.

Bradley, N. S., & Smith, J. L. (1988b). Neuromuscular patterns of stereotypic hindlimb behaviors in the first two postnatal months. II. Stepping in spinal kittens. *Developmental Brain Research, 38,* 53–67.

Bradley, N. S., & Smith, J. L. (1988c). Neuromuscular patterns of stereotypic hindlimb behaviors in the first two postnatal months. III. Scratching and the paw-shake response in kittens. *Developmental Brain Research, 38,* 68–82.

Brown, T. G. (1915). On the activities of the central nervous system of the un-born foetus of the cat; with a discussion of the question whether progression (walking, etc.) is a "learnt" complex. *Journal of Physiology (London), 49,* 208–15.

Chandler, S. H., & Goldberg, L. J. (1982). Intracellular analysis of synaptic mechanisms controlling spontaneous and cortically induced rhythmical jaw movements in the guinea pig. *Journal of Neurophysiology, 48,* 126–38.

Coghill, G. E. (1929). *Anatomy and the problems of behavior.* New York: Hafner.

Cooper, M. W. (1983). Development of interlimb coordination in the embryonic chick. Ph.D. dissertation, Yale University.

Deliagina, T. G.; Feldman, A. G.; Gelfand, I. M.; & Orlovsky, G. N. (1975). On the role of central program and afferent inflow in the control of scratching movements in the cat. *Brain Research, 100,* 297–313.

de Vries, J. I. P.; Visser, G. H. A.; & Prechtl, H. F. R. (1982). The emergence of fetal behavior. I. Qualitative aspects. *Early Human Development, 7,* 301–22.

Drachman, D. B., & Coulombre, A. J. (1962). Experimental clubfoot and arthro-gryposis multiplex congenita. *The Lancet, II,* 523–26.

Fentress, J. C. (1981). Order in ontogeny: Relational dynamics. In K. Immel-mann, G. W. Barlow, L. Petrinovitch & M. Main (Eds.), *Behavioral develop-ment: The Bielefeld Interdisciplinary Project* (pp. 338–71). Cambridge: Cambridge University Press.

Ferrington, D. G.; Hora, M. O. H.; & Rowe, M. J. (1984). Functional maturation of tactile sensory fibers in the kitten. *Journal of Neurophysiology, 52,* 74–85.

Forssberg, H.; Grillner, S.; & Halbertsma, J. (1980). The locomotion of the low spinal cat. II. Interlimb coordination. *Acta Physiologica Scandinavica, 108,* 269–81.

Gauthier, L., & Rossignol, S. (1981). Contralateral hindlimb responses to cut-aneous stimulation during locomotion in high decerebrate cats. *Brain Re-search, 207,* 303–20.

Giuliani, C. A., & Smith, J. L. (1985). Development and characteristics of airstep-ping in chronic spinal cats. *Journal of Neuroscience, 5,* 1276–82.

Grillner, S. (1981). Control of locomotion in bipeds, tetrapods, and fish. In S. R. Geiger (Ed.), *Handbook of physiology, Vol 2* (pp. 1179–236). Bethesda: American Physiological Society.

Grillner, S., & Zangger, P. (1979). On the central generation of locomotion in the low spinal cat. *Experimental Brain Research, 34,* 241–61.

Hamburger, V. (1963). Some aspects of the embryology of behavior. *Quarterly Review of Biology, 38,* 342–65.

Hamburger, V., & Balaban, M. (1963). Observations and experiments on spon-taneous rhythmical behavior in the chick embryo. *Developmental Biology, 7,* 533–45.

Hamburger, V.; Balaban, M.; Oppenheim, R.; & Wenger, E. (1965). Periodic motility of normal and spinal chick embryos between 8 and 17 days of incubation. *Journal of Experimental Zoology,. 159,* 1–14.

Hamburger, V., & Oppenheim, R. (1967). Prehatching motility and hatching behavior in the chick. *Journal of Experimental Zoology, 166,* 171–204.

Hamburger, V.; Wenger, E.; & Oppenheim, R. (1966). Motility and hatching behavior in the chick embryo in the absence of sensory input. *Journal of Experimental Zoology, 162,* 133–160.

Hooker, D. (1952). *The prenatal origin of behavior.* Lawrence: University of Kansas Press.

Hooker, D., & Nicholas, J. S. (1930). Spinal cord section in rat fetuses. *Journal of Comparative Neurology, 50,* 413–67.

Hoy, M. G., & Zernicke, R. F. (1985). Modulation of limb dynamics in the swing phase of locomotion. *Journal of Biomechanics, 18,* 49–60.

Hoy, M. G., & Zernicke, R. F. (1986). The role of intersegmental dynamics during rapid limb oscillations. *Journal of biomechanics, 19,* 867–77.

Hoy, M. G.; Zernicke, R. F.; & Smith, J. L. (1985). Contrasting roles of inertial and muscle moments at the knee and ankle during paw-shake response. *Journal of Neurophysiology, 54,* 1282–94.

Landmesser, L. T., & O'Donovan, M. J. (1984). Activation patterns of embryonic chick hindlimb muscles recorded *in ovo* and in an isolated spinal cord preparation. *Journal of Physiology (London), 347,* 189–204.

Langworthy, O. R. (1929). A correlated study of the development of reflex activity in fetal and young kittens and the myelinization of tracts in the nervous system. *Contributions to Embryology, Carnegie Institute, 20,* 127–71.

Langworthy, O. R. (1933). Development of behavior patterns and myelinization of the nervous system in the human fetus and infant. *Contributions to Embryology, Carnegie Institute, 24,* 1–57.

Loeb, G. E., & Gans, C. (1986). *Electromyography for experimentalists.* Chicago: University of Chicago Press.

Mortin, L. I.; Keifer, J.; & Stein, P. S. G. (1985). Three forms of the scratch reflex in the spinal turtle: Movement analyses. *Journal of Neurophysiology, 53,* 1501–16.

Narayanan, C. H.; Fox, M. W.; & Hamburger, V. (1971). Prenatal development of spontaneous and evoked activity in the rat *(Rattus norvegicus albinus).* *Behaviour, 40,* 100–134.

Narayanan, C. H., & Hamburger, V. (1971). Motility in chick embryos with substitution of lumbosacral by brachial and brachial by lumbosacral spinal cord segments. *Journal of Experimental Zoology, 178,* 415–32.

Narayanan, C. H., & Malloy, R. B. (1974a). Deafferentation studies on motor activity in the chick: I. Activity pattern of hindlimbs. *Journal of Experimental Zoology, 189,* 163–76.

Narayanan, C. H., & Malloy, R. B. (1974b). Deafferentation studies on motor activity in the chick. II. Activity pattern of wings. *Journal of Experimental Zoology, 189,* 177–88.

Okado, N. (1981). Onset of synapse formation in the human spinal cord. *Journal of Comparative Neurology, 201,* 211–19.

Oppenheim, R. W. (1972). An experimental investigation of the possible role of tactile and proprioceptive stimulation in certain aspects of embryonic behavior in the chick. *Developmental Psychobiology, 5,* 71–91.

Oppenheim, R. W. (1975). The role of supraspinal input in embryonic motility: A re-examination in the chick. *Journal of Comparative Neurology, 160,* 37–50.

Oppenheim, R., & Narayanan, C. H. (1968). Experimental studies on hatching behavior in the chick. I. Thoracic spinal gaps. *Journal of Experimental Zoology, 168,* 387–94.

Prechtl, H. F. R.; Fargel, J. W.; Weinmann, H. M.; & Bakker, H. H. (1979). Posture, motility and respiration in low-risk preterm infants. *Developmental Medicine and Child Neurology, 21,* 3–27.

Provine, R. R. (1981). Development of wing-flapping and flight in normal and deprived domestic chicks. *Developmental Psychobiology, 14,* 279–91.

Saito, K. (1979). Development of spinal reflexes in the rat fetus studied in *in vitro. Journal of Physiology (London), 294,* 581–94.

Smith, J. L.; Betts, B.; Edgerton, V. R.; & Zernicke, R. F. (1980). Rapid ankle extension during paw shakes: Selective recruitment of fast ankle extensors. *Journal of Neurophysiology, 43,* 612–20.

Smith, J. L.; Bradley, N. S.; Carter, M. C.; Guiliani, C. A.; Hoy, M. G.; Koshland, G. F.; & Zernicke, R. F. (1986). Rhythmical movements of the hindlimbs in spinal cat: Considerations for a controlling network. In M. E. Goldberger, A. Gorio & M. Murray (Eds.), *Development and plasticity of the mammalian spinal cord* (pp. 347–62). New York: Springer Verlag.

Smith, J. L.; Hoy, M. G.; Koshland, G. F.; Phillips, D. M.; & Zernicke, R. F. (1985). Intralimb coordination of the paw-shake response: A novel mixed synergy. *Journal of Neurophysiology, 54,* 1271–81.

Smith, J. L., & Zernicke, R. F. (1987). Predictions for neural control based on limb dynamics. *Trends in Neuroscience, 10,* 123–28.

Stehouwer, D. J., & Farel, P. B. (1983). Development of hindlimb locomotor activity in the bullfrog *(Rana catesbeiana)* studied in vitro. *Science, 219,* 516–18.

Stehouwer, D. J., & Farel, P. B. (1984). Development of hindlimb locomotor behavior in the frog. *Developmental Psychobiology, 17,* 217–32.

Stehouwer, D. J., & Farel, P. B. (1985). Development of locomotor mechanisms in the frog. *Journal of Neurophysiology, 53,* 1453–66.

Stein, P. S. G.; Camp, A. W.; Robertson, G. A.; & Mortin, L. I. (1986). Blends of rostral and caudal scratch reflex motor patterns elicited by simultaneous stimulation of two sites in the spinal turtle. *Journal of Neuroscience, 6,* 2259–66.

Stelzner, D. J.; Martin, A. H.; & Scott, G. L. (1973). Early stages of synaptogenesis in the cervical spinal cord of the chick embryo. *Zeitschrift fur Zellforschung, 138,* 475–88.

Straznicky, K. (1963). Function of heterotopic spinal cord segments investigated in the chick. *Acta Biologica of the Academy of Science of Hungary, 14,* 143–53.

Szekely, G. (1976). Developmental aspects of locomotion. In R. M. Herman, S. Grillner, P. S. G. Stein & D. G. Stuart (Eds.), *Neural control of locomotion* (pp. 735–57). New York: Plenum.

Taub, E. (1976). Movement in nonhuman primates deprived of somatosensory feedback. In J. Keogh & R. S. Hutton (Eds.), *Exercise and sport science reviews, 4* (pp. 335–74). Santa Barbara: Journal Publishing Affiliates.

Thelen, E.; Ridley-Johnson, R.; & Fisher, D. M. (1983). Shifting patterns of bilateral coordination and lateral dominance in the leg movements of young infants. *Developmental Psychobiology, 16,* 29–46.

Viala, D.; Viala, C.; & Fayein, N. (1986). Plasticity of locomotor organization in infant rabbits spinalized shortly after birth. In M. E. Goldberger, A. Gorio & M. Murray (Eds.), *Development and plasticity of the mammalian spinal cord* (pp. 301–10). Padova: Liviana Press.

Viala, D., & Vidal, C. (1978). Evidence for distinct spinal locomotion generators supplying respectively fore- and hindlimbs in the rabbit. *Brain Research, 155,* 182–86.

Villablanca, J. R., & Olmstead, C. E. (1979). Neurological development of kittens. *Developmental Psychobiology, 12,* 101–27.

Watson, S. J. (1987). A kinematic analysis of embryonic leg movements in the chick. Master's thesis, University of Colorado, Boulder.

Windle, W. F., & Griffin, A. M. (1931). Observations on embryonic and fetal movements of the cat. *Journal of Comparative Neurology, 52,* 149–88.

Windle, W. F., & Orr, D. W. (1934). The development of behavior in chick embryos: Spinal cord structure correlated wtih early somatic motility. *Journal of Comparative Neurology, 60,* 287–308.

Part II

The Development of Balance and Locomotion in Children

4

The Development of Posture and Balance Control in Children

Marjorie H. Woollacott,
Anne Shumway-Cook,
and Harriet G. Williams

A review of the literature on the development of posture control through the last century reveals that the theoretical approach of the researcher influences both the types of questions asked and the interpretation of the results of the experiments. Traditional theories on the development of neuromuscular control are based on the Sherringtonian school, which focuses on reflex function or reactions to stimuli. This approach uses research methods involving stimulating an inactive organism with abstract stimuli such as stripes (visual), clicks (auditory), or arbitrary body displacements (proprioceptive). Researchers who used this approach have concluded that overt neuromuscular activity of infants under 12–14 weeks of age is entirely reflex (Wyke, 1975). In addition, this theoretical approach models nervous-system development in terms of a strict hierarchy of levels of reflexive responses which are eventually controlled at the highest level by volitional activity. Research adhering to this reflex hierarchy approach concludes either that voluntary movement control occurs through the inhibition of reflexes by cerebral cortex pathways or that reflexes become the substrata for voluntary actions (Twitchell, 1965; Wyke, 1975). This model is commonly applied in rehabilitation medicine, with the development of numerous tests of reflex development used to determine how far up the developmental staircase a child has matured (Van Sant, 1986). In addition, the reflex hierarchy model is used to plan and sequence treatment by training the child in tasks representing successively "higher" levels of reflexes and reactions.

A more recent approach, based on the work of Bernstein (1967) and Gibson (1966), asks questions about the organism as an active agent in a continuously changing environment and thus explores the physiology of activity rather than the physiology of reactions (Reed, 1982). Instead of viewing neuromuscular control from a strictly hierarchical perspective, the approach uses a "distributed control" model, which views the nervous system as a flexible complex of systems and subsystems sharing in the control process. This contrasts with the Sherringtonian view that a movement is triggered or commanded, a concept considered inadequate to explain the control of complex behavior (Reed, 1982). A distributed control approach also models the nervous system as a perception-action system that is goal oriented, rather than a simple sensorimotor system. The function of perception in a goal-oriented organism is to identify properties of the environment which have significance to the goal. These properties have been called *affordances* (Gibson, 1979). Action, then, is organized around the perception of what the environment affords. This approach has allowed the creation of new theories concerning development. The work of von Hofsten on reaching in infancy suggests that perception is meaningful even in the neonate. In addition, infants are capable of organizing action to achieve a goal (von Hofsten, 1986).

Out of this new perspective has come a great expansion in research on the development of postural control in infants and children. Research in the area encompasses the complete spectrum of ontological development from postural movements of the fetus in utero (Prechtl, 1986) through the continued refinement of balance control in the older child (Lee & Aronson, 1974; Forssberg & Nashner, 1982; Shumway-Cook & Woollacott, 1985; Hass et al., 1986). This research has explored both static and dynamic balance control in children and has examined the role of visual, proprioceptive, and vestibular stimulation in postural control. In addition, studies on both head and hand movements of infants who are orienting toward and reaching for objects has shown that there is a strong postural component in reaching and orienting behaviors (Bower, 1982; Bullinger & Jouen, 1983; von Hofsten, 1986).

This review will focus on the development of postural control in children as an emergent property stemming from changes in perceptual, neuromuscular, and biomechanical characteristics of the child's system, and will attempt to correlate changes in neuronal development and biomechanical properties with successive behavioral modifications observed during development.

PRENATAL AND EARLY POSTNATAL STUDIES

Prechtl (1986) used ultrasound techniques to study behavior of infants during prenatal development. He has shown that spontaneous postural changes occur prenatally and notes that the fetus has the habit of changing its position and orientation in the uterus (possibly to prevent adhesions or stasis). Prechtl further described two different motor patterns responsible for these postural changes. One involves a rotation along the longitudinal body axis, initiated by a lateral turning of the head or the hips; the other consists of alternating leg movements, which result in a somersault if the legs are properly positioned against the uterine wall. He observed positional changes as often as twenty times per hour in the first half of pregnancy. The rate of change decreases with progressive gestation, perhaps due to spatial restriction.

In contrast, Prechtl (1986) was unable to activate vestibular reflexes in utero. He noted that the vestibulo-ocular reflex and the Moro response were absent prenatally but were present as soon as birth. He hypothesized that these reflexes were inhibited until the umbilical cord was broken; thus the fetus was prevented from moving every time the mother turned. Prechtl (1986) also suggested that a unique situation seems to exist in the human compared to other primates. The human newborn infant is remarkably poorly adapted to requirements of the extrauterine environment. Muscle power is minimal, and the postural control of the head and body is very weak or even absent. Prechtl (1986) reports that these signs of neuromuscular immaturity continue until the end of the second month postnatally, when there is a major transformation in the infant's sensorimotor capacity.

Bullinger (1981) and Bullinger & Jouen (1983) have shown that babies as young as sixty hours postnatally are capable of orienting themselves toward a source of visual stimulation and that they can follow a moving object by correct orientation of the head. They also showed that the organization of the movements was part of a global form of postural control which involved the head and entire body. Though Bullinger & Jouen (1983) have shown that the infant uses the entire body to orient toward visual stimuli, neuromuscular correlates of orienting and reaching movement would help to clarify the manner in which different parts of the system interacted. Von Hofsten and Woollacott have used surface electromyograms to explore the integration of arm and trunk muscle responses of infants 9-10 months of age during an arm-reaching movement requiring stablization of the trunk. They reported that infants as young as 9 months old showed activation of postural muscles of the trunk in advance of activation of voluntary muscles of the arm during some, but not all, reaching movements (see Fig. 4-1). Infants were thus capable of activating postural muscles to stabilize the trunk in advance of an arm reach in a feedforward manner. However, the system was not always activated in this manner.

A number of investigators (Butterworth & Hicks, 1977; Butterworth & Pope, 1983; Pope, 1984) have tested the effect of visual stimulation on postural control of infants as young as 2 months of age.

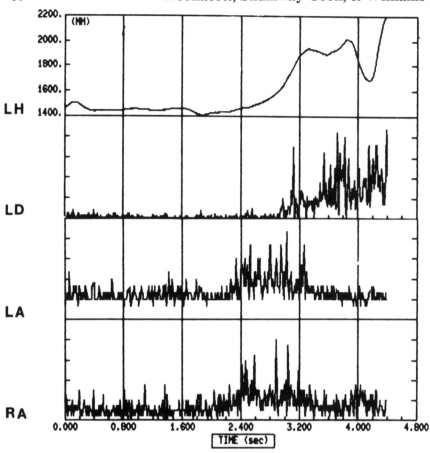

Fig. 4–1. Prime mover muscle responses and associated postural adjustments associated with a reach for an object by a 9-month-old. *LH* = forward movement of the left hand; *LD* = left deltoid EMG; *LA* = left abdominal EMG; *RA* = right abdominal EMG.

Infants were placed in an infant seat in a room with a fixed floor. The walls and ceiling of the room could be moved forward or backward to give misleading visual information simulating postural sway. Pope (1984) has shown that even before the baby can crawl, it is responsive to this discrepant visual feedback. Infants moved the head with the movement of the room, which implies that the sensorimotor system processed and interpreted the motion of the visual field as signifying body movement in the opposite direction, and compensated for this by moving the head in the direction of the visual flow. This suggests that as early as 2 months of age infants demonstrate sensitivity to visual information related to postural orientation of the head.

Pope (1984) also showed that onset of crawling, at about 6 months, coincided with a decline in the susceptibility to the effects of visual feedback from the moving room. Butterworth & Hicks (1977) noted that this pattern of high susceptibility to the pattern of visual flow with the onset of independent head control occurs again when the infant gains control over the trunk and begins to sit independently. The same pattern occurs again when the infant learns to stand (Lee & Aronson, 1974). Pope (1984) concluded that information coming from the periphery of the visual field was important in postural control in the infant, since movement of the central portion of the visual field did not lead to instability in children who had just learned to stand. These results could imply that visually induced sway is genetically predetermined and not acquired through trial-and-error experience in standing. However, in similar research that looked at the effects of a rotating visual display on postural sway (Brandt, Wenzel & Dichgans, 1976), children's posture was not affected by erroneous visual cues until they had learned to stand.

Though there may be disagreement in the literature concerning the exact age at which visual cues exert an influence on postural control (Brandt et al., 1976), most experiments provide support for the hypothesis that vision is more potent than mechanical-proprioceptive information in controlling postural sway in the young, standing child. Most authors base this conclusion on paradigms in which children were given only dynamic visual cues. No children were tested under conditions in which proprioceptive and vestibular cues indicated body sway while visual cues did not. Since all three sensory systems (visual, proprioceptive, and vestibular) appear to be functional soon after birth (Bower, 1982; Ornitz, 1983; Fiorentino, 1972), maturation of a sensory system alone cannot be used to determine dominance of a specific subsystem in posture control. Thus it is important to compare the postural responses of children under conditions that activate proprioceptive and vestibular systems, both isolated from and in conjunction with both normal and inappropriate visual cues. Only then can it be determined conclusively that visual cues are dominant in the control of posture in the young child.

It is also important to examine more closely the hypothesis which states that induced postural responses are acquired as a result of maturation rather than experience, in light of contradictory research on the effects of vision on posture in the 6-to-12-month-old seated child. Recent work on neuromuscular response organization underlying postural control in seated infants 4-14 months of age has attempted to assess the time course of the development of postural muscle response synergies as well as the relative weighting of visual, proprioceptive, and vestibular inputs in the development of balance control in children (Woollacott, et al., 1987). In this paradigm postural responses were activated by moving the infant's support surface (a hydraulically activated platform) in an anterior or posterior direction (see Fig. 4–2). The infants who were unable to sit independently were placed in an infant seat to give support to the trunk. Surface electromyograms were used to record the response of the neck flexor and extensor muscles, the trunk extensor (paraspinal) muscles, and the abdominal muscles. Infants of 4 to 6 months of age, who could not yet sit independently, showed responses only in the muscles of the neck. When visual information was present, the responses were correctly organized (neck extensor muscles were activated to bring the head back to a stable position) in only 60% of the trials for platform movements in the posterior direction, causing anterior displacement of the head. However, with vision absent (goggles were used to cover the eyes of the child), responses were correctly organized 100% of the time. These differences in postural responses with vision present versus absent imply that the visual system may be dominant in activating postural responses in infants but that it is not yet sufficiently calibrated to activate appropriate muscle responses in every instance. Proprioceptive and vestibular systems, stimulated by head movement and stretch of the neck musculature without visual information, can activate a stabilizing response with much more regularity. Such results must be viewed with some caution since it was impossible to control the direction of the infant's gaze during platform movements. If the infant was looking down or slightly to the side, visual information may have been in conflict with that of the proprioceptive system.

Postural responses of seated 8–14-month-old children included muscles of both the neck and trunk and were organized in the same manner as in adults. That is, when the support surface was moved backward, causing forward sway at the trunk, neck extensor and trunk extensor muscles were activated to bring the center of mass back to a stable position. In this age range the responses were correct with respect to directional specificity in all trials, both with and without vision. This implies that by the age of 8 months the visual system is more appropriately calibrated in its interactions with the other two sensory systems involved in postural control.

POSTURAL CONTROL IN THE NEWLY STANDING CHILD

Experiments by Lee & Aronson (1974) were the first to show a strong effect of vision on the control of posture in the newly standing

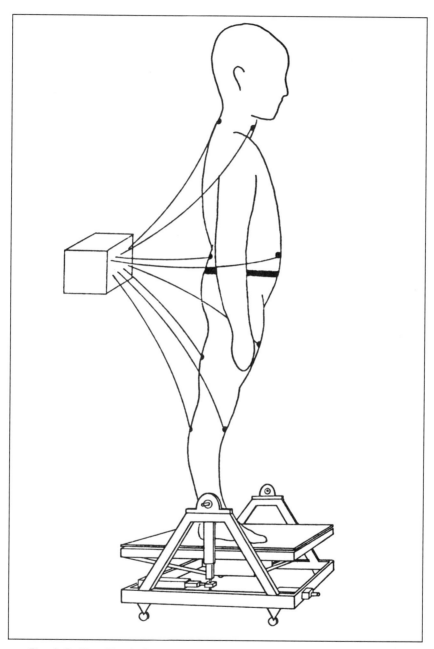

Fig. 4-2. Movable platform used for disturbing the balance of the infants and children. Movements were translations in the anterior or posterior direction, or rotations upward or downward.

child. Using the experimental techniques described above, they placed the child in a room with a stable support surface and with moving walls and ceiling. They showed that the child first learning to stand would fall, stagger, or sway in the direction of the room movement in response to misleading visual stimuli (which indicated body sway in the opposite direction). However, this effect gradually diminished over the first year of experience in standing, and by 2 years of age children tended to laugh when they experienced the room's movement rather than fall. A standing adult is very sensitive to misleading visual information as well: the head and body can be visually driven by 3-mm oscillations of the room (Lee & Lishman, 1975). However, unlike the infant, the adult is not moved off balance by such visual information under normal stance conditions. These researchers hypothesized that this is because the infant has poorer information from the ankles and feet than the adult. He suggested that the adult can be made to sway abnormally as well if asked to balance crossways on a beam, reducing the support-surface information coming from the foot.

More recent research (Forssberg & Nashner, 1982; Shumway-Cook & Woollacott, 1985; Woollacott et al., 1987) has examined the organization of postural muscle responses in the newly standing child using a movable support surface. Researchers have attempted to determine the time course of the development of the responses in the leg, trunk, and neck musculature during the transition period between sitting and standing. Experiments by Woollacott et al. (1987) were performed on children in the age range of 8–14 months (the range of stages observed in learning to stand, from no experience in independent stance at 8 months, through minimal experience at 10 months, to six weeks of experience in stance and walking at 14 months). The authors noted similarities in postural responses of children in the youngest age group (4–6 months) tested while seated (see above) and children first learning to stand. In both cases children showed an increase in neuromuscular response organization with age and experience in standing. The 8-month-old (lightly supported at the waist by the mother as an aid in standing) showed no responses to platform movements causing anterior or posterior sway. Leg, trunk, and neck muscles were either tonically active or showed no change in background activity. Thus the 8-month-old showed no postural responses as well as an inability to independently support her body weight during stance. It is possible, however, that in this younger child, the support given by the mother reduced the effect of the platform movement sufficiently to prevent stretch of the ankle musculature or, alternatively, that the support reduced the need for a postural response.

The 10-month-old showed directionally specific responses in distal muscles of the leg (gastrocnemius) during 40% of platform movements causing anterior sway. These responses were activated at very short, monosynaptic latencies (53 ± 11 msec). Upper leg muscles were activated in only one trial. Trunk and neck muscles were activated in the majority of trials but without consistent directional organization. The oldest child (14 months) showed directionally appropriate responses in leg muscles during all of the platform movements. Gastrocnemius mean latencies for anterior sway were 109 ± 24 msec. Neck and trunk responses, although often present, were not consistently organized in the temporal sequence seen in the adult.

Experiments by Forssberg & Nashner (1982) and Shumway-Cook & Woollacott (1985) on children 15 months to 10 years of age have explored transition phases that occur in postural control as children refine their balance skills. Forssberg & Nashner (1982) noted that postural adjustments of the young children were more variable and slower than those of adults. They also reported that the slower EMG responses and faster rates of sway acceleration seen in young children, due to their smaller size, resulted in sway excursions that were larger and tended to be more oscillatory than those of older children and adults. Shumway-Cook & Woollacott (1985) also observed that children 15 months to 3 years old showed clearly organized leg muscle responses to postural perturbations while standing. Distal muscles of the leg were activated before proximal muscles (as seen in adults). These postural responses were consistently large in amplitude and longer in latency and duration than those of adults, for platform movements causing anterior sway (children: 109 ± 8 msec; adults: 94 ± 11 msec, gastrocnemius). The increased duration of responses in children has been reported by others (Bawa, 1981; Berger et al., 1985). However, for posterior sway, responses were of the same latency as adults (102 ± 3 msec vs. 97 ± 12 msec, tibialis anterior). In addition, proximal muscle onset latencies for perturbations causing anterior sway showed a larger temporal delay in children than in adults (Shumway-Cook & Woollacott, 1985). More recent work has shown that the early responses found in upper body musculature in adults appeared to develop later than the leg muscle response synergy (Woollacott et al., 1987). For example, the 2-to-3-year-olds studied by Woollacott et al. (1987) exhibited responses in the trunk musculature in only 58% of trials, while adults showed responses in 84% of trials.

Experiments analyzing the onset latency and variability of leg muscle responses of children 4 to 6 years old (Shumway-Cook & Wool-lacott, 1985) revealed an unusual change in the response characteristics of this age group. The 4-to-6-year-olds appeared to regress in their postural response organization, in that leg postural response synergies were, in general, more variable and longer in latency than in the children 15 months to 3 years old, 7 to 10 years old, or adults. Though children 15 months to 3 years old showed distal muscle response onset latencies only slightly longer than those seen in adults, latencies in children 4 to 6 years old were both significantly slower and more variable. In addition, the 4-to-6-year-olds showed a significant delay in the activation of proximal leg muscle synergists for both anterior and posterior platform perturbations. Temporal delays between distal and proximal leg muscles produced increased motion at the knee joint during compensatory body sway. This was not seen in adults. The activation of proximal leg muscles of children 4 to 6 years old was apparently not sufficiently rapid to compensate for the inertial lag associated with the mass of the thigh and trunk (Shumway-Cook & Woollacott, 1985).

Studies by Woollacott et al. (1987) analyzing the responses of trunk and neck muscles in children support the observation that postural response patterns in children are characterized by high variability. Under normal visual conditions for anterior sway perturbations, neck flexor muscle responses occurred less often in children 4 to 6 years old (22% of the trials) than in 2 to 3 years old (54% of trials) or adults (84% of trials). When these responses were present they were also more variable in latency (122 ± 37 msec) than for the other age groups tested (2 to 3 years: 125 ± 21 msec; adults: 101 ± 5 msec). Trunk extensor muscle responses were also significantly longer in latency when compared to the adults. In spite of the greater variability in this age group, children 4 to 6 years old swayed less in response to platform movements than those 15 months to 3 years old (Shumway-Cook & Woollacott, 1985).

The 7–10-year-old age group exhibited postural responses essentially like those seen in the adult, in that there were no significant differences in onset latency, variability, or temporal coordination between muscles within the leg synergy, for platform movements similar to those used for younger age groups (2 cm amplitude, 250 msec duration). However, when faster platform movements were used (3 cm amplitude, 125 msec duration) neck and trunk flexors and extensors of this age group had longer latencies than those of adults under similar perturbation conditions (Woollacott et al., 1987).

POSTURAL RESPONSES WITH VISUAL CUES ELIMINATED

Removal of visual input (with opaque goggles) during horizontal platform movements had different effects on children of various ages

(Woollacott et al., 1987). In all age groups postural responses were present even when visual cues were absent. Although adults showed no significant differences in latency of muscle responses for the two conditions, children 2 to 3 years old had a reduction in latency of neck muscle responses from 125 ± 21 msec to 98 ± 17 msec with an additonal increase in the frequency of occurrence of neck muscle mono-synaptic reflexes when visual cues were eliminated. No changes were observed in the frequency of longer latency responses of neck muscles. Gastrocnemius response latencies were unchanged in the 2–3-year-old age group; there was an increase in the occurrence of monosynaptic reflexes (open: 19%; closed: 30% of trials). Children 4 to 6 years old exhibited greater variability in neck and leg muscle latencies without vision. With vision removed they also showed an increase of the frequency of occurrence of postural responses in neck muscles from activation in 22% of the trials to activation in 58% of the trials.

What is the significance of either a reduction in response latency or an increase in the frequency of occurrence of monosynaptic and longer latency responses when vision is removed? These results imply that visual cues are not required to activate postural responses in any of the age groups tested and that removal of these cues may actually increase the sensitivity of the system to remaining proprioceptive and vestibular cues. The slight reduction in latency of neck muscle responses and increased number of monosynaptic reflexes among children 2 to 3 years old with vision removed could suggest that vision is normally dominant in this age group, and that a shift occurs from the use of longer latency visual input with eyes open to shorter latency proprioceptive inputs with eyes closed.

THE DEVELOPMENT OF INTERSENSORY INTEGRATION

It is possible to use platform rotations instead of horizontal transla-tions to perturb balance, as a way of testing the ability of children to habituate or attenuate postural responses under changing environmen-tal contexts. Platform rotations, like translations, cause ankle rotations and concomitant stretch to the ankle joint musculature, but they do not initially cause body sway. Thus, ankle joint proprioceptive inputs associ-ated with horizontal platform movements are congruent with visual and vestibular inputs in indicating body sway, but ankle joint inputs associ-ated with rotations are not congruent with visual and vestibular inputs, since the former inputs indicate strong sway, whereas the latter indi-cate little or no sway. In adults, platform rotations produce postural responses in the stretched ankle muscles on initial trials. However, responses are destabilizing under these conditions and are significantly attenuated within ten trials (Nashner, 1976; Keshner & Allum, 1986). Thus dorsiflexing ankle rotations can be used to test the efficiency of ankle joint proprioceptive inputs (in isolation) in producing postural responses and of the ability of the nervous system to attenuate postural responses, when needed, in changing environmental contexts.

Forssberg & Nashner (1982) reported that responses of their two youngest age groups (1½ to 3½ yrs) to platform rotations were highly variable and that amplitude changes were not related systematically to sensory conditions. They also noted that latencies as well as amplitudes of responses were highly variable in children 5 to 7½ years old; in contrast, children older than 7½ years consistently attenuated the EMG amplitudes following exposure to the rotating support surface. They thus concluded that children under 7½ years show an inability to suppress inappropriate postural responses.

Experiments by Shumway-Cook & Woollacott (1985) have closely examined the responses of children to changing platform perturbation conditions to determine if increased exposure to changing task conditions allows children the opportunity to adapt responses. Three children between 15 and 31 months were tested with dorsiflexing rotational platform perturbations. Although monosynaptic reflexes were occasionally observed under these conditions, none showed consistent longer latency postural responses in gastrocnemius and hamstring muscles. By 3 years of age the children showed normal longer latency-response synergies in leg muscles to platform rotations. Children 4 to 6 years old also exhibited these responses. In addition, two-thirds of the 4-to-6 year-olds showed attenuation of inappropriate responses but not within the three to five trials seen in the adult. They required instead exposure to ten to fifteen trials before response attenuation occurred. Children 7 to 10 years old showed adultlike adaptation. Thus, the inability of Forssberg & Nashner to observe attenuation of responses in children under 7½ years of age may have been due to the longer time required for these children to adapt to changing environmental contexts when compared to adults.

A second approach that can be used to test the ability of children to adapt to altered sensory conditions requires the child to stand quietly for five seconds under conditions of progressively decreased redundancy of inputs relevant for balance control, until only vestibular inputs remain. These include: (1) somatosensory ankle joint, visual and vestibular inputs normal; (2) somatosensory ankle joint inputs and vestibular inputs normal, eyes closed; (3) ankle joint inputs minimized by rotating the platform in direct relationship to body sway, but vision and vestibular inputs normal; and (4) ankle joint inputs minimized (as above), eyes closed, vestibular system normal. Children's performances were measured by determining body sway as a percentage of theoretical maximum sway, with 100% indicating loss of balance.

Work by Shumway-Cook & Woollacott (1985) indicates that even under normal stance conditions the children 4 to 6 years old swayed significantly more than the older children or adults (the youngest children could not tolerate the altered conditions without crying). With eyes closed their stability decreased further, but they retained balance. However, when the support surface was rotated with body sway, thus keeping the ankle joint at approximately 90 degrees, the 4-to-6-year-olds were greatly destabilized and one lost balance. In the final condition, in which ankle joint inputs were minimized and eyes were closed, leaving only vestibular cues to aid in balance, four of the five children in this age group lost balance but none of the older children or adults needed assistance to maintain their stability.

Forssberg & Nashner (1982) noted that, under conditions in which the support surface and the visual environment were rotated with body sway to remove relevant inputs, the youngest children showed a long delay from the onset of spontaneous forward sway to the activation of the appropriate gastrocnemius muscle. Subsequently, children began to sway backward, this time initiating the appropriate anterior tibialis response only after balance had been lost. In contrast, appropriate responses were activated much more quickly among children 7 to 10 years old and oscillations remained within normal limits.

It thus appears that children under 7 years of age are unable to balance efficiently when both somatosensory and visual cues are removed, leaving only vestibular cues to control stability. Children 4 to 6 years old showed progressively decreasing stability as they lost redundant sensory inputs for postural control. They also appeared to have difficulty shifting from the use of ankle joint somatosensory cues to visual cues when ankle joint inputs were made incongruent with body sway. This may also indicate the inability of 4-to-6-year-olds to resolve intersensory conflict during postural control.

CHANGES IN LATENCY OF POSTURAL RESPONSES WITH AGE

Experiments by Haas et al. (1986) have examined latency changes in short latency (monosynaptic), medium latency, and long latency (antagonist muscle) responses to platform rotations in children from 1 to 15 years of age. They observed that, after short latency responses were normalized for body height, the time course of latency changes with age showed a decrease until 5 years of age and nearly no change thereafter. Normalized medium latency responses decreased continuously from 1 year to 15 years of age, indicating a longer time course of maturational change. However, the longer latency responses in the antagonist muscles (possibly activated by vestibular inputs indicating backward body sway) showed a much greater decrease in latency between 1 and 15 years of age. The authors concluded that the differences in maturational characteristics of the three types of responses were indicative of their different origins and of more centrally controlled pathways for antagonist, longer latency responses.

Consistent with the concept that short latency and long-latency responses have different origins are findings by Berger et al. (1985) and Shumway-Cook (1983) which show a decreasing incidence of monosynaptic activity in children above the age of 4. In contrast, longer latency postural responses become increasingly refined and effective with age.

POSTURAL RESPONSES UNDER STATIC BALANCE CONDITIONS

Williams et al. (1983) studied the neuromuscular response characteristics of children 4, 6, and 8 years of age during a variety of static balancing tasks in order to determine if with increasing age there is an increase in the ability to localize muscle activity needed to perform a given balance task. They used a variety of different static balance tasks, ranging from a pivot prone position, in which the child was lying on the stomach with trunk pivoted to the side and arms in the air, to standing on hands and knees, kneeling, standing erect, and standing on one foot. They noted that the average EMG amplitude decreased systematically between the ages of 4 and 8 years. In addition, 8-year-olds had smoother EMG profiles, and 4-year-olds had the most erratic profile. They noted that these patterns of EMG activity for children of different ages are consistent with behavioral observations of static postural task performance by normal children 6 to 11 years old (Bachman, 1961; Keogh, 1965). They concluded that younger children may be somewhat like the unskilled sports performer, in that they use excessive amounts of muscular activity to perform tasks. Older children, like the skilled performer, appear to be better able to produce the appropriate amount of muscle activity for maximum efficiency.

In a later study Williams et al. (1985) examined the duration of EMG activity in gastrocnemius, tibialis anterior, and erector spinae muscle groups during 30 seconds of standing in children of different ages and with different levels of motor development. They reported that for 4-,

8-, and 10-year-old children with normal motor development, gastrocnemius and erector spinae muscle groups seemed to provide the greatest muscular support for standing; these muscle groups were active the largest percentage of the 30 seconds of standing. The tibialis anterior was generally not active. Interestingly, for normal 6-year-olds, all three muscle groups were active a large percentage of time during standing. The authors speculated that, although co-contraction of lower leg muscles may be a part of the program of muscular control in standing for some children (6-year-olds), the overall pattern of muscular control of standing for children of all ages is one that involves a distribution of the workload across trunk and leg muscles.

Characteristic of children with motor development delays was the persistent presence of erector spinae activity for large percentages of time during standing. Lower leg muscles were active for lesser periods of time. The authors suggest that one characteristic of balance control in children with normal motor development is a more even distribution of muscular effort for standing between the muscles of the trunk and legs. In contrast, for children with motor development delays, balance control may be characterized by a pattern of muscular control in which trunk muscles contribute the largest percentage of muscular effort for standing.

BIOMECHANICAL CHANGES ASSOCIATED WITH POSTURAL CONTROL

Kugler, Kelso & Turvey (1982) offered a suggestion for why the development of motor control often occurs in a steplike or stagelike fashion. They suggested that changes seen in development of many skills may be the result of critical dimension changes in the body of the growing child. The system would remain in a state of stability until dimensional changes reached a point where previous motor programs were no longer effective in motor control. At this time the system would undergo a period of transition marked by instability and variability followed by another plateau of stability.

It may be significant that the variability in response parameters of children 4 to 6 years old found in this study occurs during a period of disproportionate growth with respect to critical changes in body form (Zeller 1964).

Recent work analyzing the movements of different segments of the body, in response to platform perturbations in both children and adults (Woollacott, et al. 1987), has shown that the kinematics of passive body movements caused by the platform translations are very similar in the 4–6-year-old, 7–9-year-old, and the adult. Figure 4–3 gives examples of the displacements of the head, shoulder, hand, hip, knee, and ankle of a 4-year-old and an adult in response to platform translations causing anterior sway. The onset times for movements of the segments for each age group are given in Table 4–1. Note that sway commences in the ankle joint immediately upon the onset of platform

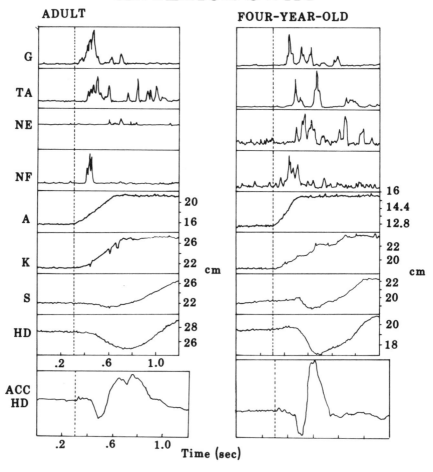

Fig. 4–3. Muscle responses and body segmental movements associated with platform translations in the posterior direction causing anterior sway. *ACC* = accelerometer placed at head level; *A* = LED movement in the anterior-posterior direction at the level of the ankle; *K* = LED at knee; *S* = LED at shoulder; *HD* = LED at head; *G* = gastrocnemius; *TA* = tibialis anterior; *NE* = neck extensor; and *NF* = neck flexor.

TABLE 4-1

Average EMG response and LED movement (AP = anterior posterior; V = vertical) onset times (in msec) of 4-6-year-olds, 7-8-year-olds, and adults in response to 3 cm platform displacements in the posterior direction

3 cm Posterior Platform Displacements

Age	Gastrocnemius	Tibialis anterior	Neck extensor	Neck flexor	Knee	Shoulder		Head	
4-6 yr	107±23	124±19	173±12	124±18	27±14	AP	126±62	AP	143±19
						V	76±9	V	34±26
7-8 yr	84±8	125±38	144±17	127±25	24±7	AP	105±20	AP	142±26
						V	53±32	V	37±17
Adult	93±7	130±24	143±8	121±22	35±11	AP	145±19	AP	164±40
						V	49±18	V	55±30

movement and progresses upward to the knee (43 ± 16 msec), hip (53 ± 22 msec), shoulder (144 ± 11 msec), and head (163 ± 20 msec) in the adult. For children of 4–6 and 7–9 years of age, platform-induced movements were not significantly different in onset time. Thus if biomechanical parameters of the body undergo changes during this period, they are not clearly demonstrated in body segmental movement parameters elicited by platform translations. It is more probable that changes in response latencies and variability seen in children 4 to 6 years old represent developmental changes in the nervous system itself.

CONCLUSIONS

We interpret our results as supporting the hypothesis that clear phases exist in the development of postural control. Visual dominance of postural control appears to reoccur at transition points in the development of posture and locomotion. Thus the infant first learning to sit independently, crawl, stand, and walk shows strong visual dependence. In children first learning to stand, neuromuscular responses tend to be long in duration, slightly longer than those of adults in onset latency and stereotyped. The age of 4 to 6 years marks a clear transition phase with responses becoming longer in latency and increasingly variable. By 7 to 10 years of age the leg muscle responses have attained adult like characteristics, although upper body responses continue to evolve during this period.

It appears that during the period of time in which children acquire basic locomotor skills (18 months to 3 years) they rely primarily on visual information. The apparent regression in postural organization that occurs between 4 and 6 years of age may represent a time during which the child begins to integrate visual, vestibular, and somatosensory inputs in the maintenance of balance. It is hypothesized that children in this age group progressively expand their reliance on sensory cues to systems other than the visual system. The fine tuning of the control of posture which results from this calibration appears to be an important stage in development, leading to adultlike postural control in which responses are both short in latency and adaptive to changing task conditions.

Research on developmental changes in the latency of postural responses to platform rotations show clear differences in the maturation time of short latency (monosynaptic), medium latency, and longer latency antagonist muscle responses. Thus the three responses appear to be activated by distinct systems. In addition, research on the control of static postures indicates that as children mature they exhibit lower levels of muscle activity and less variability in the amplitude profile, indicating a greater efficiency in performing the postural tasks.

REFERENCES

Bawa, P. (1981). Neural development in children: A neurophysiological study. *Electroencephalography and Clinical Neurophysiology, 51*, 249–56.

Berger, W.; Quintern, J.; & Dietz, V. (1985) Stance and gait perturbations in children: Developmental aspects of compensatory mechanisms. *Electroencephalography and Clinical Neurophysiology, 61*, 385–95.

Bernstein, N. (1967). Co-ordination and regulation of movements. New York: Pergamon Press.

Bower, T. G. R. (1982). *Development in infancy*. 2nd ed. San Francisco: Freeman.

Brandt, T.; Wenzel, D.; & Dichgans, J. (1976). Die Entwicklung der visuellen Stabilisation des aufrechten standes bein kind: Ein refezeichen in der kinderneurologie (Visual stabilization of free stance in infants: A sign of maturity). *Arch. Psychiat. Nervenkr., 223*, 1–13.

Bullinger, A. (1981). Cognitive elaboration of sensorimotor behaviour. In G. Butterworth (Ed.), *Infancy and epistemology: An evaluation of Piaget's theory*, (pp. 173–99). London: Harvester Press.

Bullinger, A., & Jouen, F. (1983). Sensibilité du champ de detection peripherique aux variations posturales chez le bébé. *Archives de Psychologie, 51*, 41–48.

Butterworth, G., & Hicks, L. (1977). Visual proprioception and postural stability in infancy: A developmental study. *Perception, 6*, 255–262.

Butterworth, G., & Pope, M. (1983). Origine et fonction de la proprioception visuelle chez l'enfant. In S. de Schonen (Ed.), *Le Developpement dans la première année* (pp. 107–28). Paris: Presses Universitaires de France.

Fiorentino, M. R. (1972). *Normal and abnormal development*. Springfield, IL: Thomas.

Forssberg, H., & Nashner, L. (1982). Ontogenetic development of postural control in man: Adaptation to altered support and visual conditions during stance. *Journal of Neuroscience, 2*, 545–52.

Gibson, J. J. (1966). *The senses considered as perceptual systems*. Boston: Houghton-Mifflin.

Haas, G.; Diener, H. C.; Bacher, M.; & Dichgans, J. (1986). Development of postural control in children: Short-, medium-, and long-latency EMG responses of leg muscles after perturbation of stance. *Experimental Brain Research, 64*, 127–32.

Keogh, J. (1965). *Motor Performance of Elementary School Children*. Los Angeles: Dept. of Physical Education, University of California.

Keshner, E. A., & Allum, J. H. J. (1986). Plasticity in pitch sway stabilization: Normal habituation and compensation for peripheral vestibular deficits. In W. Bles and T. Brandt (Eds.), *Disorders of posture and gait*. Amsterdam: Elsevier.

Kugler, P. N.; Kelso, J. A. S.; & Turvey, M. T. (1982). On the control and coordination of naturally developing systems. In J. A. S. Kelso and J. E. Clark (Eds.), *The development of movement control and coordination*. New York: Wiley and Sons.

Lee, D. N., & Aronson, E. (1974). Visual proprioceptive control of standing in human infants. *Perception & Psychophysics, 15*, 529–32.

Lee, D. N., & Lishman, R. (1975). Visual proprioceptive control of stance. *Journal of Human Movement Studies, 1*, 87–95.

Nashner, L. M. (1976). Adapting reflexes controlling the human posture. *Experimental Brain Research*. 26: 59–72.

Ornitz, E. M. (1983). Normal and pathological maturation of vestibular function in the human child. In Romand J. (Ed.), *Development of auditory and vestibular systems*. (pp. 479–536). New York: Academic Press.

Owen, B. M., & Lee, D. N. (1986). Establishing a frame of reference for action. In M. Wade and H. Whiting (Eds.), *Motor development in children: Aspects of coordination and control*. (pp. 287–308). Boston: Martinus Nijhoff.

Pope, M. J. (1984). *Visual proprioception in infant postural development*. Ph.D. dissertation, University of Southampton.

Prechtl, H. F. R. (1986). Prenatal motor development. In M. Wade & H. Whiting (Eds.), *Motor development in children: Aspects of coordination and control* (pp. 53–64). Boston: Martinus Nijhoff.

Reed, E. (1982). An outline of a theory of actions systems. *Journal of Motor Behavior, 14*, 98–134.

Shumway-Cook, A. (1983). Developmental aspects of postural control in normal and Down's Syndrome children. Ph.D. dissertation, University of Oregon.

Shumway-Cook, A., & Woollacott, M. (1985). The growth of stability: Postural control from a developmental perspective. *Journal of Motor Behavior, 17*, 131–147.

Twitchell, T. E. (1965). The automatic grasping responses of infants. *Neuropsychologia, 3*, 247–59.

Von Hofsten, C. (1986). The emergence of manual skills. In M. Wade and H. Whiting (Eds.), *Motor development in children: Aspects of coordination and control*. (pp. 167–86). Boston: Martinus Nijhoff.

Williams, H. G.; Fisher, J. M.; & Tritschler, K. (1983). Descriptive analysis of static postural control in 4, 6, and 8 year old normal and motorically awkward children. *American Journal of Physical Medicine, 62*, 12–26.

Williams, H. G.; McCleneghan, B.; & Ward, D. S. (1985). Duration of muscle activity during standing in normally and slowly developing children. *American Journal of Physical Medicine, 64*, 171–89.

Woollacott, M.; Debu, B.; & Mowatt, M. (1987) Neuromuscular control of posture in the infant and child. *Journal of Motor Behavior, 19*, 167–86.

Woollacott, M.; Roseblad, B.; & Hofsten, von C. (1988). Relation between muscle response onset and body segmental movements during postural perturbations in humans. *Experimental Brain Research, 72*, 593–604.

Wyke, B. (1975). The neurological basis of movement—a developmental review. In K. S. Holt (Ed.), *Movement and child development* (pp. 19–33). Philadelphia: Lippincott.

Zeller, W. (1964). *Konstitution und Entwicklung*. Gottingen: Verlag für Psychologi.

5

Preparatory Postural Adjustments and Postural Sway in Young Children

Keith C. Hayes
and Cindy L. Riach

Control of balance represents one of the many challenges facing an infant. Ensuring a stable posture is a necessary prerequisite for successful execution of limb movements aimed at exploring the child's immediate environment—for example, reaching and grasping movements. Similarly, maintenance of balance in the upright stance is a natural precursor to walking. The development of balance has long intrigued parents and scientists alike, but it is only in recent years that quantitative approaches and theoretical models have been developed for understanding the maturational processes involved.

In this chapter we consider the development of balance within the context of a theoretical model that gives explicit consideration to "feedforward" control processes. The model stems largely from the results of investigations by Belenkii and colleagues in the 1960s and more recently by Gahery & Massion (1981). Within this theoretical framework, feedforward postural adjustments constitute those changes to posture that *precede a predictable disturbance* to the body's overall equilibrium. The adjustments anticipate and reduce perturbations to the center of gravity (CG) that would occur, for example, during voluntary limb movement. In this model, sensory input is considered to subserve three roles: first, identification of the current status of the neuromusculoskeletal system so that feedforward postural adjustments are appropriate to the current needs; second, identification of and correction for any mismatch between what was ordered and what was achieved by the centrally generated feedforward postural adjustments (i.e., feedback). Third, by providing information on the effectiveness of feedforward control, feedback can help to improve the efficacy of subsequent feedforward postural commands. The model thus differs from more conventional approaches to balance control that focus on, and emphasize, the role of feedback processes in the control and regulation of changing postures *immediately following unexpected external perturbations* to equilibrium.

Our discussion starts with consideration of the characteristics of anticipatory postural control processes and the diverse ways in which they are manifest. We then briefly describe a model that incorporates explicit representation of the feedforward processes, and we present clinical evidence attesting to the usefulness of distinguishing feedforward from feedback balance-control mechanisms. The remainder of the discussion is devoted to describing two experiments conducted on healthy young children, in which their feedforward control capabilities during an arm-raise task were investigated together with their postural sway during quiet standing. The postural sway during upright standing was considered to reflect the efficacy of the feedback control system for regulating posture. Assessment of the effects of depriving the children of vision on the extent and characteristics of sway, and analysis of the frequency composition (power spectral density function) of postural sway, allow some insights into the maturation of various aspects of the feedback control processes. Finally, we attempt to integrate the results of these studies into a more global consideration of the development of balance control in children.

FEEDFORWARD POSTURAL CONTROL

Situations in which the brain uses feedforward postural control fall into three categories: (1) internally generated biological disturbances; (2) voluntary, movement-induced postural disturbances; and (3) externally induced disturbances to equilibrium. These situations are usually associated with external manifestations of anticipatory postural adjustments—for example, as alterations in the location of the center of gravity or altered kinematics/kinetics of the musculoskeletal system. Feedforward control may also be evident, however, as internal adjustments, such as alterations in the gain or threshold of reflexes likely to be invoked in the anticipated postural disturbance (cf. MacKay & Murphy, 1979).

INTERNAL BIOLOGICAL DISTURBANCES

Feedforward activation of postural musculature is thought to provide compensation for internally generated physiological disturbances in order to maintain an exact position of stable equilibrium or in order to minimize postural sway. Disturbances due to the dynamics of respiration, for example, may cause rhythmic changes in the position of CG. This ongoing and predictable disturbance appears to be compensated by an anticipatory synergic organization of postural muscles working 180 degrees out of phase to the respiratory rhythm (Gurfinkel et al., 1971), and it has been suggested that the major role in this compensation is performed by muscles at the hip joint (Gurfinkel et al., 1971). Opposing this view, however, Hunter & Kearney (1981) reported that the effects of respiration are not cancelled but are responsible for an important component of quiet standing postural sway. Conceivably, both positions have some merits and feedforward adjustments limit, but do not negate, the disturbances introduced by respiratory dynamics. Moreover, it is possible that other "physiological noise," such as cardiovascular dynamics, also contributes to postural sway and may be accompanied by some feedforward postural compensation.

It is not entirely clear whether automatic feedforward compensatory adjustments for such basic biological functions as respiration are innate or are developed in early childhood. The motor skill of marksmanship offers one example in which preparatory postural adjustments are learned. Precise, fixed patterns of compensatory synergic muscle activity in body segments are found to attenuate the instability introduced by respiratory dynamics during exact aiming in experienced marksmen. In beginners, these patterns of muscle activity are poorly organized, inconsistent, and less effective in reducing perturbations introduced by respiration (Arutyunyan et al., 1969).

MOVEMENT-INDUCED POSTURAL DISTURBANCES

When a quietly standing adult subject quickly raises the right arm, there is a marked disturbance to the body's CG unless some compensation is made beforehand (Belenkii et al., 1967). This disturbance is brought about by the transmission of forces and moments of force through the musculoskeletal system (kinematic linkage) (Hayes, 1982). Electromyography (EMG) reveals that, prior to activity in the anterior deltoid muscle that produces the arm raise, there are distinct and repeatable patterns of activity in the postural muscles of the trunk and lower limbs. The first observable change is an electrical silence in the soleus muscle, followed by activity in the biceps femoris, gluteus maximus, and erector spinae. Postural muscle activity is seen 40–60 msec prior to activity in the deltoid muscle and proceeds from distal to proximal musculature (Belenkii et al., 1967; Bouisset & Zattara, 1981; Weiss & Hayes, 1979).

The patterns of onset of postural EMG activity before a self-initiated arm movement have been shown to be predictable from the biomechanics of the arm movement (Hayes, 1982; Weiss & Hayes, 1979). Subjects raising their arms forward or backward, with or without additional load, show muscle activity patterns appropriate to mechanical demands (see also Bouisset & Zattara, 1981). The biomechanical organization of postural EMG activity is reflected in the pattern of onset of contraction in the postural muscles, which corresponds to the forth-coming dominant muscle moments of force required to stabilize the kinematic linkage during the arm movement. The EMG activity is therefore predictable from rigid-body Newtonian mechanics (Hayes, 1982; Weiss & Hayes, 1979; see also Bouisset & Zattara, 1987). Experiments conducted in reduced gravity environments have confirmed and extended these observations by showing the attenuation of preparatory muscle activity when the antigravity demands of postural adjustments are no longer present (Clement et al., 1983).

The specificity of the postural adjustments has been shown by the correspondence between changes in the preparatory postural EMG activity and the changes in movement dynamics (Hayes, 1982). In addition, preparatory adjustments have been shown to be dependent upon the initial starting position (e.g., the initial location of CG) (Legallet & Gahery, 1980; Lipshits et al., 1981). The programmed nature of the preparatory adjustments is evident from the fact that the onset of the EMG activity precedes arm movement and is therefore independent of feedback from the limb movement (see also Lee, 1980). Feedforward activity appears, therefore, to be more than just a general stiffening of the muscles about the supporting joints. It is a task-specific, pre-programmed patterning of muscle activity.

The complete mechanical function of the preparatory muscle activity is unclear. There are two obvious possibilities: (1) the muscles may be active in order to generate moments of force; (2) the muscles may be active in order to move the body segments into a dynamically more stable end position. These two functions are not necessarily mutually exclusive. The muscle activity could also serve other functions such as assisting in the transfer of momentum from the trunk to the arm.

In a study of anticipatory postural adjustments associated with self-initiated plantar or dorsiflexion reaction-time tasks, the anticipatory pattern of muscle activation in the contralateral leg was shown to become temporally linked with a warning tone (Alexeev & Naidel, 1973). Subjects who trained with a constant foreperiod of 1 second initiated anticipatory postural adjustments 300–400 milliseconds prior to the disturbance. Without the warning tone, normal subjects began postural preparation 30–70 milliseconds prior to the movement (Alexeev & Naidel, 1973). This observation that the pattern of anticipatory response can be separated from the movement pattern suggested that there were actually two separate "motor programs," one for movement and another for postural adjustments. Similar conclusions have been drawn from analyses of anticipatory postural adjustments in patients with cerebellar and Parkinson's disease (Pal'tsev & Elner, 1967; Traub et al., 1980).

Animal studies, involving stimulation of the motor cortex, red nucleus, or the output nuclei of cerebellum, have confirmed the existence of postural adjustments that precede limb flexion in cats and monkeys (Nieoullon & Gahery, 1978; Regis et al., 1976; Schultz et al., 1979). The similarity of the patterns of postural adjustment to patterns of muscle activity involved in locomotion has been recognized, and it has been suggested that the preparatory postural adjustment is a fragment of a locomotor "program" and involves the same neural circuits between limbs (Gahery & Massion, 1981). One obvious function of the postural adjustments is to reduce disequilibrium and thereby minimize the energy expenditure required for restoration of equilibrium. Another role is to maximize the stability of the body and thus avoid falls. Both objectives fit the requirements of dynamic equilibrium during locomotion as well as static balance. If the basic elements of locomotor motor programs are present at birth, as has been suggested (cf. Forssberg & Wallberg, 1980: Zelazo, Zelazo & Kolb, 1972), one might postulate that the rudiments of preparatory postural adjustments are similarly present.

EXTERNALLY INDUCED DISTURBANCES

Marsden and colleagues (1981) investigated postural reactions to externally generated arm disturbances in humans and found that compensation is made in postural supporting muscles (usually the leg) long before voluntary control intervenes (reaction time). Compensation is also made before the effects of mechanical disturbances are transmitted to the postural muscles. The postural muscle response appears to be driven not by the disturbance of the postural muscle itself, but by afferent inputs from the parts of the body which are first perturbed. The sensitivity of the response appears to be very high, as it is triggered by levels of mechanical disturbance below the threshold for conscious awareness.

Despite the short latency of these responses, they are automatically adapted to varying contexts. The specific pathways involved are not known; however, because of the adaptability of the responses, cerebral or cerebellar influences are indicated (Marsden et al., 1981). This view is supported by the loss of early anticipatory postural responses in arm perturbations of patients with severe Parkinson's disease or cerebellar dysfunction (Traub et al., 1980). The presence of external postural support can greatly reduce the amplitude of postural responses associated with arm perturbations, sometimes to the point of extinction (Cordo & Nashner, 1982). With external support present, it is presumed that anticipatory postural responses are judged not to be necessary. Indeed, even the "postural set" (i.e., the individual's perception of the state of stability and the perceived availability of external support) can influence the presence and magnitude of anticipatory postural responses (Cordo & Nashner, 1982).

CONCEPTUAL MODELS OF POSTURAL CONTROL

It is apparent that preparatory adjustments to posture are present and are manifested in diverse ways. In order to assimilate this information into a broader conceptualization of the postural control process, it is helpful to consider the two models presented in Figure 5–1. On the left is shown a conventional feedback model with various elements of the postural control mechanisms identified. Information about the desired positional state of the body serves as input to the control system. A (hypothetical) postural control center uses this information as well as knowledge of the current body position to select appropriate parameters for postural control (reference selection). A composite reference parameter, such as the "margin of stability" (Koozekanani et al., 1980), or a set of parameters is selected, specifying, for example, torque or joint stiffness about each of the links in the musculoskeletal system (the exact parameters are currently unknown). The reference selection is used by a comparator to detect discrepancies between the input reference (i) and the sensory feedback (fb). If there is a discrepancy, an error (e) signal is generated and sent to the muscles that are the effectors of the controlled musculoskeletal link system. The error signal attempts to modify the output by correcting the discrepancy between the selected reference input and the feedback. The output in a quasistatic situation is an assumed posture. If the desired posture and reference input is changing, that is, in dynamic conditions, the output can be considered an evolving posture. Visual, vestibular, and proprioceptive sensory receptors each feed back information about the current state of equilibrium.

This type of feedback control system may function in two different modes. First, when the desired posture is static, the system functions in a regulatory mode to reduce disturbances after they occur and to return the body to a position matching the fixed reference selection. Second, when a changing posture is desired, the feedback pathway works in a servo-mechanism mode, maintaining the output of the system in strict accord with the changing reference input. If the reference selection reflects a predicted adjustment to a forthcoming disturbance, muscular adjustments may also be made in advance of the disturbance, thus producing a feedforward form of servo control.

The second model, on the right of Figure 5–1, provides a more explicit representation of the feedforward component in the human postural control system. In this model a predictive controller, within the

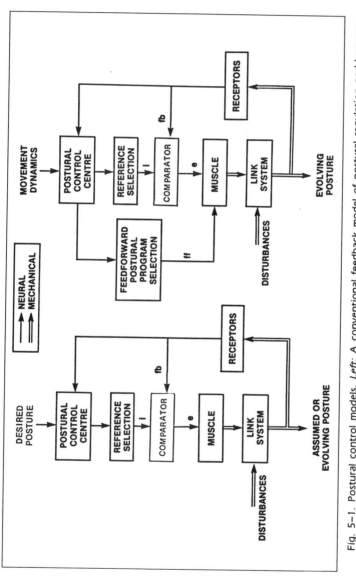

Fig. 5–1. Postural control models. *Left:* A conventional feedback model of postural regulation and/or servo-mechanism control. *Right:* A feedback model with an explicit feedforward path that provides activation of muscle synergies in advance of predictable perturbations. An essential component of this model is the capability of the hypothetical postural control center(s) to predict the dynamics of forthcoming disturbances from either internal or external sources. i = reference input; fb = feedback; ff = feedforward; e = error.

postural control center, specifies activation of a pattern of synergically organized muscles to produce a postural adjustment in anticipation of a specific disturbance. The pattern of muscle activation appears to be preprogrammed and located at a hierarchically low level of the central nervous system (cf. Nashner & Cordo, 1981). Initiation of the pattern, however, relies on the capability of higher levels of the nervous system to anticipate and predict the consequences of disturbances. The advantage of the feedforward component element in the second model is the quickness of response through direct activation of specific muscles in a pattern that is specific to the type of forthcoming disturbance.

Ideally, if the feedforward system operates correctly and accurately and feedback from previous experience (memory) is used effectively to generate an appropriate feedforward reference, the feedback will match the changing reference input and no error signal will be generated. This is asking a great deal of the feedforward control system, however, as a separate program of muscle activation would be required for every conceivable postural adaptation and the magnitude of the correction would have to be exact. In actuality, there may be a limited number of stereotyped programs to choose from; the feedforward system may select a program that functions to put the body posture in the correct ''ball park,'' while the feedback system is responsible for fine tuning of posture control. Similar views have been presented elsewhere (Gahery & Massion, 1981).

A legitimate question to pose is, what value is there in explicitly considering the feedforward component as a distinct entity when in fact it can ultimately be considered within the framework of a (more comprehensive) feedback model? Certainly the fact that feedforward postural adjustments can be experimentally distinguished from feedback postural adjustments occurring after a perturbation does not, in itself, constitute a justification. The best argument would be evidence that different physiological subsystems subserve the feedforward and feedback control elements. Some observations on patients with cerebellar damage suggest that this may be the case (Hayes, 1986).

In a clinical test of feedforward adjustments, in which a patient's ground reaction forces and moments of force are recorded prior to a rapid arm raise, a middle-aged man with pontocerebellar degeneration exhibited quite abnormal preparatory postural adjustments but an unremarkable postural sway during quiet stance (Hayes, 1986). In this study the extent and frequency composition of postural sway was assumed to reflect principally the integrity of the feedback systems. In contrast, a chronic alcoholic patient, with evidence of cerebellar anterior lobe degeneration, showed normal preparatory adjustments but a marked 3

Hz tremor during quiet standing. It was suggested that the neo-cerebellum (cerebellar hemispheres), which receives input through pontocerebellar pathways, may be instrumental in preparing the anticipatory adjustments, in addition to assisting with specification of the rapid arm-movement command. The anterior lobe of cerebellum then serves to control and regulate feedback postural adjustments mediated through spinocerebellar pathways. Such a scheme bears a close resemblance to the dynamic loop concepts suggested by Eccles (1969) and Allen & Tsukahara (1974) concerning the control of limb movement and is consistent with evidence that dentatoreticular pathways mediate activity similar to preparatory postural adjustments in monkeys following microstimulation of intracerebellar nuclei (Schultz et al., 1979).

FEEDFORWARD CONTROL OF POSTURE IN CHILDREN

All of the early published work on feedforward postural control was concerned with the control capabilities of adults. It has been unclear whether young children acquire this "skill" of making preparatory adjustments or whether such adjustments are innate. Similarly, questions remain as to whether children's feedforward adjustments develop and mature in parallel or at different rates from feedback postural control. To answer these and other questions, we undertook an investigation of the feedforward control capabilities and postural sway characteristic of thirty-three children aged 4 to 14 years and compared their results to data obtained from adults (Riach, 1985).

The children stood on a force platform and rapidly raised their right arms in response to a choice reaction-time stimulus: green light signaled an arm raise forward, red light an arm raise backward. A warning tone indicated the beginning of a random-length foreperiod (1–3 sec) prior to the visual stimulus. An accelerometer signaled the onset of arm movement, and the preparatory postural adjustments were recorded as excursions of the center of pressure (CP) of ground reaction forces that occurred prior to, or concurrent with, the onset of arm acceleration. Figure 5–2 illustrates the arm acceleration and preparatory excursions of the CP in an adult and in a 13-year-old child. Both sets of records illustrate the consistent appearance of patterns of preparatory postural adjustments made in advance of arm acceleration.[1] In these examples CP excursions in the posterior direction preceded arm acceleration in all trials. Adults typically revealed two patterns of preparatory adjustments in the lateral direction: (1) an early excursion of CP to the left, immediately followed by displacement to the right (L-R), or (2) direct excursion

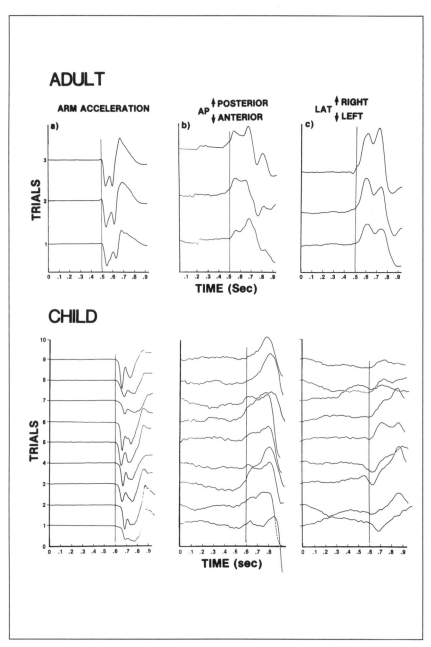

Fig. 5–2. Preparatory postural adjustments of the center of pressure (CP) of ground reaction forces in an adult (*top*) and teenage child. The vertical lines indicate onset of arm acceleration. Note the consistent posterior motion of the CP just prior to arm acceleration.

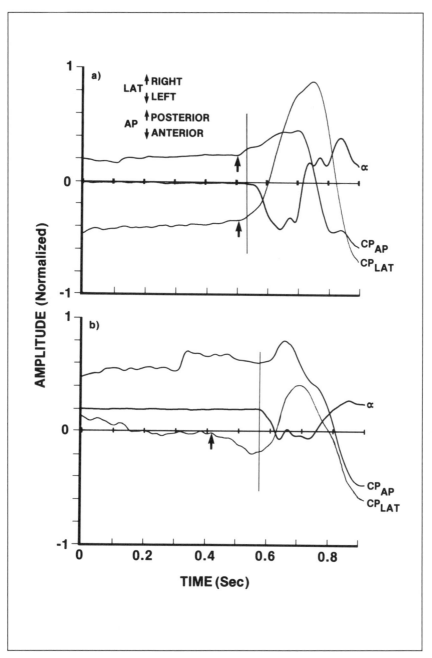

Fig. 5–3. Preparatory postural adjustments in very young children. Onset of clear, preparatory center-pressure excursions is identified by arrows.

to the right (Riach et al., 1987). Both patterns are illustrated in the records of the adult shown in Figure 5–2. These occurred early (>150 msec) or late (<150 msec) relative to arm movement (Riach & Hayes, 1987). The records of the teenage girl showed these same patterns for both the antero-posterior and lateral directions. Figure 5–3 shows the records of two 4-year-old children, both showing preparatory CP excursions in the lateral and antero-posterior directions. The lateral excursion of the CP in child A was immediately to the right, whereas child B showed the L-R pattern. The interpretation of these patterns relative to movement of the CG has been discussed elsewhere (Riach & Hayes, 1984).

TABLE 5–1

Anticipatory postural adjustments in the lateral
direction in children and adults

| | Age (years) | | | |
Timing	4–6	7–10	11–14	Adults
Early ($\geq$300 msec)[a]	8 (30%)	5 (11%)	2 (8%)	24 (27%)
Late ($\leq$150 msec)	11 (41%)	24 (53%)	10 (38%)	39 (43%)
Two	0 (0%)	2 (4%)	1 (4%)	13 (9%)
Intermediate (150–300 msec)	4 (15%)	6 (13%)	6 (23%)	8 (9%)
None	4 (15%)	8 (18%)	7 (27%)	6 (7%)
Total trials	27	45	26	90
Subjects tested	9	15	9	31
Pattern[b]				
L–R	18 (67%)	22 (40%)	10 (38%)	64 (71%)
R	5 (19%)	15 (33%)	9 (35%)	20 (22%)
None	4 (15%)	8 (18%)	7 (27%)	6 (7%)

Note: The adult values were obtained using a self-initiated arm-raise
         task instead of the two-choice reaction task.
[a] Time before arm acceleration
[b] L–R = left-right lateral pattern; R = directly right lateral pattern

TABLE 5–2

Anticipatory postural adjustments in the antero-posterior
direction in children and adults

Timing	Age (years)			
	4–7	7–11	11–14	Adults
Early	6 (22%)	13 (29%)	2 (8%)	21 (23%)
($\geq$300 msec)[a]				
Late	4 (15%)	16 (36%)	14 (54%)	29 (32%)
($\leq$150 msec)				
Intermediate	6 (22%)	8 (18%)	4 (15%)	5 (6%)
(150–300 msec)				
None	10 (37%)	6 (13%)	6 (23%)	20 (22%)
Total trials	27	45	26	90
Subjects tested	9	15	9	31

Note: The adult values were obtained using a self-initiated arm-raise
    task instead of the two-choice reaction task.
[a] Time before arm acceleration

Tables 5–1 and 5–2 show the grouped data for the children's
patterns and timing of antero-posterior and lateral excursions of CP.
These data show the number and percentage of trials in which the
various patterns were observed. In the antero-posterior direction,
preparatory adjustments were seen more frequently in the 7–14-year-
old children than in very young children. The timing of postural adjustments appeared to be more consistent in older children, with responses
in the 7–14-year-olds occurring more frequently in the late stages, that
is, in the 150 milliseconds immediately prior to arm movement.

In the lateral direction the children's preparatory adjustments of
the CP were seen regularly (81% of all trials). In all three age categories
late responses were more evident than early responses and the number
of L-R patterns exceeded the directly right patterns, as in adults. The
pattern of CP excursions appeared to differ according to age, as very
young children showed the most frequent appearance of the L-R pattern. This is curious because it is similar to the adult pattern and yet was
not so evident in older children.[2]

The reaction time of each arm raise was determined by measuring the time between the onset of the visual stimulus and the beginning of arm acceleration. There was a marked and predictable reduction in mean reaction time with increasing age, as shown in Figure 5–4 and Table 5–3.

The overall intent of this study was to determine if feedforward control was present in young children and to investigate the emergence of developing anticipatory patterns. Results suggested that the beginnings of adult feedforward control patterns were indeed present in even the youngest of children (4 years, 2 months) in both planes. However, only 56% of the young children (4–6 years) showed anticipatory CP changes in the antero-posterior plane. In addition, these younger children were less consistent than their older counterparts in the timing of the feedforward adjustments. The older children generally showed more consistency in the presence and timing of their preparatory postural adjustments. These results are in contrast to those observed by Woollacott & Shumway-Cook (1986), who studied the feedforward postural adjustments of 4–6-year-olds in a push-or-pull

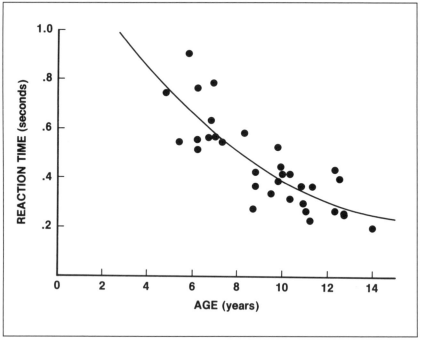

Fig. 5-4. Age-related differences in a reaction-time task involving an arm raise in response to a two-choice, visual stimulus.

arm-movement task (in the A-P plane). They found that four of the five children studied showed anticipatory postural electromyographic (EMG) activity before the prime mover muscle was activated in 100% of the trials. The fifth child showed similar activation in 80% of the trials. Thus they concluded that feedforward control is present by 4 to 6 years of age.

TABLE 5-3

Reaction times for the arm raise in
three age groups of children

Age group (years)	Reaction time mean (msec)	Standard deviation (msec)	n (trials)
4–6	673[a]	±168[a]	27
7–10	421	±115	45
11–14	296	±83	26

Regression analysis of reaction time

		Coefficients				
Model[b]	A	B	C	r	r^2
Y = A + BX	.998	−.059	—	−.82	.68
Y = A + BX + CX^2	1.328	−.136	.004	−.84	.70

[a] The reaction time of some trials (n = 3) was greater than the period of time recorded for data analysis. Both mean and standard deviation would therefore be larger than the values given.
[b] X = age (years); Y = reaction time

The differences in the characteristics of preparatory CP changes in the antero-posterior direction over the three age groups we studied may be attributed either to a differential ability among the children to anticipate and initiate postural adjustments or to varying degrees of maturation of the ability to coordinate postural control with movement under the choice reaction-time conditions.

In the lateral plane the results were quite different. Of the three age groups tested, the youngest children (4–6 years) showed the greatest number of feedforward adjustments (100% of the children showed the preparatory adjustments in more than one of the three trials). The incidence of feedforward adjustments in the lateral plane appeared to decrease with increasing age. In addition, there seemed to be a strong preference for the L-R pattern in the youngest children but not in the older children.

The left-right pattern of preparatory postural adjustment appears to be similar to the pattern of CP changes associated with gait initiation, as one arm and the contralateral leg move forward (Mann et al., 1979). Stepping movements, hypothesized to be generated by spinal pattern generators, can be seen in infants soon after birth (Forssberg & Wallberg, 1980; Zelazo, Zelazo & Kolb, 1972). It is possible that the left-to-right pattern of postural adjustments is part of an innate muscle synergy that is built into the spinal neuronal circuitry. This may explain the high incidence of anticipatory postural adjustments in the lateral direction in the youngest age group. It has been hypothesized elsewhere that the movement repertoire of the young child is governed by spinal pattern generators (Bressan & Woollacott, 1982). Further results from experiments examining preparatory postural activity showed that, despite the equal probability of a signal for forward or backward arm movements, many of the younger subjects appeared to simply prepare for a forward movement. When a signal for backward movement arrived, they responded in the wrong direction or started forward and then corrected the movement. Similar findings have been recorded for adults (El'ner, 1973). This suggests that the young children may have attempted to reduce the complexity of the task by treating the test situation as a simple reaction-time test with variable foreperiod. The backward movement trials were not recorded, but the children were unaware of this. This simple reaction-time strategy could explain the higher percentage of early responses in the lateral direction in the youngest age group compared to the 11–14-year age group. The younger children may have prepared early for an anticipated forward response, whereas the older children, more able to handle the choice reaction-time task, remained uncertain of the direction of their arm movement until the visual stimulus appeared.

The age-dependent decrease in choice reaction time found in the present study is consistent with the results of previous research (Stallings, 1982) and has been attributed to an age-related ability to attend to the stimuli (Elliot, 1964) and/or the neurological maturation of information processing (Surwillo, 1971). Several factors are likely to have influenced the reaction times of children in the present study. For example, Cordo & Nashner (1982) reported that when a background sway is induced by support-surface rotation there is an increase in time to postural adjustments and to movement initiation. Younger children have a higher level of background sway (Odenrick & Sandstedt, 1984; Riach & Hayes, 1985, 1987; see also the section that follows), and this may have been a contributing factor in the long reaction times in the youngest age group.

It has also been suggested that "the usual precession of associated postural adjustment . . . is produced by an active delay of the focal components" (Cordo & Nashner, 1982: 292). Thus, the time required for assessing and initiating postural adjustments appears to delay initiation of arm movement. The pattern of preparatory postural adjustments in the antero-posterior direction is not strongly linked in time with arm-movement initiation in the children. The reaction time may, therefore, be thought of as having two elements: (1) time required for determining and initiating postural adjustments, and (2) time required for choosing and initiating the arm-movement response. These may involve parallel processing. Both may be seen as determinants of the total choice reaction time and as dependent on age-related changes in attention and/or information processing. Both would also be influenced by the state of background stability.[3]

In summary, the longer reaction times and less consistent appearance of feedforward patterns in the antero-posterior direction suggest that young children are less proficient at correcting for anticipated postural disturbances caused by self-initiated movements and/or are less able to coordinate postural adjustments with movement execution. One factor that appears likely to influence their coordination is their high degree of background postural sway. Unlike the results in the antero-posterior plane, there was a high incidence of preparatory postural adjustments in the lateral direction in the youngest children. These adjustments decreased with increased age. There was also an age-related shift from the L-R pattern to a directly right CP pattern. The L-R pattern is similar to the CP changes seen during gait initiation. The postural adjustments may, therefore, reflect the fact that in young children CP adjustments are more closely linked to an innate, stereotyped, step-generator pattern, but as children become older, the postural adjustments become more refined and more task-specific. In any case, the mechanisms influencing anticipatory postural adjustments appear to be different for the two planes and may have different rates of maturation.

POSTURAL SWAY IN CHILDREN

The same children who were investigated in the arm-raising study also participated in a study of age-related differences in postural sway during quiet stance.[4] Of particular interest were two questions: How does the frequency composition of postural sway differ among children of different ages? Do the characteristics of postural sway follow the same time course as developmental changes involved in the feedforward regulation of posture? In view of the earlier discussion regarding possible involvement of feedforward adjustments modifying the extent of rhythmic perturbations from respiration, and so on, we must immediately acknowledge the caveat that postural sway measurements may not constitute a pure assessment of feedback control. Neither does analysis of postural sway during quiet stance elucidate the differential contribution of various physiological subsystems (e.g., visual, vestibular, proprioceptive) with the same degree of rigor that is provided by experiments involving perturbations to balance (cf. Nashner, 1981). Nevertheless, postural sway measurements in the form of Romberg's test do constitute an important part of most neurological examinations of children (and adults) (Njiokiktjien et al., 1976, 1978); and with recent advances in understanding the frequency composition of sway (Mauritz et al., 1979; Njiokiktjien et al., 1978; Kapteyn & deWit, 1972), the potential exists for characterizing age-related differences in utilization of vestibular or proprioceptive feedback.

Postural sway was measured as the time-varying excursions of CP recorded from a strain-gauged force platform. For each test the subjects stood quietly for a period of 20 seconds with their feet positioned 6 cm apart and parallel. A familiarization test was followed by two tests in which the children stood with their eyes open or closed. The order of these two tests was randomized across subjects. In order to determine the frequency composition of postural sway, the raw CP excursions were subjected to Fourier analyses and subsequent processing that yielded the power spectral density function. Additional details have been provided elsewhere (Riach & Hayes, 1987).

As was expected, there were age-related differences in postural stability (Shambes, 1984; Odenrick & Sandstedt, 1984; Williams et al., 1983). This was evident in both the lateral and antero-posterior planes and is illustrated in Figure 5–5. Considerable variability in the root-mean-square measures of the extent of postural sway was seen in the young children. This variance systematically reduced with age and with the subjects' improved stability. Regression analyses revealed that young males swayed more than young females and that males have a greater rate of improvement in lateral stability, as a function of age, than females (Fig. 5–5). Similar results have been reported elsewhere (Hirasawa, 1973; Odenrick & Sandstedt, 1984).

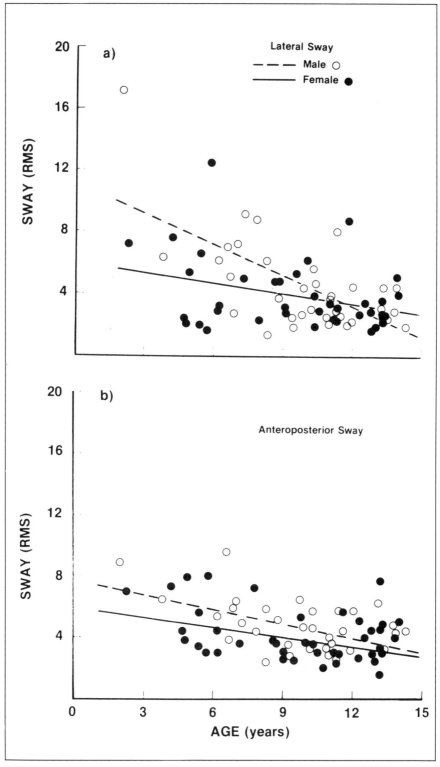

Fig. 5–5. Age-related differences in postural sway. Lines of best fit for linear regression are shown.

Also noted in this and other studies was the fact that although age was a significant predictor of sway amplitude it explained only a small proportion of the sway variance. Addition of the subjects' physical characteristics of height and weight to the regression analysis only slightly improved the total explained variance to $r^2 = .40$ for the antero-posterior direction and $r^2 = .50$ for the lateral direction. There remained much variability in the postural sway measures that cannot be attributed to age or the subjects' physical characteristics.

Differences in maturation of the underlying physiological processes, as distinct from differences in chronological age, appear to contribute to the variability in postural sway. The maturation of individual elements of the postural control process has been well documented for short- and long-loop proprioceptive reflexes (Bawa, 1981), kinaesthetic sense (Laszlo & Bairstow, 1980), postural synergy organization (Forssberg & Nashner, 1982), and vestibular (Ornitz, 1983), cortical (Rabinowicz, 1979), and visual processing (Butterworth & Hicks, 1977; Lee & Aronson, 1974). Evident from many of these studies is the large between-subject variability in maturation rate. Within subjects there may also be differences in the maturation rate of the individual physiological and psychological processes.

The effects of eye closure on the stability of stance are conventionally represented in the form of a Romberg quotient, expressing the eyes-closed sway as a percentage of eyes-open values (van Parys & Njiokiktjien, 1976). The quotient provides some indication of the contribution of vision to the maintenance of balance. Children below age 4 were unable or generally unwilling to complete the eyes-closed condition. The mean Romberg quotients for the children are presented in Figure 5–6 as a function of age. This figure illustrates remarkably low Romberg quotients recorded from three 4-year-old children (<100%) and the fact that the quotients generally increased toward adult values in the older children.

The Romberg quotients for children were lower than was expected. In the lateral plane 44% of the children exhibited values lower than 100%. Quotients lower than 100% indicate that the subject actually swayed more with eyes open than with eyes closed. When compared with adult data obtained by Lucy & Hayes (1985) and Hayes et al. (1985), 64% (lateral) and 63% (antero-posterior) of the children demonstrated Romberg values below the adult means. Unexpectedly low sway values for children with eyes closed were also reported by Odenrick & Sandstedt (1984).

A number of factors could account for the surprisingly low Romberg values. First, the magnitude of sway in the eyes-open condition was often quite large, especially for young children. As a consequence,

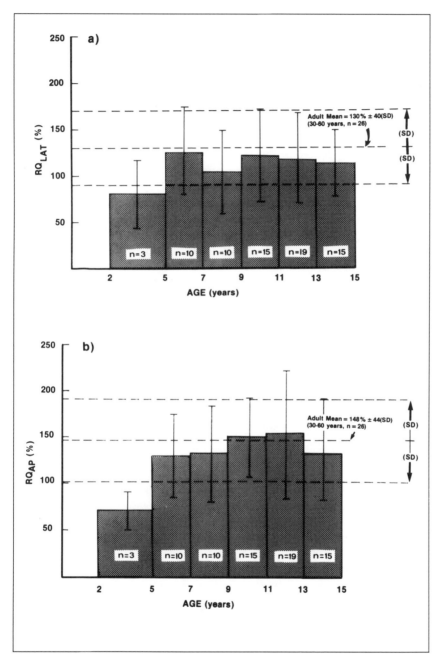

Fig. 5–6. Romberg quotients for children in different age groups showing the effects of eye closure on the stability of stance.

the change in sway amplitude with eye closure would have to be substantially greater than in adults for Romberg values to be of a comparable percentage. An alternative possibility is that processing of visual information in children may be different from that in adults. It is known that infants and young children are susceptible to destabilization by visual stimulation that conflicts with cutaneous, proprioceptive, and vestibular input. The moving-room illusion studies of Lee & Aronson (1974) and Butterworth & Hicks (1977) have suggested that "visual proprioception" (Gibson, 1966) is a more potent source of information than "mechanical-vestibular" proprioception in the control of balance. Adults are destabilized less by this visual illusion, and it has been suggested that it is the incongruence of conflicting inputs that children are unable to resolve (Forssberg & Nashner, 1982; Shumway-Cook & Woollacott, 1985).

Woollacott, Debu & Mowatt (1987) provided further insight into the role of vision in the maintenance of balance in young children. They showed that vision is not required for the activation of postural responses to platform movement in young children. However, they also observed a reduction in response latencies and an increase in monosynaptic reflexes in 2–3-year-old children when vision was removed. They suggested that vision may normally be dominant in young children and that a shift occurs from the use of longer latency visual inputs when the child stands with eyes open, to shorter latency proprioceptive/vestibular inputs when standing with eyes closed. This supports the conclusion of Lee & Aronson (1974) and Brandt et al. (1976) that vision is the dominant sensory input in young children during quiet stance and may explain our findings of reduced Romberg quotients in the very young children.

Another recent study (Riach & Starkes, 1987) has demonstrated that young children have more spontaneous visual saccades than older children or adults, even when instructed to fixate on a visual target during postural stabilization tasks. Whether increased eye movements improve or hinder postural stability is still undertermined. In any case, children are less able to visually fixate, perhaps through distractability or limited attention span. If increased visual movements are disturbing to postural control, it might explain why eye closure results in little or no reduction in stability.[5] Such an interpretation reconciles the apparently conflicting situation that in young children vision is undoubtedly a potent source of information for the control of balance but its deprivation induces less instability (i.e., lower Romberg quotients) than in adults. Zernicke et al. (1982) have also suggested that young children cannot use a fixed retinal image to reduce sway as well as adults can (Lee & Lishman, 1975).

The spectral composition of children's sway is shown as a function of age in Figure 5–7. As with adult spectra the principal power (extent of sway) for both lateral and antero-posterior sway was contained within the 0.05–0.07 Hz bandwidth. The increased sway of the very young children was reflected in the higher power contained throughout the spectrum. Increased power at the lower frequencies (0.05–0.07 Hz) may reflect qualitative differences in vestibular function (Kapteyn & deWit, 1972). Also evident in young children was a relatively greater amount of sway at high frequencies that is, in the 0.8–2 Hz bandwidth. The extent of sway at these frequencies appears to diminish as a function of age and is rarely seen in healthy young adults (Hayes et al., 1985). The high-frequency sway of very young children at these frequencies was apparent in both the lateral and antero-posterior planes.

Increased sway in the 0.8–2 Hz bandwidth may indicate impoverished proprioceptive input or processing capabilities, as it has been reported that experimental deafferentation of peripheral nerves through ischemic nerve block, peripheral neuropathy, or dorsal column pathologies leads to increased instability at 1 Hz (Lucy & Hayes, 1985;

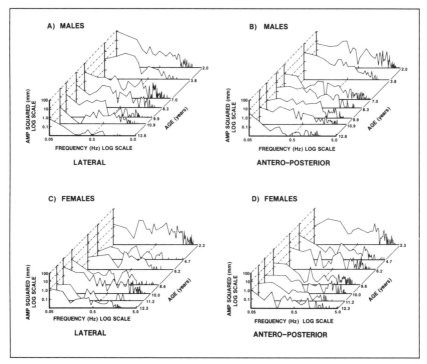

Fig. 5–7. Power spectral density functions for postural sway of children at different ages.

Mauritz & Dietz, 1980; Njiokiktjien et al., 1978). In addition, the mature functioning of long-loop proprioceptive reflexes of the type involved in postural control does not emerge until children attain about 7 years of age (Bawa, 1981).

AGE-RELATED DIFFERENCES IN POSTURAL CONTROL

At the outset of these studies it was unclear whether very young children had the capability to generate preparatory adjustments in order to minimize disequilibrium associated with predictable perturbations. It was also unclear if there existed a parallel maturation of feedforward and feedback control. Both questions were of interest from a clinical perspective; the one distinguishing the nature of balance dysfunction in young children with balance disorders may provide direction for more specific therapeutic intervention (Hayes & McKeeman, 1987). These questions also bear on theoretical and educational issues pertaining to the development of balance in healthy young children.

The first question was relatively simple to answer. Children as young as 4 years old did indeed exhibit postural adjustments in advance of arm movements. As we were unable to convince the 2-year-old children of the scientific merits of performing the test, it was not possible to determine if newly ambulatory children exhibit preparatory adjustments. It does appear, however, that, as early in life as feedforward adjustments are required, they are generated. As a child matures and learns from previous experience, the specific patterning of the adjustments becomes more refined and effective in minimizing the loss of stability.[6]

The appearance of locomotorlike postural adjustments in the lateral direction in very young children who raised their arms prompted our suggestion that the underlying motor coordination may subserve both gait and balance. This notion is consistent with the observation of innate motor organization of reciprocal stepping behavior in newborns and with more fully developed arguments concerning the ontogeny of postural control and locomotion in children (Forssberg & Wallberg, 1980).

The question of whether feedforward adjustments develop in parallel with the maturation of feedback control processes is less easy to answer. Certainly it would appear, given the asumptions of our model, that feedback processes represent an integral part of the overall organization of the preparatory adjustments. Indeed, without appropriate sensory input it seems unlikely that useful feedforward adjustments would be generated. Thus development of the feedforward system appears to be contingent upon the effectiveness of the senses in identifying the state parameters of the system (initial position, torques, etc.), in fine tuning the feedforward command, and in modifying subsequent feedforward postural program selection. It is in the last task, that of modifying subsequent feedforward adjustments, that the opportunity exists for a dissociation of the maturation of sensory feedback per se from preparatory response organization. The latter surely involves more central information processing, a form of motor learning of involuntary responses. Dissociation of the integrity of peripheral sensory processes from central processing represents a strategy for identifying the locus of impairment in balance disorders, for example, vestibular dysfunction. At best, we are able to conclude from our data that the development of feedforward and feedback control does generally appear to progress in parallel in healthy young children. The possibility exists, however, that differential maturation rates could occur in learning-disordered children.

Insights concerning the maturation of individual physiological subsystems underlying balance control (proprioception, vestibular function, and vision) have been elaborated elsewhere (e.g., Shumway-Cook & Woollacott, 1985). Our observations concerning the spectral composition of sway provide support, from a slightly different perspective, on some of these issues. In particular, demonstration that the increased sway of young children is brought about by increased energy in the power spectrum at low frequencies (0.05–0.7 Hz) as well as at higher frequencies (0.8–2.0 Hz) may be an indication that both vestibular and proprioceptive systems are functioning in an immature manner with respect to the integrative functions required to maintain balance.

As the spectrum more closely resembles the adult form by the time children attain the age of 9 years old, it would seem that by this age their sensory feedback processes have become relatively mature. We must acknowledge the possibility, however, that the altered spectral characteristics are merely a consequence of altered physical dimensions and inertial properties of the limbs and trunk or reflect the altered nerve conduction (Miller & Kuntz, 1986) and proprioceptive reflex function (Vecchierini-Blineau & Guiheneuc, 1979; Myklebust et al., 1986) that are associated with development, as distinct from maturation of balance processes per se.

Finally, the failure of eye closure to substantially increase the sway amplitude of young children in the same way that it does to adults (see also the work of Odenrick & Sandstedt, 1984) raises interesting questions about how vision is normally used by children. From the visual-mechanical illusion experiments of Lee & Lishman (1975) and Butterworth & Hicks (1977), there can be little doubt that vision is a potent source of information for maintaining stability in preambulatory and ambulatory infants. Yet these two sets of observations appear to be contradictory. Temporarily depriving a child of vision does not necessarily provide information pertinent to how that child would normally use vision. The child may simply assign greater "weighting" to input from other sensory modalities. Similarly, presenting conflicting visual and vestibular-mechanical stimulation may reflect more the child's ability to resolve the conflict (or deal with the unexpectedness of the conflict) than reveal how the underlying systems are normally used.

We have attempted to reconcile the paradox by suggesting that children may be less able than adults to use a fixed retinal image to stabilize their posture. Preliminary results (Riach & Starkes, 1987) indicate that this in turn may be related to the greater number of visual saccades generated by very young children while fixating on a stationary object. The observations of Woollacott, Debu & Mowatt (1987) that vision is not required for activation of postural responses in young children, and in children as young as 5 months may elicit less reliable muscle-response organization than proprioception alone, also pertain to this paradox. In addition, their reports of shortened response latencies and increased occurrence of monosynaptic reflexes in 2–3-year-old children when vision was removed appear to indicate a shift in weighting of the control exerted by the various sensory inputs. Proprioception/vestibular inputs may therefore be quite sufficient to maintain balance in very young children when vision is not available. It is clear that there is "more than meets the eye" when it comes to maintenance of balance in children.

NOTES

1. A sign test (Anderson & Sclove, 1978) was used to verify that the preparatory CP excursions were in a consistent direction at the onset of arm acceleration and not simply random fluctuations.

2. Studies of children's postural responses to platform disturbances have revealed a somewhat similar phenomenon. Shumway-Cook & Woollacott (1985) reported that 4-to-6-year-old children showed an apparent regression in postural response organization (compared with 15-to-31-month-old children). It was hypothesized that this age represented a transition in postural development, when children learned to integrate and alternate among visual, proprioceptive, and vestibular inputs in controlling posture. This learning would be necessary in order to enable adaptation of responses to changing sensory conditions, a process that also begins to emerge at this time (Woollacott, Debu & Mowatt, 1987).

3. It should be acknowledged that this speculation of two processes appears to be consistent with observations pertaining to the influence of cognitive "set" (Brown & Frank, 1987) but at variance with observations that stimulation of the motor cortex activates feedforward postural adjustments appropriate to the movement (Regis, Trouche & Massion, 1976).

4. The results of the postural sway characteristics from this group of children have been reported previously (Riach & Hayes, 1985, 1987). Herein we describe results obtained by pooling the data from the original group ($n = 33$) plus an additional group ($n = 43$) with similar ages (2.4–14 years) and physical characteristics. The combined results are very similar to those from the smaller sample and provide more robust information pertaining to age-related differences in postural sway.

5. An alternative interpretation might be that visual saccades and postural sway are both indicators of an underlying immaturity in the postural regulatory system.

6. Von Hofsten and Woollacott have recently documented feedforward postural adjustments associated with reaching in infants as young as 9 months of age (see Woollacott et al., this volume, Chap. 4).

REFERENCES

Alexeev, M. A., & Naidel, A. V. (1973). Rapports entre les éléments voluntaires et posturaux d'un acte moteur chez l'homme. *Agressologie, 14B,* 9–16.

Allen, G. I., & Tsukahara, N. (1974). Cerebrocerebellar communication systems. *Physiological Reviews, 54,* 957–1006.

Anderson, T. W., & Sclove, S. L. (1978). *An introduction to the statistical analysis of data.* Boston: Houghton Mifflin.

Arutyunyan, G. A.; Gurfinkel, V. S.; & Mirskii, M. L. (1969). Organization of movements on execution by man of an exact postural task. *Biophysics, 14,* 1103–07.

Bawa, P. (1981). Neural development in children—a neurophysiological study. *Electroencephalography and Clinical Neurophysiology, 52,* 249–56.

Belenkii, V. Ye.; Gurfinkel, V. S.; & Pal'tsev, Ye. I. (1967). Elements of control of voluntary movement. *Biophysics, 12,* 154–60.

Black, F. O.; O'Leary, D. P.; Wall, C.; & Furman, J. (1977). The vestibulospinal stability test: Normal limits. *Transactions of the American Academy of Ophthalmology and Otolaryngology, 84,* 549–60.

Bouisset, S., & Zattara, M. (1981). A sequence of postural movements precedes voluntary movement. *Neuroscience Letters, 22,* 263–70.

Bouisset, S., & Zattara, M. (1987). Biomechanical study of the programming of anticipatory postural adjustments associated with voluntary movement. Journal of Biomechanics, 20, 735–42.

Brandt, T.; Wenzel, D.; & Dichgans, J. (1976). Die Entwicklung der visuellen stabilisation des aufrechten standes beim kind: Ein reifezeichen in der kinderneurologie. *Archiv für Psychiatrie und Nervenkrankheiten, 223,* 1–13.

Bressan, E. S., & Woollacott, M. H. (1982). A prescriptive paradigm for sequencing instruction in physical education. Human Movement Science, 1, 115–75.

Brown, J. E., & Frank, J. S. (1987). Influence of event anticipation on postural actions accompanying voluntary movement. *Experimental Brain Research, 67,* 645–50.

Butterworth, G., & Hicks, L. (1977). Visual proprioception and postural stability in infancy. A developmental study. *Perception, 6*, 255–62.

Clement, G.; Gurfinkel, V.; Lestienne, F.; Lipshits, M.; & Popov, K. (1983). A study of mechanisms of posture maintenance in the weightless state. *Physiologist, 26*, 585–89.

Cordo, P. J., & Nashner, L. M. (1982). Properties of postural adjustments associated with rapid arm movements. *Journal of Neurophysiology, 47*, 287–302.

Easton, T. A. (1972). On the normal use of reflexes. *American Scientist, 60:* 5, 591–99.

Eccles, J. C. (1969). The dynamic loop hypothesis of movement control. In K. N. Leibovic (Ed.), *Information processing in the nervous system*. New York: Springer.

Edwards, A. S. (1943). Factors tending to decrease the steadiness of the body at rest. *American Journal of Psychology, 63*, 385–408.

Elliott, R. (1964). Physiological activity and performance: A comparison of kindergarten children with young adults. *Psychological Monographs, 78*, 1–33.

El'ner, A. N. (1973). Possibilities of correcting the urgent voluntary movements and the associated postural activity of human muscles. *Biophysics, 18*, 966–71.

Forssberg, H., & Nashner, L. (1982). Ontogenetic development of postural control in man: Adaptation to altered support and visual conditions during stance. *Journal of Neuroscience, 2*, 545–52.

Forssberg, H., & Wallberg, H. (1980). Infant locomotion: A preliminary movement and electromyographic study. In K. Berg & B. Eriksson (Eds.), *Children and exercise IX*. Baltimore: University Park Press.

Gahery, Y., & Massion, J. (1981). Co-ordination between posture and movement. *Trends in Neuroscience, 4*, 199–202.

Gibson, J. J. (1966). *The senses considered as perceptual systems*. Boston: Houghton Mifflin.

Grillner, S. (1975). Locomotion in vertebrates: Central mechanisms and reflex interaction. *Physiological Reviews, 55*, 247–304.

Gurfinkel, V. S.; Kots, Y. M.; Pal'tsev, Y. I.; & Feldman, A. G. (1971). The compensation of respiratory disturbances of the erect posture of man as an example of organization of interarticular interaction. In I. M. Gelfand, V. S. Gurfinkel, S. V. Fomin & M. L. Tsetlin (Eds.), *Models of the structural functional organization of certain biological systems*. Cambridge, MA: MIT Press.

Hayes, K. C. (1982). Biomechanics of postural control. In R. L. Terjung (Ed.), *Exercise and sport sciences reviews*. Philadelphia: Franklin Institute Press.

Hayes, K. C. (1986). Postural instability in cerebellar ataxia. *Proceedings of the Eighth Annual Conference IEEE/Engineering in Medicine and Biology Society* (pp. 1575–78), Fort Worth, Texas.

Hayes, K. C., & McKeeman, A. L. (1987). Postural control and instability. In M. Peat (Ed.), *Current physical therapy*. Burlington, Ont.: B. C. Decker.

Hayes, K. C.; Spencer, J. D.; Riach, C. L.; Lucy, S. D.; & Kirshen, A. J. (1985). Age-related changes in postural sway. In D. A. Winter et al. (Eds.), *Biomechanics IX* (pp. 383–87). IL: Champaign-Urbana, Human Kinetics Press.

Hirasawa, Y. (1973). Study of human standing ability. *Agressologie, 14C*, 37–44.

Hunter, I. W., & Kearney, R. E. (1981). Respiratory components of human postural sway. *Neuroscience Letters, 25,* 155–59.

Kapteyn, T. S., & deWit, G. (1972). Posturography as an auxiliary in vestibular investigation. *Acta Oto-laryngologica, 73,* 107–11.

Koozekanani, S. H.; Stockwell, C. W.; McGhee, R. B.; & Firoozmand, F. (1980). On the role of dynamic models in quantitative posturography. *IEEE Transaction on Biomedical Engineering. BME27,* 605–9.

Laszlo, J., & Bairstow, P. (1980). The measurement of kinaesthetic sensitivity of children and adults. *Developmental Medicine and Child Neurology, 22,* 454–64.

Lee, D. N., & Aronson, E. (1974). Visual proprioceptive control of standing in human infants. *Perception and Psychophysics, 15,* 529–32.

Lee, D. N., & Lishman, J. R. (1975). Visual proprioceptive control of stance. *Journal of Human Movement Studies, 1,* 87–95.

Lee, W. A. (1980). Anticipatory control of postural and task muscles during rapid arm flexion. *Journal of Motor Behavior, 12,* 185–96.

Legallet, E., & Gahery, Y. (1980). Influence of a diagonal postural pattern on parameters of movement and associated postural adjustments in the cat. *Experimental Brain Research, 40,* 35–44.

Lipshits, M. I.; Mauritz, K.; & Popov, K. E. (1981). Quantitative analysis of anticipatory postural components of a complex voluntary movement. *Human Physiology, 7,* 165–72.

Lucy, S. D., & Hayes, K. C. (1985). Postural sway profiles: Normal subjects and subjects with cerebellar ataxia. *Physiotherapy Canada, 37,* 140–48.

MacKay, W. A., & Murphy, J. T. (1979). Cerebellar modulation of reflex gain. *Progress in Neurobiology, 13,* 361–417.

Mann, R. A.; Hagy, J. L.; White, V.; & Liddell, D. (1979). The initiation of gait. *Journal of Bone and Joint Surgery, 61A,* 232–39.

Marsden, C. D.; Merton, P. A.; & Morton, H. B. (1981). Human postural responses. *Brain, 104,* 513–34.

Mauritz, K. H.; Dichgans, J.; & Hufschmidt, A. (1979). Quantitative analysis of stance in late cortical cerebellar atrophy of the anterior lobe and other forms of cerebellar ataxia. *Brain, 102,* 461–82.

Mauritz, K. H., & Kietz, V. (1980). Characteristics of postural instability induced by ischemic blocking of leg afferents. *Exp. Brain Res., 38,* 117–19.

Miller, R. G., & Kuntz, N. L. (1986). Nerve conduction studies in infants and children. *Journal of Child Neurology, 1,* 19–26.

Myklebust, B. M.; Gottlieb, G. L.; & Agarawal, G. C. (1986). Stretch reflexes of the normal infant. *Developmental Medicine and Child Neurology, 28,* 440–49.

Nashner, L. M. (1981). Analysis of stance posture in humans. In E. Luschei & A. Towe (Eds.), *Handbook of behavioral neurobiology,* New York: Plenum Press.

Nashner, L. M., & Cordo, P. J. (1981). Relation of automatic postural responses and reaction time in voluntary movement of leg muscles. *Experimental Brain Research, 43,* 395–405.

Nashner, L. M., & Woollacott, M. (1979). The organization of rapid postural adjustments of standing humans: An experimental-conceptual model. In R. E. Talbott & D. R. Humphrey (Eds.), *Posture and movement,* New York: Raven Press.

Nieoullon, A., & Gahery, Y. (1978). Influence of pyramidotomy on limb flexion movements induced by cortical stimulation and on associated postural adjustments in the cat. *Brain Research, 149,* 39–52.

Njiokiktjien, C.; deRijke, W.; Dieker-van Ophem, A.; & Voorhoeven-Coebergh, O. (1976). Stabilography as a diagnostic tool in child neurology. *Agressologie, 17,* 41–48.

Njiokiktjien, C.; deRijke, W.; Dieker-van Ophem, A.; & Voorhoeven-Coebergh, O. (1978). A possible contribution of stabilography to the differential diagnosis of cerebellar processes. *Agressologie, 19,* 87–88.

Odenrick, P., & Sandstedt, P. (1984). Development of postural sway in the normal child. *Human Neurobiology, 3,* 241–44.

Ornitz, E. M. (1983). Normal and pathological maturation of vestibular function in the human child. In R. Romand (Ed.), *Development of auditory and vestibular systems.* Santa Clara, CA: Academic Press.

Pal'tsev, Y. I., & El'ner, A. N. (1967). Preparatory and compensatory period during voluntary movement in patients with involvement of the brain of different locations. *Biofizika, 12,* 161–68.

Rabinowicz, T. (1979). The differential maturation of the human cerebral cortex. In F. Falkner & J. M. Tanner (Eds.), *Human growth: Neurobiology and nutrition.* New York: Plenum Press.

Regis, H., Trouche, E., & Massion, J. (1976). Movements and associated postural adjustment. In M. Shahani (Ed.), *The motor system: Neurophysiology and muscle mechanism.* Amsterdam: Elsevier.

Riach, C. L. (1985). The development of feedforward and feedback control of posture in children. Ph.D. dissertation, University of Waterloo.

Riach, C. L., & Hayes, K. C. (1984). The interaction of centre of pressure and centre of gravity in postural control. *Proceedings of the Third Bi-annual Conference of the Canadian Society for Biomechanics: Human Locomotion III* (pp. 78–80).

Riach, C. L., & Hayes, K. C. (1985). Postural sway in young children. In M. Igarashi & F. O. Black (Eds.), *Vestibular and visual control on posture and locomotor equilibrium* (pp. 232–36). Basel: Karger.

Riach, C. L., & Hayes, K. C. (1986). Feedforward postural control in children. *Proceedings of the North American Congress on Biomechanics,* Vol. 1, pp. 73–74, Montreal.

Riach, C. L., & Hayes, K. C. (1987). Maturation of postural stability in young children. *Developmental Medicine and Child Neurology, 29,* 650–58.

Riach, C. L.; Lucy, S. D.; & Hayes, K. C. (1987). Adjustments to posture prior to arm movement. In B. Jonsson (Ed.), *Biomechanics XA* (pp. 459–64. Champaign, IL: Human Kinetics.

Riach, C. L., & Starkes, J. (1987). Visual fixation and postural sway in children. *Psychology of Motor Behaviour and Sport,* Proceedings of the North American Society for the Psychology of Sport and Physical Activity, 56 (abstract).

Schultz, W.; Montgomery, E.; & Marini, R. (1979). Proximal limb movements in response to microstimulation of primate dentate and interpositus nuclei mediated by brain stem structures. *Brain, 102,* 127–46.

Shambes, G. (1984). Static postural control in children. *American Journal of Physical Medicine, 55,* 53–60.

Shumway-Cook, A., & Woollacott, M. H. (1985). The growth of stability: Postural control from a developmental perspective. *Journal of Motor Behavior, 17,* 131–47.

Stallings, L. M. (1982). *Motor learning from theory to practice*. St. Louis, MO: CV Mosby.

Surwillo, W. W. (1971). Human reaction time and period of the EEG in relation to development. *Psychophysiology, 8*, 468–82.

Traub, M. M.; Rothwell, J. C.; & Marsden, C. D. (1980). Anticipatory postural reflexes in Parkinson's disease and other akinetic-rigid syndromes and in cerebellar ataxia. *Brain, 103*, 393–412.

Van Parys, J. A. P., & Njiokiktjien, C. (1976). Romberg's sign expressed in a quotient. *Agressologie, 17B*, 95–100.

Vecchierini-Blineau, M. F., & Guiheneuc, P. (1979). Electrophysiological study of the peripheral nervous system in children. *Journal of Neurology, Neurosurgery and Psychiatry, 42*, 753–59.

Weiss, P. L., & Hayes, K. C. Postural control mechanisms. *Proc. 4th Congress of the International Society of Electrophysiological Kinesiology*, pp. 40–41, Boston, MA.

Williams, H.; Fisher, J.; & Tritschler, K. (1983). Descriptive analysis of static postural control in 4, 6, and 8 year old normal and motorically awkward children. *American Journal of Physical Medicine, 62*, 12–26.

Woollacott, M.; Debu, B.; & Mowatt, M. (1987). Neuromuscular control of vision in the infant and child: Is vision dominant? *Journal of Motor Behavior, 19*, 167–86.

Woollacott, M., & Shumway-Cook, A. (1986). The development of the postural and voluntary motor control systems in Down's Syndrome children. In M. Wade (Ed.), *Motor skill acquisition of the mentally handicapped* (pp. 45–71). Amsterdam: North-Holland.

Zelazo, P. R.; Zelazo, N. A.; & Kolb, S. (1972). Walking in the newborn. *Science, 176*, 314–15.

Zernicke, R. F.; Gregor, R. J.; & Cratty, B. J. (1982). Balance and visual proprioception in children. *Journal of Human Movement Studies, 8*, 1–13.

6

Changing Patterns of Locomotion:
From Walking to Skipping

Jane E. Clark
and Jill Whitall

Walking upright is a major achievement in the struggle for postural and movement control during the first year of life, yet it marks only the beginning of the locomotor skills that will emerge over the next 6 to 7 years. Indeed, by the time a child is 7 years old, she will have a repertoire of locomotor skills which includes running, galloping, hopping, and skipping[1] (Roberton & Halverson, 1984). Although there are developmental changes in each of these gait forms once they appear, our primary purpose here is to examine the nature of each of these later-developing locomotor skills as well as their emergence. How are the limbs organized to achieve these locomotor skills? How and why do we acquire these new gait forms which emerge after we have attained the fundamental form of upright bipedal locomotion (i.e., walking)? In the discussion that follows, we first examine the literature on the development of these gait forms in the framework within which it was originally cast, namely, the descriptive-maturational perspective. We then discuss the problems associated with this approach and argue for a change to the dynamical systems perspective. In the chapter's second section we outline the major tenets of the dynamical systems perspective as they relate to the development of the later-emerging locomotor skills. For a more detailed explanation of the dynamical systems perspective, the reader is directed to the work by Thelen and her colleagues in this volume (Chap. 2) and elsewhere (Thelen, Kelso & Fogel, 1987). In the final section we recast the story of locomotor development in early childhood within this new perspective.

THE DESCRIPTIVE-MATURATIONAL PERSPECTIVE

The earliest descriptions of locomotor development emerged from the work of developmentalists in the 1930s who sought to affirm the maturational theory of behavioral change. Because their theoretical position emphasized the unfolding of behavior, they frequently described and catalogued in great detail the appearance of behaviors in infants and young children. Not surprisingly, these behavioral catalogues were largely reports of changes in *motor* behavior, since movement is the infant's most conspicuous behavior. Though not interested in motor development per se, these early developmentalists provided the first, and in some instances the only, descriptions of early motor skill development.

The first of the upright locomotor skills to emerge is walking. Careful and thorough descriptions of the attainment of upright walking date back to the work of Burnside (1927), Shirley (1931), and McGraw (1932, 1940). These early studies and later research using more sophisticated measurement techniques provide a detailed description of the changes in the infant's walking gait from its inception to maturity. It is from this research that a vivid picture emerges of the infant's struggle to balance in the bipedal position while attempting forward locomotion. Descriptions of joint motions reveal considerable variability in joint kinematics in the first months of walking, with the knee and ankle actions showing the most noticeable differences (Burnett & Johnson, 1971; Statham & Murray, 1971; Sutherland et al., 1980) (See Fig. 6–1). In particular, the newly walking infant's knee action during stance does not show the mature double knee lock pattern in which there is knee extension-flexion-extension action during weight bearing. Ankle action is also different in the new walker, as there is a digitigrade foot action in which the toe or midsole strikes the floor before the heel (Forssberg, 1985). Plantigrade walking (heel strikes before toe) does not emerge for another 3 to 6 months.

From descriptions such as these emerges a picture of orderly and sequential change which in McGraw's words was "obviously dependent upon a degree of maturation or ripening of the nervous system"

Fig. 6–1. An infant walker

(1932: 296). For McGraw, certain behaviors appeared first as reflexes (such as the walking reflex) and then disappeared before the "controlled" behavior (i.e., the voluntary walking pattern) appeared. The inhibition of these reflexes and the emergence of voluntary movement were attributed to the neuromaturation of the cerebral cortex (McGraw, 1945/1969). Similar views on the role of neuromaturation in the development of walking persist today. For example, Forssberg (1985) argues that digitigrade walking gives way to plantigrade walking as higher centers of the nervous system mature. Similarly, Sutherland (1984) suggests that the young walker's premature muscular activity of the vastus medialis and gastrocnemius/soleus during the swing phase and the prolongation of muscular activity in a number of the muscles during the stance phase of walking are the result of neuromaturational factors such as myelinization.

Although not explicitly incorporated into such models of neural maturation or control, other forms of human locomotion which emerge after walking (e.g., running, galloping) have been described with respect to their time of emergence. Data on the time these skills emerge may not contribute directly to such models, but they would lend support to the maturational perspective if it could be found that there is an invariant order of appearance. It is therefore important to consider the evidence regarding the time of appearance of these later-developing locomotor skills.

Running is the next locomotor skill to emerge after walking and is characterized by a flight phase (see Fig. 6–2). Gesell (Gesell & Amatruda, 1947) reported that running may be present as early as 18 months of age and is well established by 2 years. Similar ages are given by Branta and her colleagues (Branta et al., 1984). Others have reported that running appears somewhere between 2.5–6 months after independent walking is achieved (Burnett & Johnson, 1971). Invariant sequences in the qualitative changes in arm and leg coordination have been hypothesized to occur after the emergence of running (Roberton, 1984; Seefeldt & Haubenstricker, 1974–1977). However, few explanations appear in the literature as to why running appears after walking or why these qualitative changes in arm and leg patterns occur.

Research on the later-emerging locomotor skills is limited. Until recently, the only evidence reporting when these skills appeared were studies by Gutteridge (1939) and McCaskill & Wellman (1938). Based on cross-sectional observations of almost two thousand children, Gutteridge concluded that by 4 years of age 33% of children could hop. A similar percentage (43%), of 4-year-olds could gallop. By 6.5 years 90% of the children were skillful at galloping and hopping. Skipping was

Fig. 6–2. The running cycle

reported to appear after galloping. However, Gutteridge found that only 14% of the 4-year-olds could skip, although by 6 years 91% had learned the basic skip pattern. More recent evidence from a longitudinal study of seven children (Roberton & Halverson, 1984) suggests that the gallop precedes the hop rather than appearing concurrently, as indicated by Gutteridge. Observations from our laboratory lend support to the order suggested by Roberton & Halverson. The conclusion that galloping and hopping emerge about the same time may have been due to Gutteridge's definition of a hop as either one-footed or two-footed. In contrast, Roberton & Halverson (1984), like us, consider a hop to be a projection of the body into the air on *one* leg and landing on the same leg, that is, a one-footed locomotion. It is quite likely the two-footed hops (or what may be called "double jumps") precede or appear at about the same time as galloping.

Examples of hopping, galloping, and skipping are displayed in Figure 6–3. As discussed above, hopping is a one-footed gait. Galloping, on the other hand, is achieved by walking with the lead limb and running with the rear limb. A skip is a combination of a step and a hop on one leg, followed by a step and a hop on the other leg.

Obvious secular differences as to the age of appearance also exist between the studies of the 1930s and more contemporary data sets. Gutteridge (1939) reported that galloping was not found until the fourth year, whereas Sinclair (1973) observed a crude pattern of galloping in 2-year-olds. Lerner (as reported by Sapp, 1980) found a high proportion of 3-year-olds (85% of boys and 99% of girls) galloping. Sapp (1980) found that 90% of the 2- and 3-year-olds she observed could be classified in one of the three developmental stages she identified for galloping, although about 60% of the children were in the most primitive stage ("a pattern resembling a rhythmic uneven run" [p. 42]).

Fig. 6–3. Hop, gallop, and skip

McCaskill & Wellman (1938) calculated the median ages for selected motor skills, including hopping and skipping. They reported the
median age for the appearance of the one-footed hop around 3½ years
and for skipping at 5 years. In a contemporary sample Halverson &
Williams (1985) found that only one 2-year-old out of a group of twenty
could perform a one-footed hop but that all 3-year-olds could hop
successfully. Contemporary data on skipping are sketchy. Branta et al.

(1984) reported that 60% of older 4-year-olds and young 5-year-olds demonstrated the first stage of skipping. Wickstrom (1987) reported anecdotal data suggesting that children as young as 3 can master a skip on one foot (a step-hop) but that it is not until 5 that the pattern can be performed on each foot alternately.

Qualitative descriptions of the development within each of these later-emerging gaits appear in the literature. For details, see Seefeldt & Haubenstricker (1974–77) and Robertson (1984) for developmental descriptions of running, Sapp (1980) for the gallop, Halverson & Williams (1985) for the hop, and Wickstrom (1987) for the skip.

In summary, the data would seem to suggest the following order for the appearance of upright locomotor gait patterns: walk, run, gallop, hop (one-footed), and skip. Previous research has contributed to our understanding of when these skills emerge and what they look like, but has fallen short in explaining how and why these developmental changes occur. The principal hypothesis as to why these skills emerge in the order they do and how they change over time has derived primarily from McGraw's (1945/1969) early speculations that the maturing central nervous system (CNS) is responsible for the behavioral change. However, there are several problems with this point of view.

First, the proof that specific human behaviors emerge or change because their CNS structure(s) matures remains indirect. Support is usually drawn from the literature on animal behavior, neurological deficit, or normative CNS development juxtaposed with normative age-of-appearance data for the selected behaviors. Direct human evidence of the link between CNS maturation and behavior is as yet unavailable and may remain so for many years. The second issue that confronts the neuromaturational perspective is one of pattern generation. If central pattern generators (CPGs) coordinate walking, are there CPGs for running, galloping, hopping, and skipping? As Kelso & Tuller (1984) point out, the notion of hard-wired CPGs for every gait is inefficient for the CNS. They cite the work of von Holst, who removed all but four or six of a centipede's legs. Faced with the loss of all but a few of its legs, the centipede was still able to locomote—albeit with a four-or 6-legged gait pattern. It is unlikely that the centipede had a four-or 6-legged CPG in its CNS as back-up circuitry in case it would have all but four to six of its legs removed! Similarly, if the later-developing locomotor skills are innate or phylogenetic skills for humans, such pattern generators would presumably be available in the CNS. Again, why do they emerge in the fixed order of appearance? Why would the walking CPG appear before any of the others?

Finally, and the most difficult issue for the neuromaturational perspective, is the problem of commanding movements. The neuromaturational perspective has relied on models of motor control in which movements are organized and regulated by complex sets of neural prescriptions. To walk or perform any of these other locomotor skills would require a set of neural commands that would continuously control the body's six hundred twenty paired muscles and two-hundred-plus bones. The problem of compiling, storing, and continuously updating these neural commands has long been recognized and referred to as the *degrees of freedom* problem (Bernstein, 1967).

The other related problem not adequately addressed by neuromaturational control models was identified by Bernstein as *context-conditioned variability*. Essentially, this means that the relationship between muscle excitation and the resulting movement is variable and that this variability is dependent upon the context within which movement occurs. In other words, a given innervational state of the muscle will result in variable movement consequences, depending on such contextual differences as angle of the muscular pull, inertia of the segment, excitability of the CNS at the time the command is issued, and so forth (Bernstein, 1967; see also Turvey, Fitch & Tuller, 1982, and Tuller, Turvey & Fitch, 1982, for more complete discussions).

In sum, although the descriptions of later-developing locomotor skills have defined the patterns of segmental actions as well as identified the normative times of appearance, they have fallen short in their ability to *explain* the development of these skills. It is thus to another perspective that we turn in our search for how it is that the newly walking infant comes to coordinate and control the later-developing locomotor skills.

DYNAMICAL SYSTEMS PERSPECTIVE

To reiterate, the two major dilemmas facing any theory seeking to explain how movements are controlled and coordinated are (1) the degrees-of-freedom problem or how to manage the vast number of choices found in the neuromusculoskeletal system, and (2) the problem of context-conditioned variability, that is, the inherent variability in a moving body in an ever-changing environment. To solve these problems, the neuromusculoskeletal system must have a style of organization which both manages the degrees of freedom but also provides flexibility and versatility in the face of change. Rather than assuming a prescriptive model of motor control, Bernstein (1967) hypothesized that the CNS solved the degrees-of-freedom problem by constraining them into units variously referred to as *synergies* (Gelfand et al. 1971), *linkages* (Waterland & Shambes, 1970), or as preferred here, *coordinative structures* (Easton, 1972; Turvey, 1977). It was Bernstein's identification of the problem of context-conditioned variability, however, which added the major ingredient for the emergence of the dynamical systems perspective. By recognizing that movements occur under dynamically different contexts, Bernstein pointed the way to seeking explanations for movement control and coordination based on dynamical principles. This approach offers a style of organization in which order and regulation *emerge* from the ensemble of muscles and bones as they move to achieve a function.

The dynamical systems perspective offers a set of principles for movement coordination and control (Kugler, Kelso & Turvey, 1982) based on a marriage of physical theories of biology (Pattee, 1971; Yates, 1982), nonequilibrium thermodynamics (Morowitz, 1970; Nicolis & Prigogine, 1977), and complex systems theory (Haken, 1983). In this perspective, movement is viewed as the result of dynamical properties of muscle collectives. Internal variables such as the limb mass, muscular stiffness, and energy all contribute to movement, as do external variables such as gravity and forces from other sources.

For those seeking to understand the development of motor skills, the dynamical systems approach has much appeal. Consider, for example, the problem facing the infant who wishes to change her location. When that infant is 2 months old, the solution to the problem may be very different than when she is 12 months old. In those 10 months there are changes in the infant that must be accounted for by the neuromuscular system if the movement goal is going to be attained. Changes in the body's morphology, CNS, muscular and postural systems all or in part affect the movement's dynamics and, therefore, require a different set of motor commands for changing locations. In a prescriptive approach the CNS would have to remember each set of commands, each set of contexts, change each motor set, and remember when and where to issue the commands. From a prescriptive perspective, change is a *problem*. From the dynamical perspective, change can be a *solution*—a source of information to be exploited.

In recasting the development of locomotor skills within the dynamical systems approach, we begin by examining the notion of the *coordinative structure* as a functional unit of action for locomotion. The principal aim here is to understand how the newly walking infant and later the toddler organize their neuromusculoskeletal system to achieve overground transport while maintaining upright postural control. Second, we analyze the *transitions* found during early childhood as the infant develops new patterns of coordination.

COORDINATIVE STRUCTURE: THE UNIT OF ACTION

The fundamental unit in dynamical systems theory is the coordinative structure (Saltzman & Kelso, 1987; Thelen, Kelso & Fogel, 1987). Originally defined by Easton (1972), a coordinative structure (CS) was an expansion of the term *reflex* in which reflexes or their neural circuits were viewed as underlying all volitional movements. Later Kugler, Kelso & Turvey (1980) redefined CS to be a muscle collective; often spanning more than one joint, which comes together to achieve a function. Coordinative structures, according to Kugler et al., were constrained units in which there was a relationship between muscles resulting in a reduction in the choices or degrees of freedom within the CNS. These collectives were considered not to be the result of inflexible, hard-wired neural circuits, but rather neuromuscular units temporarily organized to function together to meet the task demands. Evidence of such a style of organization has been shown in speech (Kelso, Saltzman & Tuller, 1986; Tuller & Kelso, 1984), two-handed movements (Kelso, Putnam & Goodman, 1983; Kelso, Southard & Goodman, 1979), handwriting (Viviani & Terzuolo, 1980), and posture (Nashner, 1977).

In locomotion the step-cycle organization within a limb may be seen as a coordinative structure. To achieve the goal of upright locomotion, the muscles within a limb (i.e., intralimb) may be constrained to act as a unit—a coordinative structure. Similarly, muscles across two limbs (e.g., the legs) may be constrained to act as a unit—that is, an interlimb coordinative structure. It is these interlimb units that are of particular interest in the study of locomotor skills, since it is the interlimb pattern of coordination that would seem to distinguish these skills.

Walking and running are patterns of interlimb coordination in which the legs are phased such that one limb is 50% out of phase with the other. That is to say, each leg goes through its own step-cycle, and its cycle is phased to the other such that as one limb is halfway through its cycle the other one starts its cycle. (Figs. 6–1 and 6–2.) Galloping, on the other hand, is an asymmetrical phasing pattern in that the leading limb begins its cycle approximately 35% of the way through the cycle of the rear limb (Whitall & Clark, 1986) (Fig. 6–3). This asymmetry is obvious if one remembers that a gallop is defined as a walk with one limb and a run with the other limb.

The changing pattern of interlimb coordination is less easily seen in hopping because only one leg is used for support. Since the swing leg never touches the ground, the calculation of an interlimb phasing relationship is problematic. However, if we examine Roberton & Halverson's (1984) data on the mature hop as to when one limb is reversing (backward to forward thigh rotation plus the so-called "hold") within the total cycle time, it would appear that one limb is reversing about halfway (47%/53%) through the phase of the other limb.

The last of the fundamental locomotor skills to appear is skipping, whose interlimb coordination is again a 50% phased one. However, it differs from running and walking in that each limb performs a walk and hop before alternating to the other foot (Wickstrom, 1987) (see Fig. 6–3). Thus within a limb the coordination is asymmetric whereas between the limbs it is symmetric.

If these patterns of locomotion are distinguishable patterns of interlimb organization, are they coordinative structures? Is there any evidence that these locomotor skills are indeed *constrained* relationships? Put another way, during a selected locomotor skill is the leg musculature constrained in a fixed manner such that knowing where one leg is in its cycle directly specifies where the other leg is in its cycle? Do these constrained units maintain their relationships when perturbed or scaled up on some parameter such as speed? And of principal importance to us here, if these are coordinative structures, how do they change developmentally?

To answer these questions an appropriate dynamical theory of interlimb coordination must be employed. To date, the model that has been the most successful for predicting interlimb coordination has been that of coupled ensembles of nonlinear, limit-cycle oscillators (Kay, Kelso, Saltzman & Schoner, 1987; Kelso, Holt, Rubin & Kugler, 1981; Kelso, Schoner, Scholz & Haken, 1987). To maintain the continuous cyclical action of locomotion, energy must be put into the cycle at some point during the pushoff phase to keep the cycle going. If no energy is put into the cycle, the cycle stops. This loss of energy is characteristic of a dissipative system and gives the system its nonlinear quality. Limit-cycle oscillators are systems that swing to and fro but have a preferred cycle or "attractive" orbit to which trajectories tend to converge (Kelso & Kay, 1987).

Coupled nonlinear, limit-cycle oscillators have three related properties: (1) entrainment; (2) phase-locking; and (3) structural stability (Kay et al., 1987; Kelso, et al., 1981, 1987; Pavlidis, 1973). *Entrainment* describes the interaction between two or more nonlinear oscillators. When two oscillators are coupled, the period of each one will be matched or will display a subharmonic ratio regardless of the natural period of either oscillator. *Phase-locking* refers to the property of nonlinear, limit-cycle oscillators whereby certain phase modes are more attractive or stable states. A limit-cycle oscillator also has the property of maintaining *structural stability* despite small perturbations which push it from its preferred phase. In effect, coupled nonlinear, limit-cycle oscillators will re-entrain and phase-lock to the nearest stable mode after encountering a perturbation.

These three properties of coupled nonlinear, limit-cycle oscillators would seem to satisfy the requirements of a coordinative structure style of organization. First, as a model, specific relationships are predicted between the limbs such that the behavior of one leg can be predicted from the behavior of the other. Second, the coupling or entrainment between the limbs signifies a unitary control over the two limbs (i.e., the many degrees of freedom are constrained to act as a single unit). Third, all three characteristics are emergent properties of a coupled system of nonlinear, limit-cycle oscillators and therefore are self-organizing processes. No CNS prescription need exist to "tell" the limbs where to go. Finally, the perturbations or challenges offered by Bernstein's context-conditioned variability problem are enjoined by the properties of entrainment, phase-locking, and structural stability.

We propose here that the leg action of the later-developing locomotor skills is constrained into coordinative structures with the properties of coupled nonlinear, limit-cycle oscillators. To support this thesis, we consider each of the skills individually for evidence of such properties.

WALKING

Although the later-developing locomotor skills are the ones of interest here, a study we conducted on the interlimb coordination of newly walking infants offers a beginning for our examination. In this cross-sectional study (Clark, Whitall & Phillips, 1988) we filmed infants when they could walk three steps independently, as well as at selected intervals for the next 6 months. Analysis of the temporal phasing[2] relationship between the limbs revealed that even newly walking infants coordinate their limbs in a 50% phasing relationship, the same as the adults. However, the young walkers differed significantly from the older walkers (i.e., those who had been walking 3 to 6 months) and adults in the variability around this mean phasing. This higher phase variability shown in the young walkers is support that the two legs are not well entrained. Well-entrained oscillators would have the same frequency and therefore minimal variability about their preferred phasing relationships. It was not until the infants had been walking about 3 months that relatively low variability (and therefore high entrainment) was observed. However, despite the lack of strong entrainment, the young walkers did have a preferred gait mode of 50% at the very onset of walking. Like coupled nonlinear, limit-cycle oscillators, the limbs appear to be phase-locked around one particular phase mode.

Only preliminary data exist on the early walking coordinative structure's stability in the face of a perturbation. This evidence comes from our longitudinal study of one infant from the time he started walking (CA = 11 months) until the present (CA = 4 years) (Clark, Whitall & Phillips, 1987). At each time of measurement we weighted one of his legs with a one-pound ankle cuff. Although the infant would not walk independently with the weight at the very onset of walking, after 2 weeks we were able to elicit walking with the weight. Without the ankle weight his overall mean phasing (49.3%) did not vary from that with the weights (50.6%). Variability also was comparable in both conditions (7.4 vs. 8.3%). However, an analysis of each limb independently revealed an asymmetry in phasing such that the weighted limb phased at 56%. One week later and thereafter for the next 6 months no such asymmetry appeared as the limbs increasingly improved their entrainment all the while maintaining the so-called attractive phase mode of 50%. Taken together with the high variability in phasing during unperturbed walking, the asymmetry found with the weight at the onset of walking suggests that the legs were not well entrained after 2 weeks of walking. Structural stability of the phase mode did not appear to be present at the very beginning of walking but emerged quickly thereafter. Interestingly, the asymmetry with the weight seen at the second week was not seen when the newly walking infant was supported with the weight on one limb or one week later when the perturbation was replicated with support. The postural demands in those first attempts at unsupported walking with the weight seemed to prevent the limbs' entrainment.

Thus from its very onset, upright independent walking seems to be constrained in a unit (i.e., a coordinative structure)(similar to that observed in adult walkers. The fact that a 50% temporal phasing relationship is found at the emergence of this upright gait argues for this phase relationship as an "attractive," or stable state (i.e., a phase-locked property of coupled nonlinear, limit-cycle oscillators). The high variability of these phasing modes demonstrated by the new walkers suggests that the limbs do not entrain well, or put another way, that they show a less stable coupling than infants who have been walking 3 months or longer. If a new walker is supported by holding her hands, this variability can be significantly reduced (Clark et al., 1988). Even in the conditions in which no perturbation is introduced, the postural demands for the newly walking infant seem to overwhelm the limbs' entrainment into a tight phase mode.

RUNNING

Do the limbs display evidence of a coordinative structure style of organization in running? Do they exhibit properties of coupled non-linear, limit-cycle oscillators? Like walking, the temporal phasing for running is such that halfway through the cycle of one limb the other limb begins its cycle (i.e., a 50% phasing). Data on the interlimb coordination of newly running infants is nonexistent, although here again our longitudinal study of one subject offers a glimpse of the prospects (Clark et al., 1987).

Seven months after taking his first three independent walking steps (CA = 18 months), our subject ran. Unlike his first attempts at walking, running was both phase-locked and well entrained at the outset. The mean phasing for this run was 50% with little variability about this mean. Indeed, at this time the variability of his walking and running phasing was essentially the same (1.5–2%). Since we were filming him every month, it is possible that his first attempts at running were unstable and we did not observe them. However, in our study on newly walking infants we found that it took the infants about 3 months to approximate adultlike phasing variability (Clark et al., 1988). Thus, we most likely would have been within one month of the run's first appearance and therefore would have captured any variability shown in that first month of running.

Additional support that running displays properties of coupled nonlinear, limit-cycle oscillators comes from work by Whitall (1988) in which children from 2 to 9 years and adults were filmed running (mean ages: 2.8, 4.2, 6.4, 9.4, and 26.1 years). Examination of both their mean and variability of phasing revealed that running was a phase-locked, stable gait mode at all ages. Although the limbs' entrainment as evidenced by phasing variability between the 2- and 4-year-old runners (M variability = 2.8%) and the adults (M = 1.5%) differed statistically, this difference was considered of little practical significance since it was within the experiment's measurement error (Whitall, 1988). When running was perturbed with a weight on one limb (approximately 4% of the subject's body weight), no effect at any age was found on the temporal phasing, that is, neither limb was perturbed away from the stable phase mode. Again this would argue for the structural stability and entrainment of a phase-locked gait at all the ages studied.

GALLOPING

With the emergence of galloping, we see the first asymmetric gait mode in the young child. When a walk on the leading leg is followed by a running step on the rear leg, an asymmetric temporal phasing of approximately 65/35% results (Whitall & Clark, 1986). Clearly, the constraint between the two limbs seen in walking and running changes qualitatively with the appearance of galloping. However, are the limbs still organized in the same dynamical way as they were for running and walking? That is, are the properties of nonlinear, limit-cycle oscillators still apparent? Our longitudinal single subject again offers a beginning point.

Some 20 months after first walking, we were able to elicit galloping in our subject, who was then 2 years 7 months (Whitall & Clark, 1987). At that time his phasing pattern was 66/33%—values very close to those found for adults (Clark & Whitall, 1986; Whitall, 1988). Whitall (1988), in her cross-sectional study of forty subjects from 2 years of age to adulthood, found two predominant phase modes among her subjects regardless of age: the 66/33 (2:1) and the 75/25 (3:1) ratios. These appear to be the two most attractive phase modes for the limbs when they cycle asymmetrically.

Variability of the temporal phasing was also low across all ages, although slightly higher than during running (Whitall, 1988). When the gallop was perturbed by placing a weight on the trailing leg, the phasing was shifted immediately away from the phase-locked mode to a slight but different phase relationship with the next four steps. With the weight on the leading limb, the phasing again shifted slightly but not significantly until the third and fourth step. In both instances the limbs did not display the properties of structural stability by re-entraining to the unperturbed phase mode. Rather, after the perturbation the limbs appeared to entrain to a slightly different phase mode.

Modeling galloping as coupled nonlinear, limit-cycle oscillators has shown that unlike running this asymmetric gait has more than one attractive state. However, despite perturbations to the limbs, a gallop is still maintained as an asymmetric mode—though not at the same phase mode as the unperturbed gallop.

HOPPING

In the three preceding skills the focus has been on the lower limbs only. Obviously, the upper limbs also are important to these later-emerging locomotor skills. From a dynamical systems perspective, the upper limbs may be studied to see if they, too, act as coupled nonlinear, limit-cycle oscillators. Only in hopping, however, has there been a direct investigation of this possibility.

Roberton & Halverson (in press) have argued that the arm and leg action of one-footed hopping may be modeled as coupled limit-cycle oscillators.[3] Their data, they have suggested, fit well with a notion in which the four limbs are seen as separate oscillators that gradually entrain over developmental time. In the earliest appearance of a one-footed hop, the swing leg is inactive (Halverson & Williams, 1985; Roberton & Halverson, in press). It is not until the age of 4 (Halverson & Williams, 1985) or 5 (Roberton & Halverson, in press) that the swing leg begins to move during the hop. When it does, the hopping leg acts as an external forcing oscillator to which the swing leg is immediately entrained. The authors have not directly tested the three characteristics of nonlinear, limit-cycle oscillators but they have provided evidence that sheds light on this hypothesis. For example, the invariance found in the phase plots of the hop and swing legs over developmental time plus the invariance found between the swing leg's peak velocity and the onset of the hopping leg's extension argue strongly that the limbs are phase-locked and entrained. The fact that these relationships are main-tained over developmental time may suggest that the phasing rela-tionship is a structurally stable one. Thus although hopping was not tested in the same manner as previous skills, Roberton & Halverson concluded that the limbs are coupled, limit-cycle oscillators—a coordi-native structure.

SKIPPING

To date, there are no data on the interlimb temporal organization of skipping. However, it is possible to make some predictions based on what has been found in the preceding skills as well as the extant qualitative descriptions of skipping. Given the fact that skipping is an alternating gait, a 50% phasing mode would almost certainly be found. It is not clear, though, whether the variability around the 50% mode would necessarily be as small as it is for walking and running. The addition of the hop to the step of the same limb may introduce more variability; however, it can be predicted that the limbs would be rela-tively well entrained in a mature skip. As to the arm coordination, it is suggested by Roberton & Halverson (1984) that the developmental sequence is from a symmetrical phasing to an alternating phasing. This order can be predicted from previous experiments on finger/hand phasing in which a symmetrical (i.e., 0 or 100%) phase is more stable (and presumably easier) than an alternating phase (Tuller & Kelso, 1984; Yaminishi, Kawato & Susuki, 1980). Interestingly, in the experiments on finger/hand phasing the phasing transition is never seen to go from symmetrical to alternating as is seen in developmental time for skipping (Roberton & Halverson, 1984) or galloping (Sapp, 1980). This may well result from the biomechanical constraints on the locomotor patterns in which the alternating arm action is used to offset the rotary forces produced by the lower limbs.

SUMMARY

So far our recasting of the development of locomotor skills has been concerned with the behavioral modeling of the skills as coupled non-linear, limit-cycle oscillators. We have provided evidence that our limbs appear to be organized like coupled nonlinear, limit-cycle oscillators in walking, running, and galloping and that all four limbs show oscillator-type properties in the hop. Further, it is clear that this oscillatory organization is apparent relatively early in the appearance of the skill (or at least as far as the lower limbs are concerned in walking, running, and galloping).

However, as developmentalists we are interested not only in the development of a skill once it has appeared, but in how and why the skill appears in the first place. That is, we are concerned ultimately with the transition from one skill to the next. Indeed, the work by Thelen and her colleagues in Chapter 4 is focused on the transition from a nonwalking infant to a walking infant. In the next section of our chapter we will focus on the transitions between later-emerging forms of locomotion.

GAIT TRANSITIONS

We first ask, what does the dynamical systems perspective offer as a theoretical overlay to this issue? One property of coupled, nonlinear, limit-cycle oscillators is that of maintaining stable phase relationships across changes in other parameters until a critical value of this other parameter is reached. For example, alternating finger movements (50% phasing) will remain constant (stable) as the speed of finger flexion-extension is increased (Kelso, 1984). When a critical speed is attained, the phasing will fluctuate and abruptly change to a simultaneous (0 or 100%) phase mode (Kelso, 1984; Kelso et al., 1987). This new phase mode is presumably the most stable relationship at this particular speed of finger flexion/extension. Although this principle of phase transition is an established one for real-time phenomena, it has not been shown but only suggested that the same principle or organization may occur in developmental time (Clark et al., 1987; Thelen, in press; Thelen et al., 1987). Specifically, it is argued that developing systems may shift into new modes by the amplification of some system-sensitive scaling parameter to the point where dynamical stability is disrupted. At this point a new form arises which is distinctly different from the previous form but is initially unstable, that is, it may easily revert back to the previous form. A system-sensitive scaling parameter denotes an internal control variable (e.g., muscular force), an external variable (e.g., gravity), or a collection of either type of variable (e.g., the postural systems). In any case, it is a parameter to which the system is sensitive such that it can cause a new form to emerge or to be held back—that is, a rate-limiter (Thelen, 1986).

The task here, then, is to identify system-sensitive scaling parameters that when scaled would allow the appearance of succeeding gaits in developmental time. At the outset it is important to say that, to our knowledge, almost no research exists which focuses on the identification of these parameters for the later-developing locomotor skills. Therefore our comments will be largely speculative.

The first transition in gaits is from walking to running. The usual distinction between the two gaits is that running has a flight phase. In order to achieve flight, sufficient ground reaction forces must be generated to propel the center of mass high enough to get the body airborne. However, it is known that adult runners at moderate speeds (4.5 ms^{-1}) create peak vertical forces at ground contact (weight acceptance) around 2x body weight (2.2 BW $\pm$ 0.4), and during pushoff the peak vertical force is slightly higher (2.8 BW $\pm$ 0.3) (Cavanagh & Lafortune, 1980). Two-year-olds encouraged to run as fast as possible demonstrate similar force absorption and thrust values (2.2 and 2.02 BW, respectively) (Fortney, 1983). It may well be that the infant's inability to create these vertical forces is the rate-limiter to the emergence of running. Once the infant can "scale up" on this parameter (i.e., vertical ground reaction force) to a critical value (perhaps 2xBW), running will emerge. Whether this scaling up of vertical ground reaction forces is the result of muscle mass increases, anthropometric changes, improved motoneuron recruitment, or some combination is as yet unknown.

Another parameter that may affect the transition from walking to running is the postural system. Although the postural system is seemingly adequate for walking about, perhaps it is not sufficiently mature to support running. The forces created in running may stress the postural system such that it cannot maintain the body in the upright position under the newly created forces. Note that from this perspective the running pattern is not considered a separate pattern generation from walking, as some have suggested (Shapiro, Zernicke, Gregor & Diestel, 1981); rather, running is viewed as a scaling up of force production while using the same pattern of interlimb coordination (i.e., a 50% phasing). Indeed, as mentioned earlier, our longitudinal case study revealed that when running emerged 7 months after walking it was immediately a stable phasing pattern (Clark et al., 1987).

The transition from running to galloping is an intentional one. Since the gallop consists of a walk with the leading limb and a run with the rear limb, it is clear that the components that may be rate-limiters for the walk or run (e.g., posture and force production) would not be factors for the emergence of a gallop. Yet the gallop does not usually appear for at least 6 months after a run emerges. Two hypotheses are forwarded. First, the production of an asymmetric gait appears to require a differentiation of force production for each limb. Conceivably, it is the ability to send different impulses to each limb (i.e., to uncouple the alternating phasing) that is the rate-limiting parameter. Second, this asymmetric gait with the limbs widespread in the sagittal plane may produce different balance requirements for the body, and thus the postural system again may be unable to handle the new skill until the toddler has been running for 6 months.

Neither of these hypotheses has been empirically tested. However, in our longitudinal case study we did notice an unusual phenomenon (Clark et al., 1987). During the first 3 months of running, the subject exhibited an equally stable (low variability) phasing pattern; however, by 6 months of running, the phasing variability for running was suddenly quite variable—almost as variable as when he first started walking. When we looked closely at the data, we found that on some trials the child had adopted a systematic asymmetry in which one leg tended to lead while the other trailed slightly. It was if the child were willfully "playing" with the system and creating an asymmetry. This was at a time when the child could not yet produce a gallop. Indeed, in her cross-sectional study of the forms of galloping, Sapp (1980) noted that an asymmetric run preceded galloping. From a dynamical systems perspective, the run-to-gallop transition can be seen as a phasing mode that has become unstable as it was scaled up on a certain parameter (asymmetry of forces) and that will shift to a new attractive phasing if this parameter is scaled beyond some critical limit.

The next transition, from the emergence of galloping to the first appearance of hopping, is slightly problematic since it is unclear that the gallop does precede the hop. Clearly, the ability to balance one's body weight on one limb for some duration is a prime candidate for a rate-limiting parameter. However, another possibility is that the child is unable to produce force in only one limb sufficient to lift the body off the ground and recover quickly enough to produce force again. Unlike the scaling of the magnitude of vertical ground reaction forces, which may be a possible rate-limiting factor for running, this particular rate-limiting parameter is concerned with the differentiation of force to one limb and/or the recovery rate for muscle excitation. Since it is known that the swing leg is inactive when the child first attempts hopping (Roberton & Halverson, in press), it is obvious that the child makes the transition to a hop by regulating one limb only while holding or freezing the other.

The final transition is from the hop to the skip. As with the gallop, the skip is comprised of movements that the child already has in her repertoire—namely, the walking step and the hop. However, in this case the skip does not require a scaling up of balance requirements (i.e., the development of the postural system) because the antecedent skill of hopping requires the ability to balance on one limb. Likewise, there is no need for any scaling of a force parameter per se, since the appearance of the hop and the other locomotor skills demonstrates that the necessary force production is already available to the child. So what are the possible rate-limiting parameters? A clue is provided by the descriptive studies of skipping. Roberton & Halverson (1984) and Wickstrom (1987) indicate that the first form of skipping to emerge is a one-sided skip, whereby one limb does a step and hop while the other does a step only. What is developing, then, is the ability to coordinate a complex limb pattern on one limb with the same pattern on the other. In other words, skipping is a coordination embedded in a coordination, i.e., an intralimb coordination embedded in an interlimb coordination. Obviously, the intralimb coordination emerges first. How this is done is as yet unclear. But it suffices to say that this transition is all the more interesting, for if we can untangle the actual rate-limiters we may well have a better understanding of how we "learn" the complex motor skills that follow these fundamental locomotor skills.

FUTURE DIRECTIONS

We began this chapter with a review of the neuromaturational/descriptive perspective on the later-developing locomotor skills. Although the developmental order across the skills and, in some instances, within some skills has been established, this perspective has not satisfactorily explained either the organization or the transition between the different movement patterns. We therefore sought to recast the development of these locomotor skills from a dynamical systems perspective. Using coupled nonlinear, limit-cycle oscillators as the coordinative structure model, we examined walking, running, galloping, hopping, and skipping for the properties of phase-locking, entrainment, and structural stability. These interrelated properties predict that interlimb coordination of any skill is organized around stable, attractive phase modes between the limbs. Furthermore, it is hypothesized that these new phase modes are accomplished by the scaling up of some system-sensitive parameter(s), which results in abrupt transitions to new phase relationships.

Given the paucity of quantitative data on the phasing relationships of the locomotor skills, we were able to show only limited evidence for stable, attractive phase modes. Interestingly, though, we note that this style of organization appears at the first onset of a gait form (at least for the lower limbs), which supports the "abrupt transition" hypothesis. Developmentally, there is only a slight increase in stability (or refinement) from the initial appearance of the skill to the adult (or mature) form of the skills. Concerning our major interest in the transitions between these later-emerging locomotor skills, we were unable to do more than speculate about the system-sensitive scaling parameters that promote the emergence of each successive skill.

Clearly, much work remains to be done if we are to explain the development of the later-appearing locomotor skills using principles derived from the dynamical systems perspective. Specifically, we point to three major gaps in the literature to date. First, with the exception of hopping, there is virtually no quantitative data on the development of the phasing relationships between the arms and between the arms and legs. Second, little attention has been paid to differences between gaits in *intralimb* coordination. Walking, running, and skipping have the same alternating (50%) *interlimb* phasing relationship for the legs but clearly differ in their intralimb coordination. Finally, and most significantly, there is no work specifically examining the transitions between gaits.[4] Identification of system-sensitive scaling and rate-limiting parameters, as Thelen and her colleagues (Chap. 4 of this volume) have done for transition from not-walking to walking, would go far in explaining early childhood motor development.

Recasting the development of the later-emerging locomotor skills within the dynamical systems perspective has enabled us to identify gaps in our knowledge of motor-skill development, gaps that we hope will be filled in the not-too-distant future.

NOTES

1. For purposes of this chapter, jumping will not be considered a locomotor skill since it is not generally performed as a cyclical, ground-covering skill. We also have chosen not to discuss leaping and sliding since both are later-developing modifications of the run (leap) and the gallop (slide).

2. It should be recognized that the amplitude (spatial coordination) phasing of the two limbs also may be organized along the lines of coupled nonlinear, limit-cycle oscillators. Discussion is limited here to temporal phasing only because very little data are available for amplitude phasing.

3. Roberton & Halverson (in press) model the limbs as linear rather than nonlinear oscillators. No evidence in their data offers a hint as to whether the limbs in hopping act as nonlinear or linear oscillators.

4. Work is currently underway in our laboratory to examine the transitions from walking to running and from running to galloping.

REFERENCES

Bernstein, N. (1967). *The coordination and regulation of movements.* London: Pergamon Press.
Branta, C.; Haubenstricker, J.; & Seefeldt, V. (1984). Age changes in motor skills during childhood and adolesence. In R. Terjung (Ed.), *Exercise and sport sciences reviews,* Vol. 12, pp. 467–520. Lexington, MA: Collamore Press.
Burnett, C. N., & Johnson, E. W. (1971). Development of gait in childhood: Part II. *Developmental Medicine and Child Neurology, 13,* 207–15.
Burnside, L. H. (1927). Coordination in the locomotion of infants. *Genetic Psychology Monographs, 2,* 284–340.
Cavanagh, P. R. & Lafortune, M. A. (1980). Ground reaction forces in distance runners. *Journal of Biomechanics, 13,* 397–406.
Clark, J. E.; Whitall, J.; & Phillips, S. J. (1987). *Changing patterns of interlimb coordination in infants and young children.* Paper presented at the biannual meeting of the Society for Research in Child Development, April, Baltimore, MD.
Clark, J. E.; Whitall, J.; Phillips, S. J. (1988). Human interlimb coordination: The first 6 months of independent walking. *Developmental Psychology, 21,* 445–56.
Easton, T. (1972). On the normal use of reflexes. *American Scientist, 60,* 591–99.
Forssberg, H. (1985). Ontogeny of human locomotor control. I. Infant stepping, supported locomotion and transition to independent locomotion. *Experimental Brain Research, 57,* 480–93.
Fortney, V. L. (1983). The kinematics and kinetics of the running pattern of two-, four-, and six-year-old children. *Research Quarterly for Exercise and Sport, 54,* 126–35.
Gelfand, I. M. Gurfinkel, V. S.; Tsetlin, M. L.; & Shik, M. L. (1971). Some problems in the analysis of movements. In I. M. Gelfand, V. S. Gurfinkel, M. L. Tsetlin & M. L. Shik (Eds.), *Models of structural-functional organization of certain biological systems,* (pp. 329–45). Cambridge, MA: MIT Press.
Gesell, A., & Amatruda, D. S. (1947). *Developmental diagnosis.* 2nd ed. New York: Harper & Row.
Gutteridge, M. V. (1939). A study of motor achievements of young children. *Archives of Psychology, 244,* 1–178.
Haken, H. (1983). *Synergetics: An Introduction.* 3rd ed. Heidelberg: Springer-Verlag.

Halverson, L. E., & Williams, K. (1985). Developmental sequences for hopping over distance: a prelongitudinal screening. *Research Quarterly for Exercise and Sport, 56,* 37–44.

Kay, B. A.; Kelso, J. A. S.; Saltzman, E. L.; & Schoner, G. (1987). Space-time behavior of single and bimanual rhythmical movements: Data and limit cycle model. *Journal of Experimental Psychology: Human Perception and Performance, 13,* 178–92.

Kelso, J. A. S. (1984). Phase transitions and critical behavior in the human bimanual coordination. *American Journal of Physiology, 246,* R1000–R1004.

Kelso, J. A. S.; Holt, K. G.; Rubin, P.; & Kugler, P. N. (1981). Patterns of human interlimb coordination emerge from the properties of nonlinear limit cycle oscillatory processes: Theory and data. *Journal of Motor Behavior, 13,* 226–61.

Kelso, J. A. S., & Kay, B. (1987). Information and control: A macroscopic basis for perception-action coupling. In H. Heuer & A. F. Sanders (Eds.), *Tutorials in perception and action* (pp. 3–32). Hillsdale, NJ: Erlbaum.

Kelso, J. A. S.; Putnam, C.; & Goodman, D. (1983). On the space-time structure of human interlimb coordination. *Quarterly Journal of Experimental Psychology, 35A,* 347–75.

Kelso, J. A. S.; Saltzman, E. L.; & Tuller, B. (1986). The dynamical perspective on speech production: Data and theory. *Journal of Phonetics, 14,* 29–59.

Kelso, J. A. S.; Schoner, G.; Scholz, J. P.; & Haken, H. (1987). Phase-locked modes, phase transitions and component oscillators in biological motion. *Physica Scripta, 35,* 79–87.

Kelso, J. A. S.; Southard, D.; & Goodman, D. (1979). On the nature of human interlimb coordination. *Science, 203,* 1029–31.

Kelso, J. A. S., & Tuller, B. (1984). A dynamical basis for action systems. In M. S. Gazzaniga (Ed.), *Handbook of cognitive neuroscience* (pp. 321–56). New York: Plenum.

Kugler, P. N.; Kelso J. A. S.; & Turvey, M. T. (1980). On the concept of coordinative structures as dissipative structures: I. Theoretical lines of convergence. In G. E. Stelmach & J. Requin (Eds.), *Tutorials in motor behavior* (pp. 3–47). New York: North Holland.

Kugler, P. N.; Kelso, J. A. S.; & Turvey, M. T. (1982). On the control and co-ordination of naturally developing systems. In J. A. S. Kelso & J. E. Clark (Eds.), *The development of movement control and co-ordination* (pp. 5–78). New York: Wiley.

McCaskill, C. L., & Wellman, B. L. (1938). A study of common motor achievements at the preschool ages. *Child Development, 9,* 141–50.

McGraw, M. B. (1932). From reflex to muscular control in the assumption of an erect posture and ambulation in the human infant. *Child Development, 3,* 291–97.

McGraw, M. B. (1940). Neuromuscular development of the human infant as exemplified in the achievement of erect locomotion. *Journal of Pediatrics. 17,* 747–71.

McGraw, M. B. (1945/1969). *The neuromuscular maturation of the human infant.* New York: Hafner.

Morowitz, H. J. (1970). *Entropy for biologists. An Introduction to thermodynamics.* New York: Academic Press.

Nashner, L. M. (1977). Fixed patterns of rapid postural responses among leg muscles during stance. *Experimental Brain Research, 30,* 13–24.

Nicolis, G., & Prigogine, I. (1977). *Self-organization in nonequilibrium systems.* New York: John Wiley.

Pattee, H. H. (1971). Physical theories of biological coordination. *Quarterly Review of Biophysics,* 255–76.

Pavlidis, T. (1973). *Biological oscillators: Their mathematical analysis.* New York: Academic Press.

Roberton, M. A. (1984). Changing motor patterns during childhood. In J. R. Thomas (Ed.), *Motor development during childhood and adolescence* (pp. 48–90). Minneapolis: Burgess.

Roberton, M. A., & Halverson, L. E. (1984). *Developing children—Their changing movement.* Philadelphia: Lea & Febiger.

Roberton, M. A., & Halverson, L. E. (in press). The development of locomotor coordination: Longitudinal change and invariance. *Journal of Motor Behavior.*

Roberton, M. A.; Williams, K.; & Langendorfer, S. (1980). Pre-longitudinal screening of motor development sequences. *Research Quarterly for Exercise and Sport, 51,* 724–31.

Saltzman, E., & Kelso, J. A. S. (1987). Skilled actions: A task-dynamic approach. *Psychological Review, 94,* 84–106.

Sapp, M. M. (1980). The development of galloping in young children: A preliminary study. Master's project. Michigan State University.

Seefeldt, V., & Haubenstricker, J. (1974–77). *Developmental sequences of fundamental motor skills.* Unpublished papers, Michigan State University.

Shapiro, D.; Zernicke, R. F.; Gregor, R. J.; & Diestel, J. D. (1981). Evidence for generalized motor programs using gait pattern analysis. *Journal of Motor Behavior, 13,* 33–47.

Shirley, M. M. (1931). *The first two years: A study of twenty-five babies, Vol I. Postural and locomotor development.* Minneapolis: University of Minnesota Press.

Sinclair, C. B. (1973). *Movement of the young child, Ages two to six.* Columbus, OH: Charles E. Merrill.

Statham L., & Murray, M. P. (1971). Early walking patterns of normal children. *Clinical Orthopaedics, 79,* 8–24.

Sutherland, D. H. (1984). *Gait disorders in childhood and adolescence.* Baltimore: Williams & Wilkins.

Sutherland, D. H.; Olshen, R.; Cooper, L.; & Woo, S. L.-Y. (1980). The development of mature gait. *Journal of Bone and Joint Surgery, 62-A,* 336–53.

Thelen, E. (1986). Development of coordinated movement: Implications for early human development. In M. G. Wade & H. T. A. (Whiting (Eds.), *Motor development in children: Aspects of coordination and control,* (pp. 107–24). Dordrecht: Martinus Nijhoff.

Thelen, E. (in press). Dynamical approaches to the development of behavior. In J. A. S. Kelso, A. J. Mandell, & M. F. Shlesinger (Eds.), *Dynamical patterns in complex systems.* Singapore: World Scientific Publishers.

Thelen, E.; Kelso, J. A. S.; & Fogel, A. (1987). Self-organizing systems and infant motor development. *Developmental Review, 7,* 39–65.

Tuller, B., & Kelso, J. A. S. (1984). The timing of articulatory gestures: Evidence for rational invariance. *Journal of the Acoustical Society of America, 76,* 1030–36.

Tuller, B.; Turvey, M. T.; & Fitch, H. L. (1982). The Bernstein perspective: II. The concept of muscle linkage or coordinate structure. In J. A. S. Kelso (Ed.), *Human motor behavior: An introduction* (pp. 239–52). Hillsdale, NJ: Erlbaum.

Turvey, M. T. (1977). Preliminaries to a theory of action with reference to vision. In R. Shaw & J. Bransford (Eds.), *Perceiving, acting, and knowing: Toward an ecological psychology* (pp. 211–67). Hillsdale, NJ: Erlbaum.

Turvey, M. T.; Fitch, H. L.; & Tuller, B. (1982). The Bernstein perspective: I. The problem of degrees of freedom and context-conditioned variability. In J. A. S. Kelso (Ed.), *Human motor behavior: An introduction* (pp 239–52). Hillsdale, NJ: Erlbaum.

Viviani, P., & Terzuolo, C. (1980). Space-time invariance in learned motor skills. In G. E. Stelmach & J. Requin (Eds.), *Tutorials in motor behavior* (pp. 525–36). Armsterdam: North Holland.

Waterland, J. C., & Shambes, G. M. (1970). Head and shoulder girdle linkage. *American Journal of Physical Medicine, 49*, 279–89.

Whitall, J. (1988). A developmental study of interlimb coordination in running and galloping. Ph.D. dissertation, University of Maryland, College Park.

Whitall, J., & Clark, J. E. (1986). The development of interlimb coordination in galloping: Theory and data. Paper presented at the North American Society for the Psychology of Sport and Physical Activity, June, Scottsdale, AZ.

Wickstrom, R. L. (1987). Observations on motor pattern development in skipping. In J. E. Clark & J. H. Humphrey (Eds.), *Advances in motor development research* (Vol. 1, pp. 49–60). New York: AMS Press.

Yaminishi, J.; Kawato, M.; & Susuki, R. (1980). Two coupled oscillators as a model for the coordinated finger tapping by both hands. *Biological Cybernetics, 37*, 219–25.

Yates, F. E. (1982). Outline of a physical theory of physiological systems. *Canadian Journal of Physiology and Pharmacology, 60*, 217–48.

Part III

Posture
and Gait Changes
in the Aging Adult

7

Aging, Posture Control, and Movement Preparation

Marjorie H. Woollacott

Though many studies on brain function and aging have shown a decline in a number of sensory and motor processes with age, scientists do not agree precisely on why or how humans age. One currently accepted model for decline in nervous system function with age assumes a linear decline over time, with various disease states appearing in individuals as neuron numbers in a specific brain area decrease below the threshold for normal function (see Fig. 7–1A). Thus Parkinson's disease would appear when cell numbers in the substantia nigra of the basal ganglia complex had been reduced to the threshold level for Parkinson symptoms. Individuals might reach this state earlier if there had been a previous incident in their lives, such as an attack by a flu virus, which reduced cell function in that region of the brain (Davies, 1987).

However, a second model of aging and brain function has also been hypothesized. In this model normal aging does not involve a continuous linear decline in neuron function. On the contrary, the nervous system continues to function at a high level until death, unless there is a specific catastrophe or the individual contracts a specific disease, which then causes a rapid decline in function in a specific brain area (see Fig. 7–1B).

It has been difficult to test these two hypotheses due to the fact that most aging studies are flawed in that they include within their population pool both individuals undergoing normal aging and individuals who have some degree of pathology. By age 85 there may be as many as 20% of individuals in a population with pathology (Davies, 1987).

In the area of posture control and locomotion there is controversy concerning the extent of change in neuronal function in the older adult. Some studies show no change in function of the neural subsystems controlling posture and locomotion with age, supporting the second model of aging, whereas others show a severe decline in function in the older adult. This appears to be due to fundamental differences in the

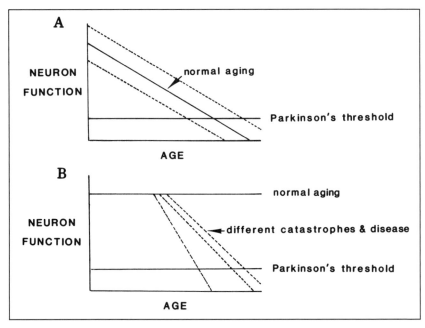

Fig. 7–1. Two models for decline in nervous system function. A: linear decline over time; B: continued high level of function unless catastrophe or disease causes rapid decline in specific brain area.

definition researchers use in classifying an individual as an "elderly" adult. For example, some researchers have classified the elderly adult as anyone over 60 years of age. A study on the effects of aging in walking ability by Imms & Edholm (1981) used this criterion for subject selection. They selected a group of 71 subjects ranging in age from 60 to 99 years using no exclusion criteria for possible pathology. These researchers noted that the mean walking velocities for the older adults were slower than any other studies had previously reported.

On the other hand, researchers have also defined the elderly adult as someone free from any pathology. In a study in which this definition was used, Gabell & Nayak (1984) screened an initial group of 1,187 individuals of 65 years and over and found only 32 who fulfilled their criteria, due to such exclusion factors as disorders of the musculoskeletal, neurological, or cardiovascular systems, or any previous history of falls. Interestingly, Gabell & Nayak found no significant differences between their young and older adult groups when comparing four parameters measuring the variability of gait. They thus concluded that an increase in variability in the gait cycle in the elderly was not normal, but always due to some pathology.

In this chapter I will review the literature on age-related changes in posture control and interactions between the postural and voluntary control systems, and in so doing will attempt to distinguish between the two models of aging described above. Subsequently, I will attempt to determine the amount of experimental support for each of the two hypotheses.

First, I will review the behavioral literature on age-related changes in postural sway in both static and dynamic balance conditions. Then I will discuss age-related changes in neuromuscular responses underlying balance control. In order to determine if deterioration of specific neuronal subsystems contributes to these changes in postural control, I will examine the literature on age-related changes in the three sensory systems (the somatosensory, visual, and vestibular systems) and in the motor systems involved in postural control.

Finally, I will review the literature on age-related changes in the interactions between the postural and voluntary control systems. We will compare the ability of young and older adults to activate postural muscles in a feedforward manner before the prime mover muscles in order to compensate in advance for changes in center of gravity caused by voluntary movements.

BEHAVIORAL STUDIES

One of the first studies on changes in the static control of posture across the life span was performed by Sheldon in 1963. To measure postural sway in his subjects, he used a triangular metal frame with U-shaped pads that fit over the shoulders of the subject. The apex of the triangle carried a pencil that registered the movements of the subject on graph paper below. He analyzed the control of sway during quiet stance under two conditions, with eyes open and with eyes closed. He noted that the performance of children from 6 to 14 years of age was surprisingly bad for both conditions, with performance improving rapidly from this age on. Performance stabilized between the ages of 16 and 59 years and once again deteriorated after the age of 60 years. The very young (6–9 years) and the very old (80+ years) showed almost identical sway excursions with eyes open, with an average sway area of 26.7 ± 10.3 squares penetrated for the children and 26.1 ± 8.6 for the older adults. However, with eyes closed the performance of the young children was significantly worse than that of the very old, with an average area under the sway curve being 105.5 ± 32.6 for the former and 76.5 ± 43 squares for the latter.

Sheldon noted that there was a distinct group of 36 subjects out of the total pool of 268 subjects who were unable to control their stance with direct visual feedback. However, with eyes closed and relying for postural control on the vestibular system, the proprioceptive afferents, and afferents from the soles of the feet, these subjects were able to significantly improve their control of sway. The subjects in this group were almost all women of advanced age, and the majority had already sustained one or more falls. They made up almost one-third of the subjects over 60 years of age.

Sheldon (1963) noted that there were great individual variations in his older adults and that these differences may have been accentuated by the presence of subjects with slight degrees of pathology, included because of his attempt to collect a random sample of older adults in his study. However, he noted that comparing the results from the sample of school children and older adults was problematic, since one can get a fairly representative sample of school children but not of older adults. Some of his older subjects were unable to perform the tests without endangering themselves, and others could not stand independently for 1 minute. Thus many subjects could not even be tested. He concluded that one tends to compare a more-or-less average sample of the younger age groups with a group made up of the physical aristocracy in their advanced years.

More recently, Hasselkus & Shambes (1975) investigated the effects of unusual or novel environmental conditions on postural sway in aging vs. young adults. They used women 20–30 years old and 70–80 years old for their population sample. They noted that the effects of age are most obvious in situations of stress, and so they analyzed sway of the two groups in the posturally threatening and more stressful forward lean position. They hypothesized that older adults would cope less effectively with this condition than younger adults and thus the two groups would show even greater differences in postural sway than in a more stable, upright position. As predicted, there was a greater effect of age on the postural sway in the forward lean stance than in the upright stance. In addition, there was a trial effect for the older adults in the forward lean position consisting of a decrease in total sway area across trials. The authors noted that the effect was probably at least partly due to greater cortical involvement in the forward lean task than in upright stance, and perhaps it was equivalent to a practice effect. They noted that not every older subject showed this phenomenon, but the overall effect across subjects was greater postural stability during the third trial.

The above studies show a clear effect of aging on static balance tasks but do not explore the effects of aging on dynamic balance control, which is required during locomotion and other voluntary motor skills. One of the first studies to explore the cause of age-related changes in walking patterns in healthy older men was that of Murray and her colleagues (1969). She examined both free and fast walking of sixty-four normal men, ranging in age from 20 to 87 years. She noted that beyond 65 years subjects had shorter and broader stride dimensions, a slower cadence, lower swing-to-stance time ratios, less shoulder flexion on forward arm swing, and less elbow extension on backward swing. There was also greater lateral head movement. However, she noted that the walking characteristics of older men did not resemble the gait of someone with pathology associated with nervous system damage, but rather appeared to be guarded or restrained, as if in an attempt to obtain maximum stability and security. She described the walking of the older men as resembling that of someone walking on a slippery surface or in the dark and thus lacking in some sensory information. She also noted that the shortened stride length appeared to provide a less precarious perimeter of support for maintaining balance. It is also of interest that the upper limbs of the older men tended toward a posture of relative shoulder hyperextension and elbow flexion, which resembles slightly the "high-guard" walking of young children.

Research by Guimaraes & Isaacs (1980) has shown that the gait of hospitalized fallers over the age of 65 years differed from that of both young adults and from other older adults in having a slow speed, short step length, narrow stride width, wide range of stepping frequency, large variability of step length, and increasing step variability with increasing step frequency. Gabell & Nayak (1984) hypothesized that this increase in the variability of gait with age could be due to a deterioration in balance mechanisms. They stated that two factors relating to balance control during locomotion are stride width and double support time, the first being a spatial and the second being a temporal parameter. They predicted that an increase in the variability of one or both of these parameters could indicate an inability to compensate for instability and thus a predisposition to falls. However, Gabell & Nayak (1984) were also interested in whether this increased variability in gait characteristics was related to age or pathology. They noted that the significantly increased step-length variability in patients who were hospitalized after a fall could have been the result of injury, shock, or hospitalization-disuse atrophy, and thus it may or may not have been present before the fall. They aimed to determine whether it was normal for older adults to show increased gait variability in the absence of pathology.

In order to rule out any form of pathology as contributing to changes in gait characteristics with age, the authors began with a subject pool of 1,187 adults over 64 years of age and excluded all those with any disorder likely to affect gait or balance. Exclusion criteria included musculoskeletal, neurological, and cardiovascular disorders; severe bilateral visual impairment or glaucoma; a history of falls or dizzy spells during the past year; the use of a walking aid; and women who habitually wore heels exceeding 4 cm in height. They found no significant difference between the variability of gait in normal young and old adults and concluded that any increase in variability occurring in the older adult is not normal but is due to a perhaps undetected pathology. They concluded that an increasingly variable pattern of gait is not a normal or inevitable concomitant of aging.

These results are supported by a study by Fernie et al. (1982) which aimed to determine if there was a relationship between the extent of postural sway during stance in the older adult and their frequency of falling. They studied a total of 205 institutionalized older adults with an average age of 82 years. They noted that the average speed of sway was significantly greater for those who fell one or more times in a year than for those who had not fallen. However, the mean sway of even the nonfallers was greater than that of noninstitutionalized elderly who had been studied previously. They thus concluded that mean speed of postural sway was only of statistical value for determining the risk of falling among the institutionalized elderly. If it is assumed that institutionalization implies the presence of some form of pathology, we may conclude that it is pathology, and not aging per se, that causes the increased sway and increased liability to fall.

ELECTROMYOGRAPHIC STUDIES

Studies by Woollacott et al. (1986, 1988) exploring the extent of neuromuscular changes associated with decreased balance abilities in the elderly have examined (1) the effects of age on the coordination of the timing and amplitude of muscle response synergies to external threats to balance and (2) the effects of age on the ability of the subject to reorganize sensory inputs and subsequently modify postural responses as a consequence of changing environmental conditions. They compared muscle response characteristics of twelve older (61–78 years) and younger (19–38 years) adults, using a platform capable of horizontal (anterior-posterior) or rotational (ankle dorsi- or plantarflexion) movements to disturb balance unexpectedly and recording the electromyographic activity of the gastrocnemius, tibialis anterior, hamstrings, and quadriceps muscles of the legs.

They noted that automatic (long latency) postural muscle responses to support surface perturbations were on the whole qualitatively similar in both young and older adult groups, though the older group showed changes in characteristics of response timing and amplitude. Increases in the absolute latency of distal muscle responses were observed in older adults, specifically in the tibialis anterior muscle, which was activated in response to anterior platform translations causing posterior sway. In addition, in five of the twelve older adults, intermittent reversals in the sequence of leg muscle contractions occurred during backward sway responses with the proximal quadriceps muscles being activated before the distal tibialis anterior. Thus the normal distal-to-proximal sequence of muscle response activation seen in young adults was occasionally disturbed, to give a less efficient activation sequence.

They also noted that older adults exhibited a large incidence of shorter latency spinal monosynaptic responses when subjected to platform perturbations rotating the ankle joint. Though these spinal myotatic reflexes can occasionally be elicited in young adults, the frequency of occurrence is low. In this study none of the younger adults showed myotatic reflexes, but seven of the older adults exhibited them. However, the effect of these reflexes may be minimal in altering postural control since they occurred in only 18% of rotation trials for older adults and were small, averaging 21% of the amplitude of the subsequent, longer latency, automatic contractions.

The ability of the older adult to balance under conditions of reduced or conflicting sensory information from somatosensory, visual, and vestibular systems was also impaired. The first test in this area required the subjects to balance on the platform when ankle joint somatosensory inputs and/or visual inputs were made incongruent with postural sway. This was done by rotating the platform and/or the visual box surrounding the subject in direct correlation with body sway. The ankle joint was thus kept at a constant 90 degrees and/or the visual world was kept stationary with relation to the body. The second test required the subjects to balance under similar ankle joint conditions but with vision absent. When first confronted with a combination of absent visual and incongruent ankle joint somatosensory inputs, half of the elderly group lost balance, although the younger adults did not. In most instances, however, the older participants were able to maintain stability during subsequent exposure to the conflicting stimuli.

CHANGES IN SOMATOSENSORY, VISUAL, AND VESTIBULAR SYSTEMS WITH AGE

As was mentioned in the previous section, information from somatosensory, visual, and vestibular systems may contribute to balance control to different extents depending on the nature of the environmental context. In young adults this redundancy of postural sensory information gives a large safety margin to ensure postural stability. It also allows the nervous system to deal effectively with environmental contexts that cause inappropriate response cues from one system by suppressing these cues and allowing inputs from other systems to elicit appropriate, though in some cases delayed, postural adjustments. This section will examine the literature on changes in these three sensory systems with age in order to determine if deterioration in these systems has caused the redundancy of sensory information normally available in young adults to be decreased in the older adult.

Research on age-related changes in cutaneous sensation and proprioception shows increased thresholds of excitability of these systems in the older adult (Birren, 1947; Whanger & Wang, 1974; Kokmen, Bossemeyer & Williams, 1978). Whanger & Wang (1974) compared the vibratory thresholds at the wrist and knee of three groups of subjects: young controls (ages 15–45 years), normal older adults (groups ranging in age from 70 to 90 years), and older psychiatric patients (groups aged from 65 to 95 years). They noted that the vibratory threshold was elevated in both older groups compared with the young controls. Their data indicate that the knee showed vibratory thresholds of 2.5 microns for the young adults and 19 microns average for the older adult groups. When the patients were separated from the older control subjects, the normal older adults showed thresholds of about 16 microns over all age groups. Seventy-year-olds showed thresholds of 14 microns and subsequent groups of subjects showed gradual declines in sensitivity to 18 microns by age 90. The authors mentioned that they had attempted to measure thresholds at the ankle joint but found a high number of subjects unable to perceive any vibration there. Since the ankle joint is one of the major axes of postural sway, one would expect that these losses would strongly affect balance abilities. After examining the relationship of pathology and nutritional factors to elevation of vibratory threshold in the elderly, the authors concluded that threshold elevation had some relation to aging per se but that it was much more related to disease and nutritional factors.

Researchers examining age-related declines in joint position sense at the knee (Skinner, Barrack & Cook, 1984) found significant deterioration with increasing age for both detecting motion and reproducing passive knee position when slow rates of knee extension were used. However, earlier studies by Kokmen et al. (1978) that explored changes in the metacarpophalangeal and metatarsophalangeal joints showed loss of joint sensation in the older adult at low but not high rates of movement. Since the difference was lost at high speeds, the investigators concluded that position sense does not vary with age. Brocklehurst, Robertson & James-Groom (1982) compared sway in 151 frail elderly (examined in residential care facilities and aged 65–85+ years) and 5 young adults and correlated sway with impairment in vibration sensitivity, proprioception, visual and vestibular function. They reported a close relationship between increased sway and impaired vibration sense in the legs but no correlation between sway and proprioceptive, visual, or vestibular impairment. They stated that the lack of correlation with proprioception may have reflected the imprecision of the test they used, since vibration sense was affected significantly. They believe that the lack of correlation between either visual or vestibular deterioration and sway confirmed the place of these senses as secondary in the maintenance of posture. They noted that vestibular impairment was found in only 6% of elderly subjects, by measurement with a tilt test (response of the body to a 20-degree tilt of the surface on which the person was sitting).

It is of interest that the exclusion criteria for pathology in this study were very limited: subjects were acceptable if they were sufficiently mentally aware to provide a reliable history, able to stand and walk independently, and had no obvious lower limb paralysis. A past history of stroke, fracture, or hip joint replacement was accepted as long as the subject fulfilled the above criteria.

Although an age-dependent loss of sensory neurons and interneurons has generally been shown within the auditory system, a similar degeneration of vestibular cell neurons has been denied by researchers (until recently) and explained as being due to the fact that these neurons are phylogenetically older structures (Mulch & Petermann, 1979). However the studies of Rosenhall & Rubin (1975) and Bergstrom (1973a, b) have shown that there is an age-dependent progressive reduction in the number of both sensory cells and nerve fibers in the peripheral vestibular system in individuals over the age of 40 years. They noted that the reduction is most pronounced in the ampullary crests, where it may reach up to 40% in individuals beyond 70 years of age. In the maculae the reduction may be as much as 20%. Bergstrom noted that the reduction is not only quantitative but also qualitative: the remaining nerve fibers become thinner with age.

The literature on age-related changes in vestibular function as evaluated by clinical tests contains a number of contradictory reports. Researchers using caloric nystagmus tests to investigate vestibular function have found everything from reduced excitability (Arslan, 1957), or normal function (Forgacs, 1957) to hyperexcitability (Schoder, 1973; Mulch & Petermann, 1979). Bruner & Norris (1971) explain this discrepancy in the following way. They theorize that peak responsivity occurs in middle age followed by hyporeactivity in senility. Thus they conclude that the vestibular system age decrement is not like that of hearing, which shows a linear decline in function but rather appears first irritative before becoming depressed. They offer a hypothesis for this process. They propose that the inhibitory control of nystagmus in the reticular formation is reduced, due to either pathology or a reduction in central neural excitability early in the aging process, causing heightened sensitivity. This is followed later by reduced peripheral sensitivity, giving rise to hyporeactivity in the very old.

Though there have been many studies on the effects of age on vestibulo-ocular reflexes, very little work has focused on the investigation of vestibulospinal reflex changes in the older adult. Graybiel & Fregly (1966) and Fregly & Graybiel (1970) examined 1,055 healthy adults aged 16 to 60 years with an ataxia battery and showed that there was a significant deterioration in function beyond the age of 40. Mulch & Petermann (1979) cite these results as indicating a decline in vestibulospinal function. However, it is difficult to conclude that these behavioral changes were due solely to changes in vestibulospinal function and not to impairment in somatosensory or visual function.

Research analyzing changes in visual sensitivity with aging has shown that there is a significant deterioration in spatial sensitivity with age (Sekuler, Hutman & Owsley, 1980). Sekuler and his colleagues have shown that older adults have diminished ability to see large and intermediate size targets. At the lowest spatial frequencies tested, the older observers needed three times as much contrast as the young subjects in order to see vertical gratings. The older adults were also less sensitive in their ability to detect slowly moving targets. Other research (Begbie, 1966; Leibowitz, Rodemer & Dichgans, 1979; Amblard & Carblanc, 1980) has shown that visually guided behaviors such as locomotion and postural stabilization depend on low frequency visual information mediated by peripheral visual inputs, and thus it is possible that certain postural stabilization problems could be due to this diminished visual sensitivity to low spatial frequencies.

If peripheral visual pathways show deterioration with age, and vision is used to help stabilize balance, one might hypothesize significant differences exist between young and older adults in postural tasks using peripheral visual cues for balance control. Recent research on postural control has addressed this problem (Woollacott et al., 1988; Manchester et al., in press). In the studies available visual inputs to the subjects were manipulated by the use of special goggles that limited vision to (1) central vision only, (2) peripheral vision only, or (3) visual feedback unrelated to body sway (translucent goggles were worn). Trials under these conditions were compared to those with eyes open (with full visual information) and with eyes closed. Thirteen young adults (mean age of 24 years) and thirteen older adults (mean age of 69 years) were tested with anterior or posterior platform movements as described in electromyographic studies above. When latencies of postural muscle responses of the leg muscles of older and younger adults were compared, no significant differences were found for any individual visual condition, including peripheral vision, indicating that if there is deterioration in peripheral visual pathways, it does not affect the latency of postural muscle responses. However, when visual conditions were combined, older adults showed significantly longer postural muscle response onsets than younger adults for the tibialis anterior muscle for platform displacements causing posterior sway.

   Though the older adults did not show significantly different latencies of postural responses when compared to young adults in the different visual conditions, they did show a difference in their ability to balance in these conditions. When the losses of balance in the two age groups were compared in different visual conditions, it was found that 15% of the older adult group lost balance more than three times in sixty trials, whereas none of the younger subjects lost balance more than three times. In addition, older adults lost balance most often with only central vision (38% of the time) or with eyes closed (24% of the time), whereas the younger adults lost balance equally often across visual conditions. Since these two conditions both eliminated peripheral visual cues, it suggests that older adults rely more on peripheral vision than young adults and that absence of peripheral vision leads to a greater number of falls.

   In addition, aging subjects showed a significant increase in postural responses in the antagonist leg muscles when compared to young adults. Whereas agonist muscles in a postural response synergy were activated with almost equal frequency in old and young adults (responses were elicited in all trials for 62% of the younger subjects and for 70% of the older subjects), antagonist muscles were activated much more frequently in older adults than in younger adults (46% of older adults showed antagonist activity on every trial for forward sway perturbations, whereas only 22% of young adults showed this activity).

   In order to determine if pathological changes in nervous system function contributed to the increased loss of balance and increased latencies of muscle responses in the older adult group, a neurological exam was performed on each of the older adults. Two subjects out of the thirteen older adults showed sensory or motor deficits (diagnoses by the neurologist as clumsiness and slight residual hemiparesis). When these two subjects were excluded from the data analysis, young and older adult groups showed much smaller differences in the number of falls and in postural muscle response latencies.

POSTURAL-VOLUNTARY RESPONSE INTERACTIONS

Many studies on voluntary reaction time have shown that there is a slowing of fast reaction time movements with age (Welford, 1977, 1982). Since postural stability also shows deterioration in the older adult and since postural muscles are often activated before voluntary movements are initiated in order to compensate in advance for any change in equilibrium caused by the movement (Belen'kii et al., 1967; Bouisett and Zattara, 1981), it could be hypothesized that slowing of reaction times for voluntary responses is caused by deterioration in the postural control system.

Research on postural and voluntary response interactions in quadrupeds has shown that the organization of the feedforward activation of postural muscles is specific to the movement, which indicates a central organization of the responses (Gahery & Massion, 1981). It has been proposed that a central command system links the anticipatory postural adjustment and the prime mover muscle activation and that the command is organized at the level of the association cortex, basal ganglia, and neocerebellum while the associated postural pattern is organized in the bulbospinal postural circuits (Massion, 1984).

Man'kovskii et al. (1980) attempted to determine if this linkage between postural and voluntary control systems deteriorates in the older adult by comparing anticipatory postural responses in younger and older adult groups during a variety of voluntary movements. In one of their experimental conditions the participants were requested to make a flexion movement of their leg at the knee while maintaining stance on the contralateral leg. When the subjects were asked to move as quickly as possible, the older adults showed a significant increase in the onset latency of the postural muscles, which causes a significant decrease in the length of time between activation of postural and voluntary muscles. The authors suggested that the delayed postural muscle response latency caused instability in the performance of the task. However, they noted that it was possible for this movement to be performed confidently when executed more slowly. They concluded that older adults perform these tasks normally, but more slowly than young adults in order to obtain optimal conditions for the maintenance of posture.

In order to determine if the slowing of postural responses seen by Man'kovskii and colleagues was associated with inefficient postural muscle response organization, as had been noted with postural responses to external threats to balance, Inglin & Woollacott (1988) compared the muscle responses of young (mean age 26 years) and older (mean age 71 years) adults on a simple and a complex reaction time task. The task consisted of pushing or pulling on a handle at chest height while standing on a platform. Surface electromyographic responses were recorded from the biceps (B) and triceps (Tr) muscles of the arm, which were the prime movers in the task, and from the postural muscles of the leg: gastrocnemius (G), tibialis anterior (TA), hamstrings (H), and quadriceps (Q). Illumination of a reaction time (RT) board with two light-emitting diodes (LEDs) placed in front of the subject was the signal for arm movement. Muscle response latencies were measured for four RT conditions: push simple RT, pull simple RT, push complex RT, and pull complex RT. In the simple RT condition, subjects were given advance information on movement direction consisting of illumination of the top LED for push or the bottom LED for pull trials, which prepared the subjects for the following response signal. In the complex RT condition, subjects were given no advance information on movement direction but simply a warning signal consisting of the illumination of both LEDs.

Previous research on young adults (Cordo & Nashner, 1982) has demonstrated that when a subject is asked to pull on a handle while standing the G muscle of the leg is activated consistently before the B muscle of the arm. Similarly, when the subject is asked to push on a handle, the TA muscle of the leg is activated before the Tr muscle of the arm. The activation of the leg muscle serves to compensate in advance for the change in the center of gravity caused by the handle pull. In young adults in the present study latencies of the G and B were 190 ± 45 msec and 260 ± 97 msec, respectively, for simple RT pull arm movements. Latencies of TA and Tr were 161 ± 35 msec and 249 ± 90 msec, respectively, for push movements. In comparing responses of older and young adults for these two movements, there was an increase in the onset latency of postural muscles for the older adult group (G: 217 ± 63 msec for pull; TA: 234 ± 76 msec for push). However, the increase in postural response latencies in older adults of 27 msec for G was nonsignificant, whereas that of 73 msec for TA was significant ($p <$ .002) for the simple RT task (see Table 7–1). These data show an interesting aging effect previously noted for postural responses to external threats to balance: a bias in aging effects on the flexor (TA) versus the extensor (G) muscles of the ankle. The data support the similarity of organization of postural adjustments to both focal move-

TABLE 7-1

Mean muscle-onset latencies (in msec) in young and older adults for simple and complex reaction-time movements

| Muscle[a] | Mean Latency (SD) | | Difference | Level of Significance |
	Young	Old		
Simple reaction time				
Push				
TA	161 ± 35	234 ± 76	73	$p < .002$
Tr	249 ± 90	372 ± 135	123	$p < .006$
Pull				
G	190 ± 45	217 ± 63	27	$p < .220$
Bi	260 ± 97	379 ± 133	119	
Complex reaction time				
Push				
TA	246 ± 36	316 ± 76	70	$p < .003$
Tr	345 ± 103	497 ± 141	152	$p < .002$
Pull				
G	269 ± 45	331 ± 78	62	$p < .018$
Bi	371 ± 45	544 ± 148	173	$p < .003$

[a]TA=tibialis anterior; Tr=triceps; G=gastrocnemius; Bi=biceps

ments and external perturbations. We also found a large increase in the onset latencies of the older adult group for activation of the prime mover muscles of the arm (B: 379 ± 133 msec; Tr: 372 ± 135 msec). Thus there were increases in latency for the prime mover muscles in the older adults of 119 msec for B (significant: $p < .015$) and 123 msec for Tr (significant: $p < .006$).

Results of trials with complex RT movements showed significant increases in latency for both postural (G: $p < .018$; TA: $p < .003$) and voluntary (B: $p < .003$; Tr: $p < .002$) muscles for the older compared to the younger adults (see Table 7-1) for both push and pull movements.

However, as in the simple RT task, the onset latencies of the voluntary muscles were slowed to a greater degree than those of the postural muscles.

Thus, differences in onset times between postural and voluntary (prime mover) muscles of the young and older adults show an additional increase in slowing of voluntary response in the older adult beyond that due to slowing of the activation of postural responses. This increase in voluntary muscle response latency resulted in an increase in the time between postural and voluntary responses in older adults.

These results may be interpreted in two ways: (1) the voluntary control system may be affected to a greater degree than the postural control system with age, limiting the speed of voluntary movement, or (2) it is possible that deterioration of the postural control system limits the speed of initial stabilization and thus delays the onset of the voluntary response. Zattara & Bouisset (1986) have shown that, in young adults given increased biomechanical requirements for the movement, voluntary movement will be initiated only after postural stabilization has occurred. These results support the second interpretation. Interestingly, young adults initiated postural adjustments on the basis of their perception of the biomechanical consequences of the forthcoming voluntary movement. Thus, older adults may perceive movement execution in this experimental paradigm as more destabilizing than younger adults.

These results have both similarities and differences with those published by Man'kovskii et al. (1980). Both studies noted increases in latencies of postural and voluntary muscle responses of the older adult group. However, Man'kovskii and his colleagues found a larger increase in the latency of the postural muscle response than in the voluntary muscle response for older adults. As a result, the latency between postural and voluntary muscle response onset was greatly reduced in the older adult group. In contrast, the present study found a greater increase in the voluntary muscle latency than in postural response latency in older adults, creating an increased latency between postural and voluntary response onsets. This could be due to a difference in task requirements: Man'kovskii used a leg-lifting task, whereas Inglin & Woollacott (1988) used an arm-movement task. This is supported by the fact that Frank et al. (1987) reported a similar increase in postural and voluntary response latencies to that of Inglin & Woollacott when asking older adults to perform either arm raises or arm pulls.

In addition to these latency differences between young and older adults, Inglin & Woollacott found differences in muscle response sequence activation patterns. The younger subjects showed a higher percentage of trials with the more classical postural response synergy, or distal-to-proximal muscle response activation on the same (anterior or posterior) body aspect for both push and pull arm movements (Fig. 7–2A). Thus, for push arm movements the activation sequence was tibialis anterior, quadriceps, triceps. However, older adults showed a slightly higher percentage of trials in which they exhibited a distal-to-proximal muscle response activation on opposite body aspects (Fig. 7–2B). Thus, for push arm movements the activation sequence was tibialis anterior, hamstrings, triceps. Therefore, distal-to-proximal postural muscle response activation appears to be altered in many older adults during RT arm movements.

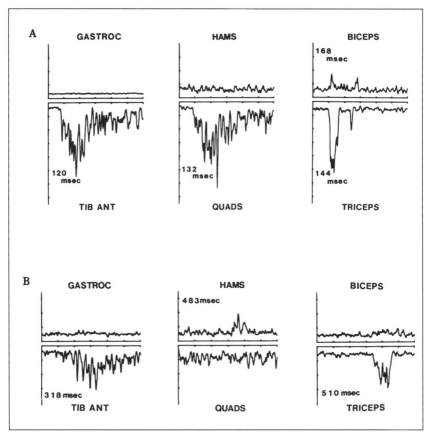

Fig. 7–2. EMG response patterns for push arm movement trials. A: most common pattern seen in young adults (Tib. Ant., Quads., Triceps); B: most common pattern seen in older adults (Tib. Ant., Hams., Triceps).

There were also changes in the temporal activation of muscle response sequences in the aging adult. For push arm movements young adults most often activated the muscle response sequence TA, Q, Tr, giving a distal-to-proximal postural response activation prior to activation of the prime mover muscle. Older adults more often activated the muscle response sequence TA, Tr, Q, activating the proximal postural muscle in a feedback manner to stabilize posture after activation of the prime mover. However, for pull arm movements, older adults more often showed the distal-to-proximal postural muscle stabilization prior to activation of the prime mover, thus using feedforward activation. It is of interest that Bouisset & Zattara (1981) and Lee (1980) found variations in the temporal pattern of muscle response sequence activation in a similar paradigm with young adults. They attribute these variations to differences in the initial posture of the subjects and in differences in individual strategy. Thus, variations in muscle response sequence between the young and older adults may be a result of differences in initial posture and the strategy of the individual.

SUMMARY AND CONCLUSIONS

If one looks superficially at the results of these studies, it may be concluded that aging significantly affects the neural mechanisms underlying postural control, with both behavioral and electromyographic studies indicating deterioration in balance control mechanisms in the older adult. Behavioral studies reveal increased sway during quiet stance in older compared to young adults with vision present, with the effect being amplified with vision absent and in novel balance tasks (Sheldon, 1963; Hasselkus and Shambes, 1975). Electromyographic studies indicate small but significant increases in onset latencies and in temporal organization of postural muscle responses in older compared to young adults when subjects are given external threats to balance. In addition, older adults have more difficulty balancing when sensory inputs contributing to balance control are reduced so that they have less redundancy of sensory information. Thus, when both somatosensory and visual inputs are made incongruent with postural sway, the older adult shows significantly increased sway compared to the young adult, and many older adults lose balance completely (Woollacott et al., 1986, 1988).

Studies on individual sensory systems that contribute to balance control also show significant deterioration in vibration sense, joint position sense, and visual and vestibular sensory systems in the older adult (Whanger & Wang, 1974; Kokmen et al., 1978; Skinner et al., 1984; Rosenhall, 1973; Sekuler et al., 1980).

In addition, studies on the feedforward activation of the postural control system to stabilize in advance for changes in the center of mass during voluntary movements have shown that older adults activate postural muscles significantly more slowly than young adults. These effects are magnified in complex reaction time conditions as compared to simple reaction time conditions and are more apparent in flexor muscles of the ankle joint than in extensors (Man'kovskii et al., 1980; Woollacott et al., 1988).

However, one may also examine the research in this area at a different level, in order to begin to weigh the number of studies supporting either of the following hypotheses concerning brain function and aging: (1) that there is a linear decline in nervous system function over time, with various symptoms of deterioration appearing in all individuals as neuron numbers in a specific brain area decrease below the threshold for normal function, or (2) that the nervous system continues to function at a high level until death, unless there is a specific catastrophe or the individual contracts a specific disease, which then causes a rapid decline in function in a specific brain area. If we attempt to correlate the studies that may have included individuals with pathology with those showing deterioration in behavior or nervous system function in the older adult, we may be able to differentiate between the two hypotheses.

As noted earlier, Sheldon's study on increased sway in the older adult mentions that there were great individual variations in the older adult population he used and that this may have been due to the presence of subjects with slight degrees of pathological change in the nervous system in his population pool, because of his effort to obtain a random sample of older adults. Fernie also notes, in his study attempting to correlate extent of sway with frequency of falling in the older adult, that his use of institutionalized elderly may have biased his results. He found that this population pool showed much more sway than non-institutionalized elderly who had been studied previously. If it is assumed that institutionalization implies the presence of some form of pathology, we may conclude that it is thus pathology, and not aging per se, that causes increased sway and increased liability to fall.

Studies on changes in somatosensory function often showed similar conclusions. Whanger & Wang (1974), in noting the increase in vibratory threshold among the elderly, concluded that the increase may have some relation to aging per se but that it was much more related to disease and nutritional factors. Brocklehurst et al. (1982), in concluding that there was a relationship between increased sway and impaired vibration sense, also noted that their exclusion criteria for pathology were very limited, and thus their population probably contained many individuals with pathology. In addition, in the study by Woollacott et al. (1988), when two subjects with neurological deficits were excluded from the data analysis, young and older adult groups showed much smaller differences in the number of falls and in the onset latencies of the postural muscle responses.

Though many of the other studies do not mention the use of neurological exams to screen for individuals with pathology, and thus it is hard to determine if such individuals may have been present in the population pool, the authors of one study, Gabell & Nayak (1984), meticulously prescreened their population pool. Theirs is also the only study showing a lack of any significant difference between the performance of their younger and older adults. They examined the variability of gait in normal young and older adults and, in finding no differences, concluded that any increase in gait variability with aging is not normal but is due to a perhaps undetected pathology.

Thus, we begin to see that the significant deterioration in balance control mechanisms in the older adult in the majority of studies presented could be attributed to the presence of some degree of pathology. However, it is difficult to ascertain the cause of the pathological changes seen in these older adults. In order to clearly differentiate between the two hypotheses concerning aging, one needs to determine whether pathology was induced by external agents or accidents, or was simply due to loss of neuron numbers with age. Davies (1987) believes this differentiation may be achieved by looking at neuron function in the very old. If these adults show significantly improved function compared to their slightly younger cohorts, he argues, it is evidence to support the second hypothesis, since the older adults with pathology have been eliminated from the population pool, leaving only their healthy counterparts with normal nervous system function. He has already shown evidence to support the second hypothesis for aging and Alzheimer's disease. It is hoped that future research in the area of postural control will be able to contribute to the more complete examination of these hypotheses.

ACKNOWLEDGMENTS

This work was supported by a National Institute of Aging grant #5 R23 AG05317 to M. Woollacott.

REFERENCES

Amblard, B., & Carblanc, A. (1980). Role of foveal and peripheral visual information in maintenance of postural equilibrium in man. *Perception and Motor Skills, 51*, 903–12.

Arslan, M. (1957). The senescence of the vestibular apparatus. *Pract. Otorhinolaryngol, 19,* 475–83.

Begbie, G. (1966). The effects of alcohol and varying amounts of visual information on a balancing test. *Ergonomics, 9,* 325–33.

Belin'kii, V. Y.; Gurfinkel, V. S.; & Pal'tsev, Y. I. (1967). Elements of control of voluntary movements. *Biofizika, 12,* 135–41.

Bergstrom, B. (1973a). Morphology of the vestibular nerve. II. The number of myelinated vestibular nerve fibers in man at various ages. *Acta Otolaryngologia, 76,* 173–79.

Bergstrom, B. (1973b). Morphology of the vestibular nerve. III. Analysis of the caliber of the myelinated vestibular nerve fibers in man at various ages. *Acta Otolaryngologia, 76,* 331–38.

Birren, J. E. (1947). Vibratory sensitivity in the aged. *Journal of Gerontology, 2,* 267–68.

Bouisett, S., & Zattara, M. (1981). A sequence of postural movements precede voluntary movement. *Neuroscience Letters, 22,* 263–70.

Brocklehurst, J. C.; Robertson, D.; & James-Groom, P. (1982). Clinical correlates of sway in old age: Sensory modalities. *Age and Aging, 11,* 1–10.

Bruner, A., & Norris, T. W. (1971). Age-related changes in caloric nystagmus. *Acta Otolaryngologia,* Supplement 282.

Cordo, P., & Nashner, L. M. (1982). Properties of postural adjustments associated with rapid arm movements. *Journal of Neurophysiology, 47,* 287–302.

Davies, P. (1987). Aging and Alzheimer's disease: New light on old problems. Paper presented at Neuroscience Society Annual Meeting, New Orleans, LA.

Fernie, G. R.; Gryfe, C. I.; Holliday, P. J.; & Llewellyn, A. (1982). The relationship of postural sway in standing to the incidence of falls in geriatric subjects. *Age and Aging, 11,* 11–16.

Forgacs, P. (1957). The cochlea and vestibular function at advanced age. *Full Orr-Gege Gy, 1,* 5–10.

Frank, J. S.; Patla, A. E.; & Brown, J. E. (1987). Anticipatory postural adjustments in adults: Aging characteristics. *Proceedings: NASPSPA Meetings, Vancouver, B. C., Canada.*

Fregly, A. R., & Graybiel, A. (1970). Labyrinthine defects as shown by ataxia and caloric tests. *Acta Otolaryngologica, 69,* 216–22.

Gabell, A., & Nayak, U. S. L. (1984). The effect of age on variability in gait. *Journal of Gerontology, 39,* 662–66.

Gahery, Y., & Massion, J. (1981). Coordination between posture and movement. *Trends in Neuroscience, 4,* 199–202.

Graybiel, A., & Fregly, A. R. (1966). A new quantitative ataxia test battery. *Acta Otolaryngologia, 61,* 292–312.

Guimaraes, R. M., & Isaacs, B. (1980). Characteristics of the gait in old people who fall. *Int. Rehabil. Med., 2,* 177–80.

Hasselkus, B. R., & Shambes, G. (1975). Aging and postural sway in women. *Journal of Gerontology, 30,* 661–67.

Imms, F. J., & Edholm, O. G. (1981). Studies of gait and mobility in the elderly. *Age and Aging, 10,* 147–56.

Inglin, B., & Woollacott, M. H. (1988). Anticipatory postural adjustments associated with reaction time arm movements: A comparison between young and old. *Journal of Gerontology, 43,* M105–13.

Kokmen, E.; Bossemeyer, R. W.; & Williams, W. J. (1978). Quantitative evaluation of joint motion sensation in an aging population. *Journal of Gerontology, 33*, 62–67.

Lee, W. A. (1980). Anticipatory control of postural and task muscles during rapid arm flexion. *Journal of Motor Behavior, 12*, 185–96.

Leibowitz, H. W.; Rodemer, C. S.; & Dichgans, J. (1979). The independence of dynamic spatial orientation from luminance and refractive error. *Perception & Psychophysics, 25*, 75–79.

Manchester, D.; Woollacott, M.; & Marin, O. (in press). Visual, vestibular and somatosensory contributions to balance control in the older adult. *Journal of Gerontology.*

Man'kovskii, N. B.; Mints, A. Y.; & Lysenyuk, V. P. (1980). Regulation of the preparatory period for complex voluntary movement in old and extreme old age. *Human Physiology (Moscow), 6*, 46–50.

Massion, J. (1984). Postural changes accompanying voluntary movements: Normal and pathological aspects. *Human Neurobiology, 2*, 261–67.

Mulch, G., & Petermann, W. (1979). Influence of age on results of vestibular function tests. *Annals of Otology, Rhinology and Otolaryngology, 88*, 1–17.

Murray, M. P.; Kory, R. C.; & Clarkson, B. H. (1969). Walking patterns in healthy old men. *Journal of Gerontology, 24*, 169–78.

Rosenhall, U. (1973). Degenerative patterns in the aging human vestibular neuroepithelia. *Acta Otolaryngologica (Stockholm), 76*, 208–20.

Rosenhall, U., & Rubin, W. (1975). Degenerative changes in the human vestibular sensory epithelia. *Acta Otolaryngologica, 79*, 67–81.

Schoder, H. J. (1973). Zur Reaktionsweise des Vestibularsystems im Alter. *Verkehrsmed Ihre Grenzgeb, 20*, 180–83.

Sekuler, R.; Hutman, L.; & Owsley, C. (1980). Human aging and spatial vision. *Science, 209*, 1255–56.

Sheldon, J. H. (1963). The effect of age on the control of sway. *Geront. Clin., 5*, 129–38.

Skinner, H. B.; Barrack, R. L.; & Cook, S. (1984). Age-related decline in proprioception. *Clinical Orthopaedics and Related Research, 184*, 208–11.

Welford, A. T. (1977). Motor performance. In J. E. Birren and K. W. Schaie (Eds.), *Handbook of the psychology of aging.* New York: Van Nostrand Reinhold.

Welford, A. T. (1982). Motor skills and aging. In J. Mortimer, F. J. Pirozzolo & G. Maletta (Eds.), *The aging motor system.* New York: Praeger.

Whanger, A., & Wang, H. S. (1974). Clinical correlates of the vibratory sense in elderly psychiatric patients. *Journal of Gerontology, 29*, 39–45.

Woollacott, M. H.; Shumway-Cook, A.; & Nashner, L. M. (1986). Aging and posture control: Changes in sensory organization and muscular coordination. *International Journal of Aging and Human Development, 23*, 97–114.

Woollacott, M. H.; Inglin, B.; & Manchester, D. (1988). Response preparation and posture control in the older adult. In J. Joseph (Ed.), *Central determinants of age-related declines in motor function.* New York: New York Academy of Sciences.

Zattara, M. & Bouisset, S. (1986). Chronometric analysis of the posturo-kinetic programming of voluntary movement. *Journal of Motor Behavior, 18*, 215–23.

8

Changes in Locomotion in the Aging Adult

Rebecca Craik

The ability to move about on one's own is a major prerequisite to independence and is of great importance to persons of all age groups. Although usually taken for granted by young healthy adults, human gait requires the coordinated control of nearly every segment of the musculoskeletal system and is, therefore, susceptible to alteration when one or more of the many components of the locomotor system changes its function.

The aging population is particularly susceptible to certain pathological conditions that substantially alter gait function. The most prevalent of these conditions include cardiopulmonary disorders, arthritis, stroke, and diabetes. In addition to the clearly definable changes in gait which accompany these and other pathological conditions, subtle but significant alterations in gait function occur as part of the aging process itself.

The need for studies on posture and gait in the elderly becomes more critical as the number of elderly within our population grows. There are currently over 2.5 million people 65 years and older, which represents an eight-fold increase in this population in the past eighty years (U.S. Senate, 1986; Woodruff & Birren, 1983). By the year 2020, 15% of the population will be 65 years or older. The responsibility of providing care for this population challenges professionals to seek a better understanding of the process of aging to appropriately evaluate, treat, and care for the older individual.

Attempts to clarify the relationship between aging and walking date back to at least 1940 and continue today. Disparate findings exist from the various studies examining the relationship between age and walking performance. Several descriptive gait studies detail age-related differences in walking patterns, but other investigators report no difference in walking behavior related to age. The results of the latter studies are surprising in view of reports that the aging neuromusculoskeletal system demonstrates a slower and more variable voluntary response time (Benton, 1977; Berlin & Wallace, 1975), de-creased muscle strength (Larsson, Grimby & Karlsson, 1979), decreased range of motion (Walker et al., 1984), and decreased musculotendinous flexibility (Aloia, 1981). The conflicting opinions on age-dependent changes in walking performance may arise from different test paradigms and the selection of different gait variables.

This chapter will focus on research describing age-related changes in walking and speculate on the relationship between these changes, walking disorders, and falls in the elderly. Also considered will be the effect of experimental methodology, including the definition of gait variables and their measurement, on the interpretation of results from gait studies in the elderly.

GAIT AND AGING

A complete analytical description of the components of ambulation requires simultaneous recording of multiple kinematic, kinetic, and elec-tromyographic variables. However, most investigators select certain variables to describe gait. A description of the most commonly cited variables can be found in several sources. The reader can refer to Craik & Oatis (1985), LeVeau (1984), and Winter (1987) for additional information.

The primary investigative approach to the study of age effects on walking has been a descriptive one. If a hypothesis was proposed, it appears to have been that there is a difference in the walking pattern of young and older persons.

CLINICAL DESCRIPTION OF WALKING DISORDERS

Ambulation is the efficient translation of the center of gravity through space, which requires the coordinated control of nearly every segment of the neuromusculoskeletal system (Inman, Ralston & Todd, 1981). The ability of a person to demonstrate a range of walking speeds is indicative of "normal" function. People appear to select a speed that is consistent with a given task—for example, window shopping may require a slow stroll whereas getting to a bus on time may require a faster gait. The ability to demonstrate this behavior requires an intact nervous system and a structural system with the needed degrees of freedom.

A number of so-called gait disorders ascribed to age alone are noted in the older clinical literature (Azar & Lawton, 1964; Barron, 1967; Critchley, 1948; Steinberg, 1966). The following walking pat-terns have been described as age-related gait disorders: (1) *apraxia of gait*, which is characterized as a slow, halting, short-stepped, shuffling or sliding gait; (2) *hypokinetic-hypertonic syndrome,* a slow and deliberate gait but without the "magnetic" attraction of the feet for the floor typical of gait apraxia; (3) *marche a petit pas,* consisting of small, rapid, shuffling steps at first followed by a slow, cautious gait, which is unsteady due to generalized limb weakness; (4) *vestibular dysfunction gait,* wherein balance difficulties occur only upon turning; and (5) *impaired proprioception gait,* characterized by a cautious gait, frequent missteps, and a tendency to watch the feet.

Spielberg (1940) was apparently the first investigator to systematically observe changes in gait which result from aging. He described three age-related stages in the decline of walking performance. Stage I (60–72 years of age) included a slower walking velocity, shortened steps, lower cadence, less vertical excursion of the center of gravity, and disturbed coordination between the upper and lower extremities. In Stage II (72–86 years of age) the normal arm-leg synergy was lost and an overproduction of unwanted movements appeared. The final stage of performance decline, Stage III (86–104 years of age), was typified by rapid disintegration of the gait pattern with arrhythmical stepping patterns. Stages II and III are reminiscent of the descriptions of the clinical gait disorders detailed above.

The hypothesis that the gait disorders just described are due to age alone is a tentative one. At the time these walking disorders were identified the effect on motor performance of such clinical disorders as multi-infarct dementia, normal pressure hydrocephalus, and Parkinson's disease had not been identified (Adams, 1984). It is unclear, therefore, if the walking disorders reflect age-related changes in walking or a combination of disease and age-related changes. The authors did not describe a detailed health screen for subjects, so the changes in walking behavior may reflect both aging and disease processes. Although Spielberg's Stages II and III are reminiscent of the other clinical walking disorders, the walking patterns are not consistent with descriptions from recent quantitative investigations of "healthy" older subjects. Therefore, though walking disorders such as *marche a petit pas* may be unique to older individuals because the disease producing this behavior is found primarily in older people, such walking disorders do not appear "typical" of the older healthy individual.

KINEMATIC DESCRIPTION OF WALKING

Footfall patterns. Ambulation can be viewed as two different subtasks, progression and "dynamic" postural control. A measure of progression is walking velocity, the result of all factors working to promote walking (Larsson, Odenrick, Sandland, Weitz & Oberg, 1980). Since walking velocity is the product of stride length and cadence, the three variables should be treated together.

Foot-contact patterns are the final outcome of the collective motions of all the major segments contributing to ambulation. The length and timing of each step indicate lower-extremity disability when patient data are compared to nonpatient data (Holden, Gill & Magliozzi, 1984). Thus, foot placement and temporal factors can indicate the integrity of the neuromusculoskeletal system. The results of reported studies in this section suggest that velocity, stride (or step) length, and cadence are sensitive enough to distinguish walking performance among subjects of various ages.

In two different studies Drillis (1961) and Molen (1973) studied footfall variables in naive pedestrians. In this approach large samples were examined without the constraint of the laboratory and accompanying instrumentation. Drillis (1961) observed 752 pedestrians walking on the sidewalk in New York City. Cadence and velocity were determined using a marked distance on the sidewalk. Step length was derived from the cadence and velocity variables. After each observation was made, the pedestrian was asked to report age, height, and weight. The whole sample of pedestrians walked an average of 1.46 m/sec (3.26 mph) with a mean cadence (step rate) of 1.9 steps per second (112.5 steps/min) and a mean step length of 76.3 cm (30.05 in). Optimal performance is commonly assumed to be a symmetrical foot-placement pattern within a velocity range of 1.2 to 1.5 m/sec and with a cadence of 1.6 to 2.0 steps/sec (100 to 120 steps/min) (Inman, Ralston & Todd, 1981). The subjects in the Drillis study were within this range, which suggests that there is face validity to the approach of observing walking behavior under nonlaboratory conditions.

Drillis (1961) stated that the age-related velocity decline observed in his results did not follow a natural exponential decay. Comparison between an exponential decay line and actual velocities selected by subjects over 45 years of age yields higher than predicted velocities for the older individuals. Drillis speculated that the higher velocities selected by the older subjects represent the individuals' "fight against aging."

Similar results to those reported by Drillis were obtained in the observation of 533 pedestrians in Amsterdam (Molen, 1973). Molen reported mean walking velocity for the 309 men as 1.39 m/sec with a mean step rate of 1.79 steps/sec and a mean step length of 77.4 cm. The 224 women walked an average of 1.27 m/sec with a cadence of 1.88

steps/sec and a step length of 67.1 cm. Such a sex-related difference in walking performance is reported consistently in gait-related research; in general, women are reported to maintain a combination of higher cadence and shorter step length.

Both Drillis and Molen reported an age-related trend in walking performance, although the statistical significance of the trend was not determined. As age increased (age range, 20–70 years), there was a decrease in walking velocity, step length, and step rate (Fig. 8–1). The slower velocity, shorter step length, and lower step rate described as features of the older subjects' walking pattern are consistent with Stage I of Spielberg's classification of walking in aging individuals (1940). The sex-related difference in walking appears to continue with age; compared to the older men, the older women demonstrated a slower velocity, higher cadence, and shorter step length (Molen, 1973).

The advantage of the investigative approach employed by Drillis and Molen was that walking was examined in the natural milieu without investigator intervention. On the other hand, constraints associated with these studies include the following: (1) the "healthfulness" of the subjects was not determined; (2) the age range of the samples was limited to 20 through 70 years; (3) the goal for walking was not examined, that is, walking to work compared to walking for window shopping may require different modes of progression; (4) stride length was derived from cadence and velocity rather than measured directly; (5) stride length was divided by two to determine step length, a method that assumes symmetry; and (6) the dynamic postural control of the walking behavior was not assessed.

Gabel, Johnston & Crowinshield (1979) reported age-related changes in foot-contact patterns from the study of twenty subjects in each of six age decades (30–90 years). An instrumented walkway was used to quantitate velocity, stride length, cadence, and swing time. The difference between this study and the Drillis and Molen studies is that subjects were screened and eliminated if they had any known disorders that would interfere with walking. In addition, the goal of walking was controlled; subjects were asked to walk at their free speed. In general, the results of the Gabel et al. study support the results reported by Drillis and Molen. The older subjects walked more slowly with a shorter stride length and a shorter swing time than the younger subjects. Cadence, however, was constant across the age ranges (Fig. 8–1). This finding is inconsistent with other literature and may be attributed to the relatively slow walking speeds selected by all of the subjects in the study. In addition, male versus female walking behavior was not addressed.

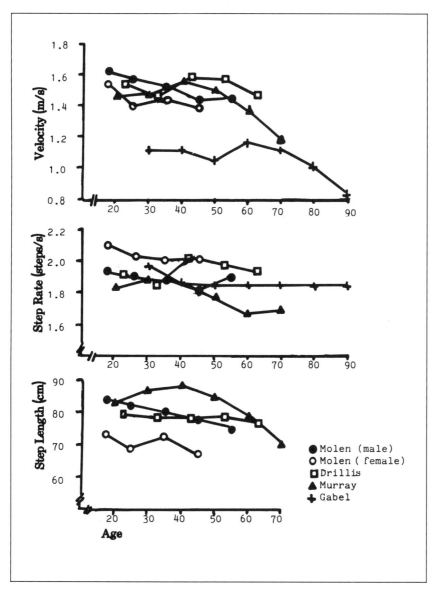

Fig. 8–1. Summary data from several authors. The general trend of the data is a diminished velocity, step rate (cadence), and step length with an increase in age. Note the variation in performance across studies. These data support the need to control for extraneous variables when the purpose of the experiment is limited to the effect of age on walking performance. These subjects represent a variety of heights, body weights, and lifestyles.

The studies just cited indicate a difference in footfall patterns between younger and older subjects but do not indicate why the differences occur. Foot-placement variables indicate the final outcome of the neuromusculoskeletal system, including compensatory mechanisms. Therefore, it is necessary to examine additional kinematic and kinetic data to try and understand why the older individual walks more slowly than the younger individual.

Descriptive laboratory studies. This section will summarize results from some of the well-known descriptive studies performed in a gait-analysis laboratory.

Murray was one of the first investigators to examine the effect of age on the intralimb events during gait under modern laboratory conditions. (Murray, Drought & Kory, 1964; Murray, 1967; Murray, Kory & Clarkson, 1969; Murray, Kory & Sepic, 1970). Multiple kinematic variables that were examined included spatial and temporal foot-contact patterns; sagittal excursion of the upper extremities, hip, knee, and ankle; excursion of the head and neck; and excursion of the pelvis and thorax in the transverse plane. The intent of the Murray series was to determine if changes in other kinematic variables accompanied changes in footfall patterns in the older individual. The purpose, then, was to compare the walking patterns of young and older individuals.

Footfall patterns of the subjects in the Murray series were similar to those already described, suggesting that the addition of instrumentation did not completely alter walking performances. Murray also measured base of support and the timing of various gait-cycle events. The first study of sixty males in five age groups (20–25, 30–35, 40–45, 50–55, and 60–65) revealed no systematic relationship between age and foot-contact measures (Murray, Drought & Kory, 1964). The men who were 60–65 years old, however, walked with shorter step lengths and wider foot angles than the younger men. The mean step lengths of the age group of 60–65 years old were significantly shorter ($p < .05$) than those of the 20–25-year-olds, and the 60–65-year-olds demonstrated a greater out-toeing than the younger subjects ($p < .01$).

A later study expanded the upper limits of the age range and included sixty-four men ranging in age from 20 to 87 years (Murray, Kory & Clarkson, 1969). The subjects were asymptomatic and were reported to have normal muscle strength and range of motion. Subjects over 65 years of age underwent physical examinations to rule out neurological deficits. The three older age groups (67–73, 74–80, 81–87) walked differently than the younger subjects. Walking speed and cadence were reduced, stride length was shorter, and the men beyond the age of 80 years showed greater out-toeing. The men beyond the age of 67 spent a longer time in the stance phase and a shorter time in the swing phase of the walking cycle. Since swing time for one limb is equivalent to single-support time in stance for the contralateral limb, the longer stance time comes from spending a longer time in the two double-support phases of the stance period.

Similar findings were reported when thirty women varying in age from 20 to 70 years were examined (Murray, Kory & Sepic, 1970). As mentioned previously, there is a sex-dependent difference in walking reported in the literature; the women compared to the men in the Murray series demonstrated a slower walking velocity, shorter step length, and higher cadence that was not related to stature or body weight. Compared to the younger women, the six older women in the 60–70-year age range had a slower walking velocity, shorter step length, longer stance, and shorter swing time.

Murray's kinematic analyses of body translation and joint rotation further characterize the walking behavior of the older compared to the younger individual. A summary of the data from the three Murray studies (1964, 1969, 1970) reveals *decreased* excursion amplitudes for the men over 67 years of age and the women over 60: vertical displacement of the head, sagittal rotation of the shoulder and elbow, transverse rotation of the pelvis, and sagittal rotation of the hip, knee, and ankle. The decreased knee excursion was noted during swing and there was less ankle plantarflexion at the end of stance. The only kinematic variable that demonstrated an *increased* displacement pattern was lateral displacement of the head.

Similar descriptive studies have been conducted by other investigators. Finley, Cody & Finizie (1969) compared walking between twelve younger women ($\bar{x}$ = 30 years) and twenty-three older women ($\bar{x}$ = 74 years). Finley et al. also examined patterns of muscle activity in the two groups. Subjects were screened to rule out conditions known to alter walking. Although inferential statistics were not used, the data for older women appeared to demonstrate similar relative changes in football to those reported by previous authors. Unlike the findings in the Murray study, there were no differences in the joint position or excursion in the hip, knee, ankle, or subtalus among subjects of different ages. A possible reason for the discrepancy in joint motions between the two studies is walking velocity, which will be discussed later. Amplitude of integrated electromyographic (EMG) activity in the rectus femoris, biceps femoris, tibialis anterior, gastrocnemius, and peroneus longus were examined at specific foot-contact events. The EMG was not normalized. In general, the older women demonstrated more EMG activity and different activation sequences among muscles than did the younger women. For example, at heel contact the older subjects demonstrated increased EMG activity in the tibialis anterior, gastrocnemius, and peroneus longus whereas the younger subjects demonstrated relatively less EMG activity in the tibialis anterior, minimal activity in the gastrocnemius, and no activity in the peroneus longus.

Some recent studies continue to use a descriptive approach to investigate the relationship between age and walking. Murray's kinematic findings are supported by Hageman & Blanke (1986), for example, who carefully controlled for anthropometric differences among the subjects. The sample consisted of thirteen young ($\bar{x}$ age = 24 years) and thirteen older ($\bar{x}$ age = 66 years) females. A health screen ruled out disabling conditions that might influence locomotion. Since body weight and stature affect walking behavior, selected subjects were within one standard deviation of the age-specific percentage of body fat, had symmetrical lower extremity lengths (< 1.9 cm between limbs), and older and younger subjects were matched for right limb lengths. Consistent with Murray's findings, the older women demonstrated a slower velocity ($p < .01$) and shorter step length ($p < .01$). Kinematic displacement variables examined were the vertical and lateral excursion of the center of gravity, pelvic obliquity, and pelvic, tibial, and ankle rotation. Age-related differences included a greater pelvic obliquity and diminished ankle excursion in the older women.

The studies just cited raise two important issues: (1) the need to be careful in generalizing to a population from a sample and (2) a limitation to the use of a descriptive model.

Hageman & Blanke compared their data to that of Murray and Finley and concluded that women walk faster today than their counterparts fifteen to twenty years ago. This conclusion is based on the finding that their subjects walked faster than did subjects reported in previous studies. Such a statement raises an issue that should be addressed. Data collected on small samples under unique laboratory conditions may be different from data collected from another laboratory and different from the "natural" performance that cannot be observed in a laboratory. The actual values derived from investigations at various laboratories cannot be compared unless measurement reliability is established. The Murray et al., Finley et al., and Hageman & Blanke studies may be used as a case in point. The gait of Murray's subjects was studied using interrupted light photography, which required the subjects to walk in darkness while a strobe light flashed. Finley et al. used a bilateral electrogoniometric assembly that was attached to the pelvis with a wide band and that included linked potentiometers centered at each of the lower extremity joints. The subjects walked on a runway that was elevated above the floor. Hageman & Blanke used high-speed cinematography under optimal lighting conditions. Small paper markers were placed on the points of anatomical interest and the only encumbrances were two 15.5 cm sticks mounted on bands that surrounded the hips and one calf. The combined free-speed velocity of the women in the Murray, Kory & Sepic study (1970) was an average of 1.3 m/sec; the older women in the Finley, Cody & Finizie study (1969) walked an average of 0.70 m/sec and the younger women walked an average of 0.82 m/sec. Hageman & Blanke's older and younger women walked an average of 1.3 and 1.6 m/sec, respectively. Differences in age, stature, leg length, or weight among women in the three studies do not account for the differences in walking velocity. Although Hageman & Blanke may be correct in assuming that women walk faster today, the validity of the statement is questioned in view of the diverse laboratory conditions. Therefore, though it is appropriate to compare *relative* change in walking performance across individuals from different laboratories, the validity of comparing actual data collected from different laboratories is questionable.

The other issue raised by the studies cited thus far is that descriptive studies do not lead to the development of a theory or model for the control or regulation of walking. The causal relationship among the gait variables presented in the Murray and Finley and Hageman & Blanke studies is, therefore, not known (Rozendal, 1986). In fact, the biomechanics of walking are not understood completely. For example, it cannot be concluded that the older subjects demonstrate a shortened step length because of less hip flexion. The diminished step length may relate to diminished pelvic rotation, decreased knee extension at heel strike, diminished plantarflexion at toe-off, or a combination of these factors. Examination of the coordination among the joints and EMG activity, and correlation of the timing of the EMG with foot contact events may help address this issue. A multiple regression or discriminant analysis may indicate the degree of relationship among gait variables and the amount of variance that is accounted for by these relationships.

Despite the lack of appropriate statistical analyses, examination of the age-related changes in walking leads to speculation on relationships among the gait variables. An image that emerges from the descriptive data is that the older individual is walking more slowly, with shorter step lengths and longer periods of double support to preserve stability.

During each stride the individual risks losing balance and then compensates for the loss of balance. Does the individual have difficulty maintaining this dynamic stability? Murray, Kory & Clarkson (1969) described the walking of older subjects as guarded or restrained. In addition to less excursion in the shoulders and elbows, the upper extremity of older individuals demonstrates a posture of relative shoulder hyperextension and elbow flexion which also implies guarded or careful walking. Finley et al. also suggest that the subjects in their study were trying to preserve stability. For example, the increased EMG activity seen in agonists and antagonists at heel strike may reflect an attempt to control progression and stability. Woollacott (1986) noted that older adults show a similar co-contraction of agonists and antagonists during postural stabilization and proposed that this strategy increases joint stiffness to compensate for decrements in other components of postural control.

In addition to the stability hypothesis, the descriptive studies just cited raise several other questions: (1) Why do the older subjects have an increased base of support? (2) Do the older individuals in the Murray series have increased lateral motion of the head because they have to shift the center of gravity further laterally within a wider base of support? (3) Is there a relationship among Murray's increased base of support and increased lateral excursion of the head, Hageman & Blanke's pelvic obliquity and hip abductor strength?

Descriptive studies have provided a range of normal expected behavior across ages, but they have not identified the necessary causal relationships. It is, therefore, not possible to say that weak musculature or slowed reaction time leads to diminished joint motion that results in slower walking velocity. The scientist does not gain insight into the effect of cellular changes on behavior. The clinician does not know where to intervene to improve behavior or if intervention will change behavior. Analysis of kinetic as well as kinematic variables may assist in the development of causal relationships. The development of a model of locomotion may also assist future investigators.

KINEMATIC AND KINETIC DESCRIPTION OF WALKING

Winter (1983) has used kinematic and kinetic variables to analyze the biomechanics of gait. Joint moments of force and joint power were derived from measures of joint rotation and ground-reaction force. Although sixteen young subjects ($\bar{x}$ age = 25.6 years) made up the sample of this study, some of the results will be presented to show the potential use of biomechanical analyses. There was a significant correlation ($r = .77$, $p < .0005$) between peak ankle power (normalized to body mass) and walking velocity during pushoff in the terminal phase of stance. Peak ankle power was also related to forward and upward acceleration of the pushoff limb. The acceleration of the pushoff limb was proposed as the primary cause of the subsequent swing of the lower limb. Therefore, an increase in the forward and upward acceleration of the pushoff limb should lead to a more forceful and rapidly swinging limb. The result of the rapid swing is a shorter swing period, commensurate increase in step length, and an increase in walking velocity. Decreased limb acceleration would result in longer swing time, shorter step length, and slower walking velocity. The advance of such an approach is that a model of behavior is presented which can be tested and proved or disproved (Olney & Winter, 1985). Until such investigations are completed, we can only speculate on the relationship among changes in EMG activity, body translation, joint rotation, and footfall patterns in the aged individual.

VELOCITY-DEPENDENT GAIT VARIABLES

The consensus thus far is that older subjects select a slower velocity than young subjects. The relevant question is, do the changes in the other gait variables produce slowed velocity, or alternatively, do the changes in the other gait variables naturally accompany a reduction in walking velocity regardless of age? The velocity-dependence of gait variables has been documented in younger individuals. The relationship between other gait variables and velocity depends on the velocity range examined. For example, cadence or step length and velocity demonstrate direct linear relationships when the range of velocities is within 0.8 through 2.0 m/sec. On the other hand, the relationships between cadence or step length and velocity are curvilinear when the lower end of the velocity range is extended to 0.3 m/sec. Single and double support are inversely proportional to velocity and demonstrate a curvilinear relationship when actual or "raw" time is used. These relationships become linear when single and double support are expressed as a percentage of stride time (Rosenrot, Wall & Charteris, 1980).

Joint rotation also diminishes with a decrease in velocity (Crowinshield, Brand & Johnston, 1978; Murray, 1967; Winter, 1983). Winter asked subjects to select a slow, natural, and fast pace, which resulted in a range of walking velocities between 2.0 and 0.7 m/sec. Knee flexion during stance and foot position at initial contact serve to illustrate the effect of velocity on joint rotation. As velocity decreased, the excursion from knee extension to flexion in early stance decreased. Mean excursion decreased from 24° to 20° and finally 14° for fast, natural, and slow walking, respectively. At foot contact and prior to the dorsiflexion that results as the leg moves over the fixed foot, fast walkers plantarflexed to 1.5°, free-speed walkers to 3.5°, and slow walkers to 6°. These data indicate that the foot comes into ground contact in a more plantarflexed position as velocity decreases.

Craik, Herman & Finley (1976) investigated the relationship between interlimb coordination and velocity in a sample of young subjects. Flexion-extension excursion and the phase relations among peak amplitudes were examined bilaterally in shoulders and hips while subjects walked from 2.0 to 0.3 m/sec. The amplitude of hip and shoulder rotation decreased with a decrease in velocity. More importantly, the pattern of interlimb coordination changed when subjects walked slowly. At free speed the contralateral shoulder flexed and extended in concert with the ipsilateral hip. At slower speeds both shoulders flexed with the hip cycles for both lower extremities. Therefore, the frequency of shoulder movement doubled during slow walking and changed from a reciprocal to an in-phase pattern. This study indicates a change in the arm-leg synergy that is velocity-related rather than age-related.

The EMG activity recorded from muscles of the lower extremity also changes with a decrease in walking speed (Eberhart, Inman & Saunders, 1947). Yang & Winter (1985) reported that a decreased amplitude in EMG of certain muscles accompanies decreasing walking velocity (1.3 to 0.75 m/sec). Muscles monitored were responsible for control of sagittal plane motion: rectus femoris, vastus lateralis, biceps femoris, tibialis anterior, soleus. A decrease in peak amplitude of EMG activity with a slower walking speed is expected if the role of certain muscle activity is primarily stabilization and deceleration of the limb during free-speed walking; the slower-moving limb requires less stabilization and deceleration in the sagittal plane. The exception to this hypothesis for muscles controlling sagittal plane motion is perhaps seen in the plantar flexion muscle activity at pushoff. It is unfortunate that little attention has been paid to frontal or transverse plane joint rotations and associated muscles in the velocity studies. If slower velocity leads to an increased base of support, increased lateral motion and increased pelvic obliquity, perhaps more muscle activity is required or different patterns of activation are necessary, as illustrated in the Finley, Cody & Finizie (1969) study cited previously.

The picture that emerges is that when healthy young individuals are asked to walk slowly a shortened step length, decreased cadence, diminished single-support time, decreased joint rotation, and diminished EMG are evident. The characteristics that have been reported to accompany aging are seen in the healthy young person who is walking slowly. Since gait variables demonstrate velocity-dependence, investigators should account for the effect of velocity in research designed to examine the effect of age on walking performance.

Velocity-matched samples. Very few studies have controlled for velocity and for age. The studies completed to date suggest that such controls may increase the sensitivity of the gait analysis. The value of velocity-matching performance across age groups is that with the speed controlled the effort of slower speed on gait variables can be separated from other indications of aging.

Gillis, Gilroy, Lawley, Mott & Wall (1986) asked their young and old subjects to walk at three speeds: slow, medium, and fast. The only variables measured were the phases of footfall. Older subjects walked more slowly than the young subjects at the medium and fast speeds so differences in the gait variables were not examined. Velocities were the same between the two samples at the slow speed. Step length was not measured. At the slow speed there was no difference in stance or in single- or double-support times expressed as a percentage of stride time. The only difference ($p < .02$) was stride time or its inverse, cadence. Conclusions cannot be drawn about performance from this study because a limited number of variables was measured. This study does illustrate the advantage of controlling velocity. Instead of concluding that the older subjects walked more slowly, the study indicates that cadence was significantly slower in the older subjects despite velocity control. Cadence, therefore, may be a variable that can discriminate between age groups.

Crowinshield, Brand & Johnston (1978) approached the velocity-dependence of gait variables by developing regression lines for velocity and age and such other gait variables as stride length and sagittal hip excursion. Twenty-six subjects demonstrated walking speeds ranging from 0.3 to 1.5 m/sec. Hip flexion-extension excursion was linearly related to the walking velocities ($p < .001$). The straight-line fit of the regression lines for the young and the old groups were significantly different in both slope and intercept. As stated previously, there is a curvilinear decrease in stride length and velocity; Crowinshield, Brand & Johnston (1978) squared the velocity terms, which produced a linear relationship between the squared velocity and stride length. The mean regression equations were again significantly different between the two age groups. The authors concluded that the older subjects walked with shorter strides and less sagittal hip excursion and that the differences in the kinematic parameters are apparently of increased significance at the higher velocities. Studies of this type conducted with large samples and which also control for such factors as stature, weight, and sex may help unravel the issue of age, velocity, and walking pattern.

In a recent study subjects were asked to walk at four speeds: super slow, slow, comfortable, and fast (Craik, Inverso, Soucy & Dawkins, 1983). Young females ($\bar{x} = 27$ years) selected the following velocities in response to the speed commands: 0.49, 0.84, 1.21, and 1.86 m/sec. Older females ($\bar{x}$ 75 years) responded with the following speeds: 0.26, 0.79, 1.16, and 1.6 m/sec. Comparing performances to each speed command reveals that older subjects selected a slower velocity even in response to the slow and super-slow commands. The velocity-dependent versus age-dependent effects on other gait variables cannot be analyzed since velocities are different in two samples. This study also indicated the importance of the range of walking velocities. The older women maintained the wide range demonstrated by the younger women but the whole range was slower. Why did these subjects walk more slowly? Studies such as these begin to focus the gait analysis onto fewer and more sensitive variables. The control of extraneous variables and the measurement of kinetic as well as kinematic variables may assist in the development or testing of a model for locomotion.

SELECTION CRITERIA

The results of the pedestrian and laboratory studies discussed thus far detail an age-related trend in walking which suggests that individuals over the age of 60 years walk differently than young individuals. These age-associated findings are refuted by investigators who have carefully screened older subjects for pathology (Busby, 1981; Gabell & Nayak, 1984). Busby correlated the results of a physical evaluation and walking behavior and reported no walking differences between young and elderly males. To be included in the study, Busby's subjects had to demonstrate normal, two-joint muscle flexibility and normal joint range of motion throughout the lower extremities. After comparing variability in step length, stride time (the inverse of cadence), stride width, and double-support time, Gabell & Nayak reported that healthy older individuals (66 to 84 years of age) walked the same as younger individuals (21 to 47 years of age). Only 32 of 1,187 individuals over the age of 64 met the strict selection criteria for this study, which ruled out any musculoskeletal, neurological, or cardiovascular disorders and any history of falls.

The question raised by the disparate findings is a valid one and focuses on the operational definition used to select an older individual. A spectrum of walking in older subjects is presented when comparing foot-contact patterns among the elite subjects from the Gabell & Nayak study, the slow, careful walkers from the Murray series (1969, 1970), and the 86–104-year-old subjects in the third stage of elderly gait from the Spielberg study (1940). It is tempting to suggest that the presence of pathology such as loss of neurons, diminished muscle-fiber diameter, and degenerative joint disease is correlated with the spectrum of walking patterns reported for the older individuals among these studies. However, there are no comprehensive studies to validate such an assumption. The level of "fitness" of older individuals is another variable that should be considered (Cunningham, 1982). It would be interesting to know if the walking behaviors among Gabell & Nayak's thirty-two older subjects would differ if walking endurance were also tested.

AGE-RELATED STANDARDS

Although the effect of aging on walking is still controversial, the use of apparently healthy older subjects as standards to examine the effects of disability on walking behavior in this population should not be ruled out. One purpose of a gait evaluation is to describe how a patient's performance differs from "normal." An accurate assessment requires that all differences between the patient's performance and the standard result from the patient's disability. Therefore, the standard used to judge performance should match the patient in terms of anthropometric characteristics, sex, age, and walking velocity. The gait variables should be selected based on a model of locomotion to yield meaningful information. An attempt to relate specific walking variables and clinical symptoms may assist in addressing the following issues: (1) the specific effect that pathology has on ambulation, (2) the severity of involvement, and (3) the ability to differentiate among different types of pathology.

The usefulness of this approach is exemplified by comparing the data derived from Smidt & Wadsworth (1973) to that of Andriacchi & Galante (1980). The walking patterns of patients with hip disease were compared to the walking patterns of healthy subjects of similar sex, height, and weight (Smidt & Wadsworth, 1973). The authors concluded that the patients had a higher cadence and shorter step length at velocities that matched the standards. However, the healthy subjects were an average 32 years of age whereas the patients were an average of 63 years. The effect of age and hip pathology are confounding variables in this data analysis. Moreover, the variables selected to describe walking performance do not distinguish hip pathology from other lower extremity disability. The same performance may occur in any patient who has pain in the lower extremity and walks with an antalgic gait.

Andriacchi & Galante compared walking performance in three different samples: patients with total hip replacement, patients with total knee replacement, and age-matched healthy subjects. The total knee patients demonstrated shorter step lengths, less knee flexion in early stance, and abnormal movements at the knee. Hip patients, on the other hand, demonstrated gait abnormalities based on the location of the reconstructed hip joint axis. If the hip joint center and the line of action of the abductor muscles had been surgically shortened, the patients demonstrated a shorter than normal stride length, reduced hip rotation, and higher than normal hip flexion movement. This study illustrates the use of the apparently healthy older individual as a standard to detect the effect of intervention on walking behavior.

Forssberg, Johnels & Steg (1984) presented the hypothesis that patients with advanced Parkinson's disease demonstrate a regression to an immature walking pattern. The gait of the patients was characterized by such features as slow velocity, diminished joint rotations, loss of heel strike at ground contact, reduced toe elevation, a forward bent posture, and reduced arm swing. The standard by which the patients were compared was not described. It is tempting to speculate that an age-matched standard would have separated age from pathology and resulted in a clearer description of the gait of the patients.

In addition to the need to focus on the relationship between pathology and functional performance, studies need to be conducted to develop norms of performance in the elderly so that they can function in the society. For example, a study was performed to determine if 79-year-olds could function as pedestrians (Lundgren-Lindquist, Aniansson & Rundgren, 1983). Functional capacity of the lower extremities was assessed in 112 women and 93 men. Subjects were asked to walk free speed and as fast as possible. Stair walking was assessed on a series of steps 10, 20, 30, 40, and 50 cm in height. Sixty-two percent of the women and 68% of the men had no symptoms that would interfere with ambulation. The rest of the sample comprised individuals who had cardiovascular, neurological, or musculoskeletal disease that altered walking ability. Walking aids were used by 27% of the women and 25% of the men. The recommended speed to cross intersections in Sweden is 1.4 m/sec. No women or men in this study achieved this speed when walking at their preferred speed. At their maximum walking speed only 32% of the women and 72% of the men reached 1.4 m/sec. All subjects climbed up and down a 10- or 20-cm step with the handrail as needed. Twenty percent of the women and 6% of the men were unable to climb up the 40-cm step height even with use of the handrail. The authors concluded that public transportation vehicles and the timing of lights at intersections in Sweden are not in accordance with the functional capacity of older persons.

The studies just reviewed should indicate the potential value of selecting the appropriate age-related norms. The limited number of studies of this type which have been completed also indicate the immediate need for such research.

FALL PREDICTION

In addition to using healthy older subjects as standards to more clearly identify the effect of pathology on walking ability, an area of vital interest is the development of tests to identify individuals who are at high risk to sustain a future injury.

An increased frequency of falls in the elderly has been verified by many investigators (Boucher, 1959; Gryfe, Amies & Ashley, 1977; Riffle, 1982; Sheldon, 1960). For the older individual, accidents are the leading cause of death, and falls are the leading cause of accidents in the home. In their review of the epidemiology of hip fracture, Lewinnek, Kelsey, White & Kreiger (1980) estimated the incidence of hip fracture in the United States to be 98 per 100,000 population in 1977. Although the lifetime risk of hip fracture among women 30 years of age is 8%, one out of five females over 80 years of age is expected to sustain a hip fracture. If the fall does not result in death, recovery from injury sustained during the fall is poorer with advancing age (Barnes & Dunovan, 1987; Cedar, Thorngren & Wallden, 1980; Jette, Harris, Cleary & Campion, 1987). Understanding why older people have a higher risk of falling is essential to discrete, differential diagnosis and to treatment planning. Ultimately, the goal must be prevention.

Much of the research on falls in the elderly has focused on the nature and cause of the falls and has stressed the complexity of the falling phenomenon. The results suggest that the cause for a fall can be subdivided into two issues: (1) the stimulus that results in the loss of balance and (2) the inability to correct for an unexpected loss of balance. Many of the proposed explanations for the decreased motor control are related to predictable changes resulting from the aging process. For example, loss of balance may be due to such self-generated stimuli as vertigo or fainting (Droller, 1955; Sheldon, 1960), to such environmental stimuli as uneven surfaces encountered during walking, or to a combination of factors. Likewise, the inability to correct for an unexpected loss of balance may be decreased reaction time (Hasselkus, 1974; Riffle, 1982), diminished central-nervous-system (CNS) integration (Droller, 1955; Isaacs, 1978), decreased strength and joint mobility (Riffle, 1982; Walker et al., 1984), or a combination of these factors.

Since no single variable reliably predicts an increased risk of falling, various outcome behaviors such as posture and ambulation have been examined to determine if they indicate early signs of neuromotor dysfunction.

Perhaps walking performance should be examined in addition to static postural ability and standard clinical tests of neuromusculoskeletal integrity. As was stated earlier, ambulation can be viewed as two subtasks, progression and dynamic postural control. What is the relationship between tests of static postural ability and gait ability? The development of studies that examine posture and gait may indicate the ability of one test to predict behavior in another task. Dettman, Linder & Sepic (1987) conducted a study that evaluated the relationships among walking performance and postural stability in a sample of patients with hemiplegia and age-matched controls. The temporal and spatial components of footfall were used to assess walking performance. Postural stability and steadiness were evaluated using a static forceplate that measured the center of pressure (CP) during upright activities: unsupported standing for 30 seconds; weight shifting in forward, backward, right and left directions. Inability to shift the CP backward and toward the paretic side correlated significantly to all measures of walking performance in the patients. The ability to maintain a degree of steadiness during standing and to shift the CP forward showed a positive relationship with walking speed and step length of the paretic limb. Force under the paretic limb during standing correlated with paretic step length and the ratio of uninvolved to involved swing time. Sensory disability did not correlate with any variables from the posture or walking tests. These investigators have begun to develop a model for locomotion and to examine what components of static postural tests relate to the dynamic task of walking. Similar studies need to be completed for the healthy elderly versus the "falling" elderly.

Another approach taken to identify fallers is to look retrospectively. Although the retrospective approach has not successfully identified fallers, studies indicate the profound effect that the fall has on gait function and support the need to try to prevent the fall. Studies examining functional recovery following hip fracture include a description of walking ability (Barnes & Dunovan, 1987; Jette et al., 1987). Examination of walking ability is usually part of an activity of daily living (ADL) test battery. Ambulation is scored as independent or dependent. Subjects are asked if they walk indoors and outdoors and if they use stairs. Although the ADL test batteries allow the investigators to determine that very few of the subjects reached prefracture independence, they do not provide any information about the quality of the ambulation. Therefore, it is difficult to identify possible predictors of falling. Future studies of hip-fracture recovery should incorporate quantitative measures of posture and gait to determine if predictive variables are present in a manner similar to the Dettman et al. (1987) study referred to previously.

Imms & Edholm (1981) purposefully selected a sample of older subjects demonstrating a variety of disabilities and level of physical activity to distinguish among them using tests of posture and locomotion. The seventy-one subjects ranging in age from 60 to 99 years filled out a questionnaire describing their medical history, history of falls, level of activity, and use of walking aids. The spatial and temporal aspects of footfall and turning-around time were selected to measure walking. Subjects also walked through an obstacle course that included rising from a chair, walking across the room, and ascending and descending stairs. Postural sway was measured as the subjects stood for 1 minute and focused on a distant object. As with previous studies, these authors demonstrated an age-dependent decrease in velocity accompanied by diminished step length, cadence, swing time, and increased stance time. The time to travel the obstacle course and the number of errors in maneuvering the course were not related to age but were related to the walking velocity obtained from the walking task. The logarithm of the postural sway score was related to age ($r = .25, p <$ .10), but postural sway scores were more strongly related to the time to traverse the obstacle course ($r = .481, p < .001$) and walking velocity ($r = -.599, p < .001$). Based on their answers in the questionnaires, subjects were classified as housebound, having limited outdoor activity, or having unlimited outdoor activity. As expected, the housebound performed the worst in means of performance in walking, successfully completing the obstacle course, and static postural sway. In general, the subjects with unlimited activity walked faster with a longer step length and completed the obstacle course faster than the other two subgroups. The regression lines developed for some of the variables yield interesting results. The regression equations for velocity and step length are remarkably similar among the three subgroups whereas the regression equations for velocity and cadence look different. These findings suggest a fixed relationship between velocity and step length regardless of activity level and pathology; the relationship between velocity and cadence may reflect activity level and pathology.

Imms & Edholm (1981) also subdivided the sample based on falling. Subjects who claimed a fall in the previous year were separated from nonfallers. The ages of the fallers and the nonfallers were the same and the incidence of falling did not vary with activity level. The only identified difference between the fallers and the nonfallers was that fallers walked more slowly and took shorter steps. Imms & Edholm concluded that changes in velocity and step length may be sensitive indicators differentiating fallers from nonfallers and that other footfall measures of gait indicate additional levels of inactivity or pathology—for example, stroke or recovery from unilateral fracture. This study highlights the sensitivity of objective measures to distinguish differences in functional performance among an age-matched sample. A discriminant analysis of the data may have indicated which variables or combination of variables predict falling while taking into account the interactions among the variables. It would have been useful to distinguish pathology from level of activity. These results should not be regarded as norms or indicators of "normal" function without anthropometric, sex, and pathology characteristics.

Gabell & Nayak (1984) suggest that consistency in walking performance may serve as an indicator of disability or a predictor of falls. The coefficient of variation was used to examine the variability in step length, stride time, stride width, and double-support time. The first two parameters are considered measures of gait patterning and the second two are considered indicative of balance. Because young and older subjects showed high variability for the balance measures compared to the gait patterning measures, the authors suggested that stride width and double-support time are not sensitive indicators of pathology. Adequate data were not presented to justify the conclusion that the coefficient of variation for step length and stride time do, in fact, indicate pathology.

Wolfson et al. (1985) stated that they can distinguish a difference in walking and balance ability between fallers and nonfallers. They stated that fallers have multiple indices of impaired gait and severely compromised balance. They also report that fallers have poor muscle strength (dorsiflexion was 10% of control values), diminished proprioception (40% of fallers were compromised compared to 13% of controls), a twofold increase in vibratory threshold, diminished sural nerve conduction velocity, and abnormal H-reflexes. These results were presented as summary data so the reader cannot critically analyze the sample, methods, or data analysis used to provide the above conclusions. In a related study Whipple et al. (1987) presented the data that support the muscle-strength findings. The results of isokinetic strength testing of knee and ankle musculature were related to the incidence of falling in an age- and sex-matched sample. Though the data support the fact that fallers have weaker musculature, there is no indication that weak musculature causes falls in the elderly.

The studies just reviewed indicate the same problems cited in the aged walking studies. The variables are not selected with a hypothesis in mind; the primary approach taken has been to select two groups and to measure walking behavior. Although the descriptive approach has produced information that can be used as standards to distinguish pathology, variables have not been identified that *predict* pathology or people at risk for falling.

SUMMARY

From this review of the efforts to describe gait in the aging population it is obvious that the description of gait and aging is unclear and incomplete. The effect of aging on walking behavior cannot be described at this time, for too many issues remain to be addressed. Depending on the investigation, the walking patterns reported for the "healthy" older subjects may reflect aging, the goal for walking, inactivity, or the presence of subtle pathology that is pain-free and not obvious to the investigator or the subject. Test conditions have been different, sample sizes are small, chronological ages do not match, and such factors as stature, height, weight, and sex often have been neglected. The most consistent finding among the studies is the choice of a slower walking velocity for free-speed ambulation. Does a slower velocity reflect a decline in postural support mechanisms, a diminished cardiovascular efficiency, a deteriorating musculoskeletal structure, decreased proprioception, or a combination of these factors? Future studies must address this issue.

The questions asked by investigators today are the same as those asked in earlier decades. With advances in technology, investigators have more sensitive instrumentation by which to examine ambulatory ability. However, the results of the studies to date suggest that all of the changes in gait patterns take place in varying degrees within individuals during the aging process. Suggestions from the more basic literature indicate that the gait changes are produced by a process of complex alterations in the neuromusculoskeletal system. Our present understanding of the relationship between the biological changes and gait is incomplete. At this time we do not even have age-appropriate norms describing healthy walking ability in older subjects. Our common clinical assumption that older subjects who have abnormal scores on tests of postural stability also demonstrate abnormal ambulation is not substantiated by research. The relationship between standard clinical tests for muscle strength, sensation, and range of motion and walking performances is yet to be established. There is an emphatic need for further study in this area.

ACKNOWLEDGMENT

I would like to thank Sandy Foreman and Tina Sweesy for technical assistance in the preparation of this chapter.

REFERENCES

Adams, R. D. (1984). Aging and human locomotion. In M. L. Albert (Ed.), *Clinical neurology of aging* (pp. 381–86). New York: Oxford University Press.

Aloia, J. F. (1981). Exercise and skeletal health. *Journal of American Geriatrics Society, 29,* 104–7.

Andriacchi, T. P., & Galante, J. O. (1980). The influence of total hip and knee replacement on gait. In *Proceedings of International Conference on Rehabilitation on Engineering,* Toronto, Canada.

Azar, G. J., & Lawton, G. H. (1964). Gait and stepping as factors in the frequent falls of elderly women. *Journal of Gerontology, 19,* 83–84.

Barnes, B., & Dunovan, K. (1987). Functional outcomes after hip fracture. *Physical Therapy, 67 (11),* 1675–79.

Barron, R. C. (1967). Disorders of gait related to the aging nervous system. *Geriatrics, 22,* 113–20.

Benton, A. L. (1977). Interactive effects of age and brain disease in reaction time. *Archives of Neurology, 34,* 369–70.

Berlin, M., & Wallace, R. B. (1975). Aging and the central nervous system. *Experimental Aging Research, 2,* 125–64.

Boucher, C. A. (1959). Accidents among old persons. *Geriatrics, May,* 293–300.

Busby, C. (1981). Gait patterns of elderly men: A comparative study using cinematography. Master's Thesis. Duke University, Durham, NC.

Cedar, L.; Thorngren, K. G.; & Wallden, B. (1980). Prognostic indicators and early home rehabilitation in elderly patients with hip fracture. *Clinical Orthopedics, 152,* 173–84.

Craik, R.; Herman, R.; & Finley, F. R. (1976). Human solutions for locomotion: Interlimb coordination. *Advances in Behavioral Biology, 18,* 51–64.

Craik, R. L.; Inverso, W.; Soucy, D.; & Dawkins, B. (1983). The influence of aging on walking behavior. *Physical Therapy, 63,* 757.

Craik, R. L., & Oatis, C. A. (1985). Gait assessment in the clinic: Issues and approaches. In J. M. Rothstein (Ed.), *Measurement in physical therapy* (pp. 169–205). New York: Churchill Livingstone.

Critchley, M. (1948). On senile disorders of gait, including the so-called "senile paraplegic." *Geriatrics, 13,* 364–70.

Crowinshield, R. D.; Brand, R. A.; & Johnston, R. C. (1978). The effects of walking velocity and age on hip kinematics and kinetics. *Clinical Orthopedics and Related Research, 132,* 140–44.

Cunningham, D. A. (1982). Self-selected walking across ages 19 to 66. *Journal of Gerontology, 37 (4),* 560–64.

Dettman, M. A.; Linder, M. T.,; & Sepic, S. B. (1987). Relationships among walking performance, postural stability, and functional assessments of the hemiplegic patient. *American Journal of Physical Medicine, 66 (2),* 77–90.

Drillis, R. (1961). The influence of aging on the kinematics of gait. In *The Geriatric Amputee*, Publication 919. National Academy of Science, National Research Council.

Droller, H. (1955). Falls among elderly people living at home. *Geriatrics, May*, 239–44.

Eberhart, H. D.; Inman, V. T.; & Saunders, J. B. (1947). Fundamental studies of human locomotion and other information related to design of artificial limbs. A Report to National Research Council Committee on Artificial Limbs, University of California, Berkeley.

Finley, F. R.; Cody, K. A.; & Finizie, R. V. (1969). Locomotion patterns in elderly women. *Archives of Physical Medicine, 50*, 140–46.

Forssberg, H.; Johnels, B.; & Steg, G. (1984). Is Parkinsonian gait caused by a regression to an immature walking pattern? *Advances in Neurology, 40*, 375–79.

Gabel, R. H.; Johnston, R. C.; & Crowinshield, R. D. (1979). A gait analyzer/trainer instrumentation system. *Journal of Biomedical Engineering, 12*, 543–49.

Gabell, A., & Nayak, U. S. L. (1984). The effect of age on variability of gait. *Journal of Gerontology, 39*, 662–66.

Gillis, B.; Gilroy, K.; Lawley, H.; Mott, L.; & Wall, I. (1986). Slow walking speeds in healthy young and elderly females. *Physiotherapy Canada, 38*, 350–52.

Gryfe, C. I.; Amies, A.; & Ashley, M. J. (1977). A longitudinal study of falls in an elderly population: Incidence and morbidity. *Age and Aging, 6*, 201–10.

Hageman, P. A., & Blanke, D. J. (1986). Comparison of gait of young women and elderly women. *Physical Therapy, 66 (9)*, 1382–87.

Hasselkus, B. R. (1974). Aging and the human nervous system. *American Journal of Occupational Therapy, 28 (1)*, 16–21.

Holden, M. K.; Gill, K. M.; & Magliozzi, M. R. (1984). Clinical assessment in the neurologically impaired: Reliability and meaningfulness. *Physical Therapy, 64*, 35–40.

Imms, F. J., & Edholm, O. G. (1981). Studies of gait and mobility in the elderly. *Age and Aging, 10*, 147–56.

Inman, V. T.; Ralston, H. J.; Todd, F. (1981). *Human walking*. Baltimore, MD: Williams & Wilkins.

Isaacs, B. (1978). Are falls a manifestation of brain failure? *Age and Aging, 7*, 97–111.

Jette, A. M.; Harris, B. A.; Cleary, P. D.; & Campion, E. W. (1987). Functional recovery after hip fracture. *Archives of Physical Medicine and Rehabilitation, 68*, 735–40.

Larsson, L.; Grimby, G.; & Karlsson, J. (1979). Muscle strength and speed of movement in relation to age and muscle morphology. *Journal of Applied Physiology, 46*, 451–56.

Larsson, L.; Odenrick, P.; Sandlund, B.; Weitz, P.; & Oberg, P. A. (1980). The phases of the stride and their interaction in human gait. *Scandinavian Journal of Rehabilitation Medicine, 12*, 107–12.

LeVeau, B. F. (Ed.) (1984). Biomechanics [special issue]. *Physical Therapy, 64 (12)*.

Lewinnek, G. E.; Kelsey, J.; White, A. A.; & Kreiger, N. M. (1980). The significance and comparative analysis of the epidemiology of hip fracture. *Clinical Orthopedics and Related Research, 35*, 35–43.

Lundgren-Lindquist, B.; Aniansson, A.; & Rundgren, A. (1983). Functional studies in 79-year-olds. III. Walking performance and climbing ability. *Scandinavian Journal of Rehabilitation Medicine, 15,* 125–31.

Molen, H. H. (1973). Problems on the evaluation of gait. Ph.D. dissertation. The Institute of Biomechanics and Experimental Rehabilitation, Free University, Amsterdam.

Murray, M. P. (1967). Gait as a total movement pattern. *American Journal of Physical Medicine, 46 (1),* 290–333.

Murray, M. P.; Drought, A. B.; & Kory, R. C. (1964). Walking patterns of normal men. *Journal of Bone and Joint Surgery, 46 (2),* 335–60.

Murray, M. P.; Kory, R. C.; & Clarkson, B. H. (1969). Walking patterns in healthy old men. *Journal of Gerontology, 24,* 169–78.

Murray, M. P.; Kory, R. C.; & Sepic, S. B. (1970). Walking patterns of normal women. *Archives of Physical Medicine and Rehabilitation, 51,* 637–50.

Olney, S. J., & Winter, P. A. (1985). Predictions of knee and ankle moments of force in walking from EMG and kinematic data. *Journal of Biomechanics, 18,* 9–20.

Riffle, K. L. (1982). Falls: Kinds, causes and prevention. *Geriatric Nursing, April/May,* 165–69.

Rosenrot, P.; Wall, J. C; & Charteris, J. (1980). The relationship between velocity, stride time, support time and swing time during normal walking. *Journal of Human Movement Studies, 6,* 323-35.

Rozendal, R. H. (1986). Biomechanics of standing and walking. In W. Bles & Th. Brandt (Eds.), *Disorders of posture and gait* (pp. 3–18). Amsterdam: Elsevier.

Sheldon, J. H. (1960). On the natural history of falls in old age. *British Medical Journal, 12,* 1685–90.

Smidt, G. L., & Wadsworth, J. B. (1973). Floor reaction forces during gait: Comparison of patients with hip disease and normal subjects. *Physical Therapy, 53,* 1056–62.

Spielberg, P. I. (1940). Walking patterns of old people: Cyclographic analysis. In N. A. Bernstein (Ed.), *Investigations on the biodynamics of walking, running and jumping.* Part II. Moscow: Central Scientific Institute of Physical Culture.

Steinberg, F. V. (1966). Gait disorders in old age. *Geriatrics, 21,* 134–43.

U.S. Senate. Special Committee on Aging. U.S. Dept. of Health and Human Services (1986). *Aging America: Trends and Projections* (Publication No. PF3377–1085), Washington, DC: U.S. Government Printing Office.

Walker, J. M.; Sue, D.; Miles-Elkousky, N.; Ford, G.; & Travelyan, H. (1984). Active mobility of the extremities in older subjects. *Physical Therapy, 64 (6),* 919–23.

Whipple, R. H.; Wolfson, L. I.; & Amerman, P. M. (1987). The relationship of knee and ankle weakness to falls in nursing home residents: An isokinetic study. *Journal of the American Geriatric Society, 35,* 13–20.

Winter, D. A. (1983). Biomechanical motor patterns in normal walking. *Journal of Motor Behavior, 15 (4),* 302–30.

Winter, D. A. (1987). *The biomechanics and motor control of human gait.* Waterloo, Ontario: University of Waterloo Press.

Wolfson, L. I.; Whipple, R.; Amerman, P.; Kaplan, J.; & Kleinberg, A. (1985). Gait and balance in the elderly. *Clinics in Geriatric Medicine, 1 (3),* 649–55.

Woodruff, D. S., & Birren, J. E. (1983). *Aging: Scientific perspectives and social issues.* Monterey, CA: Brook Cole.

Woollacott, M. H. (1986). Gait and postural control in the aging adult. In W. Bles & Th. Brandt (Eds.), *Disorders of posture and gait* (pp. 325–36). Amsterdam: Elsevier.

Yant, J. F., & Winter, D. A. (1985). Surface EMG profiles during different walking cadences in humans. *Electroencephalography and Clinical Neurophysiology, 60,* 485–91.

9

Plasticity and Exercise Effects on Aging Motor Function

Ann M. Baylor

Although the theme of this book is posture and locomotion, research on the effects of exercise on the aging motor control system has largely been limited to psychomotor tasks. One of the most distinguishing characteristics of the aging nervous system in psychomotor tasks is the loss of speed of responses; thus this chapter focuses on the effects of exercise on reactive capacity. Clearly, the initiation of rapid voluntary movements is critically linked to the ability to make rapid anticipatory postural adjustments. Woollacott et al. (1988) has reported that older subjects are slower and experience more co-contraction in postural muscles than young subjects both while compensating for postural sway and when activating postural muscles in a feedforward manner in preparation for a voluntary movement. Thus it is possible that much of the slowness in rapid movements of older subjects may be due to slower postural control systems that may be favorably affected by regular aerobic exercise.

In the past two decades the merging of two important societal trends and the research findings associated with them have focused attention on an important possibility—that the benefits of regular aerobic exercise may significantly deter many of the behavioral correlates of the aging process. If this finding is valid, it has profound implications in light of (1) the trend toward an aging population and (2) the recent importance placed on fitness (i.e., the view that vigorous exercise is an important component in a health-maintenance program). Although many organizations (e.g., American Heart Association, President's Council on Physical Fitness), physicians, and scientists are recommending vigorous exercise for health maintenance, Holloszy (1983) has cautioned that the evidence may be too meager to justify recommending strenuous exercise for the large population of sedentary and older individuals in the United States and guards against evangelistic statements that exercise retards the aging process. Although much evidence exists that exercise provides a needed stimulus for the maintenance of structural and functional integrity of the cardiovascular system, skeletal muscles, bones, tendons, ligaments, and probably the autonomic nervous system and motoneurons,, the evidence that regular exercise may protect against and have beneficial effects on coronary artery disease, diabetes, and hypertension is more fragmentary. Holloszy further argues that it does not necessarily follow that strenuous exercise has a beneficial effect on the incidence or progression of the diseases associated with aging or on the aging process itself. The need for controlled, longitudinal studies involving aerobically active middle-aged and older adults is emphasized. "If it could be documented that exercise slows some aspects of the aging process, as scattered data in the literature suggest it may, this information could, if incorporated into programs of public health and preventive medicine, have a major beneficial impact on the well-being, self-sufficiency, and productivity of elderly individuals in our society" (Holloszy, 1983: 3).

Bruce (1984) has a more optimistic view of the evidence but also emphasizes the need for controlled, longitudinal research. He argues that the decline with aging in functional aerobic capacity as defined by maximal oxygen consumption (VO2max) is twice as great in sedentary as in physically active male subjects. VO2max has been considered the international reference standard for physical fitness and can be improved through aerobic exercise at about 70% VO2max for 20 to 40 minutes, three times per week, for several weeks. The older individual responds well to aerobic training, although certain training precautions are necessary and improvement may be slower (Skinner, Tipton & Vailas, 1982).

The equivalent of VO2max for physical fitness appears to be reaction time (RT) for psychomotor functioning and speed of an individual's response to an environmental stimulus. RT is a measure of the time from the presentation of an expected, but unanticipated, signal to the initiation of a response to it. Typically, a warning signal precedes an irregular foreperiod (1 to 5 sec), after which time a stimulus to respond is presented and the subject releases a switch. As Birren, Woods & Williams (1979) have concluded, some functions, such as verbal comprehension, appear to improve with age and other functions, such as personality traits, remain remarkably stable. The most dramatic decline with aging is in speed of behavior. Although the behavioral slowness is not limited to motor responses, slowness of behavior in older individuals has been proposed as one of our best tools to assess aging of the central nervous system (CNS) see Birren, Woods & Williams, 1979, for a review. Birren et al. (1979) reported that slowing of simple RT (SRT) with age has been perhaps the most replicated finding in aging research since Galton reported from data gathered in a nineteenth-century health fair that 20-year-olds were approximately 13% faster than 60-year-olds. Birren et al. reported from their compendium of twenty-six studies that RT declines about 20% from ages 20 to 60 years. Other reviews have obtained similar results (Jacewicz & Hartley, 1987; Potvin et al., 1980; Welford, 1982). "For some it might seem that the study of speed of response in later life is a trivial pursuit; not so," stated Botwinick (1973: 154), who views slowness of behavior as the manifestation of a primary process of aging in the nervous system. This process of aging could occur within a number of nervous subsystems, including those controlling both postural and prime mover muscles involved in a RT movement. Reduction in the speed of the postural muscles would clearly affect the prime movers' response. This view is consistent with the systems model of nervous system function. Thus in addition to its obvious importance in characterizing the speed of psychomotor skills, RT movements and their underlying postural adjustments are thought to represent a behavioral "window" into the aging nervous system.

Age-related changes in performance have also been reported outside the laboratory. In a study of driving problems, young (<24 years) and old (>60 years) drivers had more frequent accidents than middle-aged drivers; however, the type of accident for older drivers was different from that for other age groups. Older drivers' accidents frequently involved improper starting and turning and failure to give right-of-way. Younger drivers were more likely to be involved in accidents resulting from excessive speed and the use of faulty equipment (McFarland, Tune & Welford, 1964). When speed of movement was related to an occupational skill, experience was found to compensate for speed changes in some complex skills (Murrell & Griew, 1965). Older typists were slower in tapping rate and in choice RT (CRT) but were not slower in speed of typing because they were sensitive to more characters before the keys were typed (Salthouse, 1984). When old drillers were required to aim an industrial drill at a mark on metal, they were not slower than younger drillers or younger naive subjects. Older drillers were faster than naive older subjects and more accurate than younger naive subjects (Murrell, Powesland & Forsaith, 1962).

This increased use of experience by older workers and the observation that age is a poor predictor of performance across the full range of employment years have contributed to the use of job performance testing as an alternative to age-based mandatory retirement (Davis & Dotson, 1987; Sharkey, 1987). Evidence suggests that older workers are more impaired than younger workers by continuous work requiring large percentages of physiological capacity (Astrand, 1968; Astrand et al., 1973) and in tasks that are not self-paced (Perone & Baron, 1982; 1983; Schonfield, 1974) or place a heavy emphasis on speed and accuracy of the response (Hines, 1979; Murrell & Tucker, 1960; Rabbitt, 1979; Salthouse & Somberg, 1982b).

It is the basic proposition of Birren (1974) that with advancing age individuals show a tendency to a slowness in response reflecting in a basic change in the speed with which the CNS processes information and that any event processed by the nervous system takes longer. His general observations are that the aging individual can do almost anything that he/she could do when younger except not as quickly. Speed of association, he contends, may well be one of the most intrinsic factors of intellectual activity. He reported that the slowing of motor skills occurred at decision points, that is, not that the movement itself was so slowed as was the time to redirect the movement in response to new information. Alternatively, this slowing could be the indirect result of decrements in another but equally vital system, such as the postural control system. In addition, some have argued that older subjects may be less motivated, but electric shock motivation studies with animals (Spirduso & Farrar, 1981) and humans (Botwinick et al., 1958) support the contentions of Pierson & Montoye (1958) that the slowness of RT with age is not a motivational issue. Clearly, the speed with which psychomotor tasks are performed by the elderly is slower than in younger adults (see Botwinick, 1973, Cerella, 1985; and Spirduso, 1980, for reviews). The important issue here is whether psychomotor speed is better retained in aged individuals who regularly participate in aerobic exercise as compared to older sedentary and to young controls.

Botwinick & Thompson (1968) were possibly the first to emphasize the role of regular aerobic exercise as a factor in RT studies. After noticing a relationship between low heart rates and faster RTs in many of their young control subjects, they categorized these subjects into two groups: (1) team athletes and others who exercised regularly four to five times per week and (2) those who exercised irregularly or not at all. When the old subjects were compared to the young groups, they were not significantly slower than the young inactive controls, but they were slower than the young active controls; however, the activity level of the older group was not addressed. Since these early findings, at least sixteen studies have focused on the relationship between regular physical activity and response speed by (1) selecting a sample of older subjects who have participated in aerobic exercise for some duration of time (two to twenty years) or (2) looking at subjects following some type of aerobic conditioning program. The data from the first category, persons who have been aerobically active on a regular basis for some time, are very promising in comparing the RTs of these individuals to various control groups.

Quite obviously, in order to evaluate the research studies contributing to this issue, a number of experimental factors must be considered. Thus these studies are discussed with respect to variables in the following four categories: exercise, practice, task complexity, and sex of subject.

EXERCISE

For how many years have the participants been active? in what type of exercise? at what intensity? at what duration? Similar issues are important to investigators studying changes within individuals progressing through an exercise program. If RT changes are to be expected from appropriate exercise programs, do they parallel changes in VO2max? Do RT changes require the same intensity and duration of training as changes in VO2max?

AEROBIC LIFESTYLE

Botwinick & Storandt (1974) studied habits of exercise as one of four variables affecting aging RT values. A brief interview categorized subjects into two levels of exercise habits: (1) non- or irregular exercisers and (2) those who exercised a minimum of 1 hour a day, at least twice a week. Subjects who reported 15 to 20 minutes of daily or near-daily exercise were excluded. Neither the main effects for activity level nor the age-exercise interaction was significant. Clearly, the frequency of exercise (twice a week) in this study was below that normally expected for VO2max improvements, and the length of time that subjects had been involved in exercise programs was unreported.

When Spirduso (1975) compared four groups of racket-sports and handball players with age-matched controls, she selected young active subjects who had been playing racket-sports for a minimum of three times per week for two years. The older active group exhibited an active lifestyle of playing racket-sports a minimum of three times per week over the past thirty years. She reported major effects for age and activity level for all variables and a significant age-by-activity interaction for all variables except discrimination RT (DRT). Both SRT and movement time (MvT) were significantly slower in the old inactive controls. Since it was possible that the findings were influenced by the daily exposure of the racket-sport players to conditions requiring numerous quick decisions and reactions, Spirduso & Clifford (1978) replicated the age and physical activity effects on RT and MvT in six groups of old and young runners, racket sportsmen, and sedentary men. The old sportsmen had been active over the past twenty years and the young over the past three years. Racket sportmen had established a pattern of playing for at least one hour, four times per week. Runners ran at least three miles, four times per week. The findings showed that older men who maintain an active lifestyle react and move significantly faster and more consistently than their sedentary peers and as least as quickly as the sedentary men who were forty years younger.

These findings have been further replicated by Clarkson (1978), who compared four groups of men and defined her old active subjects as having participated in physical activity at least three times a week for most of their adult lives. In older subjects activity level enhanced the speed of all SRTs, CRTs, and related components, with MvT showing the greatest effect. The effects of age and isometric strength on resisted response times of these subjects was reported by Kroll & Clarkson (1978), who set each subject's resistance at 10% of the maximum isometric knee extension. Although knee extension strength was lower in older subjects, the old active subjects were stronger than the old controls. Both SRT and CRT increased in the resisted condition, primarily due to the lengthening of the motor time in the resisted condition; however, the increase in resisted motor time was greater for the young groups and unrelated to physical activity level.

Hart (1980), who essentially repeated the paradigm of Clarkson with four groups of women subjects, classified her inactive women as having not regularly participated in sport or exercise programs for at least several years, nor had they engaged in a strenuous physical labor. The active women had participated in sport, exercise, or strenuous work of at least 1 hour's duration, three times weekly over the past several years. All groups were different from each other on SRT and CRT. The slowest group was the old inactive followed by the old active, young inactive, and the young active.

Additional studies substantiate this relationship. Sherwood & Selder (1979) have confirmed these findings in runners involved in rigorous training programs averaging forty-two miles per week. Both the trained and the inactive group contained eight subjects from the following decades: 20, 30, 40, 50 years. In inactive subjects they reported a gradual decline in RT as age increased, however, this trend was not present in the trained group as RT remained constant with age. Rikli & Busch (1986) studied four groups of women subjects; the active subjects were involved in vigorous physical activity (defined as strenuous enough to cause a rapid heart rate, heavy breathing, and considerable perspiration) at least three times a week for at least 30 minutes over the past three years or more (younger active group) and over at least the past ten years (older active group). Scores on SRT, CRT, balance, and two flexibility measures were better for the older active group than for the old inactive group and similar to those of the younger group. Grip strength was the only variable not showing this trend.

Spirduso et al. (in 1988) defined *active* as involved in a walk/run program for a minimum of three miles per day, three days per week for a minimum of five years and subdivided the active and inactive groups by decade as follows: 20, 50, 60, 70 years. The main effect for age was significant for all variables (SRT, DRT, discrimination time [defined as DRT-SRT] stationary tapping speed, trailmaking, digit symbol substitution, and tapping between two targets). Four of these variables were significantly related to activity (SRT, DRT, discrimination time, and stationary tapping). The SRT of physically active women was faster than that of the sedentary women in the 20- and 50-year-old groups only, but for DRT the physically active women at all ages were faster then the inactive controls. Baylor & Spirduso (1988) classified active subjects as women who had been running for at least 30 min per day for five days a week for the past five years and compared their performance to a nonexercising control group. Older women who are aerobically active were faster on SRT, DRT, and MvT than inactive controls. MacRae, Crum, Giessman, Greene & Ugolini (in preparation) verified fitness level by a submaximal bicycle ergometer test and classified older and younger women into inactive groups and running groups (those who ran a minimum of fifteen miles per week for at least the past two years). For SRT and CRT the young runners were faster than the other three groups, and the old controls were slower than the other three groups: however, the old runners did not differ from the young controls.

EXERCISE PROGRAMS

If faster RTs are found in older active subjects, an intriguing question is, do the RTs of older subjects become faster as old inactive subjects progress through an aerobic fitness program, or do older individuals who elect an active lifestyle exhibit a predisposition for faster responses in both cognitive and psychomotor abilities? The evidence on this issue is scanty and somewhat conflicting. Barry, Daly et al. (1966) tested older subjects at the highest workload that could be maintained on a bicycle ergometer for 6 min. Exercise subjects trained for three months on the bicycle ergometer, three times per week, for 40-minute sessions. Subjects performed intermittent work at submaximal loads for 10 to 15 minutes followed by 6 to 10 minutes at a near-maximal effort (work pulse of 130 beats/min). Within a session subjects performed a series of 2- or 3-minute work periods followed by a 30-second rest interval. SRT was measured prior to and following a three-month exercise program but no differences were found. The trials were few (five practice, five test), the group numbers small, and the intensity and total duration of the exercise program were not clear in terms of the recommended American College of Sports Medicine (ACSM) guidelines (ACSM, 1986; Barry, Steinmetz et al., 1966).

Dustman et al. (1984) screened volunteers aged 55 to 70 years. Healthy sedentary participants were given a modified Balke treadmill test and were assigned to one of two exercise groups: aerobic exercise training or strength and flexibility training. A third group received the performance tests and became the nonexercising control group. Exercise groups met for three one-hour sessions a week for four months. Following warm-up exercises, the aerobic group participated in fast walking and occasional slow jogging at a target heart rate of 70 to 80% of their reserve, gradually attempting to maintain this target rate for longer periods of time. Participants in the strength and flexibility exercise group monitored their heart rates but were encouraged to keep them below the threshold for improved aerobic fitness. In the pre-exercise testing, the two exercise groups did not differ on any of six physiological measures. In post-training, aerobic exercise subjects improved 27% on VO2max; whereas the strength and flexibility group improved only 9%. The aerobically trained group improved more on the neuropsychological test battery than the exercise control group, whose improvement was greater than that of the nonexercise control group. Tests purportedly measured response speed (SRT became faster, but not CRT), visual organization, memory, and mental flexibility.

These findings were supported in an animal model (Spirduso & Farrar, 1981) in which rats were divided into four groups of young and old exercisers and controls. As a measure of reactive capacity, all animals were shaped over a seven-day training period on an escape and avoidance task that produced very rapid responses (100 to 200 msec) in the shortest avoidance intervals, in which the rats learned to rapidly release a lever within a time interval to avoid a shock. Both the old and young exercise groups trained for six months by running daily on a treadmill for up to 1 hour, and both exercise groups showed high levels of training as measured by oxygen consumption per gram of gastrocnemius-plantaris muscle tissue. In the shortest avoidance intervals and in escape responses, the old trained animals were faster than the old control animals.

Recently, Lowe (1988) compared groups of old and young women and divided them into aerobic exercise and control groups. VO2max was estimated in the older subjects by a modified Bruce treadmill protocol for pre- and postaerobic training and in young subjects by a 12-minute walk run. Exercise groups received sixteen weeks (three times per week) of aerobic training for 30 minutes plus warm-up and cool-down periods. The young exercisers worked at 70% of estimated maximal heart rate while the older exercise group worked at 65 to 75% of the maximum heart rate. Lowe's CRT paradigm was fairly complex, involving combinations of four finger presses paired with each other in a two-choice CRT in which a light stimulus cued the movement. Although initially the older subjects were slower, CRT for all groups improved the same amount with no significant effects for training. It is possible that this improvement across groups represents a learning effect for CRT despite the fact that three hundred trials (fifty for each of four two-choice combinations) were given on two consecutive days, and only data from the second day were included in the analyses. Young exercisers all improved VO2max by a minimum of 20%, but only four of the fifteen old exercisers improved VO2max by 20%. In these subjects target heart rates for the young, previously inactive subjects resulted in running, whereas a walking program was the result of the target heart rates for older women.

    Very similar findings were reported in a presentation by Hornbeck & Sucec (1982), in which high (85% VO2max) and low (40% VO2max) intensities of aerobic training were compared in old and young exercisers. Initially, old and young groups differed on percent body fat, VO2max, and distance covered in a 12-min run; however, no differences existed within age categories as subjects were divided into high-intensity (85% VO2max) and low-intensity (40% VO2max) age groups. Groups differed only in the intensity of training (prescribed by individual target heart rate). Low-intensity subjects walked as high-intensity subjects ran 4800 meters three times per week for eleven weeks. Only the high-intensity group improved on VO2max, but all groups improved on SRT with no differential effect attributable to training intensity. Unfortunately, the groups were small ($n = 5$), and the number and amount of practice on SRT trials were not reported. Without adequate practice conditions, it is likely that much of this improvement in SRT was due to practice effects. Although Hornbeck & Sucec reported a significant correlation between VO2max and SRT, a low correlation was reported by Chodzko-Zajko & Ringel (1987); however, RT was correlated to a single measure of physical fitness as reduced from a battery of resting tests (pulmonary, hemodynamic, and biochemical variables) in seventy male subjects aged 63 years. VO2max was estimated in a submaximal Balke treadmill protocol in all subjects who were able to complete it (67%). High scores on the fitness index were associated with faster RTs, improved hearing at high frequencies, greater phonatory control, and improved lens accommodation.

Generally, there is support in the literature for faster RTs in persons who have trained aerobically for a minimum of three days per week for a minimum of two years. There is some evidence for RT changes in older persons as a result of an aerobic training program, but many questions are unanswered. These results should be replicated. What are the training conditions necessary to produce these changes? Do they parallel changes in VO2max? If not, what frequency, duration, and intensity of aerobic exercise are important to these changes?

Recently, Blair & Kohl (1988) reported in epidemiological data from the Aerobics Institute in Dallas, Texas, that both physical fitness as measured by a maximal exercise treadmill test and level of physical activity, as determined by self-report exercise habits are important and independent factors affecting morbidity and mortality. When age, blood pressure, cholesterol, smoking status, level of fitness, and sex were controlled, the level of physical activity affected morbidity and mortality. Similarly, when these factors and level of physical activity were controlled, physical fitness was found to make an independent contribution. The implications of these findings are not yet clear. It may be that, although physical activity can improve physical fitness within genetic limits, independently these factors are related to morbidity and mortality. These factors may have considerable bearing on studies addressing the relationship between RT and exercise, e.g., chronic activity patterns versus brief programs to improve VO2max. Clearly, the most numerous studies have looked at individuals exhibiting a lifestyle of physical activity, and eleven of the twelve studies reviewed have indicated positive effects on RT in aging individuals. The research involving programs to improve physical fitness in older populations and the effect on psychomotor speed are very few, about 50% successful and questionable in the exercise intensities and training program durations. Carefully controlled, longitudinal research is greatly needed in this area.

PRACTICE

One of the most serious methodological problems in RT studies is in the effects of practice on improving RT over trials and days. The problem of practice in the aging adult is further complicated by studies indicating that older subjects often require more practice than young subjects to reach baseline values. Botwinick & Thompson (1968) reported that older subjects require more practice for SRT to an auditory stimulus than younger subjects, especially when short warning intervals were used. Although Murrell (1970) studied the effects of practice in only three subjects, age differences in RT were eliminated with extensive practice, and the absolute improvement of the older subject was greater. Whereas his younger subjects began to improve initially,. the older subject took up to three hundred responses before improvement on CRT with high numbers (eight) of choices, but in well-practiced subjects a break of two months resulted in little loss of speed. Clarkson & Kroll (1978) reported the effects of practice on SRT, CRT, and MvT over two blocks of twelve SRT and fifteen CRT for each of two days. For SRT only, the two older groups demonstrated significant practice effects. For CRT, all groups except the old active group improved with practice. Significant improvements in MvT with practice were demonstrated only by the two inactive groups, with the greatest improvement on MvT following SRT.

MacRae et al. (in preparation) allowed three days of practice and analyzed the scores from the fastest session, which occurred on days one and two for young subjects and on days two and three for old subjects. Practice effects on speed and complexity of card sorting was reported by Falduto & Baron (1986), who found older women to be generally slower, especially with increased task complexity. Though both groups improved with practice, no age difference was evident in the gains, but there was some evidence that the age-complexity relationship was attenuated. Light (1986) studied practice affects for SRT with simple and complex hand movements in four groups ($n = 10$) of old and young practice and control. Following RT testing, the practice groups practiced for three days for one hour on RT trials while control groups practiced digit symbol tasks and experienced a health interview. Although the old were slower than the young, Light reported equal improvement in the MvT scores with the practice groups. The old practice group became equal to the young practice group in SRT with a simple movement and closer but not equal in the SRT with a complex movement. Hart (1980), who analyzed a number of variables over three days of practice, reported differences in RT related to age and activity. RT was stable across days for the old inactive and the young active groups. The young inactive group improved from day one to day two while the old active group improved significantly across all three days.

The lack of control of practice has likely affected many of the studies focused on the role of exercise on RTs of older subjects. Barry, Steinmetz et al, (1966) who did not find a significant reduction in RT following a three-month exercise program, administered only five practice trials followed by five test trials for the pretest and the posttest. Lowe (1988) showed improved CRT for all groups even following one day of practice (three hundred trials) in her complex CRT task. The amount of practice and number of days tested varies considerably in these studies. They range from no reported practice trials and few test trials to three or more days of RT testing.

TASK COMPLEXITY

As an index of perceptual difficulty, subjects were asked to judge which of two simultaneously presented lines was shorter. Older subjects were slower to make these judgments, especially when the stimulus difficulty was increased (Birren & Botwinick, 1955b). These findings were supported as old subjects reacted and moved more slowly for complex tasks than for simple (Tolin & Simon, 1968) and for bimanual coordination (Rt + MvT) (Stelmach, Amrhein & Goggin, 1988). Light (1988) studied task complexity by pairing one of four finger responses with each of the other choices in a two-choice CRT. Response speed depended upon the response pairing, that is, some combinations were more complex than others. Sixty-year-old subjects were slower than 40- and 20-year-old subjects, but only in the more difficult pairings was the 40-year-old group slower than the 20-year-old group. Although many studies have reported the effects of physical activity levels for both SRT and CRT, greater age differences have been shown in DRT (Baylor & Spirduso, in 1988; Spirduso, 1975; Spirduso et al., 1988) and CRT (Dustman, et al., 1984; Rikli & Busch, 1986) than in SRT.

Body-part responding in the RT task does not appear to affect the RT and exercise findings that have been reported for a finger release (Rikli & Busch, 1986; Sherwood & Selder, 1979; Spirduso, 1975; Spirduso & Clifford, 1978), hand release (Dustman et al., 1984), forearm flexion and extension (MacRae et al., in preparation), knee extension (Clarkson, 1978; Hart, 1980), and hip flexors (Baylor & Spirduso, 1988; Spirduso et al., 1988). The two studies not confirming the importance of activity level as a factor affecting RT both involved the upper extremity: a finger release (Botwinick & Storandt, 1974) and lifting a stylus from a metal plate (Barry, Steinmetz et al., 1966).

SEX OF SUBJECT

Findings about the effects of exercise on RT have been reported for both men (Botwinick & Thompson, 1968; Spirduso, 1975; Spirduso & Clifford, 1978; Clarkson, 1978) and women (Baylor & Spirduso, 1988;

Hart, 1980; MacRae et al., in preparation; Spirduso et al., 1988). A fitness program designed to affect RT was unsuccessful with women subjects (Lowe, 1988). Other fitness programs included a mixture of male and female participants. Barry, Steinmetz et al. (1966) reported no differences on RT with a sample of about 60% males. Dustman et al. (1984) reported significant program effects on SRT with a 70% male group. It should be noted that the ACSM exercise guidelines are based on data from men subjects, but women are believed to respond to training in the same manner; however, Pollock, Wilmore & Fox (1984) concluded that the large differences in endurance capacity seen between normal men and women beyond the age of puberty result from comparing moderately active males with relatively sedentary females.

FRACTIONATION OF RT

With numerous reports of slower RT responses in aged subjects, researchers began to define and localize the processes involved in the slowed RTs. Birren & Botwinick (1955a) reasoned that if age changes in peripheral pathways were primarily involved, the age differences in finger RT, jaw RT, and foot RT should be disproportionately slower with increased length of pathways. Although RTs of the older subjects were slower, the age change in RT was not associated with length of the peripheral path. Another method of studying the locus of RT responses has been to fractionate the RT response by recording electromyographical (EMG) potentials from agonist muscles (Weiss, 1965). This fractionation technique separates the RT response into two components: premotor time (PMT) and motor or contractile time (CT). PMT is believed to represent more central effects and is defined as the latency from stimulus onset until EMG first appears in the agonist musculature. CT, the more peripheral component, has been described as an approximation of the muscle "lag" time, or electromechanical delay, representing the biomechanical and biochemical properties of muscle contraction. Weiss (1965) used this technique to determine the locus of the commonly reported slower RTs in older subjects and concluded that the primary slowing in RT with age is in the PMT, or central component. His small difference in CT (10.2 msec) was considered insignificant and possibly reflecting strength decrements in older subjects.

This technique has also been used to study the locus of RT differences in activity level effects with old and young age groups. Clarkson (1978), who repeated Spirduso's (1975) paradigm with four groups of age and activity level differences, fractionated the RTs of male subjects executing a knee extension task. Although she reported RT and

PMT differences among the groups, she concluded that CT was lengthened slightly by the CRT condition and by age, but not by activity level. Thus CT contributes slightly more to total RT for older groups as compared to young groups. Hart (1980), who essentially repeated Clarkson's paradigm with women subjects, also reported RT and PMT differences in age and activity group but found few differences in CT and reported large intersubject variability for CT, especially in the CRT condition. MacRae et al. (in preparation) fractionated Rt in a SRT/CRT paradigm in which CT was compared among age groups in forearm flexion and extension movements. She reported RT and PMT differences with age and activity groups, but not CT differences.

Baylor & Spirduso, (in 1988) argued that the use of CRT has increased the variability associated with CT and has clouded the issue of whether there are significant age differences with activity level in this peripheral component. In the knee extension studies (Clarkson, 1978; Hart, 1980) CRT resulted in three different movements to separate targets determined by the stimulus light. Thus the SRT/CRT paradigm results in a comparison of CT in which the same movement is made in the SRT version of the task and in three extension movements to different targets in the CRT version of the task. In MacRae's study the CRT condition resulted in either a forearm flexion or an extension movement; however, these were equally represented in the SRT (50% flexion and 50% extension). We studied PMT and CT in a SRT/DRT paradigm in which the DRT response was essentially a go/no-go paradigm. The task was similar to releasing the accelerator and pressing the brake pedal of an automobile, and the first responding muscles were the hip flexors. In this paradigm MvT, RT, and both of its fractionated components were significantly faster in the older runners as compared to sedentary controls.

Two other important differences are present when the findings of Baylor & Spirduso are compared to the data of MacRae et al. (in preparation). There was no target in the arm flexion/extension CRT task; thus no "homing in" process was necessary to precisely stop the arm. The other factor is that the arm muscles were not heavily exercised in the running program; thus peripheral effects may be evident only in musculature directly involved in the exercise program. Leg musculature may also suffer more from the selective loss of the giant pyramidal cells of Betz. Scheibel et al. (1977) reported that 75% or more of the Betz cells show age-related changes by the eighth decade of life compared to less than 30% of the smaller, more numerous, surrounding non-Betz pyramidal cells, and they argued that the function of these giant cells increasingly appears to be one of temporary relaxation of extensor muscle tone across weight-bearing joints preceding a specific motor action. They suggested that the high incidence of age-related pathology and loss brings about a clinically significant decrease in the capacity for rapid initial lysis of antigravity tone in extensor muscles, resulting in symptoms and signs of pain, stiffness, and slowing in activities affecting the lower extremities and hips. The PMT findings are robust; the CT findings are small, and clearly additional work is needed in this area.

Another current fractionation technique is to study the effects of aging on stages of information processing models. Although the effects of exercise on these stages have been little reported, Carlow & Appenzeller (1981) have reviewed the favorable effects of endurance training on electroencephalography, sensory evoked responses, mental function, visual system, cerebellar control, peripheral nerve conduction, stretch reflexes, and treatment of neurologic disorders. Spirduso (1984) reviewed evidence that all of the major stages in information processing models are slowed by the aging process. Peripheral processing, including stimulus identification, feature extraction, and pattern recognition, was slower in older individuals (Salthouse & Somberg, 1982a; Simon & Pouraghabagher, 1978). Reduced somesthetic sensitivity to tactile and vibration stimuli (Era et al., 1986; Kenshalo, 1986; Verrillo, 1980) and prolonged latency of event-related potentials to auditory (Pfefferbaum et al., 1980b) and to somatosensory evoked potentials reflecting longer conduction time (Kakigi, 1987) were reported in older subjects. Attentional mechanisms (Ford et al., 1979; Guttentag & Madden, 1987; Gottsdanker, 1982; Hoyer & Familant, 1987; McDowd, 1986; Somberg & Salthouse, 1982) and both short-term and long-term memory processes (Bartus et al., 1978; Pfefferbaum et al., 1980a; Rissenberg & Glanzer, 1987; Wilkie, Eisdorfer & Nowlin, 1976) were reduced by aging. Response selection and programming were also slowed with aging (Light, 1988; Spirduso, 1984). By using research paradigms that fractionate the RT response in various ways, researchers should be able to better understand the locus of slowing with age and its relationship to chronic physical activity.

MASTER'S ATHLETES

Another line of research supporting the positive relationship between physical activity and greater functional capacity with aging is the data from master's athletes. Typically, the master's athlete is about 50 years old and has been training seriously for about twenty years. In most respects they resemble younger, inactive controls more than their own age-matched controls. Body fat is considerably lower as are resting blood pressures, and heart volume is greater. Maximum oxygen intake and the workload corresponding to 75% of VO2max are substantially greater. Loss of aerobic power with aging is slight as compared to normal sedentary subjects (Robinson et al., 1976; Shephard & Kavanagh, 1978; Webb et al., 1977). Unfortunately, the studies involving data on master's athletes have not included indices of psychomotor speed.

EXERCISE AND AGING

What are the mechanisms by which exercise might contribute to faster psychomotor speed in older individuals? Obviously, these mechanisms are not known, but several potential physiological mechanisms that might support such a relationship were reviewed by Spirduso (1980) as she organized her discussion into the general categories of brain function, cerebral circulation, and the tropic influence of physical activity on the central nervous system.

Coleman & Flood (1987) reviewed evidence of decreased neuron numbers and dendritic processes in normal aging and Alzheimer's disease and reported decreased neuronal density in the cerebral cortex with normal aging (although the extent of loss varied with brain area). Dendrites, which represent up to 95% of the receptive surface that the neuron offers for contact with other neurons, regress with aging; both the extent of dendritic branching and the number of dendritic spines (synaptic sites) decrease with aging.

It is difficult to determine how much loss of function is a result of the normal aging process and how much is associated with disease, environmental insult, poor health habits, and disuse. Spieth (1965) reviewed the relationship between cardiovascular disease and slowness of task performance and concluded that subjects suffering arteriosclerotic coronary heart disease or who show evidence of old myocardial infarctions and those with essential hypertension will perform more poorly than age-matched controls. This relationship exists for response speed and cardiovascular function (Abrahams & Birren, 1973; Birren & Spieth, 1962; Botwinick & Storandt, 1974; Light, 1978; Spieth, 1964), for response speed in cerebral diseased patients (Benton, 1977; Hamsher & Benton, 1978), and for other cardiovascular diseases and other mental functions (Hertzog, Schaie & Gribbin, 1978; Simonson & Anderson, 1966; Wilkie & Eisdorfer, 1971). The most common explanation for these relationships is that the brain of a cardiovascular diseased person is suffering from "chronic insufficiency of oxygen transport to or uptake in at least some parts of the central nervous system" (Spieth, 1965). Clearly, physical activity has been accepted as a significant health habit related to reduced mortality from cardiovascular disease (Blair, Kohl & Powell, 1987; Paffenbarger et al., 1986). Johnson (1985) addressed the issue of whether aging is physiological or pathological and defined disease simply as a reaction to injury. Thus aging would be the accumulation of incompletely repaired injuries due to countless microinsults (e.g., ionizing radiation, toxins, free radicals accumulations, mutagenic virus, trauma to vessels and to joints). He described a relationship in which biological systems have a functional reserve that steadily declines until it drops below that required for homeostasis. A specific example was given in which the continual narrowing of the coronary arteries beginning in childhood would not cause clinical disease until late in life when the arteries were more than 75% occluded. Thus by this model any activity that would increase the functional capacity or slow its rate of decline would have favorable effects on the system.

Is there a positive relationship between chronic physical activity in aging individuals and faster psychomotor responses? The evidence, although not unequivocal, is very encouraging, especially in those individuals who have participated in regular physical activity over several years. The data on longitudinal changes by exercise program intervention are scanty. The studies are few; the duration of the exercise program is short (usually three to four months), and although many programs are aimed at the ACSM guidelines (1986), the exercise intensity in older individuals participating in such a program for a few months may not be sufficient to produce the types of changes in the system reflecting faster psychomotor speed.

THEORY INTO PRACTICE

The ACSM position statement on exercise (1978) does not consider age in itself to be a deterrent to endurance training and contends that the change in VO2max is similar to that expected in younger groups, although more time is needed for the training adaptation to occur. Neither is age in the absence of symptoms and primary risk factors considered a strong indicator for requiring a physical examination or diagnostic graded exercise text before age 40 to 45 in men and 50 to 55 in women (Pollock, Wilmore & Fox, 1984). Exercise prescriptions generally have three stages: starter, slow progression, and maintenance. Clearly, the starter portion, which is usually two to six weeks of stretching, light calisthenics, and low-to-moderate-intensity aerobic exercise is important to minimize debilitating injuries to the lower extremities, and its duration is dependent upon the adaptation of the participant. Thus it should be longer with persons of low fitness levels and those who adapt to training at a slower rate. Progression should also be slower. It has been estimated that the adaptation to training load takes approximately 40% longer for each decade in life after 30; thus the amount of time at one training load before progressing to a higher load should be progressively longer with older individuals (Pollock, Wilmore & Fox, 1984).

Training programs lasting fifteen to twenty weeks may be a minimum standard for middle-aged and older participants (ACSM, 1978). Three days per week is the recommended minimum frequency of training, and about 60% of maximum heart rate reserve is the minimal threshold for improvement in VO2max. (Maximum heart rate reserve is defined as the percent difference between resting and maximum heart rate added to resting heart rate.) Thus training heart rate will be greatly reduced in older individuals because of the reduction of maximal heart rate which occurs with aging regardless of training. Since the intensity and duration of training are interrelated, the total amount of work needs to be considered. Older individuals working at low intensity (60%) should gradually work toward the longer times in the recommendation durations (15 to 60 min). Training effect appears to be independent of the mode of aerobic activity as long as the frequency, intensity, and duration of training are similar, thus consideration should always be given to nonweight-bearing exercises. In order to maintain the training effect, aerobic exercise must be continued on a regular basis at a similar intensity because significant reduction occurs after only two weeks of detraining. Generally, aerobic exercise programs for the elderly can be highly successful, but they should be carefully supervised by individuals who are well versed in exercise guidelines, prescription, and emergency procedures.

REFERENCES

Abrahams, J. P., & Birren, J. E. (1973). Reaction time as a function of age and behavioral predisposition to coronary heart disease. *Journal of Gerontology, 28,* 471–78.

American College of Sports Medicine. (1978). Position on statement on the recommended quantity and quality of exercise for developing and maintaining fitness in healthy adults. *Medicine and Science in Sports, 10* vii–x.

American College of Sports Medicine. (1986). *Guidelines for exercise testing and prescription.* 3rd ed. Philadelphia: Lea & Febiger.

Astrand, I.; Astrand, P. -O.; Hallback, I.; & Kilbom, A. (1973). Reduction in maximal oxygen uptake with age. *Journal of Applied Physiology, 35*, 649–54.

Astrand, P.-O. (1968). Physical performance as a function of age. *Journal of the American Medical Association, 205*, 729–33.

Barry, A. J.; Daly, J. W.; Pruett, E. D. R.; Steinmetz, J. R.; Page, H. F.; Birkhead, N. C.; & Rodahl, K. (1966). The effects of physical conditioning on older individuals. I. Work capacity, circulatory-respiratory function, and work electrocardiography. *Journal of Gerontology, 21*, 182–91.

Barry, A. J.; Steinmetz, J. R.; Page, H. F.; & Rodahl, K. (1966). The effects of physical conditioning on older individuals. II. Motor performance and cognitive function. *Journal of Gerontology, 21*, 182–91.

Bartus, R. T.; Fleming, D.; & Johnson, H. R. (1978). Aging in the Rhesus monkey: Debilitating effects on short-term memory. *Journal of Gerontology, 33*, 858-71.

Baylor, A. M.; & Spirduso, W. W. (1988). Systematic aerobic exercise and components of reaction time in older women. *Journal of Gerontology, 43*, 121–126.

Benton, A. L. (1977). Interactive effects of age and brain disease on reaction time. *Archives of Neurology, 34*, 369-70.

Birren, J. E, (1974). Translations in gerontology from lab to life: Psychophysiology and speed of response. *American Psychologist, 29*, 808–15.

Birren, J. E., & Botwinick, J. (1955a). Age differences in finger, jaw, and foot reaction time to auditory stimuli. *Journal of Gerontology, 10*, 429–32.

Birren, J. E., & Botwinick, J. (1955b). Speed of response as a function of perceptual difficulty and age. *Journal of Gerontology, 10*, 433–36.

Birren, J. E., & Spieth, W. (1962). Age, response speed, cardiovascular functions. *Journal of Gerontology, 17*, 390–91.

Birren, J. E.; Woods, A.. M.; & Williams, M. V. (1979). Speed of behavior as an indicator of age changes and the integrity of the nervous system. Bayer Symposium VII, *Brain Function in Old Age* (pp. 10–44). New York: Springer-Verlag.

Blair, S. N. (1988). Physical activity, physical fitness, and health. Seminar presented at the University of Texas, Department of Kinesiology and Health Education, Austin, TX.

Blair, S. N.; Kohl, H. W.; & Powell, K. E. (1987) Physical activity, physical fitness, exercise, and the public's health. In M. J. Safrit & H. M. Eckert (Eds.), *The cutting edge in physical education and exercise science research* (pp. 53–69). Champaign, IL: Human Kinetics.

Botwinick, J. (1973). *Aging and behavior.* New York: Springer.

Botwinick, J.; Brinley, J. F.; & Robbin, J. S. (1958). The effect of motivation by electric shocks on reaction-time in relation to age. *American Journal of Psychology, 71*, 408–11.

Botwinick, J., & Storandt, M. (1974). Cardiovascular status, depressive affect, and other factors in reaction time. *Journal of Gerontology 29*, 543–48.

Botwinick, J., & Thompson, L. W. (1967). Practice of speeded response in relation to age, sex, and set. *Journal of Gerontology, 22*, 72–76.

Botwinick, J., & Thompson, L. W. (1968). Age difference in reaction time: An artifact? *Gerontologist, 8*, 25–28.

Bruce, R. A. (1984). Exercise, functional aerobic capacity, and aging—another viewpoint. *Medicine and Science in Sports and Exercise, 16*, 8–13.

Carlow, T. J., & Appenzeller, O. (1981). Neurology of endurance training. In O. Appenzeller & R. Atkinson (Eds.), *Sportsmedicine* (pp. 41–47). Baltimore: Urban & Schwarzenberg.

Cerella, J. (1985). Information processing rates in the elderly. *Psychological Bulletin, 98*, 67–83.

Chodzko-Zajko, W. J., & Ringel, R. L. (1987). Physiological fitness measures and sensory and motor performance in aging. *Experimental Gerontology, 22*, 317–28.

Clarkson, P. M. (1978). The effect of age and activity level on simple and choice fractionated response time. *European Journal of Applied Physiology, 40*, 17–25.

Clarkson, P. M., & Kroll, W. (1978). Practice effects on fractionated response time related to age and activity level. *Journal of Motor Behavior, 10*, 275–86.

Coleman, P. D., & Flood, D. G. (1987). Review: Neuron numbers and dendritic extent in normal aging and Alzheimer's disease. *Neurobiology of Aging, 8*, 521–45.

Davis, P. O., & Dotson, C. O. (1987). Job performance testing: An alternative to age discrimination. *Medicine and Science in Sports and Exercise, 19*, 179–85.

Dustman, R. E.; Ruhling, R. O.; Russell, E. M.; Shearer, D. E.; Bonekat, H. W.; Shigeoka, J. W.; Wood, J. S.; & Bradford, D. C. (1984). Aerobic exercise training and improved neuropsychological function of older individuals. *Neurobiology of Aging, 5*, 35–42.

Era, P.; Jokela, J.; Suominen, H.; & Heikkinen, E. (1986). Correlates of vibrotactile thresholds in men of different ages. *Acta Neurol. Scand., 74*, 210–217.

Falduto, L. L., & Baron, A. (1986). Age-related effects of practice and task complexity on card sorting. *Journal of Gerontology, 41*, 659–61.

Ford J. M.; Hink, R. F.; Hopkins, W. F.; Roth, W. T.; Pfefferbaum, A.; & Kopell, B. S. (1979). Age effects on event-related potentials in a selective attention task. *Journal of Gerontology, 34*, 388–95.

Gottsdanker, R. (1982). Age and simple reaction time. *Journal of Gerontology, 37*, 342–48.

Guttentag, R. E., & Madden, D. J. (1987). Adult age differences in the attentional capacity demands of letter matching. *Experimental Aging Research, 13*, 93–99.

Hamsher, K. deS., & Benton, A. L. (1978). Adult age differences in the attentional capacity demands of letter matching. *Experimental Aging Research, 13*, 93–99.

Hamsher, K. deS., & Benton, A. L. (1978) interactive effects of age and cerebral disease on cognitive performances. *Journal of Neurology, 217*, 195–200.

Hart, B. A. (1980) Fractionated reflex and response times in women by activity level and age. Ph.D. dissertation. University of Massachusetts, Amherst.

Hertzog, C.; Schaie, K. W.; & Gribbin, K. (1978). Cardiovascular disease and changes in intellectual functioning from middle to old age. *Journal of Gerontology, 33*, 872–83.

Hines, T. (1979). Information feedback, reaction time and error rates in young and old subjects. *Experimental Aging Research, 5*, 207–15.

Holloszy, J. O. (1983). Exercise, health, and aging: A need for more information. *Medicine and Science in Sports and Exercise, 15*, 1–5.

Hornbeck, F. W., & Sucec, A. A. (1982). Changes in aerobic parameters and cognitive measures as a function of age and training intensity. Paper presented to the Southwest Chapter of the American College of Sports Medicine, Las Vegas, Nevada.

Hoyer, W. J., & Familant, M. E. (1987). Adult age differences in the rate of processing expectancy information. *Cognitive Development, 2,* 59–70.

Jacewicz, M. M., & Hartley, A. A. (1987). Age differences in the speed of cognitive operations: Resolution of inconsistent findings. *Journal of Gerontology, 42,* 86–88.

Johnson, H. A. (1985). Is aging physiological or pathological? In H. A. Johnson (Ed.), *Relations between normal aging and disease* (pp. 239–47). New York: Raven Press.

Kakigi, R. (1987). The effect of aging on somatosensory evoked potentials following stimulation of the posterior tibial nerve in man. *Electroencephalography and Clinical Neurophysiology, 68,* 277–86.

Kenshalo, D. R. (1986). Somesthetic sensitivity in young and elderly humans. *Journal of Gerontology, 41,* 732–42.

Kroll, W., & Clarkson, P. M. (1978). Age, siometric knee extension strength, and fractionated resisted response time. *Experimental Aging Research, 4,* 389–409.

Light, K. C. (1978). Effects of mild cardiovascular and cerebrovascular disorders on serial reaction time performance. *Experimental Aging Research, 4,* 3–22.

Light, K. E. (1986). Effects of age and practice on movements of varying complexity. Paper presented at the 5th Annual Health Care Conference on Aging, University of Texas Medical Branch, Galveston, TX.

Light, K. E. (1988). Effects of adult aging on response programming complexity and compatibility. Ph.D. dissertation, University of Texas at Austin.

Lowe, D. L. (1988). The effects of an aerobic exercise program on choice reaction time and motor programming in old and young nontrained women. Master's report. University of Texas at Austin.

MacRae, P. G.; Crum, K.; Giessman, D.; Greene, J.; & Ugolini, J. (in preparation). Fractionated reaction time responses in women as a function of age and fitness level.

McDowd, J. M. (1986). The effects of age and extended practice on divided attention performance. *Journal of Gerontology, 41,* 764–69.

McFarland, R. A.; Tune, G. S.; & Welford, A. T. (1964). On the driving of automobiles by older people. *Journal of Gerontology, 19,* 190–97.

Murrell, F. H. (1970). The effect of extensive practice on age differences in reaction time. *Journal of Gerontology, 25,* 268–74.

Murrell, K. F. H., & Griew, S. (1965). Age, experience and speed of response. In A. T. Welford & J. E. Birren (Eds.), *Behavior, aging, and the nervous system* (pp. 60–66). Springfield, IL: Charles C. Thomas.

Murrell, K. F. H.; Powesland, P. F.; & Forsaith, B. (1962). A study of pillar-drilling in relation to age. *Occupational Psychology, 36,* 45–52.

Murrell, K. F. H., & Tucker, W. A. (1960). A pilot job-study of age-related causes of difficulty in light engineering. *Ergonomics, 3,* 74–79.

Paffenbarger, R. S., Jr.; Hyde, R. T.; Wing, A. L.; & Hsieh, C-c (1986). Physical activity, all-cause mortality, and longevity of college alumni. *New England Journal of Medicine, 314,* 605–13.

Perone, M., & Baron, A. (1982). Age-related effects of pacing on acquisition and performance of response sequences: An operant analysis. *Journal of gerontology, 37*, 443–49.

Perone, M., & Baron, A. (1983). Age-related preferences for paced and unpaced tasks in chained schedules of reinforcement. *Experimental Aging Research, 9*, 165–68.

Pfefferbaum, A.; Ford, J. M.; Roth, W. T.; & Kopell, B. S. (1980a). Age differences in P3-reaction time associations. *Electroencephalography and Clinical Neurophysiology, 49*, 257–65.

Pfefferbaum, A.; Ford, J. M., Roth, W. T.; & Kopell, B. S. (1980b). Age-related changes in auditory event-related potentials. *Electroencephalography and Clinical Neurophysiology, 49*, 266–76.

Pierson, W. R., & Montoye, H. J. (1958). Movement time, reaction time and age. *Journal of Gerontology, 13*, 418–21.

Pollock, M. L.; Wilmore, J. H.; & Fox, S. M. III. (1984). *Exercise in health and disease.* Philadelphia: W. B. Saunders.

Potvin, A. R.; Syndulko, K.; Tourtellotte, W. W.; Lemmon, J. A.; & Polvin, J. H. (1980). Human neurologic function and the aging process. *Journal of the American Geriatrics Society, 28*, 1–9.

Rabbitt, P. (1979). How old and young subjects monitor and control responses for accuracy and speed. *British Journal of Psychology, 70*, 305–11.

Rikli, R., & Busch, S. (1986). Motor performance of women as a function of age and physical activity level. *Journal of Gerontology, 41*, 645–49.

Rissenberg, M., & Glanzer, M. (1987). Free recall and word finding ability in normal aging and senile dementia of the Alzheimer's type: The effect of item concreteness. *Journal of Gerontology, 42*, 318–22.

Robinson, S.; Dill, D. B.; Robinson, R. D.; Tzankoff, S. P.; & Wagner, J. A. (1976). Physiological aging of champion runners. *Journal of Applied Physiology, 41*, 46–51.

Salthouse, T. A. (1984). Effects of age and skill in typing. *Journal of Experimental Psychology; General, 113*, 345–71.

Salthouse, T. A., & Somberg, B. L. (1982a). Isolating the age deficit in speeded performance. *Journal of Gerontology, 37*, 59–63.

Salthouse, T. A., & Somberg, B. L. (1982b). Time-accuracy relationships in young and old adults. *Journal of Gerontology, 37*, 349–53.

Scheibel, M. E.; Tomiyasu, U.; & Scheibel A. B. (1977). The aging human Betz cell. *Experimental Neurology, 56*, 598–609.

Schonfield, D. (1974). Translations in gerontology from lab to life: Utilizing information. *American Psychologist. 29*, 796–801.

Sharkey, B. J., (1987). Functional vs chronologic age. *Medicine and Science in Sports and Exercise, 19*, 174–78.

Shephard, R. J., & Kavanagh, T. (1978). The effects of training on the aging process. *Physician and Sports Medicine, 6*, 33–40.

Sherwood, D. E., & Selder, D. J. (1979). Cardiorespiratory health, reaction time and aging. *Medicine and Science in Sports, 11*, 186–89.

Simon, J. R., & Pouraghabagher, A. R. (1978). The effect of aging on the stages of processing in a choice reaction time task. *Journal of Gerontology, 33*, 553–61.

Simonson, E., & Anderson, D. A. (1966). Effect of age and coronary heart disease on performance and physiological responses in mental work. *Proceedings of the 7th International Congress on Gerontology* (pp. 333–36). Vienna.

Skinner, J. S.; Tipton, C. M.; & Vailas, A. C. (1982). Exercise, physical training, and the aging process. In A. Viidik (Ed.), *Advances in gerontology* (pp. 407–39). London: Academic Press.

Somberg, B. L, & Salthouse, T. A., (1982). Divided attention abilities in young and old adults. *Journal of Experimental Psychology: Human Perception and Performance, 8,* 651–63.

Spieth, W. (1964). Cardiovascular health status, age, and psychological performance. *Journal of Gerontology, 19,* 277–84.

Spieth, W. (1965). Slowness of task performance and cardiovascular diseases. In A. T. Welford & J. E. Birren (Eds.) *Behavior, aging and the nervous system,* (pp. 366–400). Springfield, IL: Charles C. Thomas.

Spirduso, W. W. (1975). Reaction and movement time as a function of age and physical activity level. *Journal of Gerontology, 30,* 435–40.

Spirduso, W. W. (1980). Physical fitness, aging, and psychomotor speed: A review. *Journal of Gerontology, 35,* 850–65.

Spirduso, W. W. (1984). Exercise as a factor in aging motor behavior plasticity. In *Exercise and health, the American Academy of Physical Education Papers, No. 17,* (pp. 89–100). Fifty-fourth Annual Meeting. Minneapolis Champaign, IL: Human Kinetics.

Spirduso, W. W., & Clifford, P. (1978). Replication of age and physical activity effects on reaction and movement time. *Journal of Gerontology: 33,* 26–30.

Spirduso, W. W., & Farrar, R. P. (1981). Effects of aerobic training on reactive capacity: An animal model. *Journal of Gerontology, 35,* 654–62.

Spirduso, W. W.; MacRae, H. H.; MacRae, P. G.; Prewitt, J.; & Osborne, L. (1988). Exercise effects on aged motor function. *Annals of the New York Academy of Sciences, 515,* 363–375.

Stelmach, G. E.; Amrhein, P. C.; & Goggin, N. L. (1988). Age differences in bimanual coordination. *Journal of Gerontology: Psychological Sciences, 43,* 18–23.

Tolin, P., & Simon, J. R. (1968). Effect of task complexity and stimulus duration on perceptual-motor performance of two disparate age groups. *Ergonomics, 11,* 283–90.

Verrillo, R. T. (1980). Age-related changes in the sensitivity to vibration. *Journal of Gerontology, 35,* 185–93.

Webb, J. L.; Urner, S. C.; & McDaniels, J. (1977). Physiological characteristics of a champion runner: Age 77. *Journal of Gerontology, 32,* 286–90.

Weiss, A. D. (1965). The locus of reaction time change with set, motivation, and age. *Journal of Gerontology, 20,* 60–64.

Welford, A. T. (1982). Motor skills and aging. In J. A. Mortimer, F. J. Pirozzolo, & G. J. Maletta (Eds.). *The aging motor system* (pp. 152–87). New York: Praeger Scientific.

Wilkie, F., & Eisdorfer, C. (1971). Intelligence and blood pressure in the aged. *Science, 172,* 959–62.

Wilkie, F. L.; Eisdorfer, C.; & Nowlin, J. B. (1976). Memory and blood pressure in the aged. *Experimental Aging Research, 2*, 3–16.

Woollacott, M. H.; Inglin, B.; & Manchester, D. (1988). Response preparation and posture control in the older adult. In J. Joseph, Central determinants of age-related declines in motor function. *Annals of the New York Academy of Science, 515*, 42–53.

Part IV

Abnormal
Postural Control
and the
Effects of Training

10

Equilibrium Deficits in Children

Anne Shumway-Cook

The importance of understanding the underlying basis of abnormal postural control leading to balance deficits in children is rarely questioned. This importance is reflected in the numbers of books and articles devoted to describing the development of equilibrium in normal children and identifying deviations from normal postural control which contribute to balance problems. Developmental behavioral studies have been consistent in demonstrating that the neurologically impaired child achieves motor milestones at a much later chronological age than normal peers. Since it has been shown that the emergence of equilibrium function is an essential component of normal motor development, it might be expected that postural control abnormalities responsible for disruption of normal equilibrium function could account for some of the delays and deviations from normal development commonly found in the neurologically impaired child.

Studying the physiological basis for normal and abnormal postural control is important to neuroscientists concerned with neural control issues as well as to health care professionals concerned with the care of children with balance problems. Although the need for knowledge about normal and abnormal postural control is rarely questioned, there is no consensus as to the best approach for studying the problem. Indeed, the approaches used vary widely and reflect fundamental differences in assumptions about the neural basis of postural control underlying the development of equilibrium in children. These differences in approaches have affected our understanding of the neural basis for instability as well. This chapter will review research on the neural basis for equilibrium deficits in children from two different perspectives, a hierarchical/reflex approach and a distributed or systems model approach.

The first part of the chapter will discuss the neurophysiological basis for pediatric instability from a hierarchical, reflexological framework. In this framework disorders of equilibrium in children may be understood by examining the presence and or absence of hierarchically organized postural reflexes. Assessment and treatment of pediatric balance disorders using this approach are also discussed.

The second part of the chapter examines a distributed systems control approach to the study of pediatric postural control deficits. In this perspective disorders of equilibrium may best be understood by assessing problems within individual systems important to postural control. Thus problems within multiple neuro-musculo-skeletal systems and their effect on posture are considered. Implications for therapeutic intervention which arise from a distributed control approach will be discussed.

The focus of this chapter is disorders of postural control. To that end, selected research examining postural control problems in different patient populations will be presented. My purpose, however, is not to provide the reader with an in-depth understanding of the posture and movement problems associated with specific diagnoses, for example, cerebral palsy or Down syndrome, but rather to use research from patient studies to illustrate how abnormalities within different parts of the postural control system can affect equilibrium. A second goal of the chapter is to stimulate both researchers and health care professionals who are engaged in the study and treatment of postural control underlying balance disorders in children to examine more carefully the underlying assumptions of their approaches.

POSTURAL STABILITY FROM A REFLEX POINT OF VIEW

Historically, examination of reflexes has been an essential part of the study of motor development. Many developmental theorists have described the process of development as a spiraling continuum in which lower level, primitive reflex patterns evolve and are integrated into higher level, more mature reactions. It has been suggested that it is these reflexes that form the basis for mature patterns of movement behavior (Easton, 1972; Twitchell, 1975). A reflex approach to analyzing motor development is based in part on Hughlings Jackson's research, which suggests that the central nervous system (CNS) is organized as a vertical hierarchy (Jackson, 1932). It is thought that the sequential maturation of ascending levels of the CNS hierarchy results in the emergence of higher levels of behavior, which in turn modify immature behaviors organized at hierarchically lower levels within the CNS. New behaviors, then, emerge as "higher level modifications" of older, lower-level reactions (Gilfoyle et al., 1986).

The newborn infant and young child are described as being domi-nated by primitive reflexes thought to be organized at hierarchically lower levels of the nervous system. Equilibrium reactions, defined by Weiss (1938) as automatic reactions to labyrinthine inputs, are pur-ported to be controlled at the "top" of the CNS hierarchy, the cortex. In normal development, equilibrium reactions emerge only when the CNS matures to such an extent that the cortex is "in control" of lower parts of the neural hierarchy. Hence equilibrium responses emerge as part of a natural progression toward the assumption of a vertical, upright posture.

Studies providing normative data on the sequential development of postural reflexes have been extensively published (Capute et al., 1982; Paine, 1964; Haley, 1986b; Haley et al., 1986). In these studies equi-librium reactions are distinguished from righting reactions and protec-tive reactions. Righting reactions are purported to be responsible for maintaining alignment to gravity and keeping body parts in alignment to one another after rotation (Chandler et al., 1980; Effgen, 1982). Equilibrium reactions are responses to loss of balance which results when the body's base of support is disturbed by a push, pull, or tilt (Bobath, 1975a). With the emergence of equilibrium reactions, righting reactions become integrated. It has been suggested that righting reac-tions allow a child to function on a quadrupedal level, but in order to progress to a bipedal level of function the emergence of equilibrium reactions is necessary.

It is commonly assumed that a mature, or partially mature, equi-librium reaction is necessary in one position before the next develop-mental motor milestone is attained (Haley, 1986b; Milani-Comparetti & Gidoni, 1967a). Equilibrium reactions are reported to emerge first in prone (5 to 7 months), then in supine (7 to 11 months), in sitting (7 to 8 months), quadruped (8 to 12 months), and finally in standing (12 to 21 months) (Haley, 1986b; Effgen, 1982). Thus before a child can sit, she must first have developed mature equilibrium reactions in prone posi-tion; prior to standing, equilibrium reactions must be present in sitting and quadruped positions.

PRIMITIVE REFLEXES AS A BASIS FOR DYSEQUILIBRIUM

It has been hypothesized that instability in the child with neu-rologic problems results from a combination of abnormal postural re-flexes, abnormal muscle tone, and impaired muscle coordination. A variety of reflex profiles has been developed to evaluate the evolution of reflex patterns in atypical children and to correlate these results with other neurodevelopmental findings (Capute et al., 1982; Effgen, 1982; Chandler et al., 1980). Results have been used to predict motor abnormalities and eventual functional outcomes (Milani-Comparetti & Gidoni, 1967a; Capute et al., 1982). Bleck (1975) reported that assessing the presence and/or absence of five tonic reflexes and two postural reactions will successfully predict walking outcome in children with cerebral palsy. Molnar and Fordon (1976) also used the persistence of primitive reflexes to predict ambulation outcome in cerebral palsied children. However, other researchers have questioned the validity of using reflex assessment alone for predicting developmental abnormalities in children (Cambell & Wilhelm, 1985).

Persistence and dominance by primitive reflexes such as Tonic Labyrinthine Reflex, Asymmetric Tonic Neck Reflex, and Symmetric Tonic Neck Reflex are considered to be a major deterrent to independent mobility in the child with cerebral palsy (Wat, 1978; Bobath, 1975). It has been reported that in the spastic cerebral palsied child the dominance of primitive postural patterns results in spasticity and loss of mobility (Bobath & Bobath, 1984). In the ataxic cerebral palsied child equilibrium reactions are present, but movements are uncoordinated due to the presence of abnormal muscle tonus (Bobath & Bobath, 1976).

Hypotonia and persistence of primitive reflexes as an explanation for delayed motor development have also been reported in children with Down's syndrome and other types of mental retardation (Cowie, 1970; Molnar, 1978; Haley, 1986a). Rast & Harris (1986) reported that in addition to delayed emergence of postural righting reactions, four-month-old Down's syndrome infants use movement strategies to control their heads in space which were never seen in nonimpaired infants.

THERAPEUTIC IMPLICATIONS

Many techniques developed to assess and treat balance disorders are based on assumptions regarding the importance of normal reflex maturation to development (Ellison, 1983). Clinical assessment of equilibrium reactions is most commonly done by tipping a child positioned on a movable support base (Bobath, 1975; Effgen, 1982; Haley, 1986b). Presence or absence of the response or a competing response is noted.

Treatment progressions are developed with the goal of inhibiting abnormal postural reflex activity and facilitating higher-level equilibrium reactions (Bobath, 1975; Effgen, 1982). Because of the assumption that equilibrium reactions are necessary in one position before the next developmental motor milestone can be attained, time is spent within therapy stimulating righting and equilibrium reactions. This is accomplished by moving the child in such a way as to stimulate and guide an appropriate response. For example, the therapist may place a child in a seated position on a ball and gently move the ball back and forth so that the child makes the necessary head and trunk responses to counter the ball motion. Usually righting and equilibrium reactions are stimulated in an ontogenetic sequence, that is, first in prone, then supine, sitting, crawling, and finally standing (Effgen, 1982). However, the necessity for adhering to a strict ontogenetic sequence when teaching motor skills has been questioned (Forssberg, 1980; Bobath & Bobath, 1984).

In addition to the stimulation of appropriate responses by therapists, assistive devices, including seating and mobility devices, have been designed with the goal of inhibiting persistent and dominant abnormal primitive reflexes in the child with neurologic deficits (Wat, 1978).

SUMMARY

In summary, from a reflex/hierarchical perspective of CNS organization, dysequilibrium in the neurologically impaired child is associated with delay or disruption in CNS maturation resulting in the persistence of primitive reflexes. The presence of nonintegrated dominating primitive reflexes organized at hierarchically lower levels of the CNS prevents the emergence of normal equilibrium function. Since it is assumed that the development of normal voluntary behavior rests on a reflex substratum, the neurologically impaired child is blocked from achieving independence in other functional "voluntary" activities because of the presence of competing primitive movement patterns. From a therapeutic perspective, achievement of higher-level functional independence in the neurologically impaired child depends upon the therapist's ability to move the child up the CNS hierarchy, facilitating higher-level control over lower-level reflexes so that skilled voluntary movement may appear.

DISTRIBUTED OR SYSTEMS CONTROL APPROACH

In contrast to a reflex model, a distributed control or systems model of CNS control examines the maturation of various components of postural control which contribute to the development of equilibrium function. Understanding instability in children involves the systematic assessment of the individual components contributing to the task of balance and the dynamics of their interaction.

The nature of the distributed control organization itself, as well as the capacity for the immature nervous system to compensate for neural insult, makes assessment of instability difficult. Because individual components interact, abnormalities in one can disrupt normal function in the entire system. In addition, similar behavior may result from pathology in different parts of the system because loss or disruption within one component can be compensated for by those remaining. It is difficult to separate behavior that is the direct result of a neural lesion from behavior that is compensatory to the lesion. This is particularly true in the immature nervous system, where plasticity is great. Thus the effect of a neural lesion on loss of function depends in part on the extent of compensation by remaining intact components (Grimm & Nashner, 1978).

Analyzing abnormal movement behavior, in particular postural instability, involves distinguishing abnormal behavior from compensatory behavior. This is not an insignificant problem. A common view in rehabilitation medicine is that movement behavior seen in the neurologic pediatric patient is in most instances abnormal, that is, the result of a neural lesion, rather than compensatory. Long-term impact of therapy will be small, however, if efforts are directed toward changing behavior that is compensatory to a problem rather than addressing the problem directly.

A number of components of sensory motor function contribute to normal postural control in children and adults (see Woollacott, et al., Chap. 4 of this volume, for more detail). Instability can result from an abnormality in one or more of these component functions. Those discussed in this chapter include non-neural, biomechanical changes in the musculoskeletal system; abnormalities of muscular coordination; and problems in the organization of sensory information for postural orientation.

BIOMECHANICAL CHANGES IN THE MUSCULOSKELETAL SYSTEM

Few studies examine non-neural changes in the musculoskeletal system in the child with neurologic deficits. In part this paucity is due to a traditional emphasis on neurophysiological, rather than biomechanical, explanations for motor-control deficits found in the child with neurologic deficits (Gordon, 1987).

The incidence of connective-tissue and muscle contractures in the cerebral palsy child is great (Bleck, 1976). Numerous methods have been developed to correct musculoskeletal deformities, including plaster casting and surgical intervention (Sussman, 1978; Castle, 1978a).

Berger et al. (1982) examined posture and locomotion in spastic hemiplegic and diplegic cerebral palsy children. Despite clinical evidence of increased muscle tonus in the triceps surae of the involved leg, increased tension recorded in the Achilles tendon during stance phase of gait was not associated with increased electromyographic (EMG) activity in the triceps surae. This finding led to the conclusion that increased muscle stiffness found in spastic patients is due to changes in the mechanical properties of the muscle fibers themselves. This explanation is consistent with Castle's work reporting changes in the composition of muscle fibers in ambulatory and nonambulatory children with cerebral palsy (Castle, 1978b).

Stiffness regulation was examined in studies on postural control in three classes of cerebral palsied children (Nashner et al., 1983; Shumway-Cook, 1986). As expected, on clinical examination the spastic hemiplegic children demonstrated spasticity (increased resistance to passive stretch) in the triceps surae muscle on the involved leg. However, when the children were in a dynamic situation, maintaining balance in the upright position, passive stiffness in response to stretch of the ankle joint was comparable in spastic and nonspastic legs. A further surprise was the almost complete lack of myotatic reflex activity in response to imposed stretch in the "spastic" triceps surae muscle, despite the presence of enhanced deep tendon reflexes on clinical examination.

Changes in muscle-joint systems have been reported in Down syndrome children. Abnormalities reported include problems in stiffness regulation (Davis & Kelso, 1982) and changes in tendon and connective-tissue composition contributing to increased joint laxity (Harris, 1981).

These findings suggest that musculoskeletal changes may account for some of the motor-control deficits found in children with neurologic deficits. Further research in this area is essential.

MOTOR DYSCOORDINATION: TIMING PROBLEMS

Several types of motor-coordination probmems can contribute to instability in children. This section focuses on different kinds of timing problems and their role in dysequilibrium.

Onset Timing Problems. In order for postural movement strategies to be effective in returning the center of body mass to a position within the support base of the feet, the timing of muscle onset is critical (McCollum & Leen, in press; Forssberg & Nashner, 1982; Shumway-Cook & Woollacott, 1985a). Normal children, like normal adults, respond to external disturbances of equilibrium with muscle responses at latencies of approximately 95 to 110 msec (see Woollacott et al., Chapt. 4 of this volume, for more information). Delay in the onset of muscle responses can result in instability as the center of body mass moves outside the limits of stability before an effective corrective force can be generated. Using EMGs to record activity in distal and proximal leg muscles,

Shumway-Cook & Woollacott (1985b) reported normal sequencing of muscle responses but significant timing problems in children with Down syndrome. Children with Down syndrome demonstrated postural response onset latencies of 136 to 160 msec, significantly longer than the 110 to 112 msec onset latencies found in normal, age-matched children. Delayed onset of corrective muscle responses resulted in greater amounts of body sway in Down syndrome children compared to normal, age-matched peers.

Delayed onset latencies of postural responses can also be seen in children with some types of cerebral palsy. Children with spastic hemiplegia demonstrate timing asymmetries, with normal onset timing found in muscles in the uninvolved leg but delayed onset latencies in the involved leg (Nashner et al., 1983). These children have a more serious timing problem, however, which will be discussed in the next section.

Delayed postural responses can also be found in children with ataxic cerebral palsy. Unlike adults with cerebellar lesions, children with ataxia due to cerebellar lesions demonstrate not only large delays in onset of responses, but considerable trial-to-trial variation as well (Nashner et al., 1983; Shumway-Cook, 1986). As was true with Down syndrome children, timing delays produced greater than normal amounts of body sway in ataxic cerebral palsied children compared to normal children.

Intermuscle Timing Problems. Effective motor coordination requires close temporal coupling between proximal and distal muscles working synergistically to stabilize the body mass. Temporal structuring of muscle responses in normal children involves initial activation of distal muscles at about 100 msec, followed by proximal muscle activation 20 to 45 msec later. This synergistic action by proximal thigh and trunk muscles minimizes antiphase motion at the hips, resulting in little movement at the knees and hips (Shumway-Cook & Woollacott, 1985a). Disturbance of this tightly sequenced pattern of muscle activity reduces the effectiveness of a response in reestablishing stability following loss of balance.

Temporal delays of 40 to 50 msec between distal and proximal muscle synergists have been reported in children with Down syndrome and in some normal children between the ages of 4 and 6. Delayed activation of proximal muscles resulted in excessive motion at the knees and hips due to inertial lag associated with mass of the thigh and trunk (Shumway-Cook & Woollacott, 1985b).

Timing problems between distal and proximal muscle synergists have also been reported in children with spastic hemiplegia. However, rather than delays in proximal muscle activation, Nashner et al. (1983)

reported disruption in the sequencing of muscle onset such that proximal muscles were found to respond in advance of distal muscles. In addition, temporal coupling between synergists was more variable and the level of antagonist coactivation was greater. Figure 10–1 shows EMG records from leg muscles in the noninvolved and involved legs of a spastic hemiplegic child. The pattern of muscle contractions in the spastic leg is significantly different than in the noninvolved leg. In response to forward sway, the latency of the gastrocnemius response is slower (145+13 msec) and the sequence of activity is temporally reversed. The postural response begins in the hamstrings and radiates distally to the gastrocnemius. This temporal reversal between proximal and distal muscles can also be seen in responses to backward sway. The first muscle to respond is the quadriceps muscle, followed by the tibialis anterior muscle.

The mechanical consequences of inappropriate sequencing of synergistic muscles are great. Analysis of torque traces in this and other hemiplegic children indicated that despite large amplitudes of EMG activity the involved leg was not generating significant amounts of force to help compensate for postural instability. Rather, compensation for induced body sway was largely the result of action by the noninvolved leg. Another indirect consequence of abnormal coordinated muscular contractions was rapid oscillatory lateral weight shifts between the two legs.

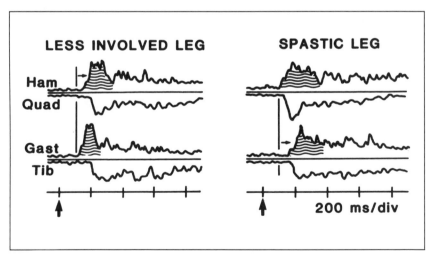

Fig. 10–1. EMG patterns to forward and backward postural perturbations in involved and noninvolved legs in spastic hemiplegic child. Spastic patterns show abnormal sequencing as well as antagonist muscle coactivation.

Abnormal patterns of muscle coordination did not correlate well with the distribution of abnormal muscle tonus in spastic hemiplegic children. Muscles identified clinically as spastic, that is, having increased resistance to passive stretch and enhanced deep tendon reflexes, showed delayed response onset even to a direct stretch input. Slowed onset and reduced amplitude in spastic muscles responding to stretch have been reported by others. Berger et al. (1985) found delayed onset and reduced amplitude of long latency muscle responses (LM2) in standing cerebral palsy children. They suggest that it is abnormal LM2 responses that result in impairment of gait and stance in cerebral palsy children. The relationship between abnormal patterns of muscle coordination and functional balance problems supports the concept that abnormal patterns of coordination are better indicators of loss of function than distribution of abnormal tonus (Milani-Comparetti & Gidoni, 1967).

The literature is inconsistent regarding the presence of abnormalities in the stretch reflex mechanism in children with abnormal muscle tonus. Nashner et al. (1983) found no increased myotatic activity in stretched spastic muscles of standing cerebral palsy children, although longer latency postural responses were delayed. In contrast, Berger et al. (1985) reported persistence of short latency myotatic activity (LM1) in spastic cerebral palsy children, though LM2 responses were delayed. Presence of normal latency myotatic activity in conjunction with delayed onset of postural muscle responses has been reported in hypotonic Down syndrome children as well (Shumway-Cook & Woollacott, 1985b). These findings raise serious questions about the traditional assumption that abnormal muscle tonus results from abnormalities within the stretch reflex mechanism (Wyke, 1976). An in-depth critical examination of this hypothesis has been presented by Burke (1983).

In contrast to current theory defining cerebellar ataxia as incoordination and dyssynergia (Harris, 1981), Nashner et al. (1983) did not find intermuscle timing problems in children with ataxia cerebral palsy. Although onset of responses was delayed, timing between distal and proximal muscle synergists was not significantly different from that of normal children.

Table 10–1 summarizes the types of timing and sequencing problems involved in motor-coordination deficits in postural control. Also presented are some of the patient groups manifesting these problems.

TABLE 10-1

Motor Coordination Deficits

Patient Group	Onset Timing	Intermuscle Timing	Sequencing
Down's syndrome	Symmetric delay	Delay	Normal
Spastic Hemiplegia	Asymmetric delay	Reversals	Reversals Coactivation
Ataxic	Symmetric delay More variable	Normal	Normal

SENSORY ORGANIZATION IN POSTURAL CONTROL

Sensory processes in balance control involve the organization of orientation inputs from somatosensory (proprioception, cutaneous, and joint) and visual and vestibular systems. Despite the availability of multiple sensory inputs, the central nervous system (CNS) generally relies on only one sense at a time for orientation information (Nashner, 1982; Shumway-Cook & Horak, 1986). It has been proposed that the preferred sensory input for the control of balance in normal adults and children above the age of 7 is somatosensory information from the feet. However, when somatosensory information reporting body movement relative to the support surface is reduced or inaccurate, such as when standing on a dense carpet or compliant foam, an alternative sensory input must be used. In cases in which there is conflict among the senses reporting orientation information, it is purported that the CNS uses orientationally accurate inputs from the vestibular system to resolve the conflict (Nashner et al., 1982). Research on normal development of postural control in children suggests that the controlling inputs to posture may be age-dependent. At 4 to 6 years of age a shift occurs from visual dependence to a more adultlike dependence on a combination of somatosensory, vestibular, and visual inputs (see Woollacott et al., Chap. 4 of this volume, for more information on normal development of postural control).

Research has shown that problems in the organization of sensory information can affect postural control in at least two ways. Disruption of the sensory component processes can adversely affect children's ability to orient in space and to coordinate movement strategies for postural control.

POSTURAL ORIENTATION PROBLEMS

Postural orientation problems can result from loss of one or more sensory inputs providing essential orientation information to the postural control system. Instability can also result from a central abnormality resulting in an inability to coordinate normal sensory inputs from vestibular visual and somatosensory systems (Horak et al., 1988; Shumway-Cook et al., 1987).

In recent years a number of studies have examined the role of the vestibular system in the development of postural stability. The vestibular system's role in the development of normal equilibrium function is controversial. Even less is known about the relationship between abnormal vestibular function and sensorimotor problems found in childhood. Disorders of the vestibular system have been implicated as the basis for developmental delays (Pignataro et al., 1979; Kantner et al., 1976), motor dyscoordination (Kaga et al., 1981), postural abnormalities (Rapin, 1974), and learning disabilities in children (DeQuiros, 1976; Ottenbacher, 1982; Ayres, 1972). Based on this premise, considerable health-care resources have been directed toward identifying and treating specific vestibular abnormalities in children.

Evidence that vestibular abnormalities underlie sensorimotor problems in children is indirect and rests largely on two assumptions: (1) that the normal development of many motor skills, including sitting, standing, and locomotion, is dependent upon maturation of normal equilibrium reactions; and (2) an intact vestibular system is necessary to the development of normal equilibrium function. Therefore, the presence of sensorimotor abnormalities such as poor eye/head coordination, decreased muscle tonus, inability to maintain prone extended posture against gravity, poor spatial orientation, and poor balance is considered indirect evidence for vestibular dysfunction. Results from several recent studies, however, have cast doubt on widely held assumptions regarding the relationship between vestibular pathology and many sensorimotor deficits found in children (Horak et al., 1988; Shumway-Cook et al., 1987).

Several studies report the effect of symmetric and asymmetric vestibular hypofunction on postural orientation skills in deaf children aged 7 to 12 (Horak et al., 1988; Shumway-Cook et al., 1986). These studies used a movable platform and visual surround to examine children's ability to alternatively use vision, somatosensation, and vestibular inputs for postural orientation. Children stood on a hydraulically controlled, movable platform, facing the center of a three-sided, movable, visual enclosure. Anterior-posterior body sway was measured while children stood for twenty seconds under six different sensory conditions. Under the first three test conditions the platform support surface was stationary, while the visual conditions consisted of (1) normal visual inputs for postural control (i.e., nonmoving visual surround), (2) absent vision (using blindfold), and (3) spatially unreliable visual inputs for orientation. In this last condition the visual surround was moved in proportion to the children's body sway, depriving the child of normal visual motion cues associated with postural sway. Thus visual cues, though present, were inaccurate for postural orientation. This required their suppression in favor of accurate vestibular and/or somatosensory inputs in order to maintain balance.

In the last three sensory conditions the support surface was no longer stationary but rotated in direct proportion to body sway, minimizing orientation information generated from the feet in contact with the support surface. The three visual conditions were repeated: (4) normal vision, (5) absent vision, (6) present but inaccurate vision. In the last two conditions (5 and 6) the only accurate sensory orientation input available to the postural control system was from the vestibular system.

Sway area was measured and normalized for each child's height and base of support. Normal limits for sway in the six conditions were defined using data from normal children.

Results from these studies suggest that the effect of loss of vestibular function on postural orientation skills is context-dependent. Because of the redundant nature of sensory inputs for postural orientation, the loss of one input (in this case, vestibular information) does not adversely affect a child's ability to remain oriented as long as visual or somatosensory orientation cues are available. Instability is seen only when a child must orient to gravity despite absent or inaccurate sensory cues from vision and/or somatosensory systems.

Identical methodology was used to examine vestibular function and balance deficits in fifteen motor-impaired, learning-disabled (LD) children (Shumway-Cook et al., 1987). Results from the six sensory organization trials suggested that, despite intact peripheral vestibular inforamtion, LD children with sensorimotor impairments could not appropriately integrate vestibulospinal inputs with visual and somatosensory inputs for postural orientation. Figure 10–2 compares body sway across the six sensory conditions in normal, deaf, and LD children. Deaf children with reduced vestibular function fell (score of 100) only when surface and visual information for orientation were unavailable and vestibular inputs alone mediated postural orientation (conditions 5 and 6). In contrast, LD children had significantly greater body sway compared to normal or deaf children in trials where there was conflict among the senses (conditions 3, 4, 5, and 6).

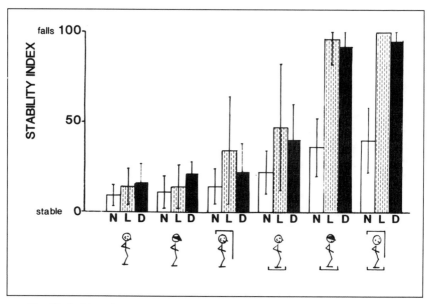

Fig. 10–2. Mean integrated postural sway area as a percentage of children's maximum sway in the six sensory conditions for the normal children (N), motor-impaired, learning-disabled children (L), and deaf children with reduced vestibular function (D).

Inability to effectively organize redundant sensory inputs for postural orientation has been reported in other postural control studies on children with CNS pathology. Ataxic cerebal palsy children demonstrate an inability to accurately maintain upright equilibrium under conditions containing conflicting orientation inputs from vision and somatosensation (Nashner et al., 1983; Shumway-Cook, 1986). This is consistent with research reporting orientation deficits in adults with cerebellar pathology (Horak et al., 1986). Because motor-coordination processes were largely normal in ataxic cerebral palsy children, dysequilibrium could not be attributed to incoordination among muscle synergists responding to loss of balance. Rather, equilibrium deficits appeared to be the result of abnormalities within central processes responsible for the organization and integration of redundant sensory inputs to the postural control system.

It is interesting to note that not all children with cerebral palsy demonstrated this type of abnormality. Contrary to our expectations, none of the children with spastic hemiplegia, even those with severe perceptual problems including hemineglect, evidenced a central sensory organization problem affecting postural orientation (Nashner et al., 1983; Shumway-Cook, 1986). It must be cautioned that the sample size in this study was extremely small (twenty-one children).

Results from this study of children are in contrast to data from a study on postural disorientation in adult hemiplegic patients following cerebral vascular accident (Shumway-Cook, unpublished observations). Almost half of the adult hemiplegic patients showed sensory organization problems leading to dysequilibrium. Surprisingly, the presence of postural orientation deficits was not limited to patients with right cerebral vascular accidents who had well-documented spatial orientation deficits.

In summary, dysequilibrium may result from sensory organization problems leading to postural disorientation. Sensory organization problems may arise from loss of a sense, as in deaf children with decreased vestibular function. In addition, orientation problems may be due to a central processing abnormality, as seen in LD children and ataxic cerebral palsy children, who could not effectively integrate peripherally intact vestibular, visual, and somatosensory inputs for postural control.

ADAPTING MOVEMENT STRATEGIES TO CONTEXT

In addition to postural orientation problems, sensory organization problems can adversely affect children's ability to adapt postural movement strategies to changes in environmental context. This section examines the development of coordinated postural movement strategies in children. Further results from the previously mentioned deaf and LD research studies are presented (Shumway-Cook, et al., 1986; Horak et al., 1988). Results from these studies suggest that loss of a sense early in life may affect postural movement coordination differently than central sensory organization problems. In addition, peripheral sensory versus central sensory problems affect overall motor-skill development in different ways.

Ninety-nine children aged 7 to 12 years participated in these combined studies: thirty hearing impaired; fifteen motor impaired, learning disabled; and fifty-four normal children. After extensive otologic testing of vestibular function, children were classified as having (1) normal sensory function for postural control; (2) reduced or absent peripheral vestibular function; or (3) abnormal sensory organization function. In the last case there was an inability to coordinate normal vestibular signals with inputs from vision and somatosensory systems for postural orientation.

The ability to coordinate postural movement strategies with changes in context was assessed while children were perturbed when standing either on a flat surface or across a beam 9 cm wide. Body kinematics and EMG responses in six leg and trunk muscles were analyzed to quantify parameters of motor coordination. Previous research on normal adults and children above the age of 7 suggests that

an ankle strategy is used to maintain balance in the flat surface condition, whereas a hip strategy, or mixture of the two strategies, is used
while maintaining balance on the narrow beam (Horak & Nashner,
1986).

Results showed that all children, regardless of sensory classification, had normally coordinated postural responses to loss of balance
while standing on a flat surface. Onset latencies of postural responses
were not significantly different in any of the children (normal children:
93 ± 19msec; reduced vestibular function: 101 ± 20msec; abnormal
sensory organization: 106 ± 11msec).

In contrast to findings on the flat surface were results from the
beam surface. Only those children classified as having normal sensory
function successfully maintained balance when perturbed while standing crosswise on a narrow beam. Children with reduced vestibular
function or central sensory organization problems were not generally
successful in maintaining balance while on the beam. Following three to
five trials of practice, normal children responded to loss of balance while
standing on the narrow beam with a normally coordinated hip postural
movement strategy. Children with reduced vestibular function lost their
balance when perturbed while standing on the narrow beam because
no postural response was triggered.

Although the learning-disabled children with abnormal sensory
organization did respond to perturbations while standing on the beam,
the responses of trunk and leg muscles were poorly coordinated even
with practice, so that the children were unsuccessful in maintaining
balance. Figure 10–3 compares EMG data averaged from the first three
trials (no practice) and the last three trials (after practice) from a normal
child who successfully maintained balance on the narrow beam. Quantification of EMG data indicated that normal children modified both
amplitude and timing parameters of muscle responses in order to successfully mix hip and ankle strategies. Critical timing changes involved
reversing the activation sequence of proximal muscles during beam
balance so that on flat surfaces hamstrings responded in advance of
quadriceps (64 ± 59 msec), whereas on the beam quadriceps responded in advance of hamstrings (50 ± 74 msec).

In contrast, Figure 10–4 shows EMG data from a motor-impaired,
learning-disabled child who was unsuccessful in maintaining balance
under the same conditions. A close inspection of EMG data indicated
that although both ankle and hip strategies were present this child did
not make sufficient timing or amplitude changes necessary to successfully coordinate both ankle and hip strategies. Loss of balance resulted
in a step off the beam.

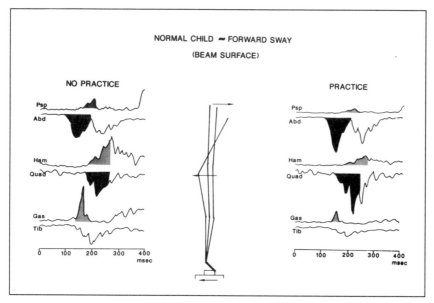

Fig. 10–3. Averaged EMG patterns from the first three trials (no practice) and the last three trials (practice) in a normal child successfully responding to a forward-sway postural perturbation while standing crosswise on a narrow beam.

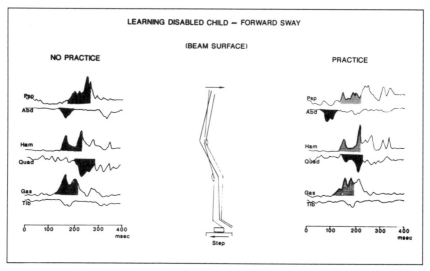

Fig. 10–4. Averaged EMG patterns from the first three trials (no practice) and the last three trials (practice) in a motor-impaired, learning-disabled child unsuccessfully responding to a forward-sway postural perturbation while standing crosswise on a narrow beam.

In summary, children with reduced vestibular function and children with abnormal sensory organization function were unsuccessful in maintaining balance while standing on a narrow beam, though for different reasons. Children with absent vestibular function lost balance because they did not trigger a response to the perturbation while standing on the beam. In contrast, children with abnormal sensory organization problems triggered a postural response that was inappropriately organized for the task.

These findings suggest that reduced or absent vestibular function early in development may affect children's ability to use some postural movement strategies but that it leaves the coordination of muscle action in remaining strategies unaffected. In our study, for example, deaf children with reduced vestibular function were unable to trigger a hip strategy but had a normally coordinated ankle strategy. Inability to trigger a hip postural response would compromise children's ability to maintain balance in situations in which this response is the strategy of choice. It has been proposed that skills requiring this type of balance strategy include balance-beam walking, heel-toe walking, and one-foot standing (Horak et al., 1988).

In contrast, sensory organization deficits early in development appear to affect children's ability to adapt essentially intact strategies to changes in environmental context. This suggests that children with central sensory organization problems would experience dysequilibrium in situations requiring the use of a well-coordinated hip strategy or a mixture of the two strategies. Hence children with reduced vestibular function and children with abnormal sensory organzation function would likely fall under the same situations but for different reasons.

THERAPEUTIC INTERVENTION

The goal of therapeutic intervention strategies using a distributed control model is to facilitate function in all components of the postural control system. Since one component does not "control" other components, the focus is on facilitating appropriate interaction among all components. This contrasts with a reflex model, in which therapeutic intervention strategies focus on facilitating higher-level control over lower levels of function.

Clinical techniques for evaluating balance assess biomechanical (musculoskeletal), sensory, and motor components of the postural control systems. Assessment includes traditional tests of strength, range of motion, coordination, and sensation. In addition, using combinations of compliant foam and various devices to occlude or distort vision, the patient's ability to remain oriented when visual and/or surface cues for postural control are absent or inaccurate is evaluated (Shumway-Cook & Horak, 1986; Horak, 1987). Also assessed is the patient's ability to execute coordinated postural movement strategies and to adapt strategies to changing task demands. Patients are timed while maintaining various positions requiring the use of either ankle or hip movement strategies—for example, one-leg stance or heel-toe stance (Shumway-Cook & Horak, 1986; Horak, 1987).

Following assessment and the identification of specific postural control problems, intervention techniques which are ecologically relevant and specific to the patients' problems are designed. These techniques prepare the patient to adapt appropriately to complex changing environments. This includes improving both the coordination of postural movement strategies and the organization of multiple sensory inputs for postural control. Treatment techniques are taken from a variety of approaches for treating sensorimotor problems in the neurologic patient (Bobath, 1975b; Carr & Shepherd, 1983; Charness, 1986; Knott and Voss, 1968).

Many approaches use similar techniques; however, the underlying rationale for using a technique may vary widely from author to author. For example, a patient may be asked to practice standing and swaying forward and backward in small ranges. Manual and verbal cues are given by the therapist to help the patient maintain good alignment, keeping hips and knees straight and moving in phase with head and shoulders. This sway technique requires the patient to have good ankle range of motion and strength in the ankle-joint musculature. One rationale for this technique could be the importance of facilitating a well-coordinated ankle strategy for controlling balance during small movements of the center of mass (Shumway-Cook & Horak, 1986; Horak, 1987). An alternative explanation emphasizes the importance of reducing proximal instability and facilitating trunk control for standing balance (Charness, 1986). Neither explanation is mutually exclusive, as the technique is successful in achieving both goals.

SUMMARY

The purpose of this chapter has been to review from two different perspectives research on the neural basis for equilibrium deficits in children. A brief examination of research on the role of abnormal reflexes in balance disorders was presented and the implications for therapeutic intervention strategies discussed. The major thrust of this chapter, however, was to review results of research examining abnormal postural control in children using a distributed control or systems model. It was shown that therapeutic strategies based on a systems model of pediatric instability differ greatly from those based on a reflex model. It is probable that development can not be successfully represented by either model exclusively, but rather some combination of the two.

Whether one embraces a reflex or systems model, however, is of less importance than the awareness that one's conception of a model for the neural control of movement consciously or unconsciously influences therapeutic decisions in important ways. This recognition dictates that researchers and health-care professionals alike must examine more carefully the underlying premises of their approaches to the study and treatment of postural control abnormalities underlying disequilibrium in children.

REFERENCES

Ayres, A. J. (1972). *Sensory integration and learning disorders.* Los Angeles: Western Psychological Services.

Berger, W.; Altenmueller, E.; & Dietz, V. (1984). Normal and impaired development of children's gait. *Human Neurobiology, 3,* 163–70.

Berger, W.; Quintern, J.; & Dietz, V. (1982). Pathophysiology of gait in children with cerebral palsy. *Electroencephalography and Clinical Neurophysiology, 53,* 538–48.

Berger, W.; Quintern, J.; & Deitz, V. (1985). Stance and gait perturbations in children: Developmental aspects of compensatory mechanisms. *Electroencephalography and Clinical Neurophysiology, 61,* 385–95.

Bleck, E. E. (1975). Locomotor prognosis in cerebral palsy. *Developmental Medicine and Child Neurology, 17,* 18–25.

Bleck, E. E. (1976). Structural changes in cerebral palsy. In *Syllabus of Instructional Courses,* American Academy of Cerebral Palsy, 26th Annual Meeting, 54–58.

Bobath, B. (1975a). *Abnormal postural reflex activity caused by brain lesions.* London: Heinemann.

Bobath, B. (1975b). *Adult hemiplegia: Evaluation and treatment.* London: Heinemann.

Bobath, B., & Bobath, K. (1976). *Motor development in different types of cerebral palsy.* London: Heinemann.

Bobath, B., & Bobath, K. (1984). The neuro-developmental treatment. In D. Scrutton (Ed.), *Management of the motor disorders of children with cerebral palsy.* London: Spastics International Medical Publications.

Burke, D. (1983). Critical examination of the case for or against fusimotor involvement in disorders of muscle tone. In J. E. Desmedt (Ed.), *Motor control mechanisms in health and disease.* New York: Raven Press.

Cambell, S. K., & Wilhelm, I. J. (1985). Development from birth to 3 years of age of 15 children at high risk for central nervous system dysfunction. *Physical Therapy, 65,* 463–69.

Capute, A. J.; Wachtel, R. C.; Palmer, F. B.; Shapiro, B. K.; & Accardo, P. J. (1982). A prospective study of three postural reactions. *Developmental Medicine and Child Neurology, 24,* 314–20.

Carr, J., & Shepherd, R. (1983). *A motor relearning programme for stroke.* Rockville, MD: Aspen Publications.

Castle, M. (1978a). Adductor transfers in cerebral palsy. In J. Wilson (Ed.), *Orthopedic aspects of developmental disabilities.* Chapel Hill: University of North Carolina Press.

Castle, M. (1978b). Histochemical analysis of spastic muscle. In J. Wilson (Ed.), *Orthopedic aspects of developmental disabilities.* Chapel Hill: University of North Carolina Press.

Cermack, S., & Henderson, A. (1985). Learning disabilities. In D. Umpred (Ed.), *Neurological rehabilitation.* St. Louis: C. V. Mosby.

Chandler, L. S.; Andrews, M. S.; & Swanson, M. W. (1980). *Movement assessment of infants. A manual.* Rolling Bay, WA: Rolling Bay Press.

Charness, A. (1986). *Stroke/head injury: A guide to functional outcomes in physical therapy management.* Rockville, MD: Aspen Publications.

Chee, F.; Kreutzberg, J.; & Clark, D. (1978). Semicircular canal stimulation in cerebral palsied children. *Physical Therapy, 58(9),* 1071–75.

Connolly, B., & Montgomery, P. (1978). *Therapeutic exercise in developmental disabilities.* Chattanooga, TN: Chattanooga Corporation.

Cowie, V. (1970). *A study in the early development of Mongols.* London: Pergamon Press.

Davis, W., & Kelso, J. S. (1982). Analysis of invariant characteristics in the motor control of Down's syndrome and normal subjects. *Journal of Motor Behavior, 14(3),* 194–212.

DeQuiros, J. B. (1976). Diagnosis of vestibular disorders in the learning disabled. *Journal of Learning Disabilities, 9,* 39–44.

Dietz, V., & Berger, W. (1982). Spinal coordination of bilateral leg muscle activity during balancing. *Experimental Brain Research, 47,* 172–76.

Dietz, V., & Berger, W. (1983). Normal and impaired regulation of muscle stiffness in gait: A new hypothesis about muscle hypertonia. *Experimental Neurology, 79,* 680–87.

Easton, T. (1972). On the normal use of reflexes. *American Scientist, 60,* 591–99.

Effgen, S. K. (1982). Integration of the plantar grasp reflex as an indicator of ambulation potential in developmentally disabled infants. *Physical Therapy, 62,* 433–35.

Ellison, P. H. (1983). Development of a scoring system for the Milani-Comparetti and Gidoni method of assessing neurologic abnormality in infancy. *Physical Therapy, 63(9),* 1414–23.

Fay, T. (1955). The use of pathological and unlocking reflexes in the rehabilitation of spastics. *American Journal of Physical Medicine, 33,* 437–51.

Fiorentino, M. R. (1973). *Reflex testing methods for evaluating CNS development.* Springfield, IL: Charles Thomas.

Forssberg, H. (1980). Motor learning: A neurophysiological review. In K. Berg and B. Erikson (Eds.), *Children and exercise, IX.* Baltimore: University Park Press.

Forssberg, H., & Nashner, L. (1982). Ontogenetic development of postural control in man: Adaptation to altered support and visual conditions during stance. *Journal of Neuroscience, 2,* 545–52.

Gilfoyle, E. M.; Grady, A. P.; & Moore, K. C. (1986). *Children adapt.* NJ: Charles Slack.

Gordon, J. (1987). Assumptions underlying physical therapy intervention: Theoretical and historical perspectives. In J. H. Carr, R. B. Shepherd, J. Gordon, A. M. Gentile, & J. M. Held (Eds.), *Foundation for physical therapy in rehabilitation.* Rockville, MD: Aspen Publications.

Grimm, R., & Nashner, L. (1978). Long loop dyscontrol. In J. E. Desmedt (Ed.), *Progress in clinical neurophysiology.* Vol. 4, Cerebral motor control in man: Long loop mechanisms (pp. 70–84). Basel: Karger.

Gunsolus, P.; Welsh, C.; & Houser, C. (1975). Equilibrium reactions in the feet of children with spastic cerebral palsy and of normal children. *Developmental Medicine and Child Neurology, 17,* 580–91.

Haley, S. (1986a). Postural reactions in infants with Down syndrome. *Physical Therapy, 66,* 17–22.

Haley, S. (1986b). Sequential analyses of postural reactions in nonhandicapped infants. *Physical Therapy, 66(4),* 531–36.

Haley, S.; Harris, S.; Tada, W.; & Swanson, M. (1986). Item reliability of the movement assessment of infants. *Physical and Occupational Therapy in Pediatrics, 6(1),* 21–39.

Harris, S. (1981). The effects of NDT on motor performance of infants with Down's syndrome. *Developmental Medicine and Child Neurology, 23,* 477–83.

Horak, F. (1987). Clinical measurement of postural control in adults. *Physical Therapy, 67(12),* 1881–85.

Horak, F., & Nashner, L. M. (1986). Central programming of postural movements: Adaption to altered support surface configurations. *Journal of Neurophysiology, 55,* 1369–81.

Horak, F.; Nashner, L. M.; & Diener, C. (1986). Abnormal scaling of postural responses in cerebellar patients. *Society for Neuroscience Abstracts, 12,* 1419.

Horak, F.; Shumway-Cook, A.; Crowe, T.; & Black, F. O. (1988). Vestibular function and motor proficiency in children with hearing impairments and in learning disabled children with motor impairments. *Developmental Medicine and Child Neurology, 30,* 64–79.

Jackson, J. H. (1932). Selected writings of John Hughlings Jackson. In J. Taylor (Ed.), *John Hughlings Jackson.* Vol. 1. London: Hodder & Stoughter.

Kaga, K.; Suzuki, J.; & Marsh, R. (1981). Influence of labyrinthine hypoactivity on gross motor development of infants. *Annals of the New York Academy of Sciences, 374,* 412–20.

Kantner, R. M.; Clark, D.; Allen, L. C.; Chase, M. F. (1976). Effects of vestibular stimulation in nystagmus response and motor performance of the developmentally delayed infant. *Physical Therapy, 59,* 414–21.

Knott, M., & Voss, D. E. (1968). *Proprioceptive neuromuscular facilitation.* New York: Harper & Row.

McCollum, G., & Leen, T. (in press). Learning to stand: Testing stability limits. *Journal of Motor Behavior.*

Milani-Comparetti, A., & Gidoni, E. A. (1967a). Pattern analysis of motor development and its disorder. *Developmental Medicine and Child Neurology, 9,* 625–30.

Milani-Comparetti, A., & Gidoni, E. A. (1967). Routine developmental examination in normal and retarded children. *Developmental Medicine and Child Neurology, 9,* 631–38.

Molnar, G. E. (1978). Analysis of motor disorder in retarded infants and young children. *American Journal of Mental Deficiency, 83,* 213–22.

Molnar, G. E., & Fordon, S. U. (1976). Cerebral palsy: Predictive value of selected signs for early prognostication of motor function. *Arch. Phys. Med. Rehabil., 57,* 153–56.

Nashner, L. M. (1982). Adaption of human movement to altered environments. *Trends in Neuroscience, Oct.,* 358–61.

Nashner, L. M.; Black, F. O.; & Wall, C. (1982). Adaption to altered support surface and visual conditions during stance: Patients with vestibular deficits. *Journal of Neuroscience, 2,* 536–44.

Nashner, L.; Shumway-Cook, A.; & Marin, O. (1983). Stance posture control in selected groups of children with cerebral palsy: Deficits in sensory organization and muscular coordination. *Experimental Brain Reserch, 49,* 393–409.

Ottenbacher, K. (1982). Patterns of postrotary nystagmus in three learning disabled children. *American Journal of Occupational Therapy, 36,* 657–63.

Paine, R. S. (1964). Evolution of postural reflexes in normal infants. *Neurology, 14,* 1036–48.

Pignataro, O.; Rossi, L.; Gaini, R.; Oldini, C.; Sambataro, G.; & Nino, L. (1979). The evaluation of the vestibular apparatus according to the age of the infant. *International Journal of Pediatric Otorhinolaryngology, 1,* 165–70.

Rapin, I. (1974). Hypoactive labyrinths and motor development. *Clinical Pediatrics, 13,* 922–37.

Rast, M., & Harris, S. (1985). Motor control in infants with Down syndrome. *Developmental Medicine and Child Neurology, 27,* 675–85.

Shumway-Cook, A. (1986). Understanding balance deficits in children with cerebral palsy. In D. Slatten (Ed.), *Pathokinesiology of cerebral palsy.* Chapel Hill: University of North Carolina Press.

Shumway-Cook, A., & Horak, F. (1986). Assessing the influence of sensory interaction on balance. *Physical Therapy, 66(10),* 1548–50.

Shumway-Cook, A.; Horak, F.; & Black, F. O. (1986). Contribution of the vestibulospinal system to development of postural coordination. *Society for Neuroscience Abstracts, 12,* 137.

Shumway-Cook, A.; Horak, F.; & Black, F. O. (1987). A critical examination of vestibular function in motor impaired learning disabled children. *International Journal of Otorhinolaryngology, 14,* 21–30.

Shumway-Cook, A., & Woollacott, M. (1985a). The growth of stability: Postural control from a developmental perspective. *Journal of Motor Behavior, 17,* 131–47.

Shumway-Cook, A., & Woollacott, M. (1985b). Dynamics of postural control in the child with Down syndrome. *Physical Therapy, 9,* 1315–22.

Sussman, M. (1978). Use of casts as an adjunct to physical therapy management of cerebral palsy patients. In J. Wilson (Ed.), *Orthopedic aspects of developmental disabilities.* Chapel Hill: University of North Carolina Press.

Sutherland, D., & Cooper, L. (1978). The pathomechanics of progressive crouch gait in spastic diplegia. *Orthopedic Clinics of North America, 9(1),* 143–54.

Touwen, B. (1976). *Neurological development in infancy.* Philadelphia: Lippincott.

Twitchell, T. E. (1975). Attitudinal reflexes. In E. Davies (Ed.), *Growth and development.* Washington, DC: American Physical Therapy Association.

Walshe, F. M. R. (1923). On certain tonic or postural reflexes in hemiplegia, with special reference to the so-called "associated movements." *Brain, 46,* 1–37.

Wat, L. (1978). Mobility module conteracting the tonic labyrinthine reflex in a cerebral palsied child. *Physical Therapy, 58,* 880–81.

Weiss, S. (1938). Studies in equilibrium reaction. *Journal of Nervous and Mental Disorders, 88,* 153–62.

Wyke, B. (1976). Neurological mechanisms in spasticity: A brief review of some current concepts. *Physiotherapy, 62,* 316–19.

11

The Role of Peripheral Vestibular Disorders in Postural Dyscontrol in the Elderly

Fay B. Horak,
Alar Mirka,
and Charlotte L. Shupert

Between 20% and 40% of people over 65 years old who live at home fall each year (Sheldon, 1948; Droller, 1955; Exton-Smith, 1977; Overstall, 1978; Prudham & Evans, 1981; Perry, 1982). In the institutionalized elderly, the incidence of falls is approximately doubled, despite more supervision and limited ambulation (Gryfe et al., 1977; Tinetti, 1987). The morbidity and mortality associated with falls in the elderly are significant and increase with age. The number of elderly adults who die within one year of a hip fracture has been reported to range between 12% and 67% (Nickens, 1985). There is certainly no doubt about the high incidence and serious consequences of falls in the elderly. The causes of this increased number of falls, however remain to be determined.

Relatively unselected samples of the elderly population have been repeatedly shown to perform poorly on qualitative tests of balance control (see, for example, Fregly 1973). Since patients with ataxias due to vestibular deficits also perform poorly on the same tests of balance (compare Fregly 1974), it has been widely hypothesized that at least some proportion of the elderly with poor balance may suffer from vestibular deficits. In support of this hypothesis, community surveys of the elderly living at home indicate that up to 47% of men and 61% of women over the age of 70 suffer from dizziness or vertigo, common symptoms of vestibular disorders (Sheldon, 1948; Droller & Pemberton, 1953; Sixt & Landahl, 1987).

Although it is tempting to make the association between falls in the elderly and vestibular deficits due to age, several important questions remain to be answered. First, what is the role of the vestibular system in postural control? The vestibular system is only one of three sensory systems that provide information about body and head motion; how does vestibular information interact with visual and somatosensory information to control posture in normal adults? Second, does the role of vestibular information in postural control change with age in the normal population? Do these changes correlate with changes in eye movement control, which also relies on information from the vestibular system? Finally, assuming that the elderly do indeed suffer from vestibular degeneration induced either by age alone or by pathology, what is the effect of peripheral vestibular deficits on sensory and motor aspects of postural control? Because the quantitative study of the role of the vestibular system in postural control in humans of any age has only recently been attempted, definitive answers to these questions are not yet available. This chapter summarizes the results of current research on the role of the vestibular system in postural control in the young and elderly and indicates some of the directions that future research must take to provide the necessary answers.

THE VESTIBULAR SYSTEM

ROLE OF THE VESTIBULAR SYSTEM IN SPATIAL ORIENTATION

The sensory information about the position and motion of the head provided by the vestibular system is used in at least two important ways. First, vestibular information is used to maintain clear vision during movements of the head. This is accomplished by means of the vestibulo-ocular reflex (VOR), which rotates the eyes in the direction opposite to the head movement at approximately the same speed. Second, information from the vestibular system is also important in the control of posture. Postural control consists of automatic, unconscious movements that maintain equilibrium and keep the head stable in space. Adequate postural control depends on the spatial and temporal integration of vestibular, visual, and somatosensory information about the active and passive motion of the head and body.

STRUCTURE AND FUNCTION OF THE VESTIBULAR SYSTEM

The vestibular end organs are membranous structures immersed in fluid which rest inside the bony labyrinth of the inner ear on each side of the head. These end organs, referred to collectively as the vestibular labyrinth, contain five pairs of sensors. Three of these sensors, the semicircular canals, detect angular accelerations of the head and transmit information about head velocity in three-dimensional space. The other two sensors, the utricle and the saccule, transmit information about linear accelerations of the head and also signal the tilt of the head with respect to gravity.

The membranous vestibular labyrinth is separated from the surrounding bony labyrinth by a fluid, called perilymph, that resembles extracellular fluid. The membranous canals are ducts filled with a slightly different fluid, called endolymph, which resembles intracellular fluid. The sensory portion of each canal is called the ampulla. The ampulla contains a gelatinous structure, the cupula, which is attached to the walls of the ampulla. The base of the cupula contacts the vestibular receptors, or hair cells. The utricle and saccule are endolymph-filled sacs, which also contain sensory structures, called maculae. The maculae consist of hair cells covered with a gelatinous material containing small calcium crystals called otoliths; the utricle and saccule are, therefore, collectively called the otolith organs.

When the head is accelerated, inertia causes the endolymph and/ or the otoliths to lag behind the head motion. This lagging deforms the gelatinous structures within the canals and the otolith organs, bending the attached hair cells. Movement of the hair cells, in turn, increases or decreases the spontaneous firing rate in the vestibular nerve in proportion to the change in the velocity of the head. Increases in firing rate signal head movements in one direction, and decreases in firing rate signal the opposite direction. The vestibular nerve carries this velocity-coded information about head movement from the peripheral vestibular system to the brainstem. Once this information reaches the central nervous system, it makes contact with the vestibular nuclei in the brainstem, the vestibulo-cerebellum, and the other structures of the central vestibular system. The structures of the central vestibular system initiate and control the reflexive eye and body movements known as the *vestibulo-ocular (VOR)* and *vestibulospinal reflexes* (see Kornhuber, 1974; Wilson & Melvill-Jones, 1979; and Wilson & Peterson, 1981, for extensive reviews).

THE EFFECT OF AGE ON THE VESTIBULAR SYSTEM AND POSTURAL CONTROL

Anatomical studies have shown evidence for the degeneration of several different components of the vestibular system with age. The number of hair cells in both the canals and the otolith organs decreases with age (Johnsson, 1971; Rosenhall, 1973). A 40% reduction in hair cells has been reported in individuals aged 70 and older compared to a control group of children and young adults (Rosenhall & Rubin, 1975). Richter (1980) has reported that the number of hair cells begins to decline starting at age 35, but the number of cells in Scarpa's ganglion (which gives rise to vestibular nerve fibers) remains constant until age 55. The number of Scarpa's ganglion cells declined by 20% between the ages of 20 and 70 in Richter's study. Finally, the number of nerve fibers in the vestibular nerve also decreases exponentially with age (see Fig. 11–1A), falling by 36% between ages 15 and 80 (Bergstrom, 1973).

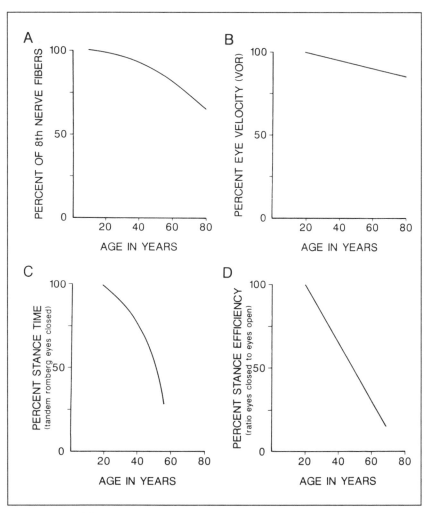

Fig. 11–1. Effect of age on the vestibular system and balance control. All measures are expressed as a percentage of the values for 20-year-olds which are arbitrarily defined as 100%. A: Loss of 8th nerve fibers with age (adapted from Bergstrom, 1973). B: Slight decline in VOR eye velocity in response to head rotation with age (adapted from Peterka et al., 1987). C: Decline in the amount of time that subjects could maintain balance in heel-to-toe stance with eyes closed as a function of age (adapted from Fregly et al., 1973). D: Decline in stance efficiency with age. Older subjects required more energy to maintain equilibrium with eyes closed than younger subjects (adapted from Black et al., 1977).

STUDIES OF VESTIBULO-OCULAR FUNCTION

A limited number of studies have been carried out in an attempt to find functional correlates of these reported age-related, anatomical changes in the vestibular system. In most studies, vestibular function has been evaluated by caloric or rotation testing of the VOR. The VOR is an eye movement approximately equal in velocity but opposite in direction to head rotation; its purpose is to maintain clear vision during movement of the head. It can be elicited either by rotating the head or, calorically, by introducing warm or cold water into the external auditory canal (see Baloh, 1984, for a description of caloric and rotation tests of the VOR used clinically). In a study of the calorically induced VOR in adults across the life span, Bruner & Norris (1971) found the highest values for maximum VOR eye velocity between the ages of 60 and 70. However, Van der Laan & Oostervald (1974) have reported maximal velocity between ages 31 and 50, with declines in the following decades. More recent studies by Mulch & Petermann (1979) and Peterka et al. (1987) show little change in the calorically induced VOR across the adult life span.

The VOR in response to head rotation has been less thoroughly studied than the caloric response in the elderly. Also, testing protocols vary widely from study to study, making systematic comparisons of findings relatively difficult. Nevertheless, several studies have shown a general decrease in VOR eye velocity in response to head velocity after age 70 (Van der Laan & Oostervald, 1974) and in subjects aged 50 to 70 as compared to those aged 20 to 40 (Wall et al., 1984). The results of a recent study of vestibular function in 216 subjects ranging in age from 10 to 80 show a very small but systematic decrement in VOR eye velocity with age (see Fig. 11–1B; Peterka et al., 1987).

STUDIES OF POSTURAL CONTROL

The role of the vestibular system in postural control in the elderly has been even less thoroughly studied than the VOR. It has been widely reported that, even among the so-called normal elderly population, balance becomes less effective with age (see Woollacott, this volume, Chap. 7). For example, elderly subjects are less able to maintain certain balance positions, and they also require more energy to maintain balance even in relatively stable positions (see Fig. 11–1C and 11–1D; Fregly et al., 1973; Black et al., 1977). However, these tests are not specific tests of vestibulospinal function. In the balance tests used in these studies, subjects had access to accurate sensory information from vision, somatosensation, or both. Thus, although these studies provide important information about the quality of balance in the elderly, they do not provide specific information about the role of the aging vestibular system in postural control.

Nevertheless, there is some evidence that the elderly may perform less well than younger people when forced to rely on vestibular information for postural control. The capacity of experimental subjects to use visual, somatosensory, and vestibular inputs to the control of upright stance can be estimated by means of a test of postural control, called *moving-platform posturography*, developed by Nashner (1982); and extended by Nashner and Black and their colleagues (Nashner et al., 1982; Black et al., 1983; Black & Nashner, 1984a, b; Black, 1985; Black et al., 1988). Moving-platform posturography provides an assessment of the amount of postural sway during six different sensory conditions (Fig. 11–2). During these tests, the subject stands on a movable platform facing into a large enclosure. This enclosure fills the subject's entire visual field. Both the platform and the visual enclosure can be rotated independently about an axis colinear with the subject's ankle joints. The subject's task is to maintain balance for 20 seconds with as little sway as possible. In Conditions 1 and 2 the subject stands on the fixed platform with eyes open and then with eyes closed. These conditions are similar to the standard Romberg test, which is frequently used clinically to evaluate postural control in patients with imbalance and ataxia.

In the remaining four conditions, sensory conflict situations are created by rotating the visual enclosure and/or the platform in proportion to the subject's sway, which is measured by attaching poten-

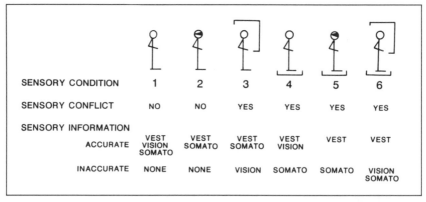

SENSORY CONDITION	1	2	3	4	5	6
SENSORY CONFLICT	NO	NO	YES	YES	YES	YES
SENSORY INFORMATION						
ACCURATE	VEST VISION SOMATO	VEST SOMATO	VEST SOMATO	VEST VISION	VEST	VEST
INACCURATE	NONE	NONE	VISION	SOMATO	SOMATO	VISION SOMATO

Fig. 11–2. Experimental protocol used in moving-platform posturography. Subjects are required to stand quietly for 20 seconds in each sensory condition. Blindfolds on stick figures indicate eyes-closed conditions. Boxes at the feet or around the head indicate that the support surface or the visual surround, respectively, are moved in proportion to the subject's sway during the condition.

tiometers to the patient's hips and shoulders with belts and systems of light rods. The rotation of the platform and the visual enclosure minimizes the sensory feedback available from visual and somatosensory cues. This technique is referred to as "sway-referencing." In Condition 3 the visual enclosure alone is sway-referenced; in Conditions 4 and 5 the platform alone is sway-referenced and patients stand with eyes open or closed; and in Condition 6 both the enclosure and the platform are sway-referenced (see Nashner et al., 1982; Black, 1985; and Black & Nashner, 1985, for more detailed descriptions).

Peterka et al. (1987) and Mirka et al. (1988) studied the effect of age on vestibular function in 216 normal subjects ranging in age from 10 to 80 years using both moving-platform posturography and caloric and rotation testing of the VOR (see Fig. 11–3). They found that the likelihood of falling in any sensory conflict condition increased with age. Also, the elderly normal subjects as a group appear to become more dependent on visual information to control posture; they tended to fall with greater frequency in Conditions 3 and 6. This is not, however, a universal finding. Woollacott, Shumway-Cook & Nashner (1986) have also carried out moving-platform posturography in normal elderly subjects. They report a tendency to rely on somatosensory information in their sample of subjects; their subjects showed increased sway and falls whenever the support surface was sway-referenced. Some elderly subjects in Peterka's study also became unstable when forced to rely on vestibular information alone. When limited to vestibular input for accurate orientation cues for balance (Conditions 5 and 6), 17% of normal subjects over age 60 fell. Only 3% of normal subjects between the ages of 20 and 30 fell in the same conditions. Thus, a larger proportion of normal elderly subjects are unable to control postural sway when the vestibular system is the only accurate source of orientation information.

SUMMARY AND DISCUSSION

The studies summarized above provide evidence that there are both anatomical and functional changes associated with age in the vestibular systems of normal adults. Nevertheless, it is probably premature to conclude that the dysequilibrium often observed in the normal elderly population is due entirely to age-related degeneration of the vestibular system. First, nothing is known about the vestibulo-ocular function and postural control of the normal subjects whose vestibular systems were studied anatomically. Thus, it is impossible to know whether the amount of vestibular degeneration found in these subjects is sufficient to cause dysequilibrium or poor oculomotor control.

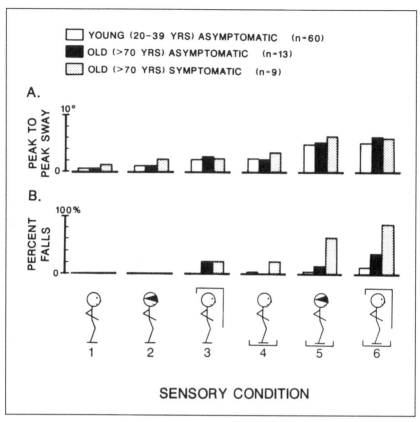

Fig. 11–3. Results of moving-platform posturography for young normal subjects (*open bars*), elderly normal subjects (*dark bars*), and elderly subjects complaining of dizziness and imbalance (*shaded bars*). A: Amount of peak-to-peak sway in each sensory condition or subjects in fall groups who did not fall. B: Number of subjects who fell in each group expressed as a percentage of the total number tested.

Second, it appears that the effect of age may be different on the oculomotor and postural control systems. For example, the rotation-induced VOR of the eight subjects in Peterka et al.'s (1987) study who fell when restricted to vestibular information (Conditions 5 and 6) was not significantly different from the VOR of the forty subjects who did not fall. This finding appears to conflict with the hypothesis that both dysequilibrium and poor VOR performance are due exclusively to degeneration of the vestibular system with age. However, this finding may reflect the fact that moving-platform posturography is not simply a test of vestibulospinal reflexes. Rather, it tests the capacity of subjects to ignore invalid sensory information from the visual and somatosensory systems, to have available and select accurate vestibular information, and to use that information to control postural sway. Deficits in any one or a combination of these functions could result in an increased tendency to fall in Conditions 5 and 6.

Finally, even if the effect of age on the vestibular system can account for at least part of the dysequilibrium of older people as a group, it is clear that the effects of age are not uniform across individuals. As Woolacott and others have pointed out (see, for example, Woollacott, this volume, Chap. 7), many older individuals enjoy normal postural control well into advanced age. Also, the older individuals in Peterka et al.'s (1987) study who did not fall showed no greater amounts of postural sway than younger individuals (see Fig. 11–3A). In order to account for these findings, it is necessary to assume either that individuals may age at markedly different rates or that the apparent effects of age in some individuals are actually the effects of age and subtle pathology, or perhaps age and lifestyle.

THE EFFECT OF PERIPHERAL VESTIBULAR DISORDERS ON POSTURAL CONTROL

CLASSIFICATION OF PERIPHERAL VESTIBULAR DISORDERS

The classification of vestibular pathologies is usually based on clinical diagnoses, such as those listed in Table 11–1. However, different vestibular pathologies often have similar functional results. Also, patients with the same pathology may show very different functional patterns depending, for example, on the stage of the disease. For this reason, categorizing vestibular disorders based on a functional classification rather than the specific etiology may be a better predictor of a given patient's postural performance. Table 11–1 lists three categories of vestibular dysfunction: *vestibular loss, vestibular distortion,* and *fluctuating vestibular function.* These dysfunction categories are based on results of tests of both the VOR and postural control, as well as clinical evaluation. They are thus based on vestibular pathophysiology, rather than on the diagnosis of a specific disease process.

Vestibular Loss. Vestibular losses result when the vestibular end organs or the vestibular nerve are so extensively damaged either bilaterally or unilaterally that vestibular information about head motion can no longer be detected and/or transmitted to the central nervous system. As shown in Table 11–1, vestibular losses may have many different etiologies, including, for example, head trauma, infections, or degenerative processes (see Schuknecht, 1974, for a comprehensive treatment of vestibular pathology). Sudden losses of vestibular function, whether bilateral or unilateral, are characterized by severe vertigo and ataxia. These symptoms disappear over time as the central nervous system compensates for the loss by learning to use information from the remaining vestibular system (in unilateral lesions) or information from other sensory systems for postural control. The central nervous system compensates for vestibular losses so effectively that slow, progressive losses of vestibular function may go unnoticed in normal sensory environments. However, symptoms of imbalance will predictably occur even in patients with well-compensated losses of vestibular function whenever visual or somatosensory information is restricted (i.e., in the dark and on uneven surfaces).

TABLE 11-1

Functional Classification of Peripheral Vestibular Disorders

Functional Classification	Clinical Disorders and Etiologies
Vestibular distortion	Benign paroxysmal positional vertigo
	Benign static positional vertigo
	Perilymph fistula
	Inner ear concussion syndrome
Vestibular loss	Vestibular degeneration
	Vestibular neuronitis
	Vascular occlusion
	Head trauma
Fluctuating function	Endolymphatic hydrops
	Perilymph fistula

Vestibular Distortion. Vestibular distortions arise whenever damage to the vestibular system results in the transmission of inaccurate information about head movement to the central nervous system. For example, in a condition known as benign paroxysmal positional nystagmus and vertigo (BPPN or BPPV), the posterior semicircular canals, which normally sense pitch rotations of the head, appear to be activated by head tilt. It has been hypothesized that this condition is caused by cupulolithiasis, which occurs when degeneration of the otolithic membranes results in loading of the posterior semicircular canal cupula with otoliths dislodged from the utricle (Schuknecht, 1974). As Table 11-1 indicates, however, other vestibular disorders may also give rise to distortion of vestibular information. Both endolymphatic hy-drops (fluid accumulation inside the vestibular labyrinth) and perilymph fistulas (membrane ruptures which permit perilymph to leak into the middle ear), for example, can cause the vestibular apparatus to falsely signal head motion when none is present.

Fluctuating Vestibular Function. Fluctuating vestibular function can result from many vestibular disorders, particulary in the early stages of progressive diseases, but the most common cause of fluctuating func-tion is endolymphatic hydrops. When vestibular function is nearly normal during some periods and distorted or reduced during other periods, effective, permanent compensation by the central nervous system is unlikely to take place.

VESTIBULAR DISORDERS IN THE ELDERLY WITH DIZZINESS AND IMBALANCE

A study of vestibular function in patients complaining of dizziness across all age groups found that approximately 40% of these patients had peripheral vestibular disorders (Drachman & Hart, 1972). However, one study of the elderly over age 65 with complaints of dizziness found that only approximately 20% had diagnosable vestibular pathology (Belal & Glorig, 1986). The remaining patients in this study were diag-nosed with "presbyastasis," a term proposed to classify patients with dysequilibrium presumed secondary to aging alone. However, the spe-cific vestibular tests performed were not described in this study. Fur-ther, even though the authors recommended that clinical tests of vestibulo-ocular function be done on elderly patients complaining of dizziness, only one-fourth of the cases studied had test results available. Therefore, the term *presbyastasis* as it is used in this study serves only to identify elderly patients with dysequilibrium in whom a specific diag-nosis has not been made.

In contrast, preliminary results from another study of elderly pa-tients with complaints of dizziness and imbalance indicate a high inci-dence of diagnosable vestibular pathology in this group (Mirka et al., 1988). All of the subjects in this study received tests of both the VOR and postural control in addition to a complete clinical evaluation. Of sixty-three patients aged 65 and older who complained of dizziness and imbalance, sixty were found to have abnormal scores on tests of ves-tibulo-ocular function and/or postural control. Table 11–2 lists the types of vestibular disorders diagnosed in these patients; it should be noted that all functional types (losses, distortions, and fluctuating function) were found. However, a specific diagnosis could not be established for 25% of the patients who had quantifiable abnormalities in tests of the VOR or postural control. Nevertheless, the results of this study are consistent with the idea that at least some, and probably a majority, of the elderly with dizziness and balance problems may suffer from measurable vestibular dysfunction.

TABLE 11–2

Etiologies of Dizziness in 63 Consecutive Elderly Patients Aged Over 65 Evaluated with Vestibular and Neuro-otologic Testing

ETIOLOGIES	NUMBER
Benign positional vertigo	28
Vestibular degeneration	27
Endolymphatic hydrops	15
Multisensory deficits[a]	8
Central vestibular disorder	6
Otosclerosis	2
Perilymph fistula	1
Parkinson's disease	1
Hyperventilation	1
No etiology found	1

[a]Deficits found in two or more sensory systems

THE EFFECT OF PERIPHERAL VESTIBULAR DISORDERS ON SENSORY AND MOTOR ASPECTS OF POSTURAL CONTROL

The systematic study of postural control in patients with vestibular disorders is just beginning. To date, almost no work has been done specifically on postural control in elderly patients with peripheral vestibular disorders as compared to younger patients with the same disorders. Nevertheless, a clear understanding of the role of the vestibular system in falls in the elderly will require a thorough understanding of the effect of vestibular pathology on the postural control of younger people as well.

Effective postural control is a sensorimotor integration task. Sensory information regarding head and body position is derived from the visual and somatosensory systems, as well as the vestibular system. Information from the senses about the characteristics of the environment and the motion of the body is used to organize appropriate motor responses. Thus, deficits in any sensory system could be expected to change not only the way sensory information is used to control posture, but also the form of the motor responses that serve postural control. In the following sections, the effects of vestibular pathology on both sensory orientation and motor coordination are summarized.

Sensory Orientation. The use of sensory information for postural control has been assessed quantitatively using moving-platform posturography in subjects with normal vestibular function (Peterka et al., 1987) and in patients with peripheral vestibular pathology, including vestibular losses (Nashner et al., 1982; Black & Nashner, 1984a; Black, 1985; Black et al., 1988), vestibular distortions (Black & Nashner, 1984a, b; Black et al., 1987; Black et al., 1988), and fluctuating vestibular function (Black, 1982; Black et al., 1983). Patients with vestibular losses typically fall or sway excessively in Conditions 5 and 6 (refer to Fig. 11–2), which require the subject to rely on vestibular information to control posture. The performance of patients with distorted and fluctuating vestibular function is more variable, however. Some show the same sway abnormalities as loss patients. Others appear to become dependent on visual information and sway excessively when provided with unreliable visual information (Conditions 3 and 6). Paradoxically, these patients appear to be able to use vestibular information to control posture when their eyes are closed. Another group of patients with distorted vestibular function sways excessivley whenever sensory conflicts are present (Conditions 3, 4, 5, and 6).

Mirka et al. (1988) are currently evaluating postural stability in a similar fashion in both normal elderly subjects and those complaining of dizziness and imbalance. Preliminary data are presented in Figure 11–3. Normal subjects aged 25 to 40 sway to a greater degree during eyes-closed or sensory conflict trials but fall infrequently. In both the normal elderly and the elderly complaining of dizziness and imbalance who did not fall, peak-to-peak sway was not significantly different from that of the young subjects (Fig. 11–3A). However, as discussed above, elderly subjects over 60 with no complaints of dizziness or falls have a higher incidence of falls than the young subjects. Previous reports have indicated that some normal elderly subjects may appear to become visually dependent, falling in Conditions 3 and 6 (Mirka et al., 1988). Other reports indicate that these subjects become dependent on surface information, falling in Conditions 4, 5, and 6. In contrast to the normal elderly in either study, the elderly complaining of dizziness or imbalance in the study by Mirka et al. show a markedly increased tendency to fall in any sensory conflict condition, especially when only vestibular information is available to resolve the conflict (Fig. 11–3B).

Motor Coordination. It is well known that patients with vestibular deficits can show gait ataxia and abnormal head- and body-righting reactions and have difficulty balancing on one leg, on balance beams, and in heel-to-toe stance (see, for example, Fregly, 1974). The wealth of clinical and qualitative studies documenting these findings will not be treated in detail here. Recent studies have attempted to quantify motor-control aspects of postural sway in patients with vestibular disorders by examining the electromyographic (EMG) and biomechanical responses of these patients to rotational or translational movements of the support surface on which they stand.

Responses to support-surface rotations. Both Nashner and Allum and their co-workers have compared the responses of normal subjects and patients with peripheral vestibular losses to support-surface rotations. Nashner and others (Nashner, 1976, 1977, 1979; Nashner, Woollacott & Tuma, 1979) reported that support-surface rotations that dorsiflex the foot at the ankle joint produced activation of the stretched muscle (gastrocnemius) at latencies between 90 and 120 msec in normal subjects. Since dorsiflexion of the ankle does not result in substantial displacement of the center of mass, activation of gastrocnemius had a destabilizing effect on the bodies of the subjects, and Nashner reported that the response adapted away after a series of similar rotations. In a study of patients with bilateral vestibular losses, Nashner et al. found that the patients showed muscle activations at latencies similar to normals, but that some (but not all) patients with bilateral vestibular losses failed to adapt normally to repeated platform rotations (Nashner et al., 1982).

Both Allum and his colleagues (Allum & Büdingen, 1979; Allum, 1983) and Diener et al. (1983), using much faster velocities of platform rotations, found activation of gastrocnemius (the stretched muscle) at monosynaptic latencies of 50 and 80 msec in addition to activation at about 120 msec, and activation of the tibialis anterior at approximately 80 and 120 msec. The tibialis response at 120 msec returned the body to an upright position. In studies of patients with bilateral and unilateral peripheral vestibular losses, Allum and others (Allum & Pfaltz, 1984, 1985a, b; Allum & Keshner, 1986; Keshner & Allum, 1986; Keshner, Allum & Pfaltz, 1987) have reported that, although patients with bilateral losses showed responses at normal latencies and amplitudes in gastrocnemius, which appeared to adapt away with repeated trials, the amount of muscle activity in tibialis was reduced at 80 and 120 msec when compared to normals, and many of the patients fell as a result.

Patients with unilateral losses responded asymmetrically to platform rotations; responses in the leg ipsilateral to the side of the loss resembled those of bilaterally absent patients.

Thus, both groups report little or no change in either the configuration of muscle activation or the muscle activation latencies for patients with vestibular losses. The differences in the muscle activation patterns and latencies for both normals and patients in Nashner's and Allum's experiments can probably be accounted for by differences in experimental protocols. In addition to using much higher rotation velocities, subjects in Allum's experiments were asked to lean backward to raise the tonic level of activity in tibialis prior to the perturbation onset. It is possible that systematic differences in muscle activation amplitudes exist between normals and vestibular-loss patients at these higher activation levels. Diener et al. (1983) and Moore et al. (1986) have also shown that initial stance positions can affect muscle activation patterns, including latencies and amplitudes. Differences in the pattern of adaptation to repeated rotations in normal subjects and patients with bilateral losses of vestibular function in Nashner's and Allum's studies may be due in part to individual variation. Nashner (1976) has reported that some normals do not show bursts of activation in the stretched muscle and, therefore, also do not show adaptation. Nashner, Black & Wall (1982) have also reported that the degree to which their loss patients adapted appeared to depend on the severity of the loss but that a few patients with vestibular loss patterns show good adaptation.

Responses to support-surface translations. Nashner and his colleagues have also studied the responses of normal subjects and patients with vestibular deficits to horizontal translations of the support surface on which they are standing (Nashner, 1976, 1977, 1979; Nashner et al., 1979; Nashner et al., 1985; Horak & Nashner, 1986; Shupert et al., 1987; Nashner et al., 1988). Horak & Nashner (1986) have demonstrated experimentally that normal subjects employ two types of postural movements, either alone or in combination, in response to support-surface translations (Fig. 11–4). In the most commonly used sway pattern, subjects sway primarily about the ankle joints and the body moves as an inverted pendulum. For this type of sway, the muscle-activation pattern proceeds in a distal-to-proximal sequence (Fig. 11–4B). In these experiments subjects activated gastrocnemius at latencies between 80 and 100 msec, followed by hamstrings and paraspinals in response to perturbations inducing forward sway. As a result of this muscle-activation pattern, subjects exert torque forces on their support

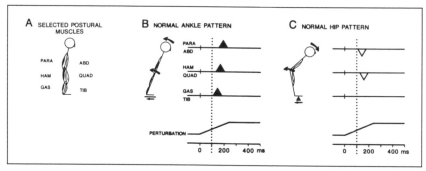

Fig. 11–4. Schematic muscle-activation patterns for two different types of postural responses to translations of the support surface which induce forward sway. A: Positions of the representative postural muscles. B: Normal ankle-sway pattern shown by most subjects in response to translations of a wide, firm support surface. Gastrocnemius is activated first, followed by hamstrings and paraspinals. C: Hip-sway pattern shown by most subjects in response to translations of a support surface smaller than the feet, such as a narrow beam. In this sway pattern, proximal muscles are activated first, followed by more distal muscles.

surface which effectively return the center of mass to a position over the feet. Most normal subjects show this pattern of sway in response to support-surface translations in situations in which these torque forces can be used efficiently—that is, when standing on a rigid, flat surface larger than the feet.

In order to balance when standing crosswise on a narrow beam, which prevents the effective use of foot torque forces for control of body position, normal subjects reposition the center of mass by exerting horizontal shear forces on the surface, with body rotation primarily about the hips instead of the ankles. In this sway pattern, muscle activation proceeds in a proximal-to-distal sequence, with the abdominal muscles becoming active at about 80 to 100 msec, followed by quadriceps in response to translations inducing forward sway (Fig. 11–4C). Normal subjects have also been observed to use combinations of hip and ankle movement patterns when subjected to very large translations on a flat surface, when leaning (i.e., when the center of mass is already close to the limits of stability), or when learning to stand on a narrow beam (Horak & Nashner, 1986; Moore et al., 1986).

Several studies have shown that patients with bilateral loss of vestibular function employ postural movements very similar to those observed in normal subjects who sway primarily about the ankles (Nashner et al., 1985; Shupert et al., 1987). Ankle muscle-response latencies and sequential activation of proximal thigh and trunk muscles in response to translations are normal, even in patients with bilaterally absent vestibular function. However, these patients appear to be restricted to the use of ankle movements for postural control, even when task constraints render that type of postural movement inefficient or ineffective. It is interesting to note that previous qualitative tests of balance in patients with vestibular losses also reported the largest differences between patients and normals in conditions requiring sway about the hips, including the tandem Romberg, heel-to-toe walking, and walking or balancing on narrow beams (Fregly, 1974).

Head-trunk coordination. Peripheral vestibular disorders may also result in abnormalities in the control of the position of the head during postural movements, depending on the type of postural movement. Shupert et al. (1987) have reported that normal subjects and patients with bilateral vestibular losses show similar head movement in response to short, low-velocity translations of their support surface. Neither the patients with bilateral vestibular losses nor the normals showed systematic activation in neck muscles. Preliminary results indicate that some patients with vestibular distortions, however, may show much poorer head control in response to support-surface translations than normals (Shupert et al., 1988).

Normal subjects appear to activate neck muscles to stabilize the postion of the head with respect to gravity both in response to high-velocity support-surface rotations (Allum & Pfaltz, 1984; 1985a, b; Allum & Keshner, 1986; Keshner & Allum, 1986; Keshner et al., 1987) and in response to translations while standing crosswise on a narrow beam (Shupert et al., 1987; Nashner et al., 1988). Allum and his co-workers have reported that some patients with bilateral or unilateral vestibular losses, especially those with uncompensated deficits, show reductions in neck muscle activity and increases in head acceleration during response to high-velocity rotations of their support surface; others show the same range of head motion as normals (see, for example, Allum, 1983). Those who show less head motion also maintain adequate balance and do not fall in responses to the perturbation. Moreover, both Nashner et al. (1985) and Shupert et al. (1987) have reported that even well-compensated patients with bilateral vestibular responses are unable either to maintain balance or to stabilize head position when translated while standing on a short beam. This finding confirms the observation reported in a previous qualitative study that patients with vestibular losses show much poorer balance than normal subjects in balance situations requiring sway about the hips (see Fregly, 1974).

Movement strategies in altered sensory conditions. Preliminary findings also indicate that different types of peripheral vestibular disorders may affect the type of postural movement pattern used by patients in different sensory environments. As discussed above, patients with bilateral vestibular losses are apparently unable to control the position of their center of mass using hip motions when translated while standing on a narrow beam (Nashner et al., 1985; Shupert et al., 1987). These patients, like normals, also appear to sway rigidly about the ankles in all the sensory conditions of moving-platform posturography. However, patients with vestibular distortions appear to rely more on hip motions to control center-of-mass position than either normals or patients with bilateral vestibular losses. Black and his co-workers studied the responses of seventy-three patients with peripheral vestibular disorders using moving-platform posturography. They compared the ratio of hip motion to ankle motion for fifteen patients with vestibular losses to the ratios for fifteen patients with vestibular distortions in Condition 6 (both the platform and the visual surround were sway-referenced). The hip/ankle ratios of patients with vestibular distortions were significantly higher than those of either normal controls or patients with vestibular losses (Black et al., 1988).

This finding is illustrated in Figure 11–5 (A and B), which shows the amount of sway about the ankles (measured at the hip) and the amount of sway about the hip (measured at the shoulder) for two patients in Condition 4 (eyes open) and Condition 5 (eyes closed). The patient shown in Figure 11–5A suffers from a bilateral vestibular loss; he shows a small amount of sway about the ankles when he has access to vision, and falls abruptly when forced to rely on vestibular information. In both trials the hip and shoulder move in unison as the subject sways about the ankles; that is, he has a low hip-motion/ankle-motion ratio in both trials. The patient in Figure 11–5B suffers from perilymph fistula (vestibular distortion); she shows large movements of the upper body in the direction opposite to lower-body motion under both conditions (high hip-motion/ankle-motion ratio). Although this subject also falls when forced to rely on vestibular information, her pattern of body movement is quite different prior to the fall, and she is able to maintain balance longer than the vestibular-loss patient.

The reason why patients with vestibular distortions adopt a hip-sway pattern is not yet clear. Normals tend to adopt hip-sway patterns when standing on support surfaces smaller than the feet. (Horak & Nashner, 1986) and when sensory feedback from the feet is disrupted by experimentally induced ischemia (Nashner, Diener & Horak, 1985). Patients with vestibular distortions may be unable to reconcile information from the somatosensory system with their distorted vestibular signals. However, normals also show hip movements when they un-

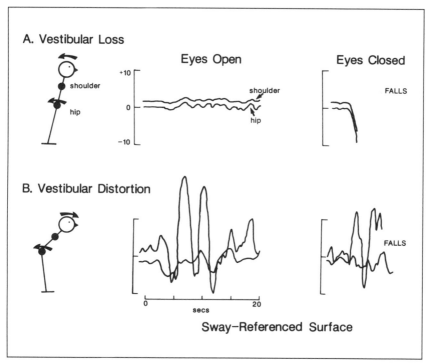

Fig. 11–5. Movement at the hip and the shoulder during attempts to stand on a platform moving in proportion to the sway of the center of mass for 20 seconds with eyes open and eyes closed for two patients with peripheral vestibular deficits. Upward trace deflections represent forward movements. *A:* Body motion for a patient with bilateral vestibular loss. The patient sways normally with eyes open and falls abruptly with eyes closed. *B:* Performance of a patient with vestibular distortion. Note the large antiphase movements of the upper body and lower body for this patient.

dergo support-surface translations while standing in leaning positions that move the center of mass close to the limits of support (Moore et al., 1986). Postural perturbations under these conditons push the center of mass past the limits of support, requiring large, fast motions about the hip to restore equilibrium. It is also possible that patients with vestibular distortions receive incorrect information about body motion from the vestibular system and therefore initiate hip motions while the center of mass is still within the base of support.

SUMMARY AND DISCUSSION

The findings of the studies summarized here indicate that the effect of peripheral vestibular disorders on postural control depends not only on the type of vestibular disorder, but on the experimental paradigm as well. Well-compensated vestibular-loss patients show only very subtle differences from normal subjects in their early motor responses to small support-surface translations. Nevertheless, these patients show markedly abnormal postural control in balance situations requiring hip sway to control center-of-mass position. Further, although these patients often show sway amplitudes within normal limits when they have access to reliable visual or somatosensory information, they fall abruptly when vestibular information is the only reliable sensory input for postural control.

Although the postural control of patients with vestibular distortions has been less thoroughly studied, the available information indicates that postural control in these patients may be different from that of patients with vestibular losses. Preliminary evidence indicates that at least some of these patients rely more heavily on hip motions to control center-of-mass position than either patients with vestibular losses or normal subjects. The abnormal postural sway patterns in response to altered sensory conditions of patients with vestibular distortions are also more heterogeneous than those of patients with vestibular losses. Like vestibular-loss patients, some patients with vestibular distortions may fall or sway excessively only when forced to rely on vestibular information. Others appear to become abnormally dependent on vision, falling in Conditions 3 and 6, or in Conditions 3, 5, and 6, whereas others sway excessively in all sensory conflict conditions (Black et al., 1988).

Preliminary studies of postural control in elderly adults who complain of dizziness and imbalance indicate that a high proportion of them are unable to quickly and accurately select the most reliable sensory information for postural control in unusual sensory environments, regardless of the type of vestibular disorder. Although the cause for this increased instability in all sensory conflict conditions, which is similar to the pattern observed in some patients with vestibular distortion, is not precisely known, some explanations have been proposed. First, multisensory deficits occur more commonly in the elderly due to the increased incidence of peripheral neuropathy, visual pathology, and vestibular degeneration in this population (Sabin & Venna, 1984; Cohen & Lessell, 1984; Rosenhall & Rubin, 1975). Second, Black, Wall & Nashner (1983) have hypothesized that the vestibular system is the only sensory system to provide an "absolute" orientation reference (i.e., the direction of gravity). The other senses provide information about body position or motion with respect to a changing environment. It is possible that a loss or distortion of vestibular information interferes with the ability to interpret sensory information from the other senses accurately. Finally, Horak et al. (1988) have identified a population of children with clumsiness and learning disabilities who appear to have normal peripheral vestibular function but who also sway excessively in all sensory conflict conditions. It has been hypothesized that in these children the central nervous system is unable to integrate the accurate sensory information it receives in a way that permits an organized motor response. The elderly are a highly heterogeneous population, and it is also possible that more than one of these hypotheses are consistent with their tendency to become unstable in unusual sensory environments.

It must be emphasized, however, that the pattern of falls shown by the elderly with complaints of dizziness and imbalance could result from still other causes. As pointed out above, postural control depends on the availability of information from the visual and somatosensory systems as well as the vestibular system. Information from all three systems must be quickly and accurately interpreted by the central nervous system in order to organize a motor response that maintains the center of mass over the base of support. Finally, an intact neuromuscular and musculoskeletal system with adequate strength and range of motion is required to execute the appropriately organized response. Failures at *any* stage of the postural control system could result in a fall. As a result, a group of elderly patients with imbalance could all fall or sway abnormally in the same sensory conditions but for many different reasons.

Although it has been shown that young and elderly patients with vestibular deficits perform slightly differently in tests of sensory integration, it is not known whether any differences exist in their patterns of muscular activation and timing. It is known, however, that the incidence of biomechanical injuries and disease increases with age. Peripheral neuropathies and losses of muscle strength and joint mobility are common in the elderly (Sabin & Venna, 1984; Pack et al., 1985; Whipple et al., 1987). Even among the normal elderly there is some evidence that the variability in the onset latency and relative timing of muscle activation in response to translations of the support surface goes up (see Woollacott, this volume, Chap. 7). It therefore seems likely that elderly patients with vestibular deficits may also show different patterns of motor abnormalities than younger patients with the same disorders.

GENERAL DISCUSSION

In normal young subjects, vestibular information interacts with information from other sensory systems to provide good postural stability over a wide range of environmental conditions. The studies presented here have shown that postural control in both normal elderly subjects and elderly subjects with dizziness and imbalance is not as good or as flexible as the postural control of young adults. These differences between young and elderly subjects become much more pronounced in altered sensory environments. Experimental evidence suggests that there are anatomical and functional changes in the vestibular system which appear to be associated with age alone. Nevertheless, further research will be necessary to resolve whether these effects are due exclusively to age and whether or not these changes can account for all or some portion of the increase in dysequilibrium commonly observed in the normal elderly population.

It is, however, also clear that vestibular pathology may play a very significant role in the increased incidence of falls among the elderly. Community surveys of the elderly living at home have shown that 47% of men and 61% of women over age 70 report dizziness or vertigo (Sheldon, 1948; Droller & Pemberton, 1953; Sixt & Landahl, 1987). Evidence is accumulating that a large proportion of the elderly who complain of dizziness and imbalance show measurable vestibular deficits and in many cases show signs of vestibular disease (Belal & Glorig, 1986; Mirka et al., 1988). Preliminary evidence also indicates that there may be some important differences in the way peripheral vestibular disorders affect postural control in young and old patients with peripheral vestibular disease.

Given the high incidence of vestibular disorders in the elderly complaining of dizziness and imbalance, a complete evaluation of falling in a given elderly individual must depend critically on an understanding of the role of the vestibular system and vestibular pathology in postural control. As discussed above, the type of vestibular deficit—whether loss, distortion, or fluctuating function—and the type of postural movement required affects the type of postural dyscontrol that will be observed. Young patients with vestibular losses rely on ankle sway to control the center of mass and may show nearly normal postural control unless other sensory cues for orientation are withdrawn. Patients with distortion may show similar patterns or may use motion about the hips to control the center of mass, and they may be unsteady even in sensory environments with accurate somatosensory or visual orientation information.

Although sensory information, including that from the vestibular system, clearly plays an important role in postural control, it is also apparent that postural control is a sensorimotor integration task. Unfortunately, relatively little is known about motor-control aspects of posture in the elderly with dizziness and imbalance. It is not known, for example, whether the normal elderly or the elderly with dizziness and imbalance use ankle sway and hip sway in the same ways that normal younger people do, or whether their muscle-activation patterns and onset latencies are similar to those of normals. Because of the complex multisensory and sensorimotor nature of postural control, a complete clinical evaluation of falling in a given elderly individual must include assessment of visual, vestibular, and somatosensory function as well as neuromuscular and musculoskeletal function. A complete scientific understanding of the problem of balance in the elderly population as a whole must also necessarily rely on multidisciplinary approaches to the study of postural control.

ACKNOWLEDGMENTS

The authors wish to thank R. J. Peterka for discussions that contributed significantly to this work, and F. Owen Black, M.D., for comments on a draft of this chapter. The support of National Institute for Neurologic, Communicator Disorders and Stroke and National Institute for Aging grants NS01094 and AG06457 to Fay Horak and NS01022 to Alar Mirka is gratefully acknowledged. Charlotte Shupert was supported by grants NS19222 and NS12661 from National Institute for Neurologic, Communicator Disorders and Stroke.

REFERENCES

Allum, J. (1983). Organization of stabilizing responses in tibialis anterior muscles following ankle flexion perturbations of standing man. *Brain Research, 264*: 297–301.

Allum, J., & Büdingen, H. (1979). Coupled stretch reflexes in ankle muscles: An evaluation of the contributions of active muscle mechanisms to human posture stability. In R. Granit & O. Pompeiano (Eds.), *Reflex control of posture and movement: Progress in brain research*, Vol. 50, pp. 185–96. Amsterdam: Elsevier.

Allum, J., & Keshner, E. A. (1986). Vestibular and proprioceptive control of sway stabilization. In W. Bles & T. Brandt (Eds.), *Disorders of posture and gait* (pp. 19–40). Amsterdam: Elsevier.

Allum, J., & Pfaltz, C. R. (1984). Influence of bilateral and acute unilateral peripheral vestibular deficits on early sway stabilizing responses in human tibialis anterior muscles. *Acta Otolaryngologia (Stockholm), Suppl., 406*: 115–19.

Allum, J., & Pfaltz, C. R. (1985a). Postural control in man following acute unilateral peripheral deficit. In M. Igarashi & F. O. Black (Eds.), *Vestibular and visual control of posture and locomotor equilibrium*, pp. 315–22. Basel: Karger.

Allum, J., & Pfaltz, C. R. (1985b). Visual and vestibular contributions to pitch sway stabilization in the ankle muscles of normals and patients with bilateral peripheral vestibular deficits. *Experimental Brain Research, 58:* 82–94.

Baloh, R. W. (1984). *Dizziness, hearing loss and tinnitus: The essentials of neuro-otology.* Philadelphia: F. A. Davis.

Belal, A., & Glorig, A. (1986). Dysequilibrium of aging (presbyastasis). *Journal of Laryngology & Otology, 100:* 1037–41.

Bergstrom, B. (1973). Morphology of the vestibular nerve: II. The number of myelinated vestibular nerve fibers in man at various ages. *Acta Otolaryngologia (Stockholm), 76:* 173–79.

Black, F. O. (1985). Vestibulospinal function assessment by moving platform posturography. *American Journal Otology (Suppl.), 6:* 39–46.

Black, F. O., & Nashner, L. M. (1984a). Postural disturbances in patients with benign paroxysmal positional nystagmus. *Annals Otology Rhinology Laryngology, 93:* 595–99.

Black, F. O., & Nashner, L. M. (1984b). Vestibulo-spinal control differs in patients with reduced versus distorted vestibular function. *Acta Otolaryngologia (Stockholm), Suppl., 406:* 110–14.

Black, F. O., & Nashner, L. M. (1985). Postural control in four classes of vestibular abnormalities. In M. Igarashi & F. O. Black (Eds.), *Vestibular and visual control of posture and locomotor equilibrium* (pp. 271–81). Basel: Karger.

Black, F. O.; Nashner, L. M.; & Peterka, R. J. (1987). Vestibulo-spinal changes following singular neurectomy for benign paroxysmal nystagmus. In M. Graham & J. Kemink (Eds.), *The vestibular system: Neurophysiologic and clinical research* (pp. 177–86). New York: Raven Press.

Black, F. O.; O'Leary, D. P.; Wall, C.; & Furman, J. (1977). The vestibulospinal stability test: Normal limits. *Tr. Am. Acad. Ophth. Otol. 84:* 549–60.

Black, F. O.; Shupert, C. L.; Horak, F. B.; & Nashner, L. M. (1988). Abnormal postural control associated with peripheral vestibular disorders. In O. Pompeiano & J. Allum (Eds.), *Vestibulo-spinal control of posture and movement: Progress in brain research,* Vol. 76, pp. 263–75. Amsterdam: Elsevier.

Black, F. O.; Wall C., III; & Nashner, L. M. (1983). Effects of visual and support surface orientation references upon postural control in vestibular deficient subjects. *Acta Otolaryngologia (Stockholm), 95:* 100–210.

Bruner, A., & Norris, T. W. (1971). Age related changes in caloric nystagmus. *Acta Otolaryngologia Suppl., 282:* 5–24.

Cohen, M. M., & Lessell, S. (1984). Neuro-ophthalmology of aging. In M. L. Albert (Ed.), *Clinical neurology of aging* (pp. 313–44). Oxford: Oxford University Press.

Diener, H.-C.; Bootz, F.; Dichgans, J.; & Bruzek, W. (1983). Variability of postural "reflexes" in humans. *Experimental Brain Research, 52:* 423–28.

Drachman, D. A., & Hart, C. W. (1972). An approach to the dizzy patient. *Neurology, 22:* 323–34.

Droller, H. (1955). Falls among elderly people living at home. *Geriatrics, 10:* 239–44.

Droller, H., & Pemberton, J. (1953). Vertigo in a random sample of elderly people living in their homes. *Journal Otolaryngology Otology, 67:* 689–94.

Exton-Smith, A. N. (1977). Clinical manifestations. In A. N. Exton-Smith & G. Evans (Eds.), *Care of elderly: Meeting the challenge of dependency.* London: Academic Press.

Fregly, A. R. (1974). Vestibular ataxia and its measurement in man. In H. H. Kornhuber (Ed.), *Vestibular system: Handbook of sensory physiology*, Vol. 6, Part 2, pp. 321–60. Berlin: Springer Verlag.

Fregly, A. R.; Smith, M. J.; & Graybiel, A. (1973). Revised normative standards of performance of men on a quantitative ataxia text battery. *Acta Otolaryngologia (Stockholm)*, 75: 10–16.

Gryfe, C. I.; Amies, A.; and Ashley, M. J. (1977). A longitudinal study of falls in an elderly population: I. Incidence and morbidity. *Age and Aging*, 6: 201–10.

Horak, F. B., & Nashner, L. M. (1986). Central programming of postural movements: Adaptation to altered support surface conditions. *Journal of Neurophysiology*, 55: 1369–81.

Horak, F. B.; Shumway-Cook, A.; Crowe, T.; & Black, F. O. (1988). Vestibular function and motor proficiency in children with hearing impairments and in learning disabled children with motor impairments. *Developmental Medicine and Child Neurology*, 30: 64–79.

Johnsson, L. G. (1971). Degenerative changes and anomalies of the vestibular system in man. *Laryngoscope*, 81: 1682–94.

Keshner, E. A., & Allum, J. (1986). Plasticity in pitch sway stabilization: Normal habituation and compensation for peripheral vestibular deficits. In W. Bles & T. Brandt (Eds.), *Disorders of posture and gait*, (pp. 289–314). Amsterdam: Elsevier.

Keshner, E. A.; Allum, J.; & Pfaltz, C. R. (1987). Postural coactivation and adaptation in the sway stabilizing responses of normals and patients with bilateral vestibular deficit. *Experimental Brain Research*, 69: 77–92.

Kornhuber, H. H., Ed. (1974). *Vestibular system: Handbook of sensory physiology*, Vol. 6, Parts 1 and 2. Berlin: Springer Verlag.

Mirka, A.; Peterka, R. J.; Horak, F. B.; & Black, F. O. (1988). Comparison of postural control in elderly with and without subjective dizziness versus normal young subjects. Presented at the annual meeting of the Association for Research in Otolaryngology, Clearwater, Florida.

Moore, S.; Horak, F.; & Nashner, L. M. (1986). Influence of initial stance position on human postural responses. *Society for Neuroscience Abstracts*, 12: 1301.

Mulch, G., & Petermann, W. (1979). Influence of age on results of vestibular function tests. *Ann. Otol. Rhinol. Otolaryngol.*, 88: 1–17.

Nashner, L. M. (1976). Adapting reflexes controlling the human posture. *Experimental Brain Research*, 26: 59–72.

Nashner, L. M. (1977). Fixed patterns of rapid postural responses among leg muscles during stance. *Experimental Brain Research*, 30: 13–24.

Nashner, L. M. (1979). Organization and programming of motor activity during posture control. In R. Granit & O. Pompeiano (Eds.), *Reflex control of posture and movement: Progress in brain research*, Vol. 50, pp. 177–84. Amsterdam: Elsevier.

Nashner, L. M. (1982). Equilibrium testing of the disoriented patient. In V. Honrubia & M. A. B. Brazier (Eds.), *Nystagmus and vertigo: Clinical approaches to the patient with dizziness*, (pp. 165–78). New York: Academic Press.

Nashner, L. M.; Black, F. O.; & Wall, C., III. (1982). Adaptation to altered support surface and visual conditions during stance: Patients with vestibular deficits. *Journal of Neuroscience*, 2: 536–44.

Nashner, L. M.; Diener, H.-C.; & Horak, F. B. (1985). Selection of human postural synergies differ with peripheral somatosensory vs. vestibular loss. *Society for Neuroscience Abstracts, 11*: 704.

Nashner, L. M.; Shupert, C.; & Horak, F. B. (1988). Head-trunk movement coordination in the standing posture. In O. Pompeiano & J. Allum (Eds.), *Vestibulo-spinal control of posture and movement: Progress in brain research,* Vol. 76, pp. 243–51. Amsterdam: Elsevier.

Nashner, L.; Woollacott, M.; & Tuma, G. (1979). Organization of rapid responses to postural and locomotor-like perturbations of standing man. *Experimental Brain Research, 36*: 463–76.

Nickens, H. A. (1985). Intrinsic factors in falling among the elderly. *Archives Internal Medicine, 145*: 1089–93.

Overstall, P. W. (1978). Falls in the elderly: Epidemiology, etiology, and management. In B. Isaacs (Ed.), *Recent advances in geriatric medicine,* pp. 61–72. New York: Churchill Livingstone.

Pack, D.; Wolfson, L. I.; Amerman, P.; Whipple, R.; & Kaplan, J. G. (1985). Peripheral nerve abnormalities and falling in the elderly. *Neurology (Suppl.), 35*: 79.

Perry, B. C. (1982). Falls among the aged living in a high-rise apartment. *Journal of Family Practice, 14*: 1069–73.

Peterka, R. J.; Black, F. O.; Newell, C. D.; & Schoenhoff, M. B. (1987). Age-related changes in human vestibuloocular and vestibulospinal reflex function. Presented at the annual meeting of the Association for Research in Otolaryngology, Clearwater, Florida.

Prudham, D., & Evans, J. G. (1981). Factors associated with falls in the elderly: A community study. *Age and Aging, 10*: 141–46.

Richter, E. (1980). Quantitative study of human Scarpa's ganglion and vestibular sensory epithelia. *Acta Otolaryngologia (Stockholm), 90*: 199–208.

Rosenhall, U. (1973). Degenerative patterns in the aging human vestibular neuroepithelia. *Acta Otolaryngologia (Stockholm), 76*: 208–20.

Rosenhall, U., & Rubin, W. (1975). Degenerative changes in the human vestibular sensory epithelia. *Acta Otolaryngologia (Stockholm), 79*: 67–81.

Sabin, T. D., & Venna, N. (1984). Peripheral nerve disorders in the elderly. In M. L. Albert (Ed.), *Clinical neurology of aging,* (pp. 425–44). Oxford: Oxford University Press.

Schuknecht, H. F. (1974). *Pathology of the ear.* Cambridge, MA: Harvard University Press.

Sheldon, J. H. (1948). *The social medicine of old age.* London: Oxford University Press.

Shupert, C. L.; Horak, F. B.; & Black, F. O. (1988). Abnormal postural coordination in patients with distorted vestibular function. *Society for Neuroscience Abstracts, 14 (9)*: 65.

Shupert, C. L.; Nashner, L. M.; Horak, F. B.; & Black, F. O. (1987). Coordination of the head and body in standing posture in normals and patients with bilaterally reduced vestibular function. *Society for Neuroscience Abstracts, 13*: 352.

Sixt, E., & Landahl, S. (1987). Postural disturbances in a 75-year-old population: I. Prevalence and functional consequences. *Age and Aging, 16*: 393–98.

Tinetti, M. E. (1987). Factors associated with serious injury during falls by ambulatory nursing home residents. *Journal of the American Geriatric Society, 35*: 644–48.

Van der Laan, F. L., & Oostervald, W. S. (1974). Age and vestibular function. *Aerospace Med., 45*: 540–47.

Wall, C., III; Black, F. O.; & Hunt, A. E. (1984). Effects of age, sex, and stimulus parameters upon vestibulo-ocular responses to sinusoidal rotations. *Acta Otolaryngologia (Stockholm), 98*: 270–78.

Whipple, R. H.; Wolfson, L. I.; & Amerman, P. (1987). The relationship of knee and ankle weakness to falls in the nursing home resident: An isokinetic study. *Journal of the American Geriatric Society, 35*: 13–20.

Wilson, V. J., & Melvill-Jones, G. (1979). *Mammalian vestibular physiology*. New York: Plenum.

Wilson, V. J., & Peterson, B. (1981). Vestibulo-spinal and reticulo-spinal systems. In V. B. Brooks (Ed.), *Handbook of physiology*, Section I: *The Nervous System*, Volume 2: *Motor Control*, Part 1 (pp. 667–702). Bethesda, MD: American Physiological Society.

Woollacott, M. H.; Inglin, B.; & Manchester, D. (1988). Response preparation and posture control in the older adult. In J. Joseph (Ed.), Central determinants of age-related declines in motor function. *Annals of the New York Academy of Science, 515*: 42–53.

Woollacott, M.; Shumway-Cook, A.; & Nashner, L. (1982). Postural reflexes and aging. In J. Mortimer (Ed.), *The aging motor system* (pp. 98–119). New York: Praeger.

Woollacott, M. H.; Shumway-Cook, A.; & Nashner, L. M. (1986). Aging and posture control: Changes in sensory organization and muscular coordination. *Int. J. Aging Hum. Dev., 23*: 97–114.

12

Influence of Athletic Training on Postural Stability

Bettina Debu, Lynda Werner, and Marjorie Woollacott

The fast-growing body of literature describing the development of posture and balance in infants and children (reviewed by Woollacott, Shumway-Cook, & Williams, Chap. 4 of this volume) is concerned with the issues of normal and pathological development. Using the adult's postural control system as a reference, researchers have explored the features of emerging balancing and postural skills and their progressive evolution toward adult characteristics. Two types of experimental designs have been used to trigger postural responses. The first design consists of manipulating the visual environment, by providing erroneous visual cues, in order to create an illusion of movement. The second type of design consists of disturbing the subject's balance by unexpectedly moving the support base on which the person stands, either in normal stance conditions or while manipulating somatosensory and visual cues. This paradigm, first introduced by Nashner (1971), has been used to determine the time course of the development of postural muscle responses.

This research on the neural mechanisms of balance and postural control has essentially focused on describing normal and pathological characteristics of the postural control system across childhood and adulthood. Very few studies have examined what happens when the system is pushed beyond the normal limits of daily life. However, Brandt, Büchele & Krafczyk (1986) have noted that the "remarkable balancing skills of steeplejacks, tight-rope artists and gymnasts indicate that congenital postural reflexes are not optimized under daily life conditions but can be adjusted to higher performance by training."

Although biomechanical and neurophysiological research investigating postural control in trained athletes is scarce, the issue has been of interest for physical educators. A review of the behavioral literature reveals a number of studies aimed at assessing whether trained athletes display improved balancing and postural abilities as compared to the "normal" population. Most of these reports show that regular practice of specific sports or physical activities (such as gymnastics, ski, or dance) can be expected to result in an improvement of balancing skills. The mechanisms underlying these changes remain mostly unexplored. Such an analysis of the postural control mechanisms in trained athletes should improve our general understanding of the postural control system, as well as prove useful for the educators and coaches teaching activities in which balancing skills are critical.

BEHAVIORAL LITERATURE

Although balance underlies many of the tasks performed by the average individual, it becomes critical in the execution of a variety of sport skills. Hence, many studies were desgined to test the prediction that trained athletes would perform better than controls on global balancing tasks. Specific tests of balance such as stabilometric performance and stability on one foot (stork stance) were chosen to test the improvement in balancing skills. Various populations of athletes were used and compared across sports disciplines and to untrained subjects. However, early research assessing balancing abilities in young athletes yielded contradictory results. Whereas some authors found that people with experience in dancing, skiing, gymnastics, or skating were far above normal in performance on the stabilometer (Travis, 1944, cited by Singer, 1970), or found a positive relationship, in the measure of body sway, between static equilibrium and ability in gross motor abilities (Estep, 1957, cited by Singer, 1970), others could not find any significant relationship between dynamic balance and athletic ability (Breitenbach, 1955, cited by Singer, 1970).

In an effort to resolve these discrepancies, Singer (1970) addressed the question of whether there is a relationship between balancing skills and athletic success. The goal of his study was to compare the balancing ability of athletes representing different sports—namely, wrestling, baseball, basketball, football, water-skiing, and gymnastics. Fifteen athletes (male) for each selected sport were tested on the stabilometer (seven trials of 30 sec duration), in addition to a group of untrained subjects and a group of female subjects. The results revealed a significant difference between groups as well as trial-to-trial differences. Gymnasts and water-skiers appeared to perform better than all the other groups, and football quarterbacks were better than the untrained subjects. It was also found that some learning occurred during the testing sessions (see also Brandt & Paulus, Chap. 13 of this volume). All of the groups improved significantly over the test session. Singer assumed that the difference observed between groups arose from a greater amount of transfer between water-skiing or gymnastics and the stabilometer test because of the similarity of the tasks. These two groups of athletes were used to balancing on a very narrow stance base. Another interesting observation reported in this study is that during the testing sessions athletes tended to experiment more with stances than did untrained subjects.

Using a similar experimental design, De Witt (1972) investigated the influence of manipulating the optic vertical upon postural sway. The aim of his experiments was to test for differences between athletes and untrained subjects in the use of redundant visual, proprioceptive, and vestibular cues to maintain balance, and further to test for differences in the ability to detect inconsistencies between these cues in athletes versus nonathletes. In these experiments De Witt recorded the excursion of the center of gravity of subjects standing on the stabilometer. He recorded both antero-posterior and lateral deviations. The experiments were conducted in a dark room, and a vertical light bar was displayed in front of the subjects as the only visual reference. Once the subjects were stable on the base, the light bar was moved to a 10-degree angle at very low frequency. The results showed that normal subjects tend to follow the light bar, a behavior called "optic sway." When the base of support became narrower (the subjects were asked to stand with one foot in front of the other), the dependence on the optic sway increased. Comparison of the performance of trained athletes with normal subjects showed that the well-trained subjects relied more on the proprioceptive cues than did the untrained subjects.

The issue of balance control has been approached with a different emphasis in the dance literature. In this field proper postural control also contributes to the aesthetic aspect of the performance by providing the dancer with a better line (aesthetically more pleasant) and an increased smoothness of movement. In addition, most of the authors in this field are educators whose concerns are oriented toward teaching. A better understanding of postural control and body mechanics brought about by research is expected to enable the design of more efficient teaching techniques and a reduction in the number of injuries. Although the main emphasis is on the decrease of stress and strain and the increase in smoothness and fluidity of movement, some empirical observations made by dance teachers support the findings made in the laboratory. In particular, many dance educators and researchers have concluded that proper skeletal alignment is essential for effective postural balance (Dowd, 1981; Sparger, 1958; Sweigard, 1974; Todd, 1929, 1937). These authors share the belief that aligning the body parts into a mechanically efficient position yields a balanced posture. Through this balanced posture efficient and effective motor behavior is achieved. Furthermore, some authors have claimed that working toward the achievement of a good posture (usually through the use of imagery), which should become as effortless as possible, will result in changes in neuromuscular patterns (Sweigard, 1974; Gardner, 1965; Todd, 1937). Specifically, Gardner (1965) stated that postural reflexes impede, rather than assist, the execution of some movements and thus have to be inhibited during the learning process.

Although postural alignment, stability, and balance have been subjects of great concern for dance researchers, very few studies were designed to directly test the balancing abilities of dancers. Shick, Stoner & Jette (1983) studied dancers' static balance on flat foot in the stork position and dynamic balance on both feet using a stabilometer. The aim of their experiment was to find out whether the balancing abilities of the subjects, as defined by their performance in the test chosen, would enable a reliable prediction for dance performance level and learning time. The hypothesis was that skilled dancers, when given a novel balancing task, would demonstrate a higher degree of controlled balance than would less experienced dancers. Three groups of subjects representing different levels of achievement in dance were tested: advanced, intermediate, and beginner. The results showed a relation between the level of performance on the stabilometric task and the level of performance in dance. Advanced dancers were significantly better than beginners on both tasks and significantly better than intermediates for the stabilometer test only. The stork-stance test did not differentiate between the two experienced groups. As for the issue of prdictability of dance performance based upon balancing performance, only 58% of the subjects could be correctly classified by this procedure. As expected, the lowest percentage of dancers correctly classified was found in the intermediate group, which encompassed the wider range in experience. The authors conclude that such a test, although very limited, could represent an objective tool to discriminate between levels of dance skill.

CLINICAL LITERATURE

A few additional studies on the effect of training on the performance of balancing tasks are found in the clinical literature. These studies were designed to assess the degree of plasticity of the postural control system. The research of Buchele, Knaup & Brandt (1984) and Brandt, Buchele & Krafczyk (1986) was motivated by the desire to find a tool that would enable clinicians to estimate the degree of rehabilitation that physical training could produce in ataxic patients. In order to obtain a reliable clinical measure for control, the first study (Buchele et al., 1984) investigated the time course of development, duration, and termination of training effects on balancing on one foot in healthy subjects. Antero-posterior and lateral body sway during free stance on one foot were measured using a stabilometer.

In the second experiment (Brandt et al., 1986) postural instability was induced by asking the subjects to stand with the head bent backward to a maximal dorsal extension (see also Brandt & Paulus, Chap. 13 of this volume). In some trials, ankle proprioceptive inputs were reduced by covering the stabilometer platform with foam rubber. The subjects included untrained students and gymnasts of both sexes. They were tested for 15 minutes with one-foot stance and for 1 hour in the head-extended position in both eyes-open and eyes-closed conditions, for five consecutive days. The results showed that in healthy subjects postural stability improved up to 50%, reaching an asymptote after three days. This effect was greater when the initial destabilization was greater. Thus, the gymnasts, whose initial stability was better, improved less than the untrained students. In addition, during a daily session the short-term improvement was greater if the subjects were standing with their eyes closed. Control measurement over forty days revealed that these balance skills were preserved for weeks after termination of training. The authors concluded that the process of sensorimotor rearrangement (recalibration of sensorimotor control loops) and the improvement are related to the degree of initial instability. They suggested that ataxic patients should be exposed to increasingly unstable postures in order to facilitate the recruitment of unused control capacities.

Finally, Haines (1974) conducted an interesting study in which he investigated the debilitating effects of inactivity on postural stability. In his experiment he tested the balancing abilities of subjects before and after prolonged inactivity. The goal of this study was to test whether the deficits in postural control and walking abilities observed in patients after prolonged bed rest were primarily due to a loss of muscular strength. Haines tested normal subjects on a battery of eleven balancing tasks before and after fourteen days of bed rest. In order to control for the importance of the loss in muscular strength, the subjects were divided into three groups: one group received isotonic leg exercise, one group received isometric leg exercise, and one group received no training during the duration of the rest. At the end of the bed rest period the isotonic exercise group was impaired in three of the eleven tests, the isometric exercise group in four of the tests, and the no leg exercise group in five. After the end of the resting period the balance skills were relearned rapidly, complete recovery being reached after three days for all the groups. Rail walk and rail stance appeared to be the most sensitive tests. Haines concluded that leg exercise does not prevent the debilitating effects of bed rest on body balance. Instead, the data suggest that balance impairment is not due to a loss of muscular strength in the legs but to a bed rest related change in the neurally coded information to the postural control center. In particular, inactivity may cause a failure of the proprioceptive loops or affect the gain of the postural reflexes.

Thus, the results of these behavioral studies appear to be in agreement with one another. All authors concluded that training, either in specific balancing tasks or in sport disciplines requiring a higher level of balance control, results in an improvement in the performance of general balancing tasks. However, some of these studies suffer from the limitations inherent in their experimental design, which included only gross measures of balance (such as ability to maintain a particular equilibrium position); these measures cannot be easily related to athletic performance in a systematic way. Moreover, these studies do not enable us to differentiate between short-term adaptations of strategy and long-lasting changes in the system. In addition, the earlier work appears to rest on the erroneous assumption that balance is a unitary concept. Thus, these authors did not try to distinguish the different components involved, such as shifts in the sensory inputs dominantly used, changes in motor coordination patterns, or changes in strategy. The notion that the postural control system is complex and involves several components is reflected in the later work. Thus, De Witt's (1972) results, for example, suggest a shift from visual to proprioceptive control of balance in trained athletes. The clinical literature reflects specific therapeutic concerns, and although the experiments were designed to systematically examine some components of the postural control system, the unusual conditions used in the tests make it difficult to generalize the results to true athletic training.

Although the exact nature of the neural modifications underlying the balance improvement remains to be investigated, most authors seem to agree that the improvement results from changes occurring at the level of the sensorimotor reflex loops. This belief is primarily justified by results of experiments on the plasticity of other reflexes involved in postural control, such as the vestibulo-ocular reflex (VOR). Information on the plasticity of the system controlling the regulation of stance can be obtained by assessing the changes occurring at the neural level. One way of approaching this problem is to take advantage of the platform paradigm and electromyographic (EMG) recordings. This design enables the experimental manipulation of human posture by simulation of environmental conditions causing instability. We will only briefly discuss the results of previous studies that have used this paradigm. For a detailed review of this literature, the reader is referred to Chapter 5 of this volume.

POSTURAL MUSCLE RESPONSES IN THE NORMAL ADULT

Perturbation of a subject's balance by unexpectedly moving the support surface on which the person stands has been shown to trigger automatic postural responses involving muscles located at different levels of the body (Nashner, 1976, 1977; Nashner, Woollacott & Tuma, 1979; Nashner & Woollacott, 1979; Woollacott & Keshner, 1984; Keshner, Woollacott & Debu, 1988). These postural responses are believed to correct for any displacement of the center of gravity and are organized in a stereotypical, distal-to-proximal sequence of muscle activation beginning close to the base of support and radiating upward. According to Nashner & McCollum (1985), this spatio-temporal organization, or ankle strategy, is the most efficient for returning the body's center of mass to its initial position. The consistent observation of an upwardly radiating activation sequence led researchers to hypothesize that the primary input responsible for triggering the synergies was the rotation of the ankle joint (Nashner, 1976, 1977; Nashner et al., 1979).

Recent research has shown that following a perturbation of stance the neck muscles are also activated (Woollacott & Keshner, 1984; Keshner et al., 1988; Woollacott, et al., 1987). The short latency as well as the variability of the neck muscle responses are not compatible with their belonging to the upward radiating synergies. This result, together with the fact that platform perturbations have been proven to stimulate a variety of sensory systems including visual, vestibular, and somatosensory (Nashner & Berthoz, 1978; Vidal, Gouny & Berthoz, 1978; Forssberg & Nashner, 1982; Bussel, Katz, Pierrot-Deseilligny, Bergero & Hayat, 1980; Allum & Keshner, 1986; Woollacott, Debu & Mowatt, 1987), has led researchers to postulate that neck muscle responses are activated by visual, neck proprioceptive, and/or vestibular inputs.

Horak & Nashner (1985) studied the organization of postural responses in relation to the properties of the support surface. They had their subjects stand on a narrow beam placed perpendicular to the length of the foot. In this situation the pattern of muscle activation elicited by a platform movement appeared to be a downward radiating sequence on the opposite side of the body from the shortened ankle musculature. The first muscles to contract were the lower trunk muscles, followed by the upper and finally lower leg muscles. The authors named this sequence the hip synergy. In some experimental conditions the subjects displayed a response pattern that appeared to be a combination of the ankle and hip synergies. Thus these results imply that the automatic postural synergies may not be rigidly hard-wired. Instead, they appear to be sensitive to the exact configuration of the stimulus triggering them.

NORMAL DEVELOPMENT OF POSTURAL CONTROL

Research on the developmental course of these postural synergies has shown that the spatio-temporal adultlike characteristics are reached at about 6 or 7 years of age for the leg muscle responses, whereas trunk and neck muscle responses undergo some additional fine tuning after 7 years of age. Typically, nonmature postural responses occur with latencies that are longer and more variable than those reported for adults. The maturational process is reflected by a progressive shortening of the muscle response latency and duration (for example, see Fig. 12–1).

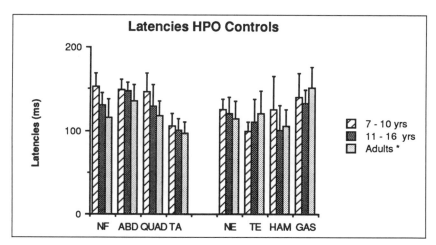

Fig. 12–1. Histogram of the latencies of postural muscle responses following anterior platform translation causing posterior body sway. Three age groups are plotted: 7–10-year-olds, 11–16-year-olds, and adults. Note the reduction in latencies occurring on the frontal aspect of the body as the subjects become older. NF = neck flexor; ABD = abdominals; QUAD = quadriceps; TA = tibialis anterior; NE = neck extensor; TE = trunk extensor; HAM = hamstrings; GAS = gastrocnemius. (Data from Debu & Woollacott, 1988, and Woollacott et al., 1987)

Developmental changes occurring in the postural responses to balance perturbation appear to follow stages characterized by different strategies for information processing (Lee & Aronson, 1974; Forssberg & Nashner, 1982; Shumway-Cook & Woollacott, 1985; Woollacott et al., 1987). Precisely, the relative dominance of the three sensory systems involved in regulation of balance (visual, vestibular, and proprioceptive) varies during the course of development. The visual system seems to be dominant early in childhood, when children are learning how to stand, and is followed by somatosensory dominance under normal sensory conditions.

The effects of initial instability on the pattern of postural responses in children (7–10 years old) and adolescents (11–16 years old) has been documented as part of studies designed to assess the effects of training on response to postural perturbations (Debu et al., 1988; Debu & Woollacott, 1988). The experimental conditions included (1) presence or absence of vision and (2) stance on one or two legs. The results showed a differential effect of these factors as a function of direction of perturbation. Specifically, following posterior platform translations causing anterior body sway, the muscle response latencies did not appear to be affected by the availability of visual information. On the contrary, when vision was removed in the case of posterior platform translations, latencies for quadriceps, abdominal, and neck flexor muscles were significantly shorter than in the presence of visual information. In addition, in the case of neck flexor muscles, the frequency of activation was higher in the eyes-closed condition than in the eyes-open condition.

For both directions of platform movement, the upper body muscle responses were also affected by the manipulation of the stance factor. Thus, when the difficulty of balancing increased, a reduction in the onset latencies of the upper body muscles was observed for the muscles located on the anterior side of the body in the case of anterior platform movement, whereas only neck muscle responses were affected for posterior platform movement. Furthermore, there seemed to be an increase in the amount of co-contraction of agonist-antagonist pairs at the trunk and neck levels. These changes in the timing of the muscle responses probably reflect the fact that a stiffer posture is used in order to keep balance on one foot.

The organization of postural responses to stance perturbation is well documented in both the normal adult and the growing child. It is therefore reasonable to investigate the organization of these responses in athletes in order to discover whether the improved balancing abilities observed in skilled subjects rely, at least partly, on modifications of the nervous mechanisms underlying balance control. In the following section, we will report the main results of recent studies aimed at exploring postural responses to stance perturbations in trained gymnasts and dancers.

POSTURAL CONTROL IN THE YOUNG GYMNAST

The goal of the first of these studies (Debu et al., 1988; Debu & Woollacott, 1988) was to investigate the automatic postural responses of young athletes of different ages and different levels of achievement in gymnastics. Two age groups (7–10 and 11–16 years of age) and three levels of training (beginner, intermediate, and advanced) were tested and their EMG responses compared to those of untrained, age-matched subjects. Anterior and posterior translations of the platform were used to trigger the stance perturbations. Four conditions were included in the experimental design in order to analyze (1) the relative importance of initial instability, by comparison of one-legged versus two-legged stance, and (2) the contribution of visual information to the stabilizing responses, by comparison of eyes-open versus eyes-closed conditions. The hypothesis was that latencies of gymnasts' postural responses would be shorter than those of untrained subjects. In addition, gymnasts were expected to be more sensitive to visual information, because of the importance of sampling visual cues in the performance of acrobatics.

The pattern of results obtained did not fully support these hypotheses, as the effects of training appeared to occur in two phases corresponding to early and later stages of practice. At first, gymnastics training seems to trigger a shortening of response latencies in upper body muscles, whereas this effect is reversed as training progresses. The advanced gymnasts displayed significantly longer response latencies than untrained control subjects in the upper body muscles. Differences were observed in the organization of responses to posterior and anterior translations. The results for the two directions of perturbations will be described separately.

POSTERIOR PLATFORM PERTURBATIONS

In response to posterior platform perturbations causing anterior body sway, a sequential pattern of muscle activation similar to that described in the literature was observed for all groups of subjects. In the 7–10-year-old group no statistically significant effect of training was observed. This result may be due to the fact that the gymnasts of this younger age group had only had two to three years of practice at the time of the experiment. Although there were no statistical differences in the response latencies of trained and untrained subjects, it is interesting to note that trunk muscle response latencies tended to be shorter in the trained group. Thus, the response latencies of this trained group appeared to be more similar to those of adults than to those of the untrained children of the same age.

Similar results were obtained following anterior translation of the platform. A nonsignificant reduction in response onset latency was observed for most of the muscles recorded (see Fig. 12–2). Thus, it is possible that gymnastics training, when started early in childhood, triggers an acceleration of the maturational processes. As a consequence, trained children's postural responses reach adultlike characteristics earlier, which may account for their greater stability. Another and nonexclusive interpretation is that, as a result of gymnastics training, the children adopt a different body alignment during quiet stance. This change in alignment involving an active engagement of the abdominal muscles could lead to a more efficient balance control, as suggested in the dance literature.

In the older age group (11–16-year-olds) the data analysis revealed unexpected effects of training. For posterior platform translations causing anterior body sway, we found that the latencies of neck muscle responses were significantly longer in the trained groups than in the untrained one. This was true for both flexor and extensor muscles. There was a trend for this delay to increase with increased duration of training (see Fig. 12–3). There was no difference in the response latencies of trained and untrained subjects for the leg muscles. As a result, the postural response of the neck muscles appeared to be uncoupled from the sequence radiating in the lower half of the body, suggesting that gymnasts use two relatively independent mechanisms to stabilize the center of mass and to stabilize the head.

ANTERIOR PLATFORM TRANSLATIONS

Similarly, following anterior platform translations causing backward body sway, responses of the upper body muscles appeared to be more sensitive to training than those of the lower body muscles. In particular, with increased duration of training, trunk and neck muscles of the anterior aspect of the body were activated after longer delays.

The characteristics of lower body muscle activation, which is critical to prevent a fall, did not show any change in timing as a function of either age or duration of training. Thus, leg muscle responses appear to be rigidly organized with a timing that is not easily modifiable even after a very long duration of training (the advanced group in this study had been practicing gymnastics for 7 to 10 years). It is likely that leg muscles

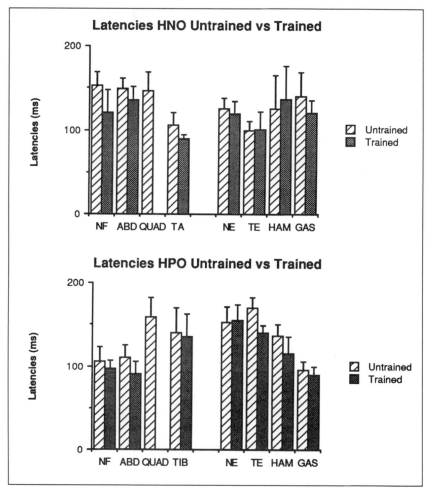

Fig. 12–2. Histogram of muscle-response latencies for untrained subjects and gymnasts 7 to 10 years old. *Upper panel,* posterior sway; *lower panel,* anterior sway. Note the reduction in latencies, for most muscles, in the trained group as compared to the untrained one. (Adapted from Debu et al., 1987, and Debu & Woollacott, 1988)

respond with optimal efficiency even in untrained subjects. As a consequence, the improvement in balance stability cannot be attributed to changes occurring at the level of the leg muscle postural responses. However, it is possible that modifications occur as a result of training in the relative amplitude of the different muscles' responses. These amplitude data were not analyzed in the experiment.

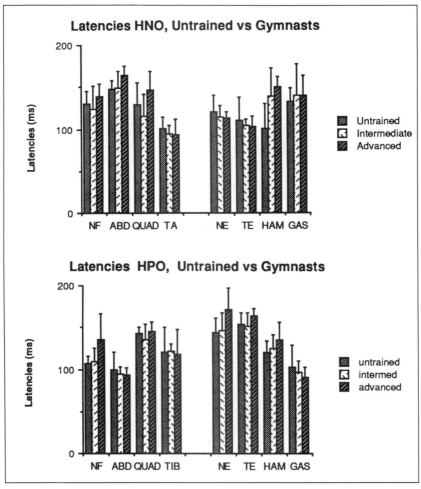

Fig. 12-3. Histogram of muscle-response latencies for 11–16-year-olds. Untrained subjects' response latencies are plotted against those of intermediate and advanced gymnasts. Note the longer upper-body muscle latencies of the advanced group of gymnasts. *Upper panel,* posterior sway; *lower panel,* anterior sway. (Adapted from Debu et al., 1987, and Debu & Woollacott, 1988)

This study also shows that the organization of upper body muscle responses is more plastic than that of leg muscle responses. In particular, the timing of activation of these muscles is susceptible to alteration. It is interesting to note that the responses of the same muscles were also sensitive to the experimental manipulations of initial stability or availability of visual information in both control and trained subjects. One could argue tht the effect observed in the latencies is only due to the different standing posture of the gymnasts. However, if this were the case, it is difficult to explain why the effect changes direction with increased duration of training. Indeed, this explanation does not seem compatible with the observation that gymnastics training first seems to trigger a shortening in muscle response latencies (cf. 7–10-year-olds), followed by a lengthening of upper body muscle response latencies as the duration of training increases. Therefore, it appears that the changes in response latencies result from modifications occurring at the neural level, rather than represent an "epiphenomenon" simply reflecting the biomechanical changes brought about by a difference in alignment. In support of this hypothesis is the fact that the changes reported for the two opposite directions of platform perturbation are not symmetrical. In other words, they seem to be dependent on the precise configuration of inputs triggered by the perturbation, as well as on the precise pattern of postural correction required to compensate for the destabilization.

POSTURAL RESPONSES IN BALLET DANCERS

In a study by Werner (1987) the postural responses of skilled ballet dancers were analyzed. The experimental setting was such as to enable (1) the comparison of dancers' and nondancers' postural responses in quiet stance (or neutral position), and (2) the analysis of the dancers' muscle responses when the difficulty of the balancing task increased. For this purpose, the subjects were tested while trying to keep balance in "relevé" (i.e., standing on the balls of their feet, with their heels high up). The balance perturbations consisted of backward platform translations causing forward body sway. As expected, the general organization of the postural responses was similar in both groups of subjects and consisted of an upward radiating sequence of activation of the muscles located on the dorsal side of the body. However, in the dancers, the activation of the neck muscles occurred very early. Thus, activation of the neck extensors preceded that of the trunk extensors by about 10 msec. On the other side of the body, activation of the neck flexor and abdominal muscles occurred at slightly, although not significantly, shorter latencies in the dancer group than in the control one (see Fig. 12–4).

Thus, it appears that the postural responses of trained ballet dancers to posterior platform perturbations are not significantly different from that of untrained subjects. In contrast with what was observed for the gymnasts, upper body muscle response latencies tended to be

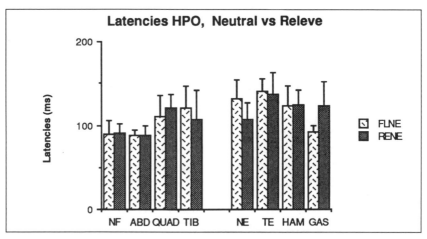

Fig. 12–4. Histogram of dancers' muscle-response latencies recorded in neutral (*FLNE*) and relevé (*RENE*) position. Note the very short latencies of the neck muscle responses. FLNE = flat surface, neutral knee; RENE = relevé, neutral knee. (Data from Werner, 1987)

shorter in the dance group as compared to normal adults. Yet both types of athletes have been reported to display better balance abilities than the normal untrained population. Possibly, improvement in balancing ability may be achieved by modifications of different components of the postural control system. This difference between the data collected with the gymnasts and that collected with the dancers supports the idea that the changes observed in the gymnast population are due to adaptive modification of the postural responses, specific to the activity practiced rather than to a difference in body alignment. Indeed, gymnastics and dance training emphasize the same type of body posture (that is, "correct alignment"), in which the abdominal and lower trunk muscles are actively engaged. Thus, if the changes reported in the timing of the gymnasts' responses were due to the different posture adopted by this population during quiet stance, one should obtain the same results with the population of ballet dancers.

The postural responses recorded in the relevé position represented a mixture of the ankle and hip strategies, observed on normal and reduced support surfaces, respectively (see section on normal adults above). In the majority of trials an early activation of abdominals was recorded, followed by quadriceps. This downward radiating sequence was followed by the activation of gastrocnemius, hamstrings, and sometimes trunk extensors on the other side of the body. Latency of activation of gastrocnemius was significantly longer than in the neutral stance condition. Videotape analysis showed that during these trials in relevé position the subjects tended to bend at the hip joint in order to maintain their balance. These results support the hypothesis of Horak & Nashner (1985) that the "hip strategy" is used when the support surface is of reduced dimensions.

More importantly, an increase in the response frequency of abdominal, neck extensor, and neck flexor muscles was observed. In this experimental condition, neck flexors and extensors were coactivated in 95% of the trials. Neck extensor response latencies were significantly shorter in this condition than in neutral stance. Thus, it again appears that upper body muscles, and in particular neck muscles, are more affected than the other muscles by both the training and the experimental conditions.

SUMMARY AND CONCLUSIONS

These studies show that the improvement in balancing abilities described in young athletes is accompanied by some modifications in the timing of postural responses to stance perturbation. Our data do not enable us to determine whether the differences observed in the automatic postural responses represent one of the factors *underlying* the acquisition of balancing skills and the better stability displayed by these athletes, or changes that arise as *a result* of the acquisition of new motor skills. However, it has been established that the efficient execution of a voluntary motor skill depends on the concomitant activation of an appropriate postural set (Belenkii, Gurfinkel & Paltsev, 1967; Cordo & Nashner, 1982; Lee, 1980). In addition, it is likely that the refinement of the postural responses reported during early childhood is at least partly responsible for the improvement in stability of growing children. Therefore, it is tempting to believe that the acquisition of complex motor skills requires some adaptation of the postural mechanisms involved in balance control, whether this adaptation consists of the inhibition of existing reflex loops, as proposed by Gardner (1965), or whether it occurs through a more complex reorganization of preexisting neural pathways (Paillard 1986). Paillard favored the selective remodeling of nervous circuitry enabling an elaborate control of basic built-in programs of posture and movement. Our results support this hypothesis, since the changes observed in the timing of the postural responses in the two groups of athletes were of opposite directions. Thus, it seems that the adaptation of the postural programs is very specific to the demands of the motor skill to be learned or performed. Possibly, the differences observed between the groups of gymnasts and dancers reflect a difference in the strategies used to keep balance, such as, for example, a difference in the sensory inputs on which the athletes rely primarily to monitor their equilibrium.

The studies summarized above do not enable us to assess the mechanisms of alteration of the postural programs. However, we believe that they demonstrate the plasticity of the postural control system. It would be useful in the future to test other populations of athletes in order to define the different patterns of modification, if they exist, and to try to relate them to the demands of the activity practiced.

REFERENCES

Allum, J. H. J., & Keshner, E. (1986). *Vestibular and proprioceptive control of sway stabilization.* In W. Bles and T. Brandt (Eds.), *Disorders of posture and gait* (pp. 19–40). Amsterdam: Elsevier.

Belenkii, V. E.; Gurfinkel, V. S.; & Paltsev, R. I. (1967). On the elements of voluntary movement control. *Biofizika, 12,* 135–41.

Brandt, T.; Büchele, W.; & Krafczyk, S. (1986). Training effects on experimental postural instability: A model for clinical ataxia therapy. In W. Bles and T. Brandt (Eds.), *Disorders of posture and gait* (pp. 353–65). Amsterdam: Elsevier.

Büchele, W.; Knaup, H.; & Brandt, T. (1984). Time course of training effects on balancing on one foot. *Acta Otolaryngologia (Stockholm), Suppl., 406,* 140–42.

Bussel, B.; Katz, R.; Pierrot-Deseilligny, E.; Bergero, C.; & Hayat, A. (1980). Vestibular and proprioceptive influences on the postural reactions to a sudden body displacement in man. In J. E. Desmedt (Ed.), *Progress in clinical neurophysiology,* Vol. 8, pp. 310–22. Basel: Karger.

Cordo, P., & Nashner, L. (1982). Properties of postural adjustments associated with rapid arm movements. *Journal of Neurophysiology, 47,* 287–302.

Debu, B., & Woollacott, M. (1988). Effects of gymnastics training on postural responses to stance perturbations. *Journal of Motor Behavior, 20,* 273–300.

Debu, B.; Woollacott, M.; & Mowatt, M. (1988). Development of postural control in children: Effects of gymnastics training. In J. E. Clark & J. H. Humphrey (Eds.), *Advances in motor development research,* Vol. 2, pp. 41–69. New York: AMS Press.

De Witt, G. (1972). Optic versus vestibular and proprioceptive impulses measured by posturometry. *Aggressologie, 13b,* 75–79.

Dowd, I. (1981). *Taking root to fly.* New York: Contact Collaborations.

Forssberg, H., & Nashner, L. (1982). Ontogenetic development of posture control in man: Adaptation to altered support and visual conditions during stance. *Journal of Neuroscience, 2,* 545–52.

Gardner, E. B. (1965). The neuromuscular base of human movement: Feedback mechanisms. *JOHPER, 36,* 61.

Haines, R. F. (1974). Effects of bed rest and exercise on body balance. *Journal of Applied Physiology, 36,* 323–27.

Horak, F. B., & Nashner, L. (1985). Central programming of postural movements: Adaptation to altered support surface configuration. *Journal of Neurophysiology, 55(6),* 1369–81.

Keshner, E., & Allum, J. H. J. (1986). Vestibular and proprioceptive control of sway stabilization. In S. Bles and T. Brandt (Eds.), *Disorders of posture and gait* (pp. 19–40). Amsterdam: Elsevier.

Keshner, E. A.; Woollacott, M. H.; & Debu, B. (1988). Neck, trunk and limb muscle responses during postural perturbations in humans. *Experimental Brain Research, 71,* 455–66.

Lee, D. N., & Aronson, E. (1984). Visual proprioceptive control of standing in human infants. *Perception & Psychophysics, 15,* 529–32.

Lee, W. A. (1980). Anticipatory control of postural and task muscles during rapid arm flexion. *Journal of Motor Behavior, 12,* 185–96.

Nashner, L. (1971). A model describing vestibular detection of body sway motion. *Acta Otolaryngologia, 72,* 429–36.

Nashner, L. (1976). Adapting reflexes controlling the human posture. *Experimental Brain Research, 26,* 69–72.

Nashner, L. (1977). Fixed patterns of rapid postural responses among leg muscles during stance. *Experimental Brain Research, 30,* 13–24.

Nashner, L., & Berthoz, A. (1978). Visual contribution to rapid motor responses during posture control. *Brain Research, 150,* 403–07.

Nashner, L., & McCollum, G. (1985). The organization of human postural movements: A formal basis and experimental synthesis. *Behavior Brain Science, 8,* 135–72.

Nashner, L., & Woollacott, M. (1979). The organization of rapid postural adjustment of standing humans: An experimental-conceptual model. In R. E. Talbot & D. R. Humphrey (Eds.), *Posture and movement* (pp. 243–57). New York: Raven Press.

Nashner, L.; Woollacott, M.; & Tuma, G. (1979). Organization of rapid responses to postural and locomotor-like perturbations of standing man. *Experimental Brain Research, 36,* 463–76.

Paillard, J. (1986). Development and acquisition of motor skills: A challenging prospect for neurosciences. In *Motor Development in Children: Aspects of Coordination and Control.* H. T. A. Whiting & M. G. Wade (Eds.). Amsterdam: Martinus Nijhoff.

Shick, J.; Stoner, L. J.; & Jette, N. (1983). Relationship between modern dance experience and balancing performance. *Research Quarterly for Exercise and Sport, 54(1),* 79–82.

Shumway-Cook, A., & Woollacott, M. (1985). The growth of stability: Postural control from a developmental perspective. *Journal of Motor Behavior, 17,* 131–47.

Singer, R. (1970). Balance skill as related to athletics, sex, height and weight. In G. Kenyon (Ed.), *Contemporary psychology of sport* (pp. 645–57). 2nd International Congress of Sport Psychology (1968).

Sparger, C. (1958). *Ballet physique.* New York: Macmillan.

Sparger, C. (1959). Ballet physique, section III, limbs. *Dance Magazine,* 74–77.

Sweigard, L. E. (1965). Better dancing through better body balance. *JOHPER, 56,* 22–33.

Sweigard, L. E. (1974). *Human movement potential: Its ideokinetic facilitation.* New York: Harper and Row.

Todd, M. E. (1929). The balancing of forces in the human being: Its application to postural patterns. Unpublished course guide, Teachers College, Columbia University, New York.

Todd, M. E. (1937). *The thinking body.* Brooklyn, NY: Dance Horizons.

Vidal, P. P.; Gouny, M.; & Berthoz, A. (1978). Role de la vision dans le declenchement de reactions posturales rapides. *Archives Italiennes de Biologie, 116,* 273–80.

Werner, L. (1987). An electromyographic analysis of balance control in dancers: On relevé, with and without hyperextended knees. Master's thesis, University of Oregon.

Woollacott, M.; Debu, B.; & Mowatt, M. (1987). Neuromuscular control of posture in the infant and child. *Journal of Motor Behavior, 19(2),* 167–86.

Woollacott, M.; Debu, B.; & Shumway-Cook, A. (1986). Children's development of posture and balance control: Changes in sensory motor integration. In D. Gould & M. Weiss (Eds.), *Advances in pediatric sport sciences: Behavioral issues* (pp. 211–33). Champaign, IL: Human Kinetics.

Woollacott, M., & Keshner, E. (1984). Upper body responses to postural perturbations in man. *Neuroscience Abstracts, 10,* 635.

13

Postural Retraining in Exceptional Populations

Thomas Brandt and Walter Paulus

Steeplejacks, tight-rope artists, and gymnasts have exceptional balancing skills indicating that postural control is not normally optimized but can be made more efficient by training. It has been shown that plasticity of the central nervous system (CNS) can compensate for peripheral or central neurological deficits by sensorimotor rearrangement, and this is the rationale for some physical therapy approaches to rehabilitating patients with acquired ataxias (Bles & Brandt, 1986). There are a number of important issues of concern to persons involved in optimizing postural control either in skilled athletes or in patients with postural instability. For example, what are the short- and long-term effects of training on postural instability? What are some of the hypothesized neural mechanisms underlying training effects? What experimental evidence exists to support the trainability of balance by stimulation of different sensory systems? Finally, is there evidence to suggest differential effectiveness of different training methods?

This chapter will discuss issues related to postural retraining and its effect in exceptional populations. First, we will discuss the effect of training on experimentally induced postural instability, such as standing with head extended or balancing on one foot, and consider the implications for retraining balance in patients with pathologies. We will demonstrate that learning by training is clearly correlated with the degree of postural instability: the greater the initial risk of falling, the greater the percentage of reduction in sway amplitudes by training. Next, we will present an approach for retraining postural dyscontrol in patients with labyrinthine lesions. Finally, we shall discuss issues related to the use of various types of biofeedback for retraining balance.

TRAINING EFFECTS ON EXPERIMENTALLY INDUCED POSTURAL INSTABILITY: A MODEL FOR CLINICAL ATAXIA THERAPY

Much insight can be gained from looking at the effects of training on experimentally induced postural instability in healthy subjects. Results from these experiments can be used to design effective therapies for retraining dysequilibrium in patients with peripheral and CNS pathologies. The following section will cover experiments related to retraining posture in healthy subjects under conditions of head extension and balance on one foot.

POSTURAL IMBALANCE WITH HEAD EXTENSION

Symptoms of to-and-fro vertigo and postural imbalance occur frequently in healthy people with head extension, elicited, for example, by overhead work while standing on an unstable, wobbling ladder or in situations in which visual cues are conflicting with proprioceptive input (looking up at moving clouds). Such a physiological instability related to head position can be demonstrated easily by attempting to balance on one foot with the eyes closed and head extended as compared with the normal head position (Brandt & Daroff, 1980a).

Posturographic measurements reveal a significant increase in body-sway amplitudes induced by head extension alone (Fig. 13–1), particularly when the "stabilizing" input of the nonvestibular sensory systems is reduced or eliminated, such as with eye closure and standing on foam rubber (Fig. 13–2, middle). Basically, the following alterations in the vestibular consequences of self-generated body sway may be responsible for the impairment of postural control in the unusual head position (Brandt et al., 1981): the utricular otoliths that transduce shear forces are beyond their optimal working range when the plane of the utricular macula (approximately parallel to the horizontal semicircular canal) is elevated relative to its normal horizontal orientation (2 degree flexion). With the head maximally extended, the saccular maculae (approximately parallel to the ipsilateral anterior semicircular canal) are significantly rotated, which causes a change in the direction of shear force action. The particular saccular contribution to postural control, however, is not known and may be less adapted, just as is the case for the semicircular canals.

Subjects were placed on the force-measuring platform and were tested for body sway during free stance under different conditions of head position with the eyes open or closed. They were instructed to maintain optimal balance with a fixed, preset foot position. A slab of foam rubber was placed on top of the stabilometer platform and covered by a second, rigid foot support. This caused a reduction in the somatosensory contribution (ankle movements) to postural control and therefore the disproportionate enhancement of the sensorial weights of the vestibular and visual systems that were under investigation.

When the subjects were standing on a firm foot support with the eyes and/or the somatosensors widely compensating for the "vestibular deficiency," postural imbalance induced by head extension was

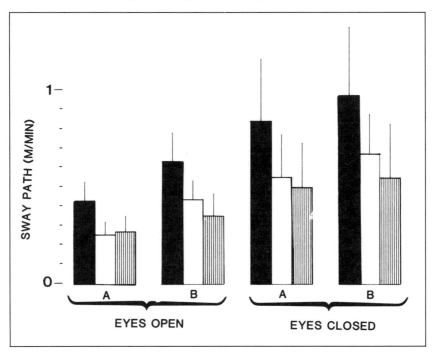

Fig. 13–1. Average body sway of upright stance on a rigid platform of twenty-four normal subjects (age range 20–50 years) with head upright vs. head extension: total sway path of the center of gravity (*black*), anterior-posterior sway path (*white*), and right-left sway path, (*vertical stripes*) are plotted in m/min. With both eyes open, sway path is most effectively reduced (*left, A*); it increases with head extension (*left, B*). With eye closure, sway path is enhanced (*right, A*), with a further destabilization by head extension (*right, B*).

comparatively weak or absent (Fig. 13–2, top). Postural balance with head extension was impaired significantly, however, with the eyes closed while the subjects were standing on the slab of foam rubber (Fig. 13–2, middle). The larger amount of fore-aft sway as compared to lateral sway seems to be not specifically related to the experimental paradigm but rather reflects mechanical joint characteristics and is prominent in most experimental and clinical ataxias. In some subjects the first trial led to an irresistible fall, but most often this was avoided by increased sway amplitudes, particularly in the low-frequency (<1 Hz) range, which seems to activate postural adjustments. Patients with sensory poly-neuropathy who lack accurate positional sense in the legs exhibit an instability with head extension similar to that of normals standing on foam rubber (Fig. 13–2, bottom). With the eyes open there was no significant increase in sway amplitudes, which is indicative of the

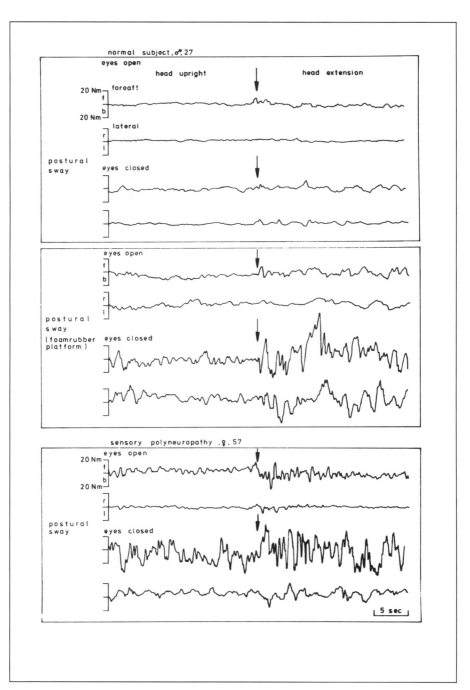

Fig. 13–2. Differential effects of head extension and normal head position upon fore-aft and lateral body sway (original recordings), with the eyes open or closed. Normal subjects standing on a firm stabilometer platform (*top*), normal subjects standing on a slice of foam rubber (*middle*), and a patient with sensory polyneuropathy standing on a firm platform (*bottom*). Postural imbalance is the most pronounced and similar for the normal subject standing on foam rubber and the patient during head extension with the eyes closed, when there is a lack of accurate positional sense from ankle movements.

redundant, multiloop control of posture, with overlapping functional ranges of the stabilizing systems, which enable them to compensate partially for each other's deficiencies (see also Woollacott et al., Chap. 4 this volume).

One hour of intermittent practice in this condition (total time of head extension 15 min) caused a remarkable improvement of balance in normal adults. The mean reduction in sway amplitudes for all subjects was 20–30% RMS (root-mean-square) value at the first trial (Fig. 13–3) and represents an exponential short-term training effect (Brandt et al., 1981). Fourier power spectra reveal a most pronounced destabilization of postural balance in the low-frequency range (1 Hz) and show that training improves sway activity over the whole frequency range below 1 Hz. Within the multiloop control of postural stabilization, each of the visual, vestibular, and somatosensory loops seems to have its own frequency range of optimal function with some overlap between the ranges. This may change—for example, in patients with deficient input from one or two sensory modalities (Paulus et al., 1987).

Figures 13–3 and 13–4 show that a short-term daily training effect and a long term training effect together form a characteristic, sawtoothlike curve of sway activity in normal adults which within five days reaches an asymptote at 40–50% of the initial sway activity (Brandt et al., 1981). After termination of training, control measurements reveal that learned balance skill without continued practice

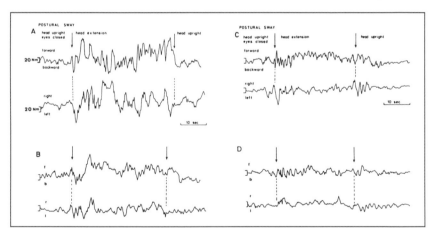

Fig. 13–3 Fore-aft and lateral body sway of normal subjects (original recordings) with the eyes closed and head extension at the beginning (A), after 1 hour of intermittent practice (B), at the beginning of the fifth training day (C), and at the end of the fifth training day (D). A short-term training effect is evident by comparison of A vs. B, and C vs. D. A long-term training effect is evident by comparison of A vs. C, and B vs. D.

becomes exponentially worse but does not reach the initial pretraining values within forty days (Fig. 13–5). On the other hand, a lack of sensorimotor exercise causes a decrement in balance performance, such as, for example, transient ataxia after bed rest (Taylor et al., 1949; Haines, 1974). This balance impairment after bed rest, which improves within one to three recovery days, is independent of muscle strength because it cannot be avoided by isotonic or isometric exercise in bed.

BALANCING ON ONE FOOT

Balancing on one foot with the head upright and the eyes closed causes a remarkable initial postural instability and in untrained subjects may even lead to unavoidable falls due to both the reduced area of foot support and the lack of normally redundant somatosensory reafferents from the ankle joint movements. A total of twenty-eight healthy subjects (twenty untrained students and eight gymnasts, selected for their equal body weights, 17–33 years of age) were employed in these experiments.

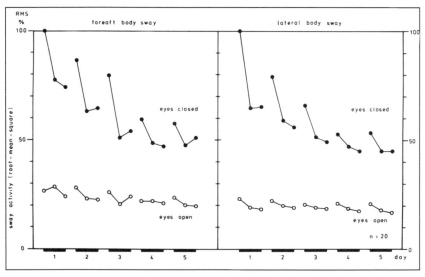

Fig. 13–4. Postural balance with head extension (effects of training). Percentage of reduction in mean RMS values of fore-aft and lateral body sway for twenty subjects during the course of a training period of five days (1 h per day; total time of head elevation with the eyes open, 8 min; eyes closed, 8 min). A short-term daily training effect (represented by the three measures during 1 h) and a long-term training effect form a characteristic sawtoothlike curve of sway activity, which reaches an asymptote at 40–50% of the initial sway activity. (From Brandt et al., 1981).

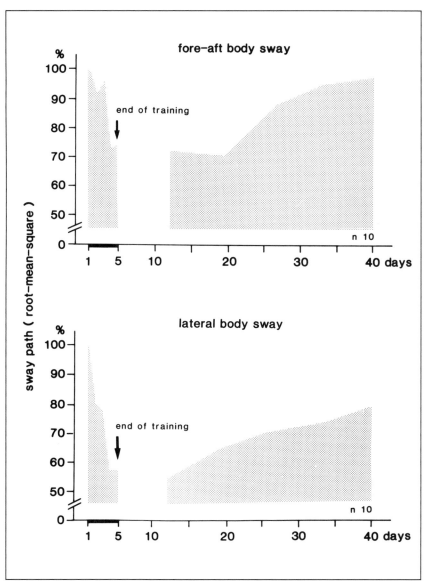

Fig. 13–5. Postural balance with head extension (outlasting training effect). The duration of the training effect on postural balance with head extension and eyes closed for ten subjects. Control measurements of body sway after a training period of five days reveal that without ongoing practice postural imbalance becomes exponentially worse, but only for fore-aft activity tends to reach the pretraining values within forty days. (From Brandt et al., 1981).

The time course of training effects on one-foot balance (1 h per day, total time of balancing on one foot 30 min) fits the data described above for the head-extension condition (Büchele et al., 1984): (1) a 20% exponential rapid improvement is obtained within the first training interval (Fig. 13–6); (2) a daily short-term training effect and a long-term effect, together, form a sawtoothlike curve of increasing postural stability with time, reaching an asymptote after 3–5 days; (3) measured postural sway activity in healthy subjects improves up to 50% within the five days of training; (4) trained gymnasts achieve weaker training effects (percentage reduction of RMS values of body sway) than untrained students, due to their better initial stability (Fig. 13–6); (5) with the eyes open there is only a 15–20% reduction in RMS values for fore-aft and lateral body sway; and (6) control measurements up to forty days following training proved that the newly acquired balance skill is stored and preserved for weeks after termination of practice or training.

IMPLICATIONS FOR CLINICAL RETRAINING OF ATAXIA

In the past, routine physical therapy of a variety of ataxias of cerebellar or sensory origin was based purely on clinical experience rather than controlled prospective studies. The differential effects of balance training on postural sway with the eyes open and the eyes closed clearly show that the process of sensorimotor rearrangement with subsequent postural stability is related to the degree of the initial instability. This finding should stimulate the clinician to make it a strategy in ataxia therapy to expose the patient increasingly to unstable body positions in order to facilitate rearrangement and recruitment of control capacities. The rapid improvement is striking in spite of the relatively short training phases, as is the long duration in weeks of newly acquired recalibration of sensorimotor control loops. Stance and gait aids seem to stabilize balance. They alleviate, however, patients' balance problems only transiently. When used continuously, they will worsen the symptoms because the multiloop control rapidly adapts to the additional feedback and support that they provide. Patients with acquired downbeat nystagmus, for example, who suffer from a tendency to fall backward (due to a combination of a central vestibular with a visual ataxia [Büchele et al., 1984]), improve their postural stability by balance training (Brandt, 1986b) despite the maintenance of the nystagmus. With physical therapy, patients with Wallenberg's syndrome due to lateral pontomedullary infarction demonstrate recovery from a tendency to fall toward the side of the lesion within days to months (Brandt & Dieterich, 1987). It is not yet clear, however, whether this

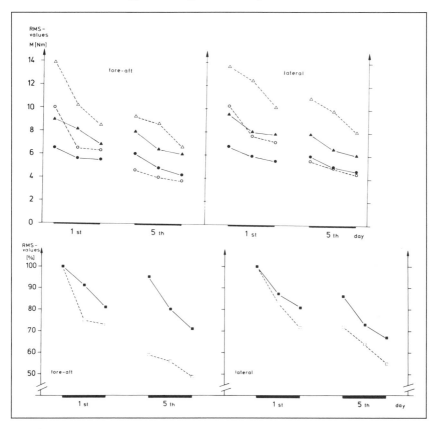

Fig. 13–6. *Top*: Absolute RMS values of fore-aft and lateral body sway during balancing on one foot with eyes closed on the first and fifth days during the course of training (O· · ·O, students; ●——● trained gymnasts; △, male, O, female). Each group consisted of four subjects selected for their equal body weights. The initial absolute instability was greater for the untrained subjects, whereas at the end of the training period the female students matched the balance skill of the female gymnasts. *Bottom*: Percentage reduction in mean RMS values for a group of eight gymnasts as compared with ten students. The effect of training appears to be smaller for gymnasts, who, however, began with better initial stability, as indicated above. (From Büchele et al. 1984)

benefit from retraining is based upon functional recovery of lesioned brainstem structures or central compensation by sensorimotor rearrangement.

POSTURAL RETRAINING IN THE PATIENT WITH LABYRINTHINE LESIONS

A number of approaches are available for managing vertigo in the patient with labyrinthine disorders. Persuaded by the pharmaceutical industry, physicians tend to overestimate the effects of antivertiginous drugs. These are indicated only for symptomatic relief of nausea and vertigo.

Central vestibular compensation for labyrinthine lesions requires reorganization of commissural brainstem connections between the vestibular nuclei and probably involves the cholinergic system. Pharmacologic and metabolic studies in animals suggest that alcohol, phenobarbital, chlorpromazine, diazepam, and ACTH antagonists retard compensation; caffeine, amphetamine, and ACTH accelerate compensation; cholinomimetics, cholinesterase inhibitors, adrenergic agents, GABA agonists, and alcohol may (re)produce decompensation. We present an alternative form of treatment involving specific exercises designed to remediate vertigo and postural imbalance in patients with two types of labyrinthine lesions: acute unilateral peripheral vestibulopathy and benign paroxysmal positional vertigo.

VESTIBULAR EXERCISES IN LABYRINTHINE LESIONS

Acute unilateral peripheral vestibulopathy. The chief symptom of the acute labyrinthine lesion (also known as vestibular neuritis) is severe rotational vertigo associated with spontaneous nystagmus, postural imbalance, and nausea. Normal vestibular end organs generate a tonic resting firing frequency equal in the right and left sides which is transmitted to the vestibular nuclei via vestibular nerves. Pathologic processes involving one end organ alter its firing frequency and thereby create a tone imbalance between the two sides. The imbalance causes most of the manifestations of the vertigo syndrome.

The fast phase of the rotational spontaneous nystagmus, as well as the initial perception of apparent body motion, are directed away from the side of the lesion. In addition, postural reactions initiated by vestibulospinal reflexes are usually opposite to the direction of vertigo. These result in both the Romberg Fall and past-pointing toward the side of the lesion (Brandt, 1986a). The symptoms abate when the tone is re-equalized by either peripheral restitution or central compensation.

Initiation, acquisition, and maintenance of equilibrium compensation (which are represented by an initial catastrophic stage, an acute and quick compensation stage, and a chronic compensation maintenance stage) require full mobilization of inputs from various sensory modalities, their appropriate modulation, and their optimal integration at many levels (Igarashi, 1986). During the first three to five days, when nausea is prominent, vestibular sedatives can be administered for symptomatic relief, such as antihistamine dimenhydrinate (Dramamine), or the anticholinergic scopolamine (Trandermscop). These drugs should not be given longer than nausea lasts because they prolong the time course of central compensation.

Further management involves physical therapy, using the Cawthorne-Cooksey exercises modified according to the current knowledge of vestibular physiology (Table 1, in Brandt 1986b). Vestibular exercises consist mainly of eye, head, and body movements designed to provoke a sensory mismatch; they enhance compensation by facilitating central recalibration, although the symptoms initially are uncomfortable. It has been convincingly demonstrated in animal experiments with unilateral labyrinthectomy that exercises promote central compensation of spontaneous nystagmus (Courjou et al., 1977) as well as postural reflexes in locomotion (Igarashi et al., 1986; Lacour & Xerri, 1980).

Compensation requires reorganization of commissural brainstem connections between the vestibular nuclei and involves the cholinergic system. Profound reorganization of commissural connections has been demonstrated in animal experiments during vestibular compensation following hemilabyrinthectomy (Dieringer & Precht, 1979; Galiana et al., 1984), and secondary lesions of commissural fibers caused reappearance of postural asymmetry in frogs that had already achieved balance compensation (Flohr et al., 1981).

Benign Paroxysmal Positional Vertigo. In benign paroxysmal positional vertigo, (BPPV); initially described by Bárány in 1921, attacks of rotational vertigo and concomitant positional nystagmus are precipitated by head extension as well as by lateral head tilt toward the affected ear. It is the most common cause of vertigo in the elderly and is hypothesized to be the result of cupulolithiasis (otoconia from the utricular macula become attached to the cupula of the posterior semicircular canal). There is frequently a natural history of spontaneous recovery. However, in those patients who do not spontaneously recover, maneuvers on a serial basis (Brandt & Daroff, 1980b) are often effective in decreasing symptoms. Schuknecht (1969) proposed that degenerated material from the utricular macula gravitates and becomes attached to the cupula of the posterior canal, which is situated directly inferior to the utricle when the head is upright. The posterior semicircular canal thus serves as a receptacle for the detached sediment. The "heavy cupula" creates an overexcitability of the posterior canal to angular accelerations in the specific plane.

Head extension at upright stance causes a rotatory positioning nystagmus as well as a vestibulospinal ataxia with the direction of fall toward the affected ear and forward (Büchele & Brandt, 1979). In the initial course of the disease, patients may also complain of other symptoms of otolithic vertigo with normal head upright position and especially of the somatosensory sensation of walking on pillows. The latter is probably due to the actual, unequal heavy loads of the two utricular otoliths and is compensated centrally by postural exercises and locomotion within one to three weeks.

The mechanism of cupulolithiasis led us to contrive a mechanical therapy by challenging these patients with precipitating head positions on a repeated and serial basis in order to promote the loosening and ultimate dispersion of the degenerated otolithic material from the cupula (Brandt & Daroff, 1980b). Thus, the rationale for the positioning maneuvers in BPPV as distinct to vestibular neuritis is labyrinth mechanics rather than facilitation of central compensation. The patients are seated with their eyes closed and tilted laterally with the lateral aspect of their occiputs resting on the bed to ensure proper plane-specific stimulation of the posterior semicircular canal. They remain in their position until the evoked vertigo subsides or for at least 30 seconds and then sit up for another 30 seconds before assuming the opposite head-down position for another 30 seconds. This sequence of positional changes is repeated about five times on a serial basis several times daily. Certainly such a regimen should be undertaken over two to four weeks in all patients with unremitting BPPV in whom a surgical procedure is contemplated. In the rare patients unresponsive to prolonged physical therapy, surgical transection of the posterior ampullary nerve via the middle ear can be considered (Gacek, 1984). This operation provides relief to vertigo; it is, however, not easy to locate the particular semicircular canal nerve surgically, and sensorineural hearing loss is a possible complication. Drug therapy with antimotion sickness medications has not proved to be particularly efficacious.

RELEVANCE OF BIOFEEDBACK FOR POSTURAL RETRAINING

In recent years various types of artificial feedback have been used during retraining balance in patients with dysequilibrium. The following section will discuss the merits of visual, acoustic, and somatosensory feedback for postural retraining. Postural strategies are often characterized in terms of feedback interaction between sensory input and motor output. In fact, reduction of body sway may be seen as an example for feedforward as well as for feedback strategies: the body has to detect and to reduce its own self-generated sway. Feedforward strategies in posture and locomotion are used to adjust the body to expected positions in space; feedback strategies react to sensed deviations from the ideal antigravity position. This "natural" feedback is usually performed subconsciously such that stabilization of posture can be achieved despite full concentration upon different voluntary, goal-directed limb movements.

With respect to posture, "biofeedback" means artificial feedback, which provides information on measured body sway via an uncommon sensory route (acoustic feedback) or with "inadequate" stimulus parameters such as a moving spot on a television screen reflecting the sway path of the center of gravity in x-y mode.

The question arises whether the multiloop control of posture can be improved by such an inadequate stimulation. With respect to physiology, this type of improvement would support a concept of a common multisensory pathway for processing of afferent information concerning postural balance posture. Improvement by biofeedback would argue against a rigid organization with fixed specific loops for each of the three sensory modalities.

VISUAL FEEDBACK

Visual stabilization of posture is subserved by visual self-motion detection, which obeys the rules of complex geometric pattern shifts of the three-dimensionally structured environments on the retina while eye and/or head are moving (Paulus et al., 1984). In visual feedback studies the subjects usually watch a moving spot on a screen coupled to lateral or fore-aft sway or both. Thus, for sway reduction, object-motion perception is used rather than perception of self-motion. Reports on this kind of feedback describe only mimimal effects on body sway (Litvinenkova & Hlavacka, 1973; Gantchev et al., 1979, 1985), smaller than the normal sway reduction of about 50% achieved by eyes open versus eyes closed (Romberg quotient: 2). Gantchev et al. (1979) found visual feedback somewhat more effective when the moving dots coded sway velocity instead of position. Litvinenkova & Hlavacka (1973) demonstrated a dependence of sway reduction on the amplification of the feedback signal, that is, the size of the area covered by spot motion. Hlavacka & Saling (1986) confirmed the effect of monitor-provided visual feedback when subjects balanced on unstable surfaces such as foam rubber. These authors claim, however, a more pronounced sway reduction if body weight was artificially increased by weights.

We were interested in the amount and time course of sway reduction by visual feedback with short training periods over days. In contrast to the experiments described above, a force-measuring platform equipped with twelve force transducers (Kistler) was used. The sway path was calculated in m/min as described by Hufschmidt et al. (1980). The subjects stood on a rigid plate that covered the slab of foam rubber on the platform. The recording period was 25 seconds with a sample rate of 40 Hz. In addition, head sway path was directly monitored by aid of a camera system mounted above the subjects and which traced two-dimensionally anterior-posterior (A-P) and right-left (R-L) movements of an infrared LED attached to the subject's head.

Subjects stood 1 m in front of a screen and fixated the moving spot, the gain of which was adjusted such that 1 cm of displacement of the center of gravity caused a displacement of the spot of 1 cm. Body sway to the right induced a spot displacement to the right as well and vice versa. With forward body sway the spot moved upward, with backward sway, downward. Only a subtle, insignificant decrease as compared to the sway before training occurs, while head sway, paradoxically, increases (Fig. 13–7). Although several authors have suggested the possibility of decreasing body oscillation by use of artificial visual feedback, measurable effects on normal subjects are insignificant. It is unclear whether this approach would benefit patients with various types of ataxias.

ACOUSTIC FEEDBACK

Some acoustic stabilization of posture already occurs under natural stimulation conditions. Fixed sound sources in space may reduce body sway (Edwards, 1946; Takeya et al., 1976; Marme-Karelse & Bles, 1977). Even reflected acoustic stimuli subserve spatial orientation, particularly in the blind (Edwards 1942, 1946; Takeya et al., 1976; Marme-Karelse & Bles, 1977), Artificial acoustic feedback is commonly provided by modulation of tone frequency or loudness, coupled either to position or velocity of the measured sway path.

Quantitative studies on acoustic feedback in normal subjects showed a disappointing amount of reduction in body sway similar to the results obtained with visual feedback. Gantchev et al. (1979) described a 5 to 10% reduction of sway with eyes closed, which occurred only if the feedback signal was coupled to sway-path velocity rather than position.

We tried to increase the amount of sway reduction by using head sway in addition to body sway as the feedback signal. Tone frequency of four loud speakers (in front, at the back, and on both sides of the subject) was modulated from a basic 40 Hz tone to 3 KHz. Sway-path reduction by feedback almost never exceeded the net training effect measurable without feedback (Fig. 13–8, left column in each quadrant). Feedback information from head sway initially destabilized both head and body sway. This increment in sway was reduced after training to previous levels of sway path without feedback. We conclude that feedback of head sway is even less helpful than platform feedback since an initial body sway increase was caused. Repeated training over four days did not significantly enhance the training effect, as demonstrated in Figure 13–9. From day 1 to day 4 measured body sway before and after training remained unchanged. From these data we conclude that

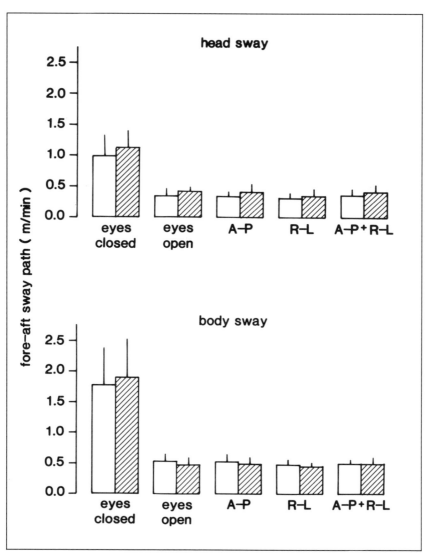

Fig. 13–7. Fore-aft head (*top*) and body sway (*bottom*) with visual feedback of the sway of the center of gravity (*A-P*: anterior-posterior; *R-L*: right-left; *A-P + R-L*: combined A-P and R-L feedback) as compared to body sway with eyes open and eyes closed without feedback. After 3 min of practice over four days with visual feedback, body sway shows only a subtle, insignificant decrease (*hatched columns*) as compared to the sway before training (*open columns*). Head sway, paradoxically, shows a slight increase.

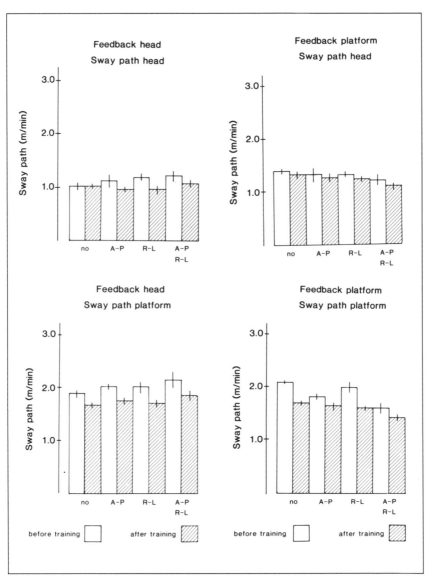

Fig. 13–8. Differential effects of the acoustic feedback of head or body sway on head and body sway. The figure represents either measured body (*bottom*) or head sway (*top*) for acoustic head (*left*) or body feedback (*right*), combining posturographic and optical tracing methods of head sway. Each of the four quadrants represents four pairs of data: no feedback, anterior-posterior, right-left, or combined A-P and R-L feedback. Sway path was recorded at the onset (*white columns*) and after 3 min of practice (*hatched columns*).

the effects of artificial acoustic feedback in normal subjects are disappointing, and we remain cautious as to their relevance in ataxia therapy.

SOMATOSENSORY FEEDBACK

An unusual kind of somatosensory feedback was realized by use of a pendulum attached to the ceiling such that it contacted the subject's forehead without exerting too much pressure. By increase of skin pressure with forward sway and loss of contact with backward sway a very sensitive, additional somatosensory cue of A-P head sway was provided. As is evident in Figure 13–10, there was a selective significant ($p < .05$) reduction of A-P head sway only (which consequently produces a total head sway reduction also). This points toward a transition of postural strategy under these circumstances, since body sway was not affected. The head was successfully fixed in space in A-P plane in order to keep the pressure changes of the pendulum minimal, whereas increased hip movements hindered concurrent stabilization of the center of gravity.

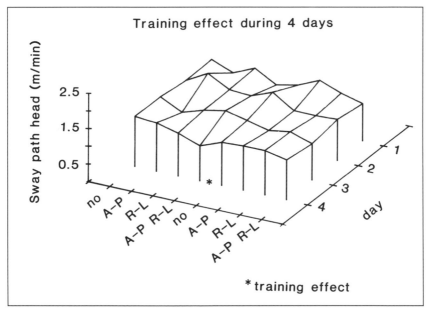

Fig. 13–9. Training effects of acoustic feedback to posture over a period of four days. Head sway path has been plotted on the Y-axis for the four different conditions: without feedback; with A-P, R-L, and combined A-P/R-L feedback; before (left) and—indicated by an asterisk—after training (right). Data of days 1 to 4 are plotted on the Z-axis, the four conditions before training on the left side of the X-axis. No consistent effects can be observed during the four days.

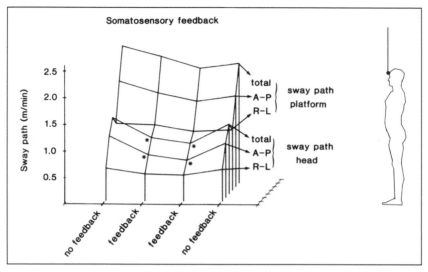

Fig. 13–10. Influence of an unusual somatosensory feedback on body and head sway provided by a pendulum contacting forehead skin. Six different parameters are plotted: total sway, A-P and R-L sway for either body or head. The experimental sequence involved four measurements: the standard condition without feedback, the two feedback measurements, and a second control standard condition. The only significant effect is the selective reduction of A-P head sway, which contaminates total head sway also. Despite a decreased head sway, body sway remains unaffected due to a change in postural strategy with larger hip movements.

Results from these experiments suggest that biofeedback methods for training balance are not efficacious in normal subjects; however, their viable application to patients with acquired ataxias is yet to be determined.

SUMMARY

This chapter has focused on issues relevant to retraining postural control in patients with various pathologies. We have shown that simple training of postural balance with either head extension or standing on one foot improves body sway activity by 30 to 50% within five days. A typical, sawtoothlike time course is formed by the interaction of a short-term and a long-term training effect. The rapid improvement is striking in spite of the relatively short training phases, as is the long-term retention of training effects resulting from newly acquired recalibration of sensorimotor control loops.

We have found that the differential effects of balance training on postural sway is related to the degree of the initial instability; the greater the initial risk of falling, the greater the percentage of reduction in sway amplitudes by training. This suggests that an appropriate strategy in ataxia on balance therapy is to expose the patient to increasingly unstable body positions in order to facilitate rearrangement and recruitment of control capacities.

It has been convincingly demonstrated that exercises promote central compensation of spontaneous nystagmus as well as postural imbalance in patients with acute unilateral labyrinthine lesions. The amount of rapid improvement by training within 1 hour makes it possible to predict the long-term benefit of the type of physical therapy in patients with peripheral or central vestibular pathologies.

In contrast, we have found only a minor improvement of postural balance using artificial sway feedback. This has been demonstrated for visual, auditory, and somatosensory feedback. Therefore, we are cautious regarding the overall benefit of feedback methods for retraining balance in patients with ataxia.

REFERENCES

Bárány, R. (1921). Diagnose von Krankheitserscheinungen im Bereich des Otolithenapparates. *Acta Otolaryngologia, 2,* 434–37.

Bles, W., & Brandt, Th., (Eds.) (1986). *Disorders of posture and gait.* Amsterdam: Elsevier.

Brandt, Th. (1986a). Vertigo and dizziness. In A. K. Asburg, G. M. McKhann & W. I. McDonald (Eds.), *Diseases of the nervous system.* (pp. 561–76). Philadelphia: Saunders.

Brandt, Th. (1986b). Episodic vertigo. In R. E. Rakel (Ed.), *Conn's Current Therapy* (pp. 741–46). Philadelphia: Saunders.

Brandt, Th., & Daroff, R. B. (1980a). Physical therapy for benign paroxysmal positional vertigo. *Archives, Otolaryngology, 106,* 484–85.

Brandt, Th., & Daroff, R. B. (1980b). The multisensory physiological and pathological vertigo syndromes. *Annals of Neurology, 7,* 195–203.

Brandt, Th. & Dieterich, M. (1987). Pathological eye-head coordination in roll: tonic ocular tilt reaction in mesencephalic and medullary lesions. *Brain, 110,* 649–66.

Brandt, Th.; Krafczyk, S.; & Malsbenden, I. (1981). Postural imbalance with head extension: Improvement by training as a model for ataxia therapy. *Annals of the New York Academy of Science, 374,* 636–49.

Büchele, W., & Brandt, Th. (1979). Vestibulo-spinal ataxia in benign paroxysmal positional vertigo. *Aggressologie, 20,* 221–22.

Büchele, W.; Knaup, H.; & Brandt, Th. (1984). Time course of training effects on balancing on one foot. *Acta Otolaryngologia (Stockholm), Suppl., 406,* 140–42.

Courjou, J. H.; Jeannerod, M.; Ossuzio, I.; & Schmid, R. (1977). The role of vision in compensation of vestibulo-ocular reflex after hemilabyrinthectomy in the cat. *Experimental Brain Research, 28,* 235–48.

Dieringer, N., & Precht, W. (1979) Synaptic mechanisms involved in compensation of vestibular function following hemilabyrinthectomy. In R. Granit & O. Pompeiano (Eds.), *Progress in brain research*, Vol. 50. *Reflex control of posture and locomotion* (pp. 607–15). Amsterdam: Elsevier.

Edwards, A. S. (1942)., The measurement of static ataxia. *American Journal of Psychology, 55*, 171–88.

Edwards, A. S. (1946). Body sway and vision, *Journal of Experimental Psychology, 36*, 526–35.

Flohr, H.; Bienhold, H.; Abeln, W.; & Macskovics, I. (1981). Concepts of vestibular compensation. In H. Flohr & V. Precht (Eds.), *Lesion-induced neuronal plasticity in sensorimotor systems* Berlin: Springer. (pp. 153–72).

Gacek, R. R. (1984). Cupulolithiasis and posterior ampullary nerve transection. *Ann. Otology Rhinology and Otolaryngology, 93*, Suppl. 112, 25–29.

Galiana, H. L.; Flohr, H.; & Melvill Jones, G. (1984). A reevaluation of intervestibular nuclear coupling: its role in vestibular compensation. *Journal of Neurophysiology, 51*, 242–59.

Gantchev, G. N.; Draganova, N. I.; & Dunev, S. (1979). The role of the sensory feedback in the control of postural-tonic activity. *Aggressologie, 20*, 155–56.

Gantchev, G. N.; Draganova, N. I.; & Dunev, S. (1985). Influence of the stabilogram and statokinesigram visual feedback upon the body oscillations. In M. Igarashi & F. O. Black (Eds.), *Vestibular and visual control of posture and locomotor equilibrium* (pp. 135–38).

Guegen, J.; Leroux, J,; Domenger, J. C. & Poulard, G. (1976). Sur l'influence du retour visuel sur la regulation de la posture. *Aggressologie, 17*, 63–66.

Haines, R. F. (1974). Effect of bed rest and exercise on body balance. *Journal of Applied Physiology, 36*, 323–27.

Hlavacka, F., & Litvinenkova, V. (1973). First derivative of the stabilogram and postural control in visual feedback conditions in man. *Aggressologie, 14*, 45–49.

Hlavacka, F., & Saling, M. (1986). Compensation effect of visual biofeedback in upright posture control. *Activ. Nerv. Sup. (Praha), 28*, 191–96.

Hufschmidt, A.; Dichgans, J.; Mauritz, K. H.; & Hufschmidt, M. (1980). Some methods and parameters of body sway quantification and their neurological applications. *Arch. Psychiat. Nervenkr., 228*, 135–50.

Igarashi, M. (1986). Compensation for peripheral vestibular disturbances—animal studies, In W. Bles and Th. Brandt (Eds.), *Disorders of posture and gait* (pp. 337–52). Amsterdam: Elsevier.

Lacour, M., & Xerri, C. (1980). Compensation of postural reactions to free-fall in the vestibular neurectomized monkey. Role of the visual motion cues. *Experimental Brain Research, 40*, 103–10.

Litvinenkova, V., & Hlavacka, F. (1973). The visual feedback influence upon the regulation of the upright posture in man. *Aggressologie, 14*, 95–99.

Marme-Karelse, A. M., & Bles, W. (1977). Circular-vection and human posture, II. Does the auditory system play a role? *Aggressologie, 18*, 329–33.

Paulus, W.; Straube, A.; & Brandt, Th. (1984). Visual stabilization of posture: Physiological stimulus characteristics and clinical aspects. *Brain, 107*, 1143–63.

Paulus, W.; Straube, A.; & Brandt, Th. (1987). Visual postural performance after loss of somatosensory and vestibular function. *Journal of Neurology, Neurosurgery, and Psychiatry, 50*, 1542–45.

Schuknecht, H. F. (1969). Cupulolithiasis. *Advances in Otolaryngology, 90,* 765–78.

Takeya, T.; Sugano, H.; & Ohno, Y. (1976). Auditory and visual feedback of postural sway. *Aggressologie, 17,* 71–74.

Taylor, H. L.; Henschel, A.; Brozek, J.; & Keys, A. (1949). Effect of bed rest on cardiovascular function in work performance. *Journal of Applied Physiology, 2,* 223–39.

Zee, D. S. (1985). Perspectives on the pharmacotherapy of vertigo, *Archives of Otolaryngology, 111,* 609–12.